GRAVESTONE I[
BELF/
VOLU]

THE NEW
BURYING GROUND

OLD BELFAST FAMILIES
and
THE NEW BURYING GROUND

from

Gravestone Inscriptions,

with Wills *and*

Biographical Notes

•

compiled by
A.C.W. MERRICK
edited by
R·S·J·CLARKE

ULSTER HISTORICAL FOUNDATION
WITH FINANCIAL ASSISTANCE FROM THE BELFAST CITY COUNCIL

Published 1991
by the Ulster Historical Foundation
12 College Square East
Belfast
BT1 6DD

All Rights Reserved. No part of this publication may be reproduced, stored in a retrieval system or transmitted in any form or by any means, electronic, mechanical or otherwise without the prior permission of the publisher.

© 1991 The Ulster Historical Foundation

ISBN 0 901905 47 X

Typesetting by Joe Passmore at
the Ulster Historical Foundation

Printed by
Coleraine Printing Company
70A Union Street
Coleraine
Co. Londonderry

This book has received financial assistance
under the **Cultural Traditions Programme**
which aims to encourage acceptance and
understanding of cultural diversity.

Grateful Acknowledgement is also made to the
Belfast Natural History and Philosophical Society

and to

Belfast City Council

Cover Design by Wendy Dunbar

CONTENTS

List of Illustrations vi

Introduction vii

Bibliography xv

The New Burying Ground, Clifton Street 1

List of Subscribers 311

LIST OF ILLUSTRATIONS

Portrait of Arthur, 5th Earl and 1st Marquess of Donegall viii
Coffin guard from the days of the body-snatchers x
Photograph of George Andrews of Ardoyne, damask weaver 8
Engraving of the top of the Batt tomb. 17
Tomb of Edward Benn of Glenravel 21
Memorial to Thomas Blain at the R.B.A.I. 24
Portrait of William Cairns 38
Memorial to Adam Dickey 62
Headstone of the Rev. William Steel Dickson, United Irishman 65
Portrait of Dr William Drennan, United Irishman 68
Medallion of Sarah Dunville, before re-erection 74
Photograph of Sir William Quartus Ewart, 2nd baronet 85
Advertisement of William Gilbert, jeweller 103
Advertisement of Grattan & Co. of Corn Market 109
The Haliday vault before its destruction 115
Portrait of Hill Hamilton, Junior 121
Heron monument before restoration 131
Headstone of Robert Hodgson, bookseller 134
Memorial to Robert Hyndman of Portview, Ballymacarret 141
Portrait of Valentine Jones, merchant 151
Portrait of Henry Joy 153
Memorial to the Journeyman Coopers of Belfast 159
Arms on Lennox gravestone 164
Photograph of Mary Ann McCracken 180
Portrait of Dr Andrew Marshall 199
Memorial to Dr John Mattear 203
Portrait of Hugh Ritchie, shipbuilder 240
Portrait of William Ritchie, shipbuilder 242
Advertisement for the posting establishment of John Robson 246
Memorial to Robert Stevenson, surgeon 274
Memorial to Thomas Weir, linen manufacturer 297
Memorial tablet to Professor John Young 309
The cholera ground, looking west, in the 1950s 310

INTRODUCTION

Belfast grew up round the junction of the rivers Farset and Lagan. The Farset was still open, along the line of the present High Street, and remained so until well into the nineteenth century. The old Corporation Church with its graveyard stood on the south bank of the Farset where St George's Church now stands. In mediaeval times it had been a chapel of Shankhill Parish Church but, by the early seventeenth century it had become the parish church of Belfast and, though it suffered during the Cromwellian war, it was restored again soon afterwards. It was probably neglected, however, during the following century and finally had to be demolished in May 1774. It was replaced on a new site in Donegall Street in October 1776 by a church dedicated to St Anne, itself later to be pulled down to make way for the Cathedral.

The old graveyard round the Corporation Church was the main burying place for the city and here reposed such notables as the Pottinger and Collier families, the Rev. James Saurin, Vicar of Belfast from 1747 to 1772, and six of the 1798 insurgents including Henry Joy McCracken. By 1798, however, the nuisance caused by the tidal flooding and its unsightly state led to its official closure and further interments were forbidden. A few years later the Rev. Edward May is said to have levelled the graveyard and torn up the headstones, in spite of the protests of many who had relatives buried there. He eventually had a Bill passed in Parliament giving power to dispose of the outlying parts of the graveyard, which he did for the area next to Ann Street. The last remains of the old church and graveyard were removed when the present St. George's was built, between 1812 and 1817. Most of the gravestones were then lost but part of the Pottinger memorial was removed to Old Kilmore graveyard (see *Gravestone Inscriptions, County Down*, Vol. 3) and other stones were taken to the New Burying Ground (e.g. LENNOX and McILWAIN).

The other ancient graveyards which were used down the centuries should also be considered—Shankill and Friar's Bush. The former is the mother church of Belfast, being mentioned in the 1306 Papal Taxation, and it is described fully in the first volume of the Belfast series of *Gravestone Inscriptions*. Friar's Bush also dates from mediaeval times but there are few gravestones or records from before 1800. Its pre-1900 inscriptions are included in *Gravestone Inscriptions, Belfast*, Vol. 2. Each of these graveyards was, of course, well outside the city until the beginning of the nineteenth century.

While the changes in the churches were taking place in the late eighteenth century, the condition of the poor was causing increasing concern. A Charitable Scheme was established in 1752 to raise money to build a Poor House and Hospital. Things proceeded slowly and it was not until 1770 that the 5th Earl of Donegall gave the land for a building and in the following year Stewart Banks, the Sovereign of Belfast, laid the foundation stone. The Society was formally incorporated in 1774 and was involved from its inception in caring for the needy, both adults and children. Its members were also instrumental in starting the General Hospital. In addition, it took up the task of providing work in the form of spinning and weaving, first of linen and later of cotton. Their other principal area of activity was in providing a water supply

Old Belfast Families

Portrait of Arthur, 1st Marquess of Donegall (1739-1799) by Thomas Gainsborough (Ulster Museum).

Introduction

for Belfast (see Strain: *Belfast and its Charitable Society* (1961)).

It was in this context, therefore, that the General Board of the Charitable Society recommended on 27 October 1795 'appropriating one of the fields up the lane for the purpose of a burying ground.' The lane was Buttle's Loney which ran along the south and west side of the Poor House, and continued on to Vicinage, the home of Thomas McCabe. In the following month they resolved that the field 'lately in the possession of the Revd. Mr Bristow be enclosed in with a wall and appropriated for a burying ground.' While one purpose was to provide a New Burying Ground worthy of the citizens of Belfast, it was seen mainly as a means of raising money for the Charitable Society, with the sale of lots commencing in January 1797. The oldest stone truly belonging to the graveyard dates from 1799 (LOWRY), though earlier eighteenth century stones were brought there for safe keeping.

The wall was constructed slowly over the years, not only to protect the graveyard from public nuisance, but to provide the more valuable wall-lots for sale. By November 1819 only the east side, nearest the House, was incomplete. It was calculated that the income since 1798 had been £2,097 and, deducting the value of the land, the cost of building the wall and maintenance, the profit had been £1,548. The potential value of the remainder of the upper ground, even allowing for paupers' plots, was a further £654. At that time it was decided to take possession of the lower field, then let to Mr. W. McClure, and by 1828 this was done and the extension also walled in. The next phase in the maintenance was the erection of a gate-lodge in 1840, but it must have been rather a poor affair as by 1884 it had been declared unfit for habitation. By then, the aproaches to the Burying Ground had been greatly improved by the construction of Henry Place and a good road as far as the entrance to the Military Barracks. The old lodge was replaced by a properly built house, which has only recently been abandoned. A resident caretaker was still employed, but much later the house was occupied by the Society's engineer, who was responsible for opening and closing the gates and for general supervision. A groundsman was employed to tend the graves and the upkeep of the ground.

One of the problems faced by the New Burying Ground, like other graveyards of the early nineteenth century, was that of 'body-snatchers'. Anatomy had been taught at the Academical Institution since 1818 and in subsequent years there was a steady trade in disinterring fresh corpses for sale to the anatomists of Belfast and across the water. We only know for certain of one episode which occurred here in 1824, in which an infant's coffin, several years interred, was lifted and left unopened on the ground. Public alarm reached its height in 1828 with the trial in Edinburgh of Burke and Hare for committing several murders to provide corpses. The whole subject is discussed by Dr. John Fleetwood in *The Irish Body Snatchers* (1988) as well as in Strain's *History* above-mentioned and in Skillen's *The resurrectionists in County Antrim* (1939).

In response to these developments, several devices were used to protect the corpse until such time as decomposition had rendered it valueless to the grave robbers. One was an iron cage in which the entire coffin was enclosed prior to interment, an example of which is preserved in the Ulster Museum. A heavy gravestone also gave some protection but of course was valueless for a new grave, as it was not usually placed in position for some weeks. Night watchmen were sometimes employed to deter would-be grave robbers but, after some disturbances in the New Burying Ground, a rule was made in 1830 forbidding them from taking firearms into the graveyard at night. This was not sufficient and in 1833 it appears that the watchmen fired several shots during the night, which went into the barracks nearby. Body snatching ceased to be a problem when the Anatomy Act, legalising the supply of bodies for dissection, was passed in 1832.

Coffin guard from the days of the body-snatchers in the early nineteenth century, dug up from the New Burying Ground during grave digging operations. (Ulster Museum).

Although the graveyard was planned mainly as a means of raising funds for the Society, it was agreed as early as 1799 that those who had no funds were to be buried within the graveyard. In 1819 60 lots were allocated to the poor and in 1832 Dr Drummond was permitted to have a single grave in the Paupers' Ground for the interment of subjects granted to the Anatomical School.

However, by 1832 a much larger problem was reaching Belfast — the Asiatic cholera — and the Fever Hospital in Frederick Street had special wards added to cope with the epidemic. Of course, the water-borne nature of the disease was not understood until later, and isolation of the victims and of the healthy in the Poor House seemed to be the only possible precaution against infection. It is therefore to the credit of the doctors and nurses of the Fever Hospital that by 12 November the number of deaths in Belfast was only 418 out of a total of 2,827 cases. Only 23 of these were buried in the New Burying Ground. The cause of death is rarely given on a gravestone but it may be noted in passing that Dr Thomas Simpson of Moira is recorded as having died of cholera in this epidemic (*Gravestone Inscriptions, County Down*, Vol. 18). Other epidemics followed in 1834, 1836 and 1837 and because of pressure of space in 1840 the Committee decided to confine the interment of paupers to those who died in the Poor House. They did, however, allow the committees of the Lying-in Hospital and the Belfast District Lunatic

Introduction

Asylum to bury their dead in the New Burying Ground 'only that they shall be at the expense of digging the graves'.

The real crisis came in 1845-7 with the potato blight, subsequent famine and widespread deaths from cholera, typhus, relapsing fever, dysentery and smallpox. The fever was brought into Belfast by starving country people and quickly spread through the city. Deaths became so numerous that the New Burying Ground was again opened for burials from all over the city and as many as 20 deaths in one day were often accommodated. Among the casualties were the surgeons Alfred Anderson and James McCleery (q.v.). Strain gives the following figures for burials during 1847 as due to fever, 812; dysentery, 131; smallpox, 42; and bodies from other places without diagnosis, 64. The area where most of the poor were buried was known as 'the cholera ground' and it is essentially the part of the upper field nearest to the gap in the dividing wall. In the nature of things there were no gravestones in this plot, indeed the emptiness was much more obvious when the rest of the ground was covered with gravestones. Friar's Bush graveyard was also used for mass burial of victims of epidemics.

The year 1847 did not mark the end of the epidemics, but certainly there was never again such a major catastrophe in the city. In the epidemic of 1849, for instance, there were only 35 pauper burials, none of which came from the Poor House itself. This was fortunate because the graveyard was filling up rapidly and by 1856 the last of the lots had been sold, although residents of the Poor House continued to be buried there until 1882 and lots were re-let as late as 1884. Henceforth there would be no more profit, only the expense of upkeep. Interestingly, the last burial took place as recently as 1984.

Despite the Society's efforts, the state of the burying ground was getting worse, judging from the Annual Report of 1884, in which appears the following:

'The state of the graveyard has long occupied the attention of the Committee. Considerable pains and expense have been devoted to its improvement, but the result is still far from satisfactory. The difficulty lies chiefly in the fact that many lots in the proprietary parts of the ground have suffered from time and weather. Headstones and monuments have become dilapidated, railings are eaten away with rust, and gates unhinged and fallen. In several cases there are no representatives of the families to whom such places of interment belonged. In some other cases the representatives have almost wholly neglected the resting place of their fathers. The funds of the Charity are not available to keep proprietary monuments and lots in repair, hence the discreditable state into which some parts of the graveyard have fallen. The case demands prompt measures in the application of a remedy, and is now submitted to the Corporation i.e. the General Board. It is suggested that the Corporation urgently appeal to families having places of interment in the ground that requisite attention and care be bestowed upon them; that a subscription list be opened by persons interested in the burying ground to enable the Committee to keep in proper condition such places of sepulture as have not any representative to care for them.

The Committee has closed the common ground against further interments in accordance with the report of the Chief Sanitary Officer of the Borough, and have planted trees and shrubs that will improve the aspect of that portion of the graveyard and the neighbourhood generally. But much more remains to be done, and a considerable expense must be incurred, if the necessary improvement is to be effectively completed.'

As a result of a public appeal sum of £409 18s 8d. was received towards the cost of putting the ground in order and this improvement seems to have been maintained until the end of the World War I. The Annual Report for 1915 comments as follows:-

'In consequence of age and the weather it is difficult to keep it in such order as one would wish, principally because of the large number of iron railings surrounding many of the graves. Many owners have renewed and improved their plots, and when necessary the Society has spent on those committed to its care.'

In 1930, after further deterioration, a fresh appeal was made to all the families owning plots who could be traced. The result was not very encouraging as few relatives were forthcoming. Nevertheless, a full-time groundsman was employed and the general condition was greatly improved. What could not be done was to halt the deterioration of much of the stone and ironwork, the sandstone tablets being particularly vulnerable. Heavy headstones erected on inadequate foundations were no less liable to suffer from the effects of wind and weather. After World War II it became increasingly difficult to find groundsmen willing to undertake this kind of work and, when the last groundsman left in the autumn of 1969, he was not replaced. From time to time it had been suggested that the Belfast Corporation should take over the graveyard and in 1967 the Superintendent of Parks and Cemeteries, after consultation with the Town Solicitor, again rejected the proposal. It was felt that legal problems with many of the owners of plots still using the ground would lead to difficulties.

In the spring of 1970 the army took over the graveyard, essentially to protect the Glenravel Street police station from attack. This ensured its preservation though not, of course the upkeep. However, when they left in 1973 the worst phase in the graveyard's history began, with destruction of stones by vandals on a massive scale by smashing and daubing with paint, while the trees were hacked and partly burned. When this had gone on for some years the Parks and Cemeteries Department finally changed its mind and took over the maintenance in 1979, though formal acceptance was not until 1984. Since then an effort has been made to clean some memorials and restore others, at the same time rendering the burying ground more manageable with mechanical equipment and making it safe even for the vandals! Unfortunately, because of the loss of stones and the tidy transecting paths, the New Burying Ground will never again have the natural charm which some of us remember in the 1950s and 1960s.

While all graveyards are important genealogically, the New Burying Ground is particularly interesting as a source for the social history of Belfast during the first half of the last century. The political world of the United Irishmen and the 1798 rising is represented by such key figures as Henry Joy McCracken (whose remains were brought here to be beside his sister Mary Ann), the Rev. William Steel Dickson and Dr William Drennan. The shipbuilding industry has the graves of William, John and Hugh Ritchie who really established it in the centre of Belfast as early as 1800. Happily their

Introduction

memorials are well preserved, but the stone of William Pirrie, father of Viscount Pirrie, was smashed by the vandals of the 1970s.

The occupation which is best represented in the new Burying Ground is that of medicine. There is generally a much larger concentration of medical men in urban than in rural graveyards, and this is the case in Clifton Street. The principal names encountered in this respect are William Aickin, Alfred Anderson, John Milford Barnett, Robert Coffey, William Drennan, John S. Drennan, Edward Gribbin, Alexander H. Haliday, William Haliday, Thomas McCabe, James McCleery, Robert McCluney, Andrew Marshall, John Mattear, William Moffatt, John Neilson, Alexander Officier, John Quinn, James Maxwell Sanders, Samuel M. Stephenson, Robert Stevenson, Thomas Thompson, Samuel Smith Thomson, John Vint, James Wilson and Thomas Wilson. Many of them were closely associated with the Charitable Society: Dr Robert Stevenson, for example, bequeathed the large sum of £1,000 to the Society. One of the most notable of the Belfast physicians, Dr Andrew Malcolm, was buried at Dunmurry but, in his *History*, he mentions many of the above group, referring lovingly to Dr S. S. Thomson as the "Father of the profession" in Belfast. Although, as mentioned earlier, two surgeons died during the Great Famine, Dr Andrew Marshall survived a period as naval surgeon under Admiral Gambier in the Baltic to become the first secretary and treasurer of the Medical Society (and later its president) and eventually died in 1868 at the age of 88.

Natural history is represented by such names as George Crawford Hyndman and John Templeton of Cranmore and it is satisfying to see that the two greatest benefactors of the Charitable Institute, Edward Benn and John Charters, are buried here. There are several booksellers, publishers and paper-makers such as the Blows, the Greers, the Kennedys, the Simms and two of the families most involved in the *Belfast News Letter*, the Joys and Mackays, as well as Frederick Dalzell Finlay, founder of the *Northern Whig*. Finally most of the business families of Belfast during the nineteenth century are commemorated: Boomer, Batt, Bristow, Dobbin, Dunville, Eakenhead, Ewart, Herron, Jones, Mulholland, Murray, Workman, etc.

There is no burial register for the early years of the graveyard, but from 1831 there are burials registered as follows:-

1831-1841	2,600
1841-1864	5,940
1865-1978	3,097
Total	11,637

These records are of great interest medically in their curious descriptions of causes of death, such as "decay of nature" or "break up of constitution" and they also have value to the social historian, especially for the period of the great epidemics when this was the principal graveyard for the city. The burial register is kept in Clifton House and, while it has been consulted frequently, no complete collation with the inscriptions was carried out in the preparation of this volume.

In 1907 it was decided to compile a transcript of all the headstones and tablets. The transcription occupies three volumes, and it has been one of the main sources for this book. However, the surviving headstones were again copied by one of us (A.C.W.M.) in 1973-4 and checked against the 1907 text. Finally, a

Old Belfast Families

further check on surviving stones was made in 1991. The figures, sadly, show an even faster rate of loss than in most graveyards since, of a total of approximately eleven hundred inscriptions listed here, almost all pre-1907 in date, nearly twenty per cent had disappeared by 1973 and a further fifty per cent by the present day. It should be said that a few stones listed as lost may be still extant, though face downwards or buried, and a few more survive but are virtually unrecognisable. Where there is a description of a stone and the phrase "now lost" it usually means that the stone has disappeared since 1973. We can only be grateful to the 1907 copyist for his early record and glad that further recording could be done before the destruction of the 1970s.

Ecclesiastical records of baptism, marriage and burial were kept erratically in Ireland during the 18th and 19th centuries and particularly for Presbyterians and Roman Catholics. In addition, for over one thousand parishes of the established church pre 1870 baptismal and burial registers and pre 1845 marriage registers were deposited in the Public Record Office in Dublin and destroyed there in 1922. Civil registration of Protestant marriages only started in Ireland in 1845 and registration of births, marriages and deaths of all denominations in 1864. Thus although burial registers exist for the parish of St. Anne's, Belfast from 1745, these inscriptions for Clifton Street graveyard for the period 1797-1864 are often the only record of deaths for many of the citizens of Belfast.

While Clifton Street may have suffered more than many graveyards, its problems highlight the need to publish as many as possible of our old inscriptions so that the information may be preserved. As well as this, genealogists abroad with roots in Ireland will welcome a printed record to avoid the problems of sorting out the subtleties of parish and congregation.

We are grateful to the Society for allowing the transcription to take place and to the late Mr T. Nolan of Clifton House for making available the records of burials, gravestone transcripts and other records of the Society; to Mr Joseph Baker who recently transcribed the surviving gravestones, for help and information; to Dr John Logan for information about Drs Coffey and Sanders; to Miss Eileen Black of the Ulster Museum for information on Dr Thomas Thompson; to Dr H.A. Hezlett for information on the Steen family; to Dr R.W.M. Strain for lending so many of the photographs and for writing the *History of the Charitable Society* which ranks with Benn's *History* in its value for the nineteenth century in Belfast; to the Trustees of the Ulster Museum for permission to reproduce so many of the illustrations and the Deputy Keeper of the Public Record Office of Northern Ireland for permission to reproduce the photograph of Hill Hamilton (ANT 4/6/2). Ray Anderson Paul O'Hora and Ronald Ringland carried out the will searches; Mrs Maxine McKinnon typed the text; Joe Passmore typeset the pages; Mr George Brittain of Brittain Laboratories helped prepare the book for the printer, and Trevor Parkhill again gave editorial advice. Finally, we would like to thank the Belfast City Council, the Belfast Natural History and Philosophical Society and the Cultural Traditions Programme of the Community Relations Council for financial assistance towards publication costs.

R.S.J. Clarke
A.C.W. Merrick
June 1991

BIBLIOGRAPHY

Adams, J.R.R.: *The Printed Word and the Common Man. Popular Culture in Ulster 1700-1900.* Belfast 1987.

Addison, W.I.: *The Matriculation Albums of the University of Glasgow, from 1728 to 1828.* Glasgow, 1913.

Allen, Robert: *The Presbyterian College, Belfast, 1852-1953.* Belfast, 1954.

Allison, R.S.: *The Seeds of Time, being a short history of the Belfast General and Royal Hospital, 1850-1903.* Belfast, 1972.

Anderson, J.: *History of the Belfast Library and Society for Promoting Knowledge, commonly known as the Linen Hall Library...* Belfast, 1888.

Andrews, S.: *Nine Generations, a History of the Andrews Family, Millers of Comber.* Belfast, 1958.

Anonymous: *Catalogue of Loan Exhibition of Irish Portraits at Belfast Municipal Museum, March, 1927.* Belfast, 1927.

Anonymous: *The Industries of Ireland, Part I, Belfast and Towns of the North,* London, 1891. Reprint, Belfast, 1986.

Anonymous: *The New Burying Ground with the Inscriptions on the Tombstones.* Belfast, 1907. (Privately printed).

Bailie, W.D. (ed.): *A History of Congregations in the Presbyterian Church in Ireland, 1610-1982.* Belfast, 1982.

Barkley, the Rev. J.M.: *Fasti of the General Assembly of the Presbyterian Church in Ireland, Part I, 1840-1870.* Belfast, 1986. Part II, 1871-1890. Belfast, 1987. Part III, 1891-1910. Belfast, 1987.

Batt, Rev. N.G.: Belfast sixty years ago: recollections of a septuagenarian. *Ulster Journal of Archaeology,* second series, 1896, 2, 92-95.

Beckett, J.C. (ed.): *Belfast, The Making of the City, 1800-1914.* Belfast, 1983.

Belfast Commercial Chronicle, 13 December 1943.

Belfast Literary Society, 1801-1901, Historical Sketch with Memoirs of some Distinguished Members. Belfast, 1902.

Belfast Street Directory, 1807 to 1904.

Benn, George: *A History of the Town of Belfast.* Belfast, 1823.

Benn, George: *A History of the Town of Belfast from earliest times to the close of the eighteenth century.* Vol. 1, London, 1877. Vol. 2, London, 1880.

Biggar, Francis Joseph: The Belfast Poor's House. *Ulster Journal of Archaeology,* second series, 1896, 2, 191-193.

Brett, C.E.B.: *Buildings of Belfast, 1700-1914.* 2nd edition, Belfast, 1985.

Burke, Sir Bernard: *A Genealogical and Heraldic History of the Landed Gentry of Ireland.* London, 1912.

Burke, Sir Bernard: *Burke's Genealogical and Heraldic History of the Landed Gentry of Ireland.* London, 1958.

Burke's Irish Family Records. London, 1976.

Burke's Peerage and Baronetage. 105th edition, London, 1978.

Burtchaell, G.D. and Sadleir, T.U.: *Alumni Dublinenses.* London, 1924.

Calwell, H.G.: *Andrew Malcolm of Belfast, 1818-1856, Physician and Historian.* Belfast, 1977.

Campbell, A.A.: *Belfast Newspapers, Past and Present.* Belfast, 1921.

Chambers, G.: *Faces of Change — The Belfast and Northern Ireland Chambers of Commerce and Industry*. Belfast, 1983.

Chart, D.A.: *The Drennan Letters, being a selection of the Correspondence which passed between William Drennan, M.D., and his brother-in-law and sister, Samuel and Martha McTier during the years 1776-1819*. Belfast, 1931.

Clarke, R.S.J.: *Gravestone Inscriptions, County Down*, Vol.2, 2nd edition, Belfast, 1988. Vol. 3, Belfast, 1969. Vol.4, Belfast, 1969. Vol. 5, 2nd edition, Belfast 1984.

Clarke, R.S.J.: *Gravestone Inscriptions, Belfast*. Vol. 1, Belfast, 1982. Vol. 3, Belfast, 1986.

Crookshank, Rev. C.H.: *History of Methodism in Ireland*. Three volumes. Belfast 1885-1888.

Deane, A. (ed.): *The Belfast Natural History and Philosophical Society, Centenary Volume, 1821-1921*. Belfast, 1924.

Dictionary of National Biography, with Supplement to 1911. London, 1913.

Ferrar, M.L.: *Register of the Royal School, Armagh*. Belfast, 1933.

Fisher, J.R. and Robb, J.H.: *Royal Belfast Academical Institution, Centenary Volume, 1810-1910*. Belfast, 1913.

Fleetwood, John: *The Irish Body Snatchers*. Dublin, 1988.

Gaffikin, T.: *Belfast Fifty Years Ago*. Belfast, 1894.

Gallagher, Rev. R.H.: *Pioneer Preachers of Irish Methodism*. Belfast, 1965.

Garner, Margaret A.K.: *Robert Workman of Newtownbreda, 1835-1921*. Belfast, 1969.

Gracey, Diane: The Decline and Fall of Marcus Ward. *Irish Booklore*, 1971, 1, 186-202.

Hayward, Richard: *Belfast through the Ages*. Dundalk, 1952.

Hill, E.D.: *Northern Banking Company Limited, Centenary Volume*. Belfast, 1925.

Jamieson, J.: *The History of the Royal Belfast Academical Institution, 1810-1960*. Belfast, 1959.

Jefferson, H.: *Viscount Pirrie of Belfast*. Belfast, [c. 1948].

Journal of the Irish Memorials Association or Memorials of the Dead (M.D.). 1909, VII, 511-513. 1918, X, 159-161. 1921, XI, 1.

Kernohan, J.W.: *Rosemary Street Presbyterian Church, Belfast*. Belfast, 1923.

Killen, J.: *A History of the Linen Hall Library, 1788-1988*. Belfast, 1990.

Kilpatrick, Rev. T.: *Millisle and Ballycopeland Presbyterian Church, A Short History*. Newtownards, 1934.

Latimer, W. T.: *Ulster Biographies relating chiefly to the Rebellion of 1798*. Belfast 1897.

Leslie, Rev. J.B.: *Ferns Clergy and Parishes*. Dublin, 1936.

Leslie, Rev. J.B.: *Raphoe Clergy and Parishes*. Enniskillen, 1940.

Leslie, Rev. J.B. and Swanzy, the Rev. H.B.: *Biographical Succession Lists of the Clergy of Diocese of Down*. Enniskillen, 1936.

Logan, J.S.: Doctor Sanders' silver lancet case. *Ulster Medical Journal*, 1991, 60, 93-95.

Loudan, J.: *In Search of Water, being a history of the Belfast Water Supply*. Belfast, 1940.

Loughridge, the Rev. Adam: *Fasti of the Reformed Presbyterian Church of*

Bibliography

Ireland, Part 1. Belfast, 1970.
McConnell, the Rev. J.: *Fasti of the Irish Presbyterian Church, 1613-1840.* Belfast, 1951.
McNeill, Mary: *The Life and Times of Mary Ann McCracken, 1770-1866.* Dublin, 1960.
McNeill, Mary: *Little Tom Drennan.* Dublin, 1962.
McNeill, Mary: *Vere Foster, 1819-1900, An Irish Benefactor.* Newton Abbott, 1971.
McTear, T. and Biggar, F.J.: Personal recollections of the beginning of the century. *Ulster Journal of Archaeology,* second series, 1899, 5, 162-174.
Madden, R.R.: *Antrim and Down in Ninety-eight.* Glasgow, n.d.
Malcolm, A.G.: *The History of the General Hospital, Belfast, and the other Medical Institutions of the Town.* Belfast, 1851.
Marshall, J.J.: *Old Belfast, the Origin and Progress of the City.* Belfast, 1894.
Merrick, A.C.W.: Some gleanings from Belfast's New Burying Ground. *North Belfast Historical Magazine,* 1984, No. 1, 6-20 and 1986, No. 2, 13-20.
Merrick, A.C.W.: *Gravestone Inscriptions, Belfast.* Vol. 2, Belfast, 1984.
Millin, J. Shannon: *Sidelights on Belfast History.* Belfast, 1932.
Millin, J. Shannon: *Additional Sidelights on Belfast History.* Belfast, 1938.
Millin, S. Shannon: *History of the Second Congregation of Protestant Dissenters in Belfast.* Belfast, 1900.
Moody, T.W. and Beckett, J.C.: *Queen's, Belfast 1845-1949. The History of a University.* Two volumes. London, 1959.
O'Byrne, Cathal: *As I Roved Out.* Belfast, 1946.
O'Laverty, Rev. James: *An Historical Account of the Diocese of Down and Connor, Ancient and Modern.* Vol. II, Dublin, 1880.
Owen, D.J.: *A Short History of the Port of Belfast.* Belfast, 1917.
Owen, D.J.: *History of Belfast.* Belfast, 1921.
Pim, E.W. (ed.): *The Acts of Parliament constituting the Belfast Charitable Society ... together with a chronological statement, drawn up by order of the Board in 1879.* Belfast, 1899.
Praeger, R.L.: *Some Irish Naturalists, a Biographical Notebook.* Dundalk, 1949.
Roddie, I.C.: *An Excellent Medical School.* Belfast, 1965.
Simpson, Noel: *The Belfast Bank, 1827-1970.* Belfast, 1975.
Skillen, J.: The resurrectionists in county Antrim. *Ulster Journal of Archaeology,* third series, 1939, 2, 22-25.
Stewart, A.T.Q.: *Belfast Royal Academy. The First Century, 1785-1885.* Belfast, 1985.
Stewart, Rev. David: *The Seceders in Ireland with Annals of their Congregations.* Belfast, 1950.
Strain, R.W.M.: *Belfast and its Charitable Society.* London, 1961.
Stuart, James: *Historical Memoirs of the City of Armagh.* New edition, revised, etc. with introduction by the Rev. Ambrose Coleman. Dublin, 1900.
Swanzy, H.B.: *Succession Lists of the Diocese of Dromore.* Belfast, 1933.
Wilson, A: *Fragments that Remain.* Belfast, 1950.
Young, R.M. and Pike, W.T.: *Belfast and the Province of Ulster in the 20th Century.* Brighton, 1909.

CLIFTON STREET BURYING GROUND, BELFAST
O.S. Antrim 61. Grid Ref. 335752

ADAIR
[Stone now missing from upper ground.] Erected by Hugh Adair in affectionate remembrance of his son Charles D.L. Adair died 24th October 1862 aged 4 years. Also his beloved daughter Martha Ainsworth Adair who fell asleep in Jesus, 16th January 1875 aged 13 years.

ADAMS
[Broken and flaking.] Erected to the memory of Gilbert Adams of Belfast who died July 10th 1818 aged 27 years.

ADAMS
[No longer extant, but recorded in the Society's Inscription books.] Erected by Robert Adams in memory of his ... (John) Adams who departed this life on the (30)th June 1834 aged 54 years.

AGNEW
[Marble tablet in a large pedimented headstone, topped by a draped urn, now lost.] Erected by James Agnew, Belfast, in memory of his beloved wife Jane who departed this life on the 25th Sept. 1855 aged 39 years. Also his son George Alexander who died on the 20th August 1850 aged 14 months. And his son John who died on the 12th Feby 1866 aged 18 years. The above James Agnew died 23rd April 1866 aged 62 years. Also his daughter Lizzie, the beloved wife of Daniel DIXON, of Belfast, who died 4th June 1868 aged 27 years. Also his son James who died 15th February 1871 aged 27 years. Also his daughter Mary Jane who died 25th Feby 1910 aged 72 years.

[The will of James Agnew late of Prospect Terrace Belfast in the county of Antrim, timber merchant, who died 23 April 1866 at same place, was proved at Belfast 30 May 1866 by the oaths of William McNeill of Upper Crescent and James Agnew Junior and William Agnew, both of Propect Terrace (all in Belfast aforesaid), merchants, the executors. Effects under £8,000.

Daniel Dixon (1843-1907) was the last Mayor of Belfast, becoming its first Lord Mayor in 1893, having been knighted the previous year. He also served several terms as Lord Mayor in the 1900s at which time he lived outside Holywood.]

AGNEW
[This stone in the lower portion of the graveyard is no longer extant and was probably replaced by the Celtic cross below.] Sacred to the memory of Robert Agnew, engineer, who died 27th May 1859 aged 50 years. Also five of his children who died in infancy. This monument is erected by a few of his friends, and the workmen of the Shipyard Foundry, Belfast, as a mark of respect to his memory. Thomas Agnew, son of the above Robert Agnew, who died 24th April 1871 aged 25 years. Also his wife Elizabeth who died 31st Oct. 1887 aged 74 years.

AGNEW

[Polished granite Celtic cross (now laid flat), adorned with interlacing, and in a low enclosure.] In loving memory of Robert Agnew who died 27th July 1859 aged 50 years. Of his son Thomas Agnew who died 24th April 1871 aged 25 years. Of his wife Elizabeth Agnew who died 24th October 1887 aged 68 years. And of his daughter Mary Teresa Leslie KELLY, beloved wife of John Kelly, who died 26th July 1920 aged 61 years. "Requiescant in pace". Erected by John Kelly.

AICKIN

[Very badly flaked, now lost] Sacred to the memory of (Francis) Aickin who departed this life the (19th) day of Feby. (1826) aged 7(2) years. "My (flesh) shall (also rest in hope). The Lord (gave) and the Lord hath (taken away). Blessed be the name of the Lord"

AICKIN

[Raised slab, which was badly flaked and smashed into four pieces, now lost.] To the memory of William Aickin (late of Corn Market, Belfast, Surgeon, (who depart)ed (this life) Ap(ril) 15th 1837 (aged 41 years) A most affectionate and dutiful son, a truly loving brother and tender husband, his sincere and unostentatious piety and his well directed intelligence will long be cherished by those who knew him. "The sweet remembrance of the just shall f(lourish) when he sleeps in dust". And here are buried Samuel B. Aickin and Graves Chamney his children who died you(ng) ... Here also are interred the remains of Margaret (Aicki)n, da(ughter of) the (la)te Francis Aickin of Lur(gan who die)d the 22nd day of December 18(35). Also Jane wife of Surgeon ... John Aickin who died 1(6th) March 1(855). And two of their children John and Thomas. (Gr)aves Thos Aickin died Dec 19th 1859 aged 69. Frances his wife died Sept, 18(5)0 aged 35. Frances his daughter died Jan. 28, 18(5)7 aged 13. Jane his daughter died April (17), 1845 aged 6 mo.

AICKIN

See SMITH

AIKEN

Erected by Richard Aiken in memory of his son Thomas who died 16th Octr. 1847 aged 10 months. Also his son Richard who died 29th April 1849 aged 4 years. Underneath lies the remains of the above named Richard Aiken who departed this life on the 2nd of January 1852 aged 44 years. Also his daughter Mary Aiken who died 15th January 1854 aged 4 years. Also Ann Aiken, wife of the above named Richard Aiken, died 29th February 1885 aged 69 years. Also their son William Aiken died 9th February 1911 in his 76th year.

AINSWORTH

See McCREEDY

ALD(ERDICE)

[Very badly flaked headstone.] ... Frances Ald(erdice who departed) this life March 20th (in the year o)f Our Lord 180(3) aged (48) years. Also

James (Alderdice died November 2nd in the) year (of Our Lord 1812) aged (38 years).

ALEXANDER

[Broken sandstone, badly flaked near top.] Sacred (to the) memory of John (Alex)ander, Peter's Hill, (who depar)ted this life January the 2( ), 1832 aged 84 (years). John Alexander junr departed this life Decr the 13th 181(7) [7 over 3] aged 39 years. Sarah Alexander departed this life December the 12th 1814 aged 57.

[For several generations the Alexander family kept an inn on Peter's Hill, and it was in John Alexander's ownership when it was raided by the Monaghan Militia in 1797, as they had received information that it was a meeting place of the United Irishmen. In the *Belfast Directory* of 1808, he is described as owning a carman's inn at No. 11, Peter's Hill, and in the 1819 *Directory*, the address is given as No. 27.]

ALEXANDER

[At base of marble cross against north wall.] In memory of John Alexander of Ardmoulin, Belfast, died 23rd December 1821 aged 86 years. Also his second son, Andrew Alexander, Sovereign of Belfast, died at Ardmoulin 24th October 1824 aged 43 years. Also James Alexander of St. Clair, Holywood, died 9th February 1882 aged 63 years.

[Andrew Alexander was co-sovereign with John Agnew for only a few months. James Alexander whose family originally hailed from Milford House, near Carlow, Co. Carlow was a partner of John Alexander & Co., Belfast Flour Mills, Falls Road. For the last few years of his life he was a Town Commissioner of Holywood.

Letters of administration of the personal estate of James of James Alexander late of St. Clair Holywood Co. Down, Esquire J.P. who died 9 February 1882 at same place were granted at Belfast 20 March 1882 to Lucia Margaret Alexander of St. Clair, Holywood, the widow. Effects £43,545 12s.6d.]

ALEXANDER

[Formerly in lower ground and now missing.] Erected to the memory of the Revd. Edwd. Alexander of Belfast, who died 12th Nov. 1832 aged 58 years.

[The Rev. Edward Alexander was born near Kilmood, county Down, entered the Belfast Academical Institution and obtained the General Certificate in 1820. He was licenced by the Belfast Presbytery in 1823 and ordained Minister of Carlow Presbyterian Church on 23 June 1825. He resigned, presumably because of ill health on 5 April 1828. See Fisher and Robb: *The Royal Belfast Academical Institution, Centenary Volume* (1913); McConnell: *Fasti of the Irish Presbyterian Church* (1951).]

ALEXANDER

[Now lost] Erected by John Alexander of Antrim, in memory of his beloved daughter Jane Alexander who departed this life in Belfast, 14th March 1841 aged 9 years and 5 months. "I know that my Redeemer liveth, and that He shall stand at the latter day upon the earth: and though after my skin worms destroy this body, yet in my flesh shall I see God".

ALEXANDER
[Raised horizontal slab, now lost.] Sacred to the memory of Robert Alexander, of Belfast, who departed this life 26th October 1852 aged 54 years. And his children: Robert, James, Alicia and Alice Jane who died young. Also his brother Thomas Alexander, of Ballymena, who died 10th November 1848 aged 60 years.

ALEXANDER
[Worn sandstone plaque set into north wall probably of c.1820-60.] (The bur)ying ground of the (Alexander) and CRANSTON families.

ALLEN
[Flaking headstone now lost.] Erected to the memory of John Allen who departed this life September 24th 1821 AE 43 years. Also his son William who departed on the 1 of May 1810 AE 4 months. Likewise his son Archibold [sic] who departed on the 9 of Sept 1811 AE 2 years and his son John who departed on the 9 of Sept 1814 AE 6 years.

ALLEN
[Top broken off.] E(rected by) James Allen to the memory of his brother Robert who died the 8th of May 1833 aged 24 years. The above named James Allen died 9th November 1865 aged 67 years. Also his wife Rachel who died 30th July 1866 aged 72 years. Also his daughter in law Agnes Allen, who died 23rd July 1885 aged 49 years. Also his son James Allen who died 23rd August 1892 aged 61 years. Also Rachel, daughter of the last named James Allen, who died 17th October 1912 aged 47 years.

[The will of James Allen late of Belfast in the county of Antrim, tailor who died 9 November 1865 at same place was proved at Belfast 11 April 1866 by oath of Edward Gribben, watchmaker and jeweller, and James Allen Junior, (salesman) both of Belfast aforesaid, the executors. Effects under £800.]

ALLEN
[Large headstone, now lost — copied from Inscription book.] To the memory of three sisters, the Misses Allen, Donegall Place, Belfast: Bess, who died on 29th Nov. 1851 aged 63 years, Susanna, 4th Dec. 1853 aged 74 years, Jane, 20th March 1854 aged 60 years.

ALLEN
[Worn marble in surround now lost.] Sacred to the memory of my beloved husband Richard Allen C.E., who was drowned in Belfast Lough, 27th May 1866 AE (34) years. "He is not lost, they who are (Christ's) ...ing with him at his coming". Also his father William Allen C.E. who departed this life 19th July 1852, AE 54 years. Also Anna, eldest daughter of Richard Allen C.E.

Here shall I bathe my weary soul
(in) seas of heavenly rest,
And not a wave of trouble rolls

across my peaceful breast.
Also Christian, second daughter died January 23rd 1909.

ALLEN
See COATES, GIBSON and McCONNELL

ALLEY
See BYRTT and THOMSON

ANDERSON
[Stone in upper ground and now missing. The plot was bought by Henry Anderson in February 1828.] To the memory of Eliza the beloved wife of Henry Anderson who died 5th June ..... [A text of scripture followed but it was indecipherable even in 1907.]

ANDERSON
[Raised horizontal slab, now lost.] Erected by the children of James Anderson in memory of their father who departed this life 21st of July 1833 aged 48 years.

ANDERSON
[Small undated headstone looking of c.1870-1900, now lost.] The family burying ground of James Anderson, Belfast.
[James Anderson bought this plot in October 1846.]

ANDERSON
[Worn marble headstone now lost.] In memory of (Alfred Anderson) who died on Sunday the third day of (October 1847), in the (2)5th year of his age, of malignant fever contracted in the (furtherance) of his duty, as Resident Surgeon of the Belfast General Hospital.
[Alfred Anderson had been house surgeon in the Belfast General Hospital, which was situated in Frederick Street, for only a few months when he died as a result of attending the very large numbers of people who had been struck down by typhus and relapsing fever during the Great Famine and epidemic of 1847. See Allison: *The Seeds of Time* (1972).

ANDERSON
[Completely weathered in the middle and now lost.] Erected (by) William (And)erson in mem(ory of his) children, Marga(ret who) departed this life 1st No(vember 1847 aged) 2 years. James, 21st February 1854 aged 3 yrs. Margt Ann, 28th March 1855 AE (2), Mary Ann, 26th Septr 1869 AE 8. Also (his mother-in-law Martha GORDON) who died on 26th (March 1851 aged 6)6 years.

ANDERSON
[Marble tablet in sandstone surround, supporting a draped urn, laid flat.] In memory of Drummond Anderson, the affectionate husband, the kind father, the faithful friend: who died on the (2)0th day of July 18(49) aged (73) years. This tablet is erected by his widow and children.

ANDERSON
[White limestone, lying flat.] In memory of Helen, the loving and

beloved wife of John C. Anderson, died 23rd day of September 1849. Also John Crossley Anderson died 22nd Sep. 1888. Also his beloved wife Jane MONTGOMERIE, died 26th February 1915. And their children Alfred and Annie and Thomas.

[The will of John Crossley Anderson of 8 The Mount, Mountpottinger, county Down, gentleman who died 22 September 1888 at same place was proved at Belfast 1 September 1890 by Jane Montgomerie Anderson and Francis Anderson, bank clerk, both of 8 The Mount, Mountpottinger the executors. Effects £660.]

ANDERSON
[Laid flat, top now missing.] Erected by James Anderson, of Belfast, in memory of his mother Mary Anderson who died 19th September 1854 aged 50 years.

ANDERSON
[Broken marble with lead letters, in fallen headstone, now lost.] Here resteth the remains of William Jones Anderson, born 20 March 1856, died 24 October 1857, eldest son of John Anderson, No. 19, Donegall Street, Belfast, and Holywood, Justice of the Peace, and of Jane JONES his wife ...... said John was born 8 July 1815, died [left blank]. Said Jane was born 3 Febuary [sic] 1822, died 23 May 1891. .... their second son, also named William Jones Anderson was born 19 November 1858, died 8 July 1879, having lost his life in a storm on Lough Allen in the West of Ireland when on a canoeing expedition with his friend Kenneth S. REED, of London.

ANDERSON
[Corroded iron plaque in low-railed enclosure, now lost.] The family burying ground of William Anderson, (1868).

ANDERSON
[Polished granite in low enclosure, laid flat.] Sacred to the memory of Joseph Anderson who entered into rest 16th December 1897, aged 77 years. "Light is sown for the righteous, and gladness for the upright in heart". Psalm XCVII., 11. And his wife Amelia Anderson who fell asleep 19th February 1900, aged 79 years. "Absent from the body ... present with the Lord". II Corinthians v.8 Also their children:
Thomas Alexr died April 1852 aged 1 year
James Dickson died 26th Feb. 1859 aged 1 month
John Dickson died 1st Oct. 1871 aged 8 3/4 years
Joseph Dickson died 16th April 1875 aged 15 years

[Probate of the will 11th February 1898 of Joseph Anderson late of 3 Easton Gardens, Cliftonville, Belfast gentleman who died 16 December 1897 at Colwyn Bay, North Wales, granted at Belfast 11 February 1898 to Samuel Anderson of 6 Easton Crescent, Belfast, and Thomas Anderson of 3 Easton Gardens, Cliftonville, Belfast, merchants. Effects £3,028 18s.6d.]

ANDERSON
See NEILL and YOUNG

ANDREWS

[Large twin tablets in a large pedimented memorial now broken, flaking and laid flat.] Sacred to the memory of Thomas Andrews of Belfast who died 10th June 1809, and of his widow Anne FORDE who died in 1814. Also of Elizabeth MEEK who died 15th March 1841, the relict of Michael Andrews, of Castlewellan, who is interred at Wigton in England, where he died in 1805.

Dedicated by Michael Andrews, Ardoyne, to the memory of his wife Sarah D. McWILLIAM, who departed this life 11th December 1813, and of their two children, Michael deceased 5th February 1814, Thomas deceased 24th August 1829. Also of his second wife Margt McCAMMON, ob. 20th March 1844, and their son Joseph, ob. U.S.A. June 1855. Also of Isaac Robert, son of Michael and Eliza ORMISTON Andrews, ob. 19th May 1867 aged 14 years. Here also are interred the mortal remains of Michael Andrews, Ardoyne, ob. 20th December 1870 aged 82 years. Also Thomas Corbitt Andrews, son of the above died on the 30th of April 1875 aged 25 years. And here also Eliza Ormiston Andrews, widow of Michael Andrews, Ardoyne, who died 19th October 1900 aged 87 years. George their youngest son died 3rd July 1920 aged 66. And his wife Eugenie died 28th November 1936 aged 80 years.

Dedicated to the memory of Thomas John Andrews who departed this life 16th June 1842. Also of his son Wm S. Andrews, who died 4th Oct. 1858 aged 38, and of his widow Elizabeth Andrews who died 12th Feb. 1859 aged 69. And of Jane Hardie Johnston Andrews daughter of Thomas Andrews, M.D., F.R.S., born, 30th Nov. 1849, died 7th Aug. 1861. Michael Andrews died 15th May 1889 aged 70 years. Also his daughter Isabella Jane Johnston Andrews died 27th December 1870 aged 12 years. Jane Johnston Andrews, daughter of the above Thomas John Andrews & Elizabeth Andrews died 5th February 1897 aged 81 years. Margaret Andrews wife of the above Michael Andrews, died 14th Oct. 1905 aged 85 yrs. Also their son Randal W.J. died 3rd Jan. 1906 aged 50, was interred in Paris.

[The will (with two codicils) of Michael Andrews late of Ardoyne near Belfast, county Antrim, linen merchant and damask manufacturer, who died 20 December 1870 at same place, was proved at Belfast 18 January 1871 by the oaths of William Walker of Banbridge, county Down, linen manufacturer, and William Borthwick of Belfast aforesaid, merchant, the executors. Effects under £30,000.

Letters of administration with the will annexed of the personal estate of Thomas Corbitt Andrews formerly of Glendivis, near Belfast and late of Ardoyne Cottage, near Belfast, linen merchant, who died 13 April 1875 at latter place were granted at Belfast 8 March 1876 to Marion Andrews of Orsett, county Essex, the widow and a legatee. Effects under £5,000.

The will of Elizabeth Andrews late of Upper Crescent Belfast in the county of Antrim, widow, who died 12 February 1859 at Upper Crescent aforesaid, was proved at Belfast 30 May 1859 by the oaths of Thomas Andrews of Queens College Belfast M.D. and of James Stevenson Andrews, No. 15 Broad Street London, merchant, the executors. Effects under £8,000.

Photograph of George Andrews of Ardoyne, damask weaver.

The will of Michael Andrews late of 14 University Square Belfast, esquire, who died 15 May 1889 at same place was proved at Belfast 12 July 1889 by Margaret Andrews of 14 University Square, Belfast, widow, the sole executrix. Effects £10,084 9s.3d.

Probate of the will of Jane Johnston Andrews formerly of Belfast, county Antrim and late of Finglas, county Dublin, spinster, who died 5 February 1897 at latter place, granted at Dublin 12 April 1897 to James Stevenson Andrews of 161 Cromwell Road, South Kensington, London, esquire. Effects £5,817 8s.8d.

The Andrews family were well-known linen merchants with offices in the Donegall Street and York Street area in the early 19th cent.

John Andrews of Comber (1721-1808), linen bleacher and flour miller, married in 1746 Mary Corbitt, daughter of Michael Corbitt of Newtownards and had 6 sons (as well as 4 daughters):

1. Thomas Andrews of Belfast (1747-1809), see above.
2. Michael Andrews of Castlewellan (c.1749-1805) married in 1779 Elizabeth Meek, see above.
3. John Andrews of Comber (c.1751-1770).
4. Robert Andrews (b.c.1757), went to London.
5. William Andrews of Comber (c.1761-1784).
6. James Andrews of Comber (1762-1841) was father of John Andrews of Comber whose descendants were flax-spinners and Isaac Andrews of Belfast whose descendants were flour-millers.

The above Michael Andrews had 3 sons (as well as 3 daughters),

1. Thomas John Andrews of Belfast (1781-1842) married in 1813 Elizabeth Stevenson, see above.
2. George Miller Andrews of Jamaica (c.1785-1860) died unmarried.
3. Michael Andrews of Ardoyne House, Edenderry (1788-1870) was a prominent figure in Belfast business and cultural life. He married (1) in 1810 Sarah McWilliam, died in 1813; (2) in 1817 Margaret McCammon who died in 1844; (3) in 1845 Elizabeth Ormiston who died in 1900.

The family of Michael Andrews, junior is mainly buried here.

See Young and Pike: *Belfast and the Province of Ulster* (1909); Andrews: *Nine Generations* (1958); *Burke's Irish Family Records* (1976); Clarke: *Gravestone Inscriptions, County Down*, Vol. 5 (2nd ed. 1984.]

ANDREWS

[In upper ground and now missing. This plot was bought by William Andrews in August 1803.] In memory of Hugh Andrews who died 16th May 1846 aged 75 years. "I am the Resurrection and the Life. He that believeth in me though he were dead, yet shall he live, and whosoever liveth and believeth in me, shall never die". John XI Chap. 25th, 26th verses.

ANDREWS

[Tablet of polished red granite, secured to east-wall.] The family burying place of James Andrews, solicitor, Belfast. His first wife Isabella Anna Andrews, died 29th Sept. 1854. His son James Andrews, junr, died 4th July 1864 aged 30 years. His grandson George Edward Andrews, died 4th Sept 1865 aged 3 years. James Andrews, Solr. died 29th Nov. 1875 aged 75 years. "Genial and generous, honoured in his profession, and loved by his friends". His second daughter Fanny died 30th Nov. 1901 aged 72 years. His eldest daughter Anna Robertson, died 11th Sept 1905 aged 78 years.

[Letters of administration of the personal estate of James Andrews Junior, late of Greenisland, near Carrickfergus, in the West Division of the county of the town of Carrickfergus, solicitor, who died 1 July 1864 at same place, were granted at Belfast 2 January 1865 to Eliza Bozilia Andrews of Greenisland, (Belfast) aforesaid, the widow of said deceased. Effects under £1,500.]

ANDREWS
[In high-railed enclosure.] Sacred to the memory of Martha K. Andrews, born Oct. 6 1828; died Mar. 2 1894. Also her infant sons, John and William. [On base.] William Andrews.

ANDREWS
See CORBITT and MILLIKEN

ARCHER
[Now lost, but recorded in Inscription book.] In memory of Samuel Archer, of Belfast, Mary his wife and their children: Margaret, Ann, William, Mary, Stephen, Samuel, Henry, Isabella and Sarah. Also of Francis (buried in Liverpool), and Elizabeth (buried in Dingle).

[The plot was purchased by Samuel Archer in February 1842. This was the Samuel Archer, of Archer & Sons, Stationers, printers and lithographers, at this time of 27, Castle Place. The family also owned the Ballyclare paper mills. He later became a J.P.]

ARCHER
See SINCLAIR

ARMOUR
See SINCLAIR

ARMSTRONG
[Very badly flaked sandstone.] In memory of Mary Armstrong, the beloved mother of John Armstrong Esq., (40th Regt) who died (at Belfast), on the 9th Dec(ember 1857) aged (60 years.)

ARNOLD
[In a low railed enclosure.] Erected by Jane Arnold, in memory of her beloved husband Captn. Robt Arnold, who departed this life March 9th 1946 aged 34 years. Also his daughter Jane Eliza who died August 1st 1846 aged 4 years. Also the above named Jane Arnold died 5th January 1895 aged 81 years. Also their daughter Robertina, born 16th March 1846, died 17th August 1898. Also their eldest daughter Helen Arnold died 20th April 1919. Also their daughter Sarah Ann Arnold, died 17th July 1930.

[The will of Jane Arnold late of 3 Cranbrook Terrace, Lisburn Road,

Belfast, widow, who died 5 January 1895 at same place was proved at Belfast 10 April 1895 by Helen Arnold, Sarah Ann Arnold and Robertina Arnold all of 3 Cranbrook Terrace, Lisburn Road, Belfast, spinsters, the executors. Effects £1,162 7s.6d.

Probate of the will of Robertina Arnold, late of 43 Cranbrook Terrace, Lisburn Road, Belfast, spinster, who died 17 August 1898 at Belfast granted at Belfast 22 December 1898 to Helen Arnold and Sarah Arnold both of Cranbrook Terrace, spinsters. Effects £536 14s.5d.]

ARNOLD

[Almost completely obliterated marble in a large headstone in a low enclosure, now lost.] In memory of the family of John Arnold ...... Arnold died 22nd January 1850. Susannah, daughter of John Arnold, died August 27th 1863. Lydia Arnold, daughter, died (5th Decr) 1867. Also the above-named John Arnold, born 3rd Novr 1803, died 26th Septr 1882.

[The will of John Arnold, late of Dunmurry, county Antrim, gentleman, who died 26 September 1882 at same place was proved at the Principal Registry 13 January 1883 by Robert James Arnold of Dunmurry, Presbyterian Minister, one of the executors. Effects £40.]

ARTHUR

[Undated plaque in the shape of a shield, secured to north wall — probably c.1850-1880.] The family burial ground of James Arthur, solicitor, Belfast.

[Ground bought by Mr Arthur in 1807.]

ARROTT

[Large tablet secured to dividing wall.] In memory of Revd Andrew Arrott, Minister of Newton, Caithness, who died on the 19th Dec. 1831. Also his wife Magdeline who died on the 2nd Feb. 1832. Also their son Isaac Arrott, merchant, Belfast, who died on the 1st Sept. 1862 aged 76 years. Also his wife Jane who died on the 13th Nov. 1880.

[The will of Jane Arrott late of University Road, Belfast, widow, who died 13 November 1880 at same place was proved at Belfast 17 January 1881 by the oaths of the Reverend Robert Knox of Windsor Park, Belfast, D.D., Presbyterian Minister, and Francis Brown of 34 Mill Street, Belfast, rent agent, two of the executors. Effects under £1,500.]

ASH

[Two smashed marble tablets, formerly with surrounds in a high-railed enclosure.] Sacred to the memory of Sally Ash, died 31st May 1833 aged 17 years. "Behold, thou hast made my days as it were a span long". "O consider this, ye that forget God".

(In memoriam) George Ash, junior aged 24 years, died 18th Decr. 1854. "Yea, speedily was he taken away lest that wickedness should alter his understanding or deceit beguile his soul". George Ash, aged 79 years died 3rd August 1863. Also Mary SWAN (his wife), born 3rd (August 1790, died 5th April 1888.)

[The will of George Ash, formerly of Belfast in the county of Antrim, merchant, and late of Holywood, in the county of Down, who died 3

August 1863 at Holywood aforesaid, was proved at Belfast 28 August 1863 by the oath of Mary Ash of Holywood aforesaid widow of deceased, one of the executors. Effects under £2,000.

The will of Mary Ash late of Holywood, county Down, widow, who died 5 April 1888 at same place was proved at Belfast 15 February 1889 by the Reverend John Armstrong Crozier of Newry, said county, Presbyterian Minister, one of the executors. Effects £51 14s.6d.

The elder George Ash, in partnership with William Berwick from 1824, was a grocer and general provision merchant at the corner of Waring Street and Donegall Street, their premises being known as the "Exchange" shop. George Ash is better remembered as the compiler of *George Ash's Book* which chronicled the Patrol Guard's activities during the 1810-1820 period, and so constitutes a fascinating record of the maintenance of law and order prior to the opening of Belfast first town prison in Ferguson's Entry, off Smithfield.]

ASHENHURST

[Now missing from lower ground.] Sacred to the memory of Hugh (M. Ashenhurst who departed this life March 7th 1848 aged 21 years.)

ASHMORE

[In low-stone enclosure.] Died on the 7th April 1821, Mary Ashmore, widow of the late Samuel Ashmore, of Belfast, merchant aged 80 years. Mary Ashmore her second daughter died on the 2nd April 1827 aged 54 years. John Ashmore her son died on the 22nd September 1827 aged 61 years. Also to the memory of the late Richard Ashmore her son who departed this life on the 2nd February 1839 aged 63 years.

ATKINS

[Flaking sandstone headstone with urn carved at the top, now lost.] Michael Atkins Esqr, 40 years a Member of the Northern Theatres, the (favourite) and justly admired actor, having (stru)tted his hour upon the (stage) finished the last scene (of the great) drama of life on the (10)th April 18(12) aged 6(6) years. (Mrs At)kins's glass was run on the 1(.) October 1808 aged (5.). years the best of mothers and the best of friends. Mrs MURPHY'S glass was run on the 28th July 1817 aged 38 years, the best of wifes and the best of (friends) lamented by all that (knew) her worth. Also Wm Murphy who died 18th January 1819 aged 38 years [sic].

[Michael Atkins, originally from Dublin, was for a time manager of "The Vaults" theatre in Ann Street before starting a theatre in Rosemary Street in 1784. His most important achivement was the building of the Theatre at the corner of Arthur Street and Castle Lane in 1793. This soon became the most fashionable place in Belfast, and some of the personalities who acted here under Atkins' management included such names as Mrs Siddons, Edmund Kean and Garrick.]

ATKINSON

[In low-railed enclosure.] Erected by Richard Atkinson in memory of his daughter Anna who departed this life 13th March 1850 aged 4 years and 6 months. Also two of his children Ann and JaneAnn who died young. The above named Richard Atkinson departed this life 5th February 1860 aged 48 years. Also his beloved wife Mary Atkinson who departed this life 27th January 1868 aged 54 years. Also his son James Atkinson who died July 1874 aged 24 years. Also his eldest son John Atkinson who died 11th January 1879 aged 42 years. Also his grandson Edmund Atkinson who died 15th August 1890 aged 37 years. Also three children of Edmund Atkinson who died young. Also Fred, the beloved son of the above named Edmund Atkinson who died 8th July 191(3).

[The will of Richard Atkinson of Antrim, publican who died 5 February 1860 at Cromac Street aforesaid, was proved at Belfast 28 February 1860 by the oaths of Mary Atkinson of same place, widow, and John Vint of Market Street, Armagh, merchant, the executors. Effects under £5,000.

Letters of administration of the personal estate of Mary Atkinson late of Cromac Street, Belfast, county Antrim, widow, who died 27 January 1868 at Belfast aforesaid, were granted at Belfast 14 March 1868 to Elizabeth Green, wife of Joseph Green of Denmark Street, Belfast aforesaid, grocer and spirit dealer, the daughter and one of the next of kin of said deceased. Effects under £450.]

ATKINSON
See MATHERS

BAGLEY
[Undated and flaking headstone, probably c.1860-1880, now lost.] Rev. John Bagley. In memory of his beloved children, viz: Ellen aged 13, Martha aged 8, John aged 6, Ebenezer aged 2. (Eliza aged 1.)

BAILEY
[Small egg-shaped tablet set into a low wall in upper ground.] Erected by Robert Bailey, Belfast, A.D. 1825.

BAILIE
[In upper ground and now missing. Plot bought by John Bailie in December 1810.] The family burying ground of John Bailie, Belfast.

BAILIE
See HYNDMAN

BAIN
See BOWDEN

BAIRD
[Flaking headstone.] Sacred to the memory of Ann Baird who departed this life Octr 14th 1807 aged 56 years. Also hir [sic] husband James Baird who departed this life Decr 20th 1809 aged 52 years. Likewise their son James Baird who died August the 9th 1816 aged (25) years.

BAIRD
See LYONS

BAKER
[Badly flaked — probably c.1800-1830, now lost.] This stone ..... S.tt.n Baker .... memory of .... (mer)chant, ... 40 A.

BAMMER
[Flaking headstone now lying flat.] Erected by William Bammer in me(mory of) Isabella who departed this life (13)th October 1824 aged 32 years. Also her daughter Jane who departed this life 20th April 182(5) aged 1 year and 9 months. Also the above William Bammer, born 8th October 1788, died 3rd July 1874 aged 86 years.

BARBER
See SMITH

BARBOUR
See DUNLOP

BARKLIE
[Missing.] The burial place of Latimer Barklie who died on the 7th of Feby 184(7) aged 28 years.

BARNETT
[Large monument in wall plot in upper ground and no longer extant, but recorded in Society's Inscription book.]

The family burying place of John Barnett. Sacred to the memory of John Barnett, late of Belfast, formerly of Ballyacherty, County of Down who closed a life of public usefulness and private worth on the 19th day of March A.D. 1835, AE 65. Jane GIBSON, wife of John Barnett, died 13th March 1864 in her 95th year. James Barnett, son of the above, died 26th March 1861 aged 65 years. Eliza his wife died 23rd Septr 1859 aged 55 years. The infant son of John Barnett and three of his grandchildren are also interred here. James MONTGOMERY of Wolfhill, son-in-law to John Barnett, who died 2nd December 1877 aged 67 years. Anna Barnett, wife of James Montgomery died June 3rd, 1891 aged 78 years. In hope of eternal life.

[John Barnett was the first Secretary of the House of Industry, situated in Smithfield, and in 1817 he was one of the first Spring Water Commissioners. James Montgomery of Wolfhill House was a well-known linen merchant.]

BARNETT
[Large obelisk (fallen) with inscription on three sides of the pedestal, and in a large high-railed enclosure.] This monument is erected by Sarah C. Barnett, in memory of her beloved husband Richard Barnett who departed this life 29th January 1867 aged 65 years. "I am the Resurrection and the Life: he that believeth in Me, thou he were dead, yet shall he live; and whosoever liveth and believeth in Me shall never die. Believest thou this?" Sarah C. Barnett, fell asleep in Jesus on the 2nd January 1890 aged 80 years. "I know whom I have believed and am persuaded that He is able to keep that which I have committed unto Him against that day" II. Tim. 1 12.

[South-west face.] Helen, wife of Robert MEGAW and eldest daughter of Richard Barnett, died 12th April 1862 aged 26 years. "We believe that

Jesus died and rose again: even so them which also sleep in Jesus will God bring with Him". Margaret Barnett, third daughter of Richard Barnett, fell asleep in Jesus, 10th June 1898 AE 57. Isabella, widow of the late Robert CARSON, and second daughter of the late Richard Barnett, died 5th October 1911 aged 72 years. Jeremiah, 23. 28. 1 Peter 1,3,4,5. "There is a land of pure delight".

[North-east side.] In memory of Mary E.C. JOHNSTON, the beloved wife of Surgeon J. Milford-Barnett M.D., H.M. Indian Army. She fell asleep in Jesus, 16th Feb. 1875.

[On enclosure.] The burial place of Richard Barnett. A.D. 1848.

[The will (with two codicils) of Richard Barnett late of Ardmore Terrace, Hollywood, county of Down, Esquire, who died 29 January 1867 at same place, was proved 22 February 1867 at Belfast by the oath of Sarah Barnett of Ardmore Terrace, Hollywood, aforesaid, widow, and John Grattan (apothecary) and James Hamilton (merchant) both of Belfast, three of the executors. Effects under £6,000. Re-sworn at Belfast 21st March under £8,000.

The will of Sarah Barnett formerly of Ardmore Terrace, High Hollywood, county Down and late of Cannes, France, widow, who died 2 January 1890 at Redhill, Surrey, was proved 11 April 1890 at the Principal Registry by Margaret Barnett of Heather Lodge, Redhill, county Surrey, spinster, the sole executrix. Effects £152 16s.9d.

Probate of the will of Margaret Barnett, formerly of Marlborough Park, Belfast, and late of Fernbank, Hollywood, county Down, spinster, who died 10 June 1898 at latter place, granted 26 August 1898 at Belfast to John M. Barnett of Norfolk House, Stockleigh Road, St. Leonards on Sea, county Sussex, M.D. and Richard W. Barnett of 10 Bedford Court Mansions, Bedford Square, London B.L. Effects £6,818 11s.6d.

Richard Barnett was a dentist of Wellington Place and Robert Megaw was a partner in the firm of Hamilton, Megaw and Thomson, general merchants of Corporation Street, Belfast.

This branch of the Barnett family are descended from Andrew Barnett of Warwickshire who settled in Ballyagherty, near Smithfield. Earlier members are buried in Saintfield Church of Ireland Graveyard.

Surgeon John Milford Barnett was born on 28 September 1830, educated at Trinity College, Dublin and Edinburgh; M.D. Edinburgh 1852; MRCS Eng. 1852. He joined the Bombay Artillery in 1852 and passed in Hindustani. He had an exciting career in India with a shipwreck, a cyclone and various campaigns before he retired in 1869. He was involved with the temperance movement and Presbyterian charities generally. He married (1) in 1859 Mary E. C. Johnston, daughter of John Johnston of Ashley Lodge, county Down and Agnes Gemmill. He married (2) on 28 September 1875 Selina Boyd, daughter of General Brooke Boyd of St Leonards. J. M. Barnett had moved to Bexhill-on-Sea, Sussex and is presumably buried in England. He had 1 son John Gemmill Barnett, born 1862 at Deesa, Bombay, educated at Lurgan College and Heversham, agent in Argentina for various British businesses. See Young and Pike: *Belfast and the Province of Ulster* (1909); Clarke: *Gravestone Inscriptions, County Down*, Vol. 3 (1969).]

BARNETT
See CAVART and GEMMILL

BARRETT
See HAMILTON

BARRY
See BINGHAM

BARTER
See EWART

BARTON
Erected by Stewart BEGGS, to the memory of his brother-in-law, Joseph Barton, who departed this life November 13th 1842 aged 39 years. Also the above named Stewart Beggs, who departed this life November 17th 1844 aged 63 years. Also Margaret NUGENT who departed this life 17th Septr 1858 aged 58 years. Also John Nugent who died 29th Decr 1889 aged 23 years.

BATHURST
[Marble tablet in the plinth of a fallen obelisk.] Erected by William Bathurst jun., in memory of his father Wm Bathurst, who departed this life at Consbrook, Co. Down, 23rd November 1867 aged 68 years. "Blessed are the dead which die in the Lord". Also two of his grandchildren who died in infancy.

[William Bathurst, senior, owned coach factories both in Chichester Street and Police Square, the latter place now called Victoria Square.]

BATT
[M.D. X 159. Worn tablet in worn carved sandstone entablature in low stone enclosure secured to west wall.] Erected by Narcissus Batt Esq., of Belfast, banker. Here lieth the remains of his brother Robert Batt Esq., who died 8th May 1811 aged 38 years. Also his mother Mrs P..... Batt who died 24th April 183(5) aged (7)9 years. Also his niece Cat(herine Bat)t who died 2nd March 1818 aged (18) years.

[According to the Inscription Book Mrs P. Batt died in 1816 and not 1835.

The Batt family played an important role in the rapidly developing commercial life of Belfast in the first half of the 19th century. A certain Captain Robert Batt had come to the north of Ireland from Co. Wexford in 1760 and married a daughter of Samuel Hyde of Hyde Park, Co. Antrim. His five sons included Narcissus and Robert (see above) and the Rev. William (see below). Narcissus Batt who lived for a time in the Marquis of Donegall's former town house in Donegall Place and subsequently in Purdysburn House which he built, was a founder of the Belfast Bank in 1808 and also of the Belfast Banking Company in 1827. He was also, for a time, Chairman of the Ballast Board. Narcissus died in 1840 and was also buried here though his monument seems to have disappeared by 1907. His brother Thomas was a founder of the Belfast Banking Company and a member of Ballast Board. Narcissus's two sons Robert and Thomas Greg were also founders of the Belfast Banking Company, the latter being a director for over thirty years. See

Engraving at the top of the Batt tomb.

Batt: *Belfast Sixty Years Ago* (1896).

There is also a Batt family vault in Drumbo Church of Ireland churchyard at Ballylesson, Co. Down. See Clarke: *Gravestone Inscriptions, County Down*, Vol. 2]

BATT

[Beside the above.] Here lieth the body of Francis Turnley Batt, the dearly beloved son of the Rev. William Batt and Arminella Batt, who died 24th day of February 1835 aged 35 years. Restored by William Batt, 1905.

[Francis Turnley Batt was a grandson of Francis Turnley (d.1802) who owned much property in Ann Street and on the Quays and was a partner of Turnley and Batt, the brewers. Francis Turnley's son, also called Francis, built Drumnasole House, near Carnlough, Co. Antrim. The family also owned Rockport House and Richmond Lodge, both near Holywood, Co. Down. See Burke's *Landed Gentry of Ireland*, 1958 ed.]

BATT

[Tablet with surround, secured to east wall, and in high-railed enclosure with Alexander Turnly's memorial.] Here lieth the body of Arminella Batt, wife of the Rev. William Batt, who died the 30th day of July 1840 aged 69 years. Robert Batt, died 15th Nov. 1841 aged 44 years. Rev. William Batt died 14th June 1855 aged 87 years. Also in remembrance of Arminella Hannah, youngest daughter of the late Rev. William Batt, of Belfast who died at Black Rock, Co. Dublin 24th

October 1871. "There remaineth therefore a rest for the people of God". [contd. on plinth of surround.] Also Jane Batt, eldest daughter died May 1874. And William Batt, eldest of family, died January 1885, and interred in Balmoral Cemetery, Belfast.

[The Rev. William Batt was a brother of Narcissus (see above) and was the last member of the family to reside in Donegall Place. His house was near the corner of Fountain Lane. He was also an active Committee member of the Belfast Charitable Society. See Clarke: *Gravestone Inscriptions, Belfast*, Vol. 3, pp.8-9.]

BATT
See TURNLY

BAXTER
Erected by Richard Baxter, of Belfast, in memory of his three sons, viz: William Dawson Baxter who died 30th Dec. 1834 aged 3 years, Thomas James Baxter who died 20th April 1855 aged 16 years, Dawson Baxter who died 26th Oct. 1865 aged 24 years. Here also are interred the remains of the above named Richard Baxter who died 26th December 1875 aged 75 years. Also his wife Martha Baxter who died 19th April 1885 aged 88 years. His son William Baxter who died 28th Novr 1899 aged 64 years. Also his son Richard Baxter who died 27th March 1922 aged 89 years.

[Probate of the will of William Baxter, formerly of Strandtown, county Down and late of 1 Chlorine Place, Belfast, county Antrim, insurance agent, who died 28 November 1899 at latter place, granted 20 January 1900 at Dublin to Richard Baxter, insurance agent. Effects £10,526 3s.8d.

The Baxters were well-known insurance agents, working for the Sun Fire and Life Insurance Company amongst other activities.]

BEATTY
See GORDON

BEGGS
See BARTON and GIBBS

BELL
[Flaking near the bottom.] Erected in memory of William Bell who departed this life 4th of August 1819 aged 74 years. Also Ann, relict of the above named William Bell, who died 22nd April 1836 aged 90 years. Here also lies Margaret, wife of James Bell, who died December 16th 1827 aged 35 years. Also three of their children who died in infancy. And the (above n)amed James Bell who d(eparted this) life on the 15th day of (Sept 1846) aged 49 years.

BELL
[Headstone lying flat and broken.] I.H.S. Sacred to the memory of Captain Thomas Bell who departed this life 17th of March 1821, in the 60th year of his age. Also the remains of Mary his wife who departed this life 13th of January 1823 aged 64 years. Also Ellenor their youngest daughter, the beloved wife of Captn. John FALOON, who departed this life 13th of April 1844 aged 46 years. Also Captain John

Faloon who departed this life 26th September 1849 aged 54 years. Also to the memory of their beloved daughter Mary Teresa Faloon who departed this life on the 19th of May 1877, aged 49 years.

BELL

[Badly flaking, now lost.] Erected by (Sarah) Bell in memory of her husband Isaac Bell, who departed this life the 7th May 1825 aged (4)9 years. Also of his daughter Sarah who died (2.)th July 1818 aged 3 years. Here also is interred the above mentioned Sarah Bell who departed this life the 10th Decr 1834 aged 54 years.

BELL

[Small metal shield on a low railed enclosure. The plot was bought by William Bell in October 1824.] W.B.

BELL

[Slate in large headstone now laid flat in a railed enclosure.] Erected by William Bell, of Belfast, in memory of his beloved wife Susanna who departed this life June 2nd 1853 aged 37 years. Also the above named William Bell departed this life on the 7th July 1859 aged 48 years. Also his brother Samuel Bell who died 14th November 1879 aged 58 years. Also Robert, son of Samuel Bell, who died 4th September 1863 aged 3 years. Also Frances Bell, wife of Samuel Bell, who died 26th April 1888 aged 62 years. Also William Bell, son of the above named Samuel Bell, who died 5th April 1899 aged 39 years.

[Probate of the will of William Bell, late of 15 Great Victoria Street, Belfast, gentleman, who died 5 April 1899, granted at Belfast 15 May 1899 to Jane Bell, spinster, and Thomas Guilfoyle, gentleman, both of 15 Great Victoria Street, Belfast. Effects £3,862 7s.8d.]

BELL

See CURRAN, HOLMES, McCLELLAND and O'HAGAN

BELLAMY

See BYRTT

BELLANY

See THOMSON

BENN

[Decorated headstone (now badly damaged) in a low-railed enclosure with Edward Benn's stone.] In memory of John Benn, late of Glenravel House, County of Antrim, who died 16th March 1853 aged 86 years, of his wife Elizabeth CRAIG, who died 29th August 1859 aged 89 years, of their eldest daughter Anne who died 25th August 1838 aged 46 years, and of their grandson John son of Professor HODGES M.D., of Belfast, who died 9th of April 1847 aged 7 years, all of whom are buried here. Also James Benn, eldest son of the aforesaid John Benn who died June 1866 aged 76 yrs. His wife Margaret DUNNE, who died Nov. 1844 aged 52 yrs. And her mother Diana Dunne, who died 1828 aged 82 yrs. His children, Diana who died in 1818, an infant, Croasdaile 1832 aged 15 yrs Frances in 1842 aged 17 yrs.

[John Benn's family fortune derived from their interest in the iron ore works at Glenravel near Ballymena, Co. Antrim. Two of his sons were Edward the distinguished philanthropist (see below) and George the historian, the latter being buried in the City Cemetery. Dr John F. Hodges was a Professor of Chemistry and was a founder of the Chemico-Agricultural Society of Ulster.]

BENN

[Large polished granite block in enclosure with above.] Edward Benn, third son of John Benn, formerly of Belfast, afterwards of Glenravel, in the County of Antrim is here interred. He died 3rd August 1874 aged 76 years.

[It was Edward Benn who purchased a considerable tract of land at Glenravel, Co. Antrim and built Glenravel House in the 1830s. He developed the iron ore workings and used the resulting wealth to improve the district, and, more importantly to Belfast, to endow various medical foundations in the rapidly-growing town. He paid for two extensions to the Belfast Charitable Society's premises, as well as founding the Samaritan Hospital on the Lisburn Road. He also founded the Benn Hospital for diseases of the eye, ear and throat in Glenravel Street. His collection of Irish antiquities was said to be the largest private one of its kind in the north of Ireland and its donation in 1879 to the Belfast Museum was a major addition to that institution. His brother George (1801-82) wrote the well-known *History of Belfast*, published 1823 and 1877/80. See also Strain: *Belfast and its Charitable Society* (1961).]

BENSON

Erected by Patrick Benson in memory of his wife Martha who departed this life 25th October 1827 aged 52 years. Also the above named Patrick Benson who died on the 14th of November 1841 aged 68 years, A.D. Also Martha LYNAS who died Decr 24th 1865 aged 58 years. Also his son John Benson, pilot, died July 13th 1865 aged 55 years. Also his wife Esther Benson died November 23th (sic) 1909 aged 87 years.

[In the early 19th century pilots were engaged to guide sailing vessels up the tortuous channel in to the harbour which at that time included the Town Dock in High Street.]

BENSON

[Worn stone, now lost.] In memory of John Benson who died 10th May 1838 aged (82) years. Also Ann (McCor)mick Benson who died 1st Decr 1860 aged 27 years. Also Isabella Benson who died 26th August 187(4) aged 83 years. Also Elizabeth S. Benson who died 19th December 1902. Also Margaret Benson who died 19th June 1913.

BERESFORD

[Worn headstone in "Cholera Ground", now lost.] In memory of George De La Poer Beresford (died) November 14th 1838 (aged 4) years.

BIGGAR
See DUFFIELD

Tomb of Edward Benn of Glenravel, philanthropist and antiquarian.

BINGHAM
[Flaking headstone at the end of a flat slab.] Erected by Ann Bingham in memory of her husband John Bingham who died 23rd August 1827 aged 47 years.

BINGHAM
[Raised flat slab beside John Bingham's stone.] Erected by Henry BARRY, of Belfast, in memory of his mother-in-law Ann Bingham, who departed this life Der. the 9th 1839 aged 59 years.

Her happy spirit dwells' on high,
Her guardian angel pointed out the way,
She'll rise again no more to die,
But live with God thro never ending day.

Also his beloved wife Maria Louisa who departed this life January the 9th 1841 aged 28 years.

In silent anguish, oh, my spouse,
When I recall thy worth,
Thy lovely life time's early end,
I feel estranged from earth.

And his beloved daughter Margaret who departed this life March the 22nd 1842 aged 8 years.

Departed shade they sorrowing Parent here,
On this tomb he drops the embittered tear,
T'is all alas his grieving heart can do
Yet, oh! too little for a Child like you.

Also the above named Henry Barry who departed this life the 28th of November 1850 aged 50 years.

BIRKMYRE
[Worn marble in very large headstone, now lost.] Erected by John and Catherine Birkmyre to the memory of their beloved beloved parents, viz: their mother Catherine who was born in Scotland on the (2)5th March (1786) and died at Belfast on the (16)th March 183(5). And their father Thomas Birkmyre, also born in Scotland and who died at Belfast on the 24th May 1846 aged (68) years. ("In death, both were enabled to realize those immortal) hopes of which the (Gospel is at once the origin and the evidence"). And John Birkmyre, grandson of the above C. and T. Birkmyre, and son of John and E. Birkmyre, of the City of Londonderry, and died at Belfast on the (4)th April 18(5)6 aged (17) years. John Birkmyre, senr, of Derry, died at Belfast, 14th March 1877. Also Elizabeth Birkmyre, his wife, who died 16th May 1857. "Blessed are the dead which die in the Lord"

BLACK
[In upper ground and now missing.] Here lie Margaret Black who (depart)ed this life 27th September 1807 aged ... years. Margaret Black, relict of the late Thomas Black, died October 15th 1823 aged 89 years ...ah Black their daughter.........

BLACK

[White limestone, laid flat.] Erected by Eliza G. Black, in memory of her beloved husband John Black who departed this life 1st August 1858 aged 60 years. Also their son Samuel M. Black who died 20th April 1853 aged 23 years. Also her father Samuel MACLURCAN, who died April 1849 aged 95 years. Also her mother Agnes Maclurcan, who died Sept. 1854 aged 90 years. Here also lieth the remains of the above named Eliza Gregg Black, relict of the late John Black Esq., who departed this life 27th July 1865 aged 67 years. Also last surviving child of above Agnes Gregg Black died at Bangor, 18th Feby 1910.

[The will of John Black, late of Donegal Street, in the town of Belfast, and county of Antrim, gentleman, who died 1 August 1858 at same place, was proved at Belfast 16 August 1858 by the oath of Robert John Black of No. 6 Amelia Place, South Gate Road, London, Doctor of Medicine, one of the executors. Effects under £2,000.

John Black, silk mercer of 111 Donegall Street, was one of the first councillors of the reformed Town Council which was elected in 1842.]

BLACK

[Now removed.] The family burying place of James Black, High Street, Belfast, 1854.

BLACK

See COOPER

BLACKLEY

See MONTGOMERY

BLACKWELL

[Polished granite in a low stone enclosure.] Sacred to the memory of William Blackwell and his wife Jane Hamilton Blackwell, who died within a few weeks of each other in 1810. "They also who sleep in Jesus will God bring with him."

BLACKWELL

[Undated headstone, now lost, probably of c.1810-1835.] The burial place of Alex Blackwell. [This plot was bought by Alexander Blackwell in October 1800. He was a linen draper of High Street and was connected with the Belfast Charitable Society. See Strain: *Belfast and its Charitable Society* (1961).]

BLACKWOOD

[Worn and badly flaked.] Here lieth (the) body of (Elizabeth) Blackwood who departed this life the 9th of October 1809 aged (1)2 years.

BLACKWOOD

[Polished granite.] In memory of Charles Blackwood, born 11 April 1804, died 4 July 1862, and his wife, Abby Purss WILSON, born 16 June 1825, died 17 March 1897. Also their children: John Wilson born 6 Jan. 1859, died 9 April 1876, Charles, born 25 Jan. 1858, died 26 Feb 1879, Elizabeth, born 6 March 1861, died 6 Dec. 1889.

Memorial to Thomas Blain at the R.B.A.I. where he was head of the English School.

BLACKWOOD
[Headstone has disappeared from upper ground since it was copied in 1907.] Erected by John Blackwood to the memory of his parents, Charles Blackwood who died 22nd May 1848 aged 76 years. And Matilda BURNS his wife who died 9th January 1844 aged 69 years.

BLAIN
[Now lost.] John Blain's family burying place. Underneth are deposited the remains of William Blain, born 7th March 1825, died 26th June 1845 aged 20 years. Also Catherine Blain, beloved wife of the above John Blain, born Sep 10th 1786, died Sep. 19th 1850 aged 64 years. Also the above named John Blain, died June 7th 1874 aged 90 years.

BLAIN
[Broken marble with lead letters in surround, now lost.] Erected by Thomas Blain, LL.(D), in memory of his wife Frances BRIDGE who departed this life 16th November 1835. Also his second wife Letitia IRELAND who departed this life 17th April 1851. "Hinc subrectura". Here also are interred the remains of the above named Thomas Blain, Head Master of the English Department of the Royal Academical Institution, Belfast, from 1845 to 1861, who departed this life 16th November 187(9) aged 87 years. Here also are interred the remains of his third wife Anne ORR who departed this life 5th April 1893 "When Christ, our Life, shall appear, then shall ye also appear with him in glory".

[Dr Blain was born at Guiness, Dromara, Co. Down, in March 1792, eldest son of William Blain, farmer, and received his early education at Ballynahinch. He entered Glasgow University in 1812 but obtained no degree before his LL.D. in 1856. He taught under the celebrated Dr Bruce at the Belfast Academy in Academy Street, then was a Classical master at the Royal Belfast Academical Institution before starting a succession of his own schools in Belfast, Donaghadee and Bangor. He returned to "Inst" as Head Master of the English Department in 1845 and such was his method of teaching and relationship with the pupils that few masters at the Institution have been as highly esteemed either before or since. After his death the Blain Prize in English was founded in his honour. See Fisher and Robb: *Royal Belfast Academical Institution, Centenary Volume* (1913); Addison: *Matriculation Albums of the University of Glasgow* (1913); Jamieson: *History of the Royal Belfast Academical Institution* (1959).]

BLAIN
See MACLURCAN

BLAIR
Here lies the remains of Mrs Elenor Blair, relict of the late Alexr Blair Esqr, of Ballyclover, near Antrim, who departed this life the 25th Octr 1822 aged 80 years.

BLAIR
[Now missing from upper ground.] Erected by William and Mary Blair to the memory of their beloved mother Jane who departed this life June

29th 1847 aged 50 years. "The memory of the just is blessed".

BLAIR
[Polished granite.] The burial ground of William Blair of Castledawson, and Springfield, Belfast, who died Sept. 1847 aged 66 years.

BLAIR
See DUNLAP

BLAKE
[Formerly in lower ground, but now gone.] The family burying place of James Blake, High Street, Belfast, 1854.

BLOOMFIELD
[Undated headstone, looking of c.1850-1870, now removed.] Erected to the memory of William Bloomfield, late of John Street, Belfast.

[This plot was purchased by Edward Bloomfield in 1852. Several members of this family worked as tinsmiths and metal-workers in the John Street and Donegall Street area at that time.]

BLOW
See CUNNINGHAM and MILLER

BOAG
See STEVEN

BODELL
[Marble in large headstone, now removed.] Erected by James Bodell in memory of his four children who died in childhood. "The Lord gave and the Lord hath taken away, blessed be the name of the Lord". James Bodell, father of above, who died 17th July 1888 aged 74 years. And of Eliza Bodell, widow of James Bodell, who died 1st December 1894 aged 80 years.

BOOKER
[Marble headstone with lead letters broken and laid flat.] Erected to the memory of William Booker, of Belfast, who died 10th March 1877 aged 73 years. Also John Booker, third son of the above, who died 23rd Oct. 1849 aged 4 years. Also his son George William who died 31st Jan. 1912 aged 70 years. "For I know that my Redeemer liveth". Job. XIX, 25-27.

BOOMER
[Large tablet in ornate entablature surmounted by three urns and secured to north wall.] Erected in memory of James Boomer, late of Belfast who departed this life, 7th September 1820 aged 53 years. Also his son William who died 19th December 1808 aged 7 years, and his daughter Jane who died 25th December 1808 aged 5 years.

[James Boomer of Waring Street was one of the most prosperous cotton spinners in Belfast in the early years of the 19th century. He also lived in a substantial house in Mill Street, formerly occupied by the well-known Sinclair family. The firm later turned to flax spinning and passed out of existence in the 1850s.]

BORLASE
   See STEWART

BOUCHER
   [Broken in three pieces and lying flat.] In memory of James, the beloved husband of Elizabeth Adair Boucher, who departed this life 17th Decr 1849 aged 52 years. Also his infant son James aged 6 months. Also Ann HEPBURN, daughter of Miles Hepburn, died 14th Octr 1897 aged 70 years. Also the above named Elizabeth Adair Boucher, and daughter of Miles Hepburn, died 6th Octr 1893 aged 76 years. Also Reb [blank] Hepburn, [this line left blank.] Sarah Hepburn.

BOURDOT
   [Flaking headstone.] Here lieth the body of Nicholas Bourdot, of Chaumont in Bossigni in Champagne, who departed this life on the 12th December 1816 aged 78 years. Also two of his grandchildren who died young. Nicholas Bourdot died 17th August 1891 aged 21 years.
   [Nicholas Bourdot was captured during Thurot's attack on Carrickfergus in 1760 and lodged with fellow French prisoners in the old barracks in Ann Street. Following his release on the termination of the Seven Years War in 1763, he decided to remain in Belfast, becoming a barber, as did his son after him.]

BOWDEN
   [Sandstone laid flat and flaking near bottom.] Erected by James Bowden, of Belfast, in memory of his daughter Charlotte who departed this life 22nd September 1814 aged 7 years and 6 months. Also my wife Charlotte who departed this life 24th April 1817 aged 47 years. Also Joseph Bowden who departed this life 10th March 1829 aged 26 years. Also Elizabeth Bowden my wife who departed this life the 12th of April 1834 aged 59 years. The above James Bowden died 12th Feby 1836 aged 70 years and was buried here. Also his son-in-law Donald BAIN who died 9th May 1837 aged 34 years. His daughter-in-law Jane Bowden who died June 1839 aged (2)8 years. His son James Bowden who died 29th July 1849 aged 38 years. His daughter Ann Bowden who died 28th Octr 1850 aged 49 years. His daughter Susannah Bowden who died 28th May 1881 aged 64 years. His daughter Jane died 10th March 1890 aged 85 years, widow of Donald Bain.

BOYD
   [Headstone missing from upper ground, but recorded in 1907.] To the memory of Francis Boyd of Belfast who departed this life .... Oct. 1811 aged .. years. Where also are interred two of his children: viz, John who died 17th July 1823 aged 31 years. And Eliza who died 28th March 1823 aged 21 years.

BOYD
   This stone was erected to the memory of Nathaniel Boyd, late of Berry Street, Belfast, who departed this life 20th day of Jan. A.D. 1813 aged 57 years. Also Jane Boyd, wife to the above Nathaniel Boyd, who died

16th September 1831 AE 70 years.

[Nathaniel Boyd was a tavern-keeper.]

BOYD

[Worn.] Erected by Dr Boyd L.R.C.S.E. in memory of his grandfather Hugh Boyd who died 4th Jan. 1815 aged 6(4) years. Also his brother William Boyd who died Dec. 1840 aged 17 years. Also his brother Hugh Boyd, Divinity Student of the General Assembly's College, Belfast, who died Feb. 1841 aged 18 years. And two children who died young. Also his father William Boyd who died 4th February 1861, in the 81st year of his age. "Blessed are the dead who die in the Lord: yea, saith the Spirit for they rest from their labours and their works do follow them" Also his mother Ann Boyd who died 21st March 1875 aged 89 years.

BOYD

[Inscription at base of marble cross, now lost.] (Elizabeth, 1832-1837, Ellen, 1837-1837.) Children of Robert & Mary Boyd.

BOYD

[Twin marble tablets in a pedimented entablature attached to the south wall, largely destroyed.] Burial place of John Boyd. Sacred to the memory of, Mary daughter of John Boyd, who died 3rd Decr 1842 aged 11 months. Edward, son of John Boyd, who died 28th January 1849 aged 15 years nearly. Jane, daughter of John Boyd who died 10th August 1852 aged 14 years. John Boyd who died 28th May 1860 aged 74 years. James H., son of John Boyd, who died 24th August 1862 aged 30 years nearly. Elizabeth F., daughter of John Boyd, who died 25th August 1868 aged 24 years. Frances Boyd, wife of John Boyd, who died 20th March 1871 aged 60 years.

Sacred to the memory of Jane H., daughter of John K. Boyd, who died 21st December 1854 aged 7 months. Emma, wife of John K. Boyd, who died 29th October 1855 aged 22 years. Anna H., daughter of John K. Boyd. who died 25th March 1858 aged 6 months.

[The will with one codicil of John Boyd, late of Great Victoria Street, Belfast, in the county of Antrim, merchant, who died 28 May 1860 at Armagh, was proved at Belfast 16 November 1860 by the oath of John Hind of Durham Street, Belfast aforesaid, merchant, one of the executors. Effects under £4,000.

The Boyd family were proprietors of the Durham Street flax spinning mills.]

BOYD

[Marble tablet in large headstone, topped by a draped urn, now lost.] Erected by Samuel Boyd in memory of his beloved (wife) Ellen who died 7th March 1856 aged 56 years. (Also th)eir son John who died 14th February 1852 aged 28 years. And three of their children who died in early life. Also their daughter Eleanor Coburn who died 20th October 1857 aged 21 years. Thomas ROWELL died 26th Sept 1861. Mary Jane McCLINTON died 18th August 1897.

BOYD

[In large headstone of neo-Egyptian style, now removed.] Erected by Henry Boyd in memory of his son Henry who died 19th April 1855 aged 10 mos. Died on 15th March 1862, the above named Henry Boyd aged 46 years.

BOYD

[Worn marble in a low-railed enclosure.] Erected to the memory of Jane Boyd, widow of the late James Boyd of (Beech Lodge), Castlereagh, who died (on the 13th June) 1867 aged 7(7) years. Also to the memory of (her grandson), William MAWHINNY (who died on the 10th of June 1867 aged 24 years. Also Eliza Mawhinny, daughter of the above Jane Boyd who died on the 7th March 1900 aged 79 years. Here lieth (the body of) Margaret HANNA (wife of) Hans Hanna (of Belfast) who died on the (22nd) June (1815) aged (27 years). The above Hans Hanna of Belfast, departed this life on the 2(1)st of July 1832, at Leghorn, Italy in the (44)th year of his age.

[James Boyd was proprietor of the starch works at 35-37, Boyd Street which thoroughfare was named after him.]

BOYD

[Polished granite tablet in carved surround in walled enclosure, now lost.] Hugh Henry Boyd, Parkville, died 3rd May 1889 aged 86 years. Also his wife Isabella WEIR, died 8th December 1893 aged 86 years. "As for me, I will behold thy face in righteousness; I shall be satisfied when I awake with thy likeness". Psalm XVII, 15.

[The will (with 6 codicils) of Hugh Henry Boyd, late of Parkville, Belfast, esquire, who died 3 May 1889 at same place, was proved at Belfast 24 June 1889 by the Rev. James Martin, Presbyterian Minister, Hugh Aikin, travelling school agent, John Edgar Magill, estate agent, and Hugh Rankin, secretary for Sabbath School Society, all of Belfast, the executors. Effects £7,296 17s.5d.]

BOYES

[Polished granite headstone.] Sacred to the memory of Francis Boyes who departed this life 4th February 1829 aged 43 years. And three of his children. Also Jane, widow of James Boyes, formerly of Belfast, who departed this life 12th January 1892 in the 82nd year of her age.

[The will (with one codicil) of Jane Boyes, late of Hanover Street, Portadown, county Armagh, widow, who died 12 January 1892 at same place, was proved at Armagh 17 June 1892 by John Buckly Atkinson of Portadown, solicitor, one of the executors. Effects £2,425 6s.4d.]

BOYES

See BRYSON

BOY(LE)

[Very worn altar-tomb, now lost.] Here lie the remains of Mr Robert Armstrong Boy(le, merchant), of Kingston, Jamaica, (native of this town) who died in his (71)st year in his .... he .... of .an .... (..th Aug. 1800).

BOYLE

[Now lost, copied from Society's Inscription book.] Erected by the three youngest sons in memory of their father, Saml Boyle, merchant, Ann Street, Belfast, who died 17th January 1854. Also their mother Mary who died 16th March 1854.

BOYLE

[In large carved surround, now lost.] Erected by Joseph Boyle, Belfast, to the memory of his beloved and only son Alexander Arthur Boyle, who died on the 4th of May 1864 aged 17 years and 8 months. "The Lord gave, and the Lord hath taken away, Blessed be the name of the Lord", The above named Joseph Boyle who died 16th June 1881 aged 79 years. "For as in Adam all die even so in Christ shall all be made alive". 1 Corin. XV, 22. Also Matilda, widow of the above Joseph Boyle, who died 18th April 1904 aged 85 years.

[The will (with one codicil) of Joseph Boyle, late of Belfast, gentleman, who died 16 June 1881 at Portstewart, county Londonderry, was proved at Belfast 10 August 1881 by the oaths of Edward Porter Cowan and William Mullan, both of Belfast, merchants, the executors. Effects £7,753 8s.8d.]

BRADDELL
See McGAHAN

BRADFORD

[Large slate, now lying flat.] Erected by James Bradford, Belfast, in memory of his father John Bradford, merchant, Belfast, who died 16th February 1815 aged 42 years. And his two daughters, Jane, who died 22nd July 1838 in the fifth year of her age, and Eliza who died 22nd Nov 1846 aged 19 years. Also his son John who died 16th January 1868 aged 31 years.

BRAN(NEN)

[Very badly weathered and flaked, now lost.] (Gra)teful to (the re)collection (of Abr)aham B(r)a(nnen) who departed (this) life 22nd Ju(ne 18..) aged (7)2 years. And also his wi(fe ... Ma)rgaret who departed this (life .... 1826). aged (.. years.).

[This plot was bought by Abraham Brannen in March 1800. He was a nailer and joiner by trade and lived at 14 Cole's Alley, off Church lane.]

BREAKEY
See MILLER

BRIDGE
See BLAIN

BRIGS

[Very badly flaking, now lost.] Here lie deposited the remains of Jane (B)rigs, wife of Robert Brigs, of Belfast, who died in the (2)8th year of her age, 9th (June) 1813. "Innocence, good nature and benevolence combined with the ...ly which excites to the performance of every social and moral duty were prominent features in the character of this excellent young woman, who will long be remembered with respect and affection by all those who had an opportunity of observing her amiable disposition and the greatness of her heart". (Here also lie) the remains (of her) children who all died in infancy, (and to) whom she was a fond and faithful mother". (Here also lie) the remains of (Rober)t Brigs, (muslin manufacturer, Belfast, who died 21st August 1840. He was a loving husband, an affectionate father and a true friend. He was an .... a class read scholar and a poet. This humble record is raised by his son Addison who hopes to meet him in a better world.

BRINKMAN
[Large headstone, with top missing.] Erected by Elizabeth Brinkman, in memory of my dearly beloved husband William John Brinkman who died 25 April 1856 aged 36 years.

BRISTOW
[Twin slate tablets in pedimented entablature secured to east wall in a high-railed enclosure.] Sacred to the memory of Joseph, son of James Bristow, of Belfast, banker, who died the 22nd April, 1844 aged 12 years. Letitia who died the 4th March 1852 aged 28 years, Mary RIPPINGHAM, who died the 14th Oct. 1858 aged 27 years, both daughters of James Bristow, above mentioned. Also of Jane Bristow, otherwise SMITH, his wife who died the 24th June 1863 aged 65 years.

Mary, daughter of James THOMSON, of Coleraine, surgeon, who died the 26th Novr 1846 aged 75 years. Samuel Smith Thomson, of Belfast, M.D., son of James Thomson, of Coleraine, who died the 30th April 1849 aged 71 years. Anne, daughter of the late James Thomson, of Coleraine, who died the 13th day of August 1849 aged 88 years. Also of Joseph Bristow, of Belfast, banker, who died the 26th Sept. 1858 aged 63 years.

[The will of Joseph Bristow, late of No. 38 College Street, Belfast, in the county of Antrim, esquire who died 21 September 1858 at same place, was proved at Belfast 12 October 1858 by the oath of James Bristow of Wilmont in the said county, esquire, one of the executors. Effects under £4,000.

James Bristow was born near Coleraine in 1795, the grandson of the Rev. Skeffington Bristow, Vicar-General of Connor. He and his twin brother Joseph came to Belfast to live with their mother's brother, the celebrated Dr. Samuel Smith Thomson who obtained for them positions in the private bank of Orr, McCance, Montgomery & McNeile, soon (in 1824) to become the Northern Bank. Chief adviser to the private concern, though still only in his twenties, James Bristow, subsequently, in 1828, became one of the first Directors of the Northern Bank, such was the esteem in which he was generally held. He was several times President of the Belfast Chamber of Commerce and in 1844 he was called upon to testify before a Select Committee of the House of Commons, his mercantile knowledge particularly impressing Sir Robert Peel. In 1866 he died at Wilmont House, a fine residence he had built for himself and his family in what is now the Sir Thomas and Lady Dixon Park, near Drumbeg. His son and grandson later also became Directors of the Northern Bank. He was buried at Drumbeg. See Clarke: *Gravestone Inscriptions, County Down*, Vol. 3, p.5.

James Bristow's uncle, Dr Samuel Smith Thomson was one of the most eminent physicians in Belfast in the early 19th century. Described by Dr

A. Malcolm as the "father of the medical profession in Belfast", he was the first President of the Belfast Medical Society, founded in 1806. A very active member of the Belfast Charitable Society, he was closely associated with the founding in 1815 of the Fever Hospital in Frederick Street, later the Belfast General Hospital and was consulting Physician to the latter body. A thoroughly charming man, he was also an accomplished scholar and a keen musician, being instrumental in the founding of the Belfast Anacreontic Society, later the Belfast Philharmonic Society.

Dr S. S. Thomson's mother was Ellen, youngest daughter of Samuel Smith (1693-1760). He was one of the founders of the Belfast Charitable Scheme in 1752 and was also the father of John Galt Smith who married Valentine Jones's daughter and became the ancestor of a large and widely respected family.

James Bristow married his second cousin, his father-in-law, Samuel Smith of Balnamore near Ballymoney, being a son of John Galt Smith and grandson of Samuel Smith (1693-1760).

James Bristow's paternal uncle was the Rev. William Bristow (1735-1808), Vicar of Belfast from 1772 to his death and one of the most respected Sovereigns of the town, serving no fewer than eleven annual terms between 1786 and 1798. On the establishment of the Belfast Charitable Society by Act of Parliament in 1774, he was one of its first Committee members and took a most active and valuable part in its affairs. He donated the field in which the original portion of the New Burying Ground was laid out in the late 1790s. He was also a first cousin of the famous Henry Grattan.

Joseph Bristow, who died unmarried, was sub-agent in the Belfast branch of the Bank of Ireland. See Benn: *A History of the Town of Belfast* Vol. I (1877), and Vol. II (1880). Strain: *Belfast and its Charitable Society* (1961); Calwell: *Andrew Malcolm of Belfast* (1977).]

BRITTEN

Erected by Alexander Britten in memory of wife Martha who departed this life the 31st August 1817 aged 34 years. Also his brother William who departed this life the 24th August 1815 aged 40 years. Likewise their son John who died in infancy.

BRO...

See FRYER

BROADLEY

[Flaking and now lost.] This stone was erected by Benjamin Broadley, of Belfast, to the memory of his son Frederick Broadley who departed this life August the 18th 1824 aged 4 months. Also the remains of the above named Benjamin Broadley who departed this life June 22nd 1825 aged 45 years.

[According to the Society's burial book Benjamin Bradley died in 1845 and not 1825.]

BROW

[Rusty iron shield in low railing, now lost.] The family burying ground of William Brow, 18(66.)

BROWN
Erected by Abigail Brown, Belfast, in memory of her husband William Brown who died 7th June 1814 aged 40 years. Also her son James Brown who died 24th Jany 1840 aged 35 years. Also her son John Brown who died 13th April 1842 aged 41 years.

BROWN
[No longer extant.] Burial place of William Brown, late of Clady Print Works, 1830.

BROWN
[Very badly fragmented headstone now lost.] Erected by Thomas Brown of Belfast, in memory of his daughter Jane who d(eparted this) life 29th March (1837) aged 2(4) years.

BROWN
[Very badly weathered.] (Erecte)d by Elizabeth Brown, (in memory of her) husband (James Brown who departed this life January 23rd 1840.)

BROWN
[Missing from lower ground.] Sacred to the memory of A. H. Brown who departed this life .. of August 1840.

BROWN
[Iron shield, no longer extant, but recorded by Society.] The family burying ground of William Brown, 1846.

BROWN
[Partly weathered and now lost.] 1848. Erected by Margaret Brown, in me(mory) of her husband Robert Brown, merchant, Belfast, ob(ituary) February 1848 aetatis 40. Also the children of James McCALLUM, Belfast; Robert died Augt 29th 1852 aged 6 months, James died Decr 7th 1860 aged 2 months, William died September 28th 1892, Agnes McKENZIE died January 23rd 1932. His wife Ann Francis died December 23rd 1866. The above named James McCallum died February 15th 1868.

BROWN
[Small oval tablet on headstone.] Erected by Robert Brown in memory of his wife Eleanor who died 16th Dec. 18(55) aged (53) years.

BROWN
[Polished granite.] Erected by Henry Brown in memory of his children:
    Sarah who died 17th Jany 1839 aged 8 years,
    Jane who died 10th July 1843 aged 12 years,
    Elizabeth who died 2nd May 1847 aged 13 years,
    Henry who died 22nd March 1859 aged 21 years,
    Margt WRIGHT, 22nd March 1865 aged 26 years.
Here lie also the remains of the above named Henry Brown who died 28th May 1874 aged 71 years. Sarah, relict of Henry Brown, who died 24th Novr 1884 aged 74 years.

[The will of Henry Brown, late of Granstone Place, Antrim Road, Belfast, sea-captain, who died 26 May 1874 at same place, was proved at Belfast 12 June 1874 by the oaths of Sarah Brown, widow, and James Brown, master mariner, both of Granston Place, Antrim Road, Belfast aforesaid, two of the executors. (Deceased died domiciled in Ireland). Effects in U.K. under £6,000.]

BROWN
[Undated iron shield in a low-railed enclosure.] The family burying place of Robert Brown, Belfast. [The ground was purchased by Robert Brown in December 1840.]

BROWN
See FORRESTER, MULLIGAN and RICHARDSON

BRYAN
See SMITH

BRYSON
[Polished granite pillar surmounted by an urn in a low-railed enclosure.] Erected by Mary Bryson in loving memory of her dear father and mother: William Bryson, Rugby Terrace, Belfast, died 16th Nov. 1883, Mary McKeand Bryson his wife died 22nd July 1854. "Them also which sleep in Jesus will God bring with him". 1. Thess. IV. 14. Also her great-grandmother died 1845. Cousin Frank BOYES died 1845.

[East side.] Also her grand-parents: James Bryson died 1840, Jane Bryson his wife died 1830. And several of their children who died young. "The memory of the just is blessed" Prov. X. 7.

BRYSON
[Broken slate headstone.] Here lyeth the body of James Bryson who died at Macedon on the 16th of August 1847 aged 62 years. Also the body of Daniel JOHNSTON who died at Macedon, 23rd July 1858 aged 55 years.

[James Bryson was a domestic servant.]

BRYSON
[Decorated marble with lead letters.] In memoriam. Thomas Bryson, who died 1st June 1867 aged 61 years. Margaret Bryson who died 3rd Dec. 1889 aged 82 years. Ellen Bryson who died in 1853 aged 8 years. Helen Bryson who died 26th Dec. 1893.

BRYSON
[Polished granite, laid flat.] Erected by Jane Bryson in loving memory of her husband William Bryson who died 9th October 1926. "Mors janua vitae".

BUCHANAN
[Elegant headstone with inscription set in an ellipse.] Erected in memory of Capt. Robert Buchanan, of Maryport, who departed this life at Belfast, the 5th of September 1811 aged 44 years.

(BUCHANAN?)
[Very worn sandstone, with urn and rosettes carved at the top, but no sur-

name apparent, formerly beside Capt. Robert Buchanan's but now lost.] In memory (of) his (two) sons David and (Hir)am who died in infancy, 1812.

BUCHANAN
See LE PAN

BULLICK
[Flaking badly.] Erected to the memory of George Bullick who departed this life 26th Mar(ch 1822) aged 64 yers. Also Isabella his wife who departed this life 1st August 1822, in the 67th year of her age, George Bullick, their son died 19th November 1837. Elizabeth Bullick, wife of Samuel Bullick, died 18th July 1849. Here are interred two of their infant children.

[George Bullick senr. was principal of the English and Mercantile Academy in High Street, near the corner with Skipper Street. It was in existence until the 1850s.]

BUNTING
[Worn marble tablet in a carved surround with pediment broken off, and secured to north wall, now lost.] Erected in memory of John Bunting, who died 18th Oct. 1828 aged 52 years. Harriet Bunting died 12th Jan. 1830 aged 2(3) years. Thomas Ash Bunting died 17th Nov. 18(33) aged 21 years. Mary Bunting died 17th January 1837 aged 21 years. Sarah Bunting, died (21st May) 1837 aged 6(7) years. The first and last on this tablet were the parents of the intervening three, their beloved and only children.

[John Bunting ran a school for young ladies at 1 Donegall Place. In the 1800s it was situated at 67 Donegall Street. His brother Edward Bunting is famous for having chronicled so much of Ireland's old music.]

BURGESS
[Very badly flaked.] (In memory of Mary Ann, wife of ...... Burgess. Serjt-Major 3rd [K.O.] .... Dragoons who dep(arted) this life) May the 20th 1826, aged 25 years.

Pluckd from my children in their youthfull days,
When most their mother's tender care they need,
Oh, let a faithfull friend direct their ways,
In that bright path which will to Heaven lead.

BURNETT
Erected by Simpson Burnett, of Belfast, to the memory of his beloved child Rebecca who departed this life on 13th of May 1839 aged 13 months.

BURNS
[Badly weathered sandstone, now lost.] Erected (by William) Burns, of Belfast, in memory of his wife Susanna who departed this life (3)0th May 18(11) aged (..) years. Also to the memory of his father, (brother) and son. Also to the memory of the above Wm. Burns who died at (sea). Also to the memory of his son Matthew who died (in) Jamaica. Also to the memory of his daughter Susan who died in Saint (Louis) 185(0) aged (40).

BURNS
Interred here Jane Burns, wife of Robert Burns, who departed this life

on the 2nd day of August 1835 aged 43 years. Also four of their children who died in infancy.

BURNS
[Missing from lower ground.] Elizabeth Burns, died 28 March 1857 aged 80.

BURNS
See BLACKWOOD

BURNSIDE
[No longer extant. Plot bought by Thomas Burnside in December 1810.] The family burying place of Thomas Burnside, Belfast.

BURROWS
See CRAIG

BUSBY
See GILL

BUTLER
See DIGBY

BYERS
[Flaking and broken.] Erected by James Byers to the memory of William Byers, muslin mercht, who departed this life the 8th February 1822 aged 56 years.

BYERS
See SLOAN

BYRTT
[Twin marble tablets with sandstone entablature, formerly secured to west wall, but now lost.] In memory of William Byrtt, who died 23 March 1788. Juliana his wife who died 2 March 1801 aged 40 years. William Byrtt, their son, late surgeon 24th Regt, who died at Belfast 9 Oct. 1845 aged 59 years. Mary Ann Harriet LEWIS his wife who died 27 Sept. 1847 aged 41 years.

The burying place of Samuel THOMSON, merchant, Belfast, Sacred to the memory of Sophia BELLAMMY, his beloved wife departed this life 4th June 1866 aged 70 years. Also Elizabeth Agnes their eldest daughter, wife of Wm H. ALLEY died 28th Feb. 1869 aged 41 years. Also above named Samuel Thomson who died 7th November 1873 aged 76 years.

[This was the Byrtt family, several of whose members were Sovereigns of Belfast between 1721 and 1757, and after whom Byrtt's Entry, near Bluebell Entry, off High Street, was named.

In the late 18th century a Miss Edith Maria Lewis had married into the Bellamy family, one of whose members was a banker in the 1820's.

Samuel Thomson, who was one of the Thomsons of Jennymount, was the Director of the Provincial Bank at 1 Corporation Street.

There is a memorial tablet in Christ Church, Belfast. See Clarke: *Gravestone Inscriptions, Belfast*, Vol. 1, p.163; Benn: *History of Belfast*, Vol. I (1877), pp. 583 and 727-728.]

CAIRD
    See GRAHAM

CAIRNS
    [Broken tablet which is now lost, formerly in enclosure with Prof. James Thomson's.] (In) memory of (Re)vd Wm Cairns LL.D., for (33) years Professor of Logic (&) Belles Lettres in the Belfast Academical Insti(tution) died on the 21st April (1848) aged 64. (And of) his wife (Margaret) HARVEY (who died on the 8th) Nov. 1851. "But go thou thy way till the end be, for thou shalt rest and stand in thy lot at the end of the day" Daniel XII. 13.)
    [The Rev. William Cairns was born c.1784 in Rutherglen, Scotland, the eldest son of William Cairns, farmer. He entered Glasgow University in 1795, graduated M.A. in 1802 and LL.D. in 1838. He was Antiburgher (Secession) Minister in Johnstown 1808-15. He then came over to Belfast as Professor of Logic and Belles Lettres at the (Royal) Belfast Academical Institution 1815-45. See Fisher and Robb: *Royal Belfast Academical Institution, Centenary Volume* (1913); Addison: *Matriculation Albums of the University of Glasgow* (1913).]

(C)ALDBECK
    [Flaking horizontal slab on the ground.] Here lies the body of Ri(chard Ca)ldbeck, Esqr, late of Rath(cr...., in) the Queen's County, who departed this life on the 28th of January 1817 in the 45th year of his age.

CALDWELL
    [White limestone laid flat.] Erected by Julia Caldwell, in memory of her beloved husband John Caldwell, Minister of the Lord Jesus Christ, who fell asleep in Him, 18th April 1841 aged 29 years. Also of their two children, Jane who died 25th Decr 1839 aged 8 months, and John who died 21st Decr 1840 aged 4 months. "Thy dead men shall live, together with my dead body shall they arise. Awake and sing ye that dwell in dust: for thy dew is as the dew of herbs, and the earth shall cast out the dead." Isaiah XXVI. 19.

CALLENDER
    [Formerly in lower ground and now missing.] Erected by James Callender, (Mill) Street, Belfast, in memory of five of his children who died in infancy.
    Ere sin could blight or sorrow fade
    Death came with tender care,
    These lovely buds to Heaven conveyed,
    And bade them blossom there."
    Also his son James who departed this life 6th May 1849 aged 1 year and 8 months.
    [He was publican, carrier and leather merchant at 21 and 23 Mill Street, now Castle Street.]

CAMERON
    [Polished granite laid flat.] James Cameron, of Tulloch, Perthshire, died 1851 aged 97. Margaret Stuart, his wife, died 1853 aged 94. James

Portrait of William Cairns, Professor of Logic, Rhetoric and Belles Lettres at the R.B.A.I.

Cameron, son of the above, died 1879 aged 81. Sarah BARRON, his wife, and their children: James, Alexander, Margaret, who died in childhood, also Robert who died 21st January 1909 aged 66. Margaret Cameron died 7th November 1933, the last survivor of the family of James Cameron.

CAMERON
[Large slab on the ground.] In loving memory of John Cameron, formerly of Belfast, died Melbourne, Australia, 13 Feby. 1872 aged 78 yers. Arabella Cameron his wife died Melbourne, 5th April 1889 aged 77 years. And of their daughters: Arabella, died Melbourne, Australia aged 49 years, Jessie, died Belfast, buried here aged 18 years. Kathleen MARKS died Casterton, Australia aged 29 years. Also in memory of these buried here: Robert Bothwell McCUNE aged 27 years. Elizabeth DUGAN nee McCune aged 39 years. Jane Cameron aged 87 years, Anna Maria WALKINGSHAW aged 12 years. This stone laid by surviving sons and daughters, 19 March 1900.

CAMPBEL
See HANNAY

CAMPBELL
[In upper ground, but no longer extant.] Erected by James Campbell to the memory of his father William Campbell of Belfast who departed this life on the 26th of December 1814 aged 38 years. Also his brother John who was drowned on the 20th day of April 1828 aged 18 years. And his brother Thomas who died in infancy. Also Martha Campbell, wife of the above James Campbell died the 24th of January 1848 aged 44 years. Also the said James Campbell died at Rio Grande 25th of April 1850 aged 46 years.

CAMPBELL
[Very badly flaked sandstone.] Erected (by) Mary (Cam)pbell, (in mem)ory (of her) dearly beloved (mother Grace Colgan) Campbell (late of Randalstown, who after a life of much) trouble (but of pious use)fulness (died) in this (place, 25th) January 182(6) or (2) aged (56) years.

CAMPBELL
[Badly flaking and now lost.] Erected by John Campbell (in memory of) his daughter (Elizabeth) who departed this life (on the 9th July) 182(5) or (9) aged 13 months.

CAMPBELL
[Flaking slate, now lost.] Erected by William C. Campbell in memory of his beloved wife Elizabeth Campbell who departed this life Feby 14th 1827 aged 71 years. Also the above named William Campbell who died 12th Sept 1842 aged 78 years. Also his son-in-law Joseph WARD who died 17th Jany 1828 aged 33 years. Also Ellen Campbell, daughter of the above named William who departed this life the 12th of Feby 1844 aged 58 years.

CAMPBELL
[Polished granite tablet in sandstone pedimented surround, secured to

dividing wall.] In memory of James Campbell, died 31st January 1874 aged 82 years. Nancy his wife died 29th October 1830 aged 33 years. And their children, James died 21st March 1835 aged 19 years, William died 7th April 1840 aged 13 years, Lydia died 29th July 1853 aged 28 years, Anna died 23rd March 1905 aged 84 years.

[James Campbell lived at Cultra, near Holywood.]

CAMPBELL

[Twin tablets in sandstone monument, secured to dividing wall, and in a high-railed enclosure.] Erected by Edward and Samuel Campbell, Belfast, 1832 in memory of William their brother who died 4th January 1831 aged 35 years. And of Jane Eliza, the wife of Samuel Campbell, who died 2nd Feb. 1836 aged 27 years. The above named Samuel Campbell died 12th August 1850 aged 49 years. Anne Campbell, daughter of Edward and Sarah Campbell, born 8th Jany 1839, died 6th Oct 1923.

In memory of Elizabeth the beloved wife of Edward Campbell who died 14th July 1832 aged 28 years. The above named Edward Campbell died 29th August 1850 aged 57 years. William Campbell, eldest son of the above Edward Campbell, who died 11th April 1880 aged 39 years. Margaret DEMPSTER born 18th June 1823, died 23rd April 1900. Sarah Campbell, wife of the above named Edward Campbell, born 5th March 1815, died 10th February 1904. Edward H. Campbell, born 26th September 1872, died 20th September 1905.

[Edward and Samuel Campbell were general provision merchants and soap manufacturers in North Street.]

CAMPBELL

[Pitted.] Erected by John Campbell, (No)rth Queen Str., Belfast, in memory of his beloved wife Jean who died 14th February 1835 aged 42 years.

CAMPBELL

[Broken cast-iron plaque.] The family burying place of James Campbell, Belfast, June 22 1846.

CAMPBELL

[Worn sandstone, with dove bearing an olive leaf at the top, in low-railed enclosure.] Erected by James Campbell, master mariner, of this port, in memory of his beloved wife Mary MILBURN who died 2(6th) Feby 1872 aged 61 years. "A kind mother and loving wife". Also five of their children who died young. Also their son John Campbell, master mariner, who died 21st Nov. 1866 aged 29 years. Also their son David Campbell, provision merchant, who died 7th Feby 1876 aged 32 years. Also James Campbell husband and father of the above who died 4th November 1887 aged 78 years. "Blessed are the dead who die in the Lord".

CAMPBELL

[White limestone with carved surround laid flat in a low-stone enclosure.] Erected 1872, in memory of Samuel Campbell and his daughters, Jane, Eliza and Dorothea. Also of his son William Campbell of 23 University Road, who died at Donaghadee, 28th August 1885 aged 70 years. "God's finger touched him and he slept".

CAMPBELL
[In upper ground. The stone is now missing and even in E.W. Pim's time it was excessively worn. It was next to Thomas McComb's grave.] Erected by Margaret Campbell of Belfast.

CAMPBELL
See KENNEDY

CARLILE
[Decorated headstone.] Erected by John Carlile, junr of Belfast, in memory of his beloved mother Mary Carlile who departed this life 23rd Oct. 1858 aged 40 years.

Thou art gone to thy rest dear Mother,
We will not weep for thee,
For thou art now where oft on earth
Thy spirit longed to be.

Thou art gone to thy rest, dear Mother,
Thy toils and cares are o'er,
And sorrows pain and suffering now
Shall ne'er distress thee more'.

CARLILE
See CLARKE

CARLISLE
[Enamelled iron shield lying loose, now removed.] The family burial place of David Carlisle, 1878.
[Granite block, locking of c.1930-1950.] Carlisle. CULLEN.

CARR
[Large headstone, now lost.] 1846. (Sacred) to the memory of James Carr, late Qtr. Master, 64th Regt., who died 22nd August 1845 aged 65 years. His son James died in Sydney, 21st Sept. 1843 aged 31 years. Erected by his beloved wife and children. His daughter Matilda died 11th April 1866 aged 47 years. Elizabeth Carr, relict of the above James Carr, died 20th April 18(67) aged 77 years.

CARROLL
See WARD

CARSON
[Polished granite memorial, attached to south wall, in enclosure that was formerly high-railed.] A.D.1846. The family burial place of William Carson, merchant, Belfast. His son Samuel, born 16th Sep. 1833, died 7th Oct. 1855.

CARSON
[Polished granite, in a low stone enclosure.] In memory of Robert Matthews Carson, born 16th July 1813, died 24th April 1874. Also his children: Anna, Jane and John Lindsay who died in infancy. Also of his daughter Mary who entered into rest 27th November 1878. Also his wife Marianne LINDSAY,

born 15th February 1812, died 3rd September 1890."He that believeth in me though he were dead yet shall he live". John XI, 25. "He that believeth in me though he were dead yet shall he live." [sic]

[The will of Robert Matthews Carson late of Belfast, merchant, who died 24 April 1874 at same place was proved at Belfast 15 May 1874 by the oath of Marianne Carson of Newington Terrace, Belfast aforesaid, widow, the sole executrix. (Deceased died domiciled in Ireland). Effects in U.K. under £2,000.

He owned a large timber yard and seed stores at 130 Corporation Street.]

CARSON

[Small white marble stone.] In loving memory of Jane Carson, a faithful servant, died 9th August 1912. Also James B. OWEN died 4th September 1916. Also his daughter Fanny STEVENSON, died 12th July 1930. Also his daughter Margaret died 25th December 1967.

CARSON

See BARNETT

CARTER

[Corroded iron shield difficult to identify.] The family burying ground of John T. Carter, Monkstown, (1861).

CARTER

See McTIER

CATTERNACH

[Stone now missing from upper ground. The plot was bought by Charles Catternach in January 1804.] .... in memory of his daughter Elizabeth Catternach who departed this life on the 30th .... aged 10 months.

CATTO

See FOLINGSBY

CAUGHEY

[Flaking badly.] Thomas Caughey, son to Captain (Jo)hn Caughey, died October (the) 18th 1800 aged 23 (mon)ths. Also Isabella Caughey (relic)t of the said Captain John Caughey (died) March 15th 1832 aged 68 (years. Also) Margaret Caughey (daug)hter of the late Captain John Caughey died May 24th 1869 aged 77 years.

CAUGHEY

[Flaking badly.] Erected in memory of (Capt Jas. Caughey), of Belfast, who de(parted this life the) 12th day of April (1832 aged 61 years.) Here also lieth the (remains of Sarah) PATTERSON, (wife of the late Capt. Jas. Patterson), of Belfast, who died the 13th Decr 1805 aged 65 years. And Mary WARNICK, her sister. Likewise of Mary Eliza McCLEERY, daughter of Surgeon Jas. McCleery, of Belfast, who died the 28th Feb 1827 aged 13 months. Also John aged 2 years, and Mary an infant, son and daughter of Jas. Caughey, Church Street. Here also lieth Mary, wife of the above named Captn Caughey, died 1st Augt 1845 aged 73 years.

[See also Surgeon James McCleery's gravestone below.]

CAUGHEY

[Badly flaking.] Sacred (to) the memory of Alexander Cau(ghey) who departed this life the 20th June 18(44) aged (43) years. And his fourth son (Will)iam Henry H(arper) who died (8)th December 18(65) aged 27 years. Also his second son James A. Caughey who died on his passage to Australia, 2nd February 1867 aged 34 years.

CAUGHEY

See LAMONT

CAVAN

See FRAZER

CAVART

[Four tablets in entablature secured to south wall in low-walled enclosure.] Erected to the memory of Henry Cavart. Jane Cavart his daughter departed this life 26th Septr 1809 aged 20 years. Henry Cavart departed this life 13th Nov. 1817 aged 63 years. John Cavart his son departed this life 16th March 1821 aged 27 years. Isabella Jane Cavart, daughter to John departed this life 18th March 1822 aged 10 months. Ann LOGAN sister to Henry departed this life 21st Sept. 1826 aged 83 years. Isabella, wife of Henry departed this life 26th Aug. 1841 aged 83 years.

(b) [Marble tablet] (Samuel GIB)SON, Esq. (died March) 1817, aged 52 years. Mary, daughter of the late John BARNETT Esq. and wife of Rev. R WILSON departed this life on the 9th of March 1837, two days after the death of her infant.

(c) [Small marble tablet beneath above.] In memory of Henry, son of John Cavart, who died at Hong Kong, August 12th 1844 aged 24 years.

(d) [In pedimented entablature.] The family burying place of John Barnett. Sacred to the memory of John Barnett, late of Belfast, formerly of Ballyacherty, County of Down who closed a life of public usefulness and private worth on the 19th day of March A.D. 1835, AE 65. Jane Gibson wife of John Barnett died 13th March 1864 in her 95th year. James Barnett, son of the above died 26th March 1861 aged 65 years. Eliza his wife died 23rd Septr 1859 aged 55 years. An infant son of John Barnett and three of his grandchildren are also interred here. James MONTGOMERY, of Wolfhill, son-in-law to John Barnett who died 2nd December 1877 aged 67 years. Anna Barnett, wife of James Montgomery, died June 3rd 1891 aged 78 years. "In hope of eternal life".

[John Cavart was an attorney and lived in Castle Street. The Rev. Robert Wilson was Professor of Biblical Criticism to the General Assembly of the Presbyterian Church in Ireland; see below under WILSON.

The Montgomery family which lived in Wolfhill House were well-known flax-spinners.]

CHAMBERS

[Small headstone, now lost.] Beneath lieth the body of William Chambers, 2nd child of John and Rosella Chambers, 64th Regt, died 11th of

February 1831 aged 1 year and 7 months.
N....... ast of time can
That only thee..........
.... to...... p,
The happy soul in Heaven.

CHAMBERS
[Polished granite in low-stone enclosure.] In loving memory of our parents, John Chambers died 9th February 1899 aged 59 years, Elizabeth Chambers died 19th August 1898 aged 52 years. Also our grandmother Annie FINLAY, died 16th November 1863 aged 39 years.

CHAMBERS
See RITCHIE and STEPHENS

CHAPMAN
[Now lost but copied from Society's Inscription Book.] Erected by Juliana Chapman in memory of her beloved husband William Chapman who departed this life 31st March 1836 aged 46 years. Also their child Isabella who died young. The Rev. R. M. DOLAN, A.B., T.C.D., died 28th Feby 1876 aged 54 years. Also the above-named Juliana Chapman died 19th May 1876 aged 83 years. Also Juliana, daughter of the above William Chapman and widow of the above Revd. R. M. Dolan, died 18th Octr 1883 aged 53 years.

[The will of Reverend Robert Dolan, late of High Street, Holywood, county Down, Clerk in Holy Orders, who died 28 February 1876 at same place, was proved at Belfast 7 April 1876 by the oaths of Julia Anna Dolan of High Street, Holywood, widow, and George May of 14 University Street, Belfast, yarn merchant, the executors. Effects under £3,000.

The Rev. Robert Mussen Dolan was born in 1821 in Bangor, son of William Dolan, ship's captain, educated at the Royal Belfast Academical Institution 1836-40 and entered Trinity College, Dublin in November 1840. He graduated B.A. in 1845, was ordained deacon in 1847 and was curate of Aghaderg (Loughbrickland), county Down 1861-63 (sic). See Fisher and Robb: *The Royal Belfast Academical Institution, Centenary Volume* (1913); Burtchaell and Sadler: *Alumni Dublinenses* (1924); Swanzy: *Succession Lists of the Diocese of Dromore* (1933).]

CHAPMAN
[Flaking and now lost.] Sacred to the memory of James Chapman, Master of the brig "Tyne", of Cardiff, who died in Belfast Lough, on the 1(0)th November 1852 aged (63) years.

CHARNOCK
See McDOWELL

CHARTERS
[Large marble tablet in carved entablature formerly topped by a draped urn, secured to east wall in high-railed enclosure.] In memoriam, Mary H. Charters, wife of John Charters, died March 9th 1853. James B. Charters, son of John and Mary Charters, died January 8th 1849. John Charters jun. died

September 26th 1865 aged 40 years. John Charters died August 13th 1874 aged 78 years. Anna Boomer Charters died July 14th 1891 aged 69 years.

[The will (with two codicils) of John Charters late of Craigowen, county Down, esquire, who died 13 August 1874 at same place, was proved at Belfast 31 August 1874 by the oath of George Washington Charters of Craigavad, same county, esquire, the sole executor (deceased died domiciled in Ireland). Effects in United Kingdom under £180,000.

John Charters, senr. of Ardmoulin House, Falls Road, was proprietor of the Falls Flax Spinning and Weaving Company, at that time one of the leading concerns of its kind in Ulster. He was one of Belfast's more noted philanthropists, and one of his chief interests was the promotion of education, particularly among the less privileged. Two institutions which benefited were the R.B.A.I. and the Model School. He had close connections with the Belfast Charitable Society and built the Charters Wing behind Clifton House in 1868. As a person he was most likeable, and was highly esteemed both in private and public life. See Fisher and Robb: *The Royal Belfast Academical Institution, Centenary Volume* (1913); Strain: *Belfast and its Charitable Society* (1961).]

CHEW
> See GIBBS

CHIRMSIDE
> [Broken sandstone headstone worn on one side and partly buried.] Sacred to the memory of (Eliza) Chirmside, wife of (John) Chirmside, (of) Belfast. ...... very endearing ...... on, both of mind ....n; this young and ...... woman was suddenly .... the bosom of her .... (parents) on the ...... (181)7 aged 19 years.

CHIRMSIDE
> [In low stone enclosure.] This stone was erected by Thomas Chirmside, of Belfast in memory of his mother Ann Chirmside who departed this life the 5th of November 1818 aged 59 years. Also his son Thomas who died this 9th of August 1826 aged 18 months. And of his beloved wife Mary who departed this life on Saturday 9th of September 1854. Also Martha McCLELLAND, daughter of the above died 21st of May 1875. Also the above named Thomas Chirmside who died on the 12th November 1875 in his 85th year. Here lies also Hugh McClelland, husband of the above Martha McClelland died 19th January 1891 in his 68th year. Also Hugh McClelland, son of the above Hugh McClelland, who died 16th August 1896 aged 33 years. And Annie M. Chirmside, born 3rd March 1826, died 21st December 1900. [Continued on plinth] Also Mary Chirmside, youngest daughter of above named Thomas Chirmside, born 6th August 1832, died 2nd May 1912. "A meek and quiet spirit".

[Thomas Chirmside was a woollen draper in Bridge Street, and later was a flax merchant; and he lived latterly in Marine Parade, Holywood.]

CHISHOLM
> See LARMOUR

CINNAMOND
[Very badly weathered and now lost.] Erected in memory of James C(inn)amond who departed (this) life the (..) ..... 182(6 aged 4. ye)ars.

CINNAMOND
[Flaking near the top.] Erected by Helena Cinnamond, in memory of her beloved husband George Cinnamond who departed this life on the 15th April 1851 aged 61 years. Also 6 of her sons who died as follows: viz, Robert James 22nd December 1834 aged 7 months, William Arthur, 10th March 1840 aged 20 months, George, 16th September 1839 aged 14 months, George, 27th December 1847 aged 11 months, James, 10th March 1851 aged 6 years & 11 months. Also the above named Helena Cinnamond, who departed this life on the 20th July 1884 aged 78 years.

CINNAMOND
[Worn marble in carved entablature, now lost.] In memory of John the beloved son of John Cinnamond, of Belfast, who departed this life 25th Oct. 1860 aged 29 years. "Looking unto Jesus". Also Mary his beloved wife who departed this life 18th Nov. 1866 aged 72 years. The above John Cinnamond died 1879 aged 82 years. Also their four children, viz: Henry, Mary, Anna and John. Their nephew William GILLESPIE.

[John Cinnamond, senr. was the proprietor of a well-established firm of boot and shoe merchants in High Street and Arthur Street.]

CLARK
Erected by Hugh Clark in memory of his wife Jane who departed this life on the 8th September 1834 aged 35 years. His son William who died 30th November 1834 aged 2 years. His son John who died 5th May 1835 aged 6 years.

CLARK
[Marble in low-railed enclosure.] Sacred to the memory of Thomas Clark who died on the 5th January 1840 aged 49 years. Also Mary his wife who died on the 1st June 1852 aged 52 years. Also Margaret Joyce Clark their eldest daughter who died on the 24th February 1883 aged 59 years. Also their youngest son Thomas Clark, Brigade Surgeon A.M.D., formerly of 69th Regt, died 23rd Dec. 1891 aged 59 years. "He shall raise us up, and we shall live in his sight".

CLARK
[Large slate in entablature, now lost.] The burying place of Ledlie Clark Belfast. Ledlie Clark died 25th Sepr 1842 aged 8 months. Ledlie Clark, senr died on the 21st May 1854 aged 52 years.

[Ledlie Clark was a brewer of 130 Ann Street.]

CLARK
See HARPER and THOMPSON

CLARKE
[Polished granite headstone secured to north wall in high-railed low-

walled enclosure.] Sacred to the memory of John Clarke who was buried in the old parish ground at St. George's Church, 1775. Also of Catherine Anne Clarke his wife, here interred, died 17th January 1823 aged 87 years. And their son William Clarke died 11th June 1839 aged 73 years. Also six of his children who died young.

Also his wife Mary Anne Clarke, died 20th July 1843 aged 63 years. And their youngest son Henry Wray Clarke, died 14th October 1861 aged 39 years. Also John Clarke, eldest son of William Clarke, died 22nd April 1863 aged 70 years. And Catherine Anne CARLILE, daughter of William Clarke, died 14th April 1875 aged 77 years.

[The Clarkes were a noted and respected family in Donegall Place for much of the first half of the 19th century. William Clarke was a J.P. and his brother John (d.1800) had been an assistant curate to the Rev. William Bristow, Vicar of Belfast, and was active in the founding of the town Dispensary in 1792.

William's son John was also a J.P. and was one of the original aldermen of the newly formed Town Council of 1842, becoming Mayor of Belfast in 1844. He was Chairman of the Belfast Harbour Board from 1855 until his death in 1863.

Another son of William's was Edward Harris Clarke (d.1889), early in his career a barrister and subsequently a Director of the Belfast Banking Company from 1850 to 1880. He was descended from Valentine Jones (1711-1805) through his mother. See Benn: *History of Belfast*, Vol. II (1880); Simpson: *The Belfast Bank*, 1827-1970 (1975).]

CLARKE

[Flaking slate, badly damaged.] Sac(red) to the memory of James Pritchard Clarke, son of James Clarke, of the Royal Artillery who departed this life 22nd June 1805 aged three mon(ths).

Grieve not my parents dear,
I am not dead but sleepeth here,
My debts are paid and that you see,
Prepare for death and follow me.

CLARKE

See SINCLAIRE (2)

CLAYTON

In memory of Joseph Clayton, a native of Banff, Scotland, Commander of the barque "Helen", of Belfast who departed this life on the 7th day of Jany 1847 aged 34 years. Erected by his uncle William HOSSACK.

CLELAND

See PATTERSON and YOUNG

CLEMENTS

[Now lost.] Erected by David Clements, in memory of three of his children who died young. Also the above named David Clements, who died 11th December 1866 aged 79 years. Also Elizabeth his beloved wife who died 4th January 1870 aged 76 years. Also Sarah their daughter who died 21st February 1882 aged 51 years. Also their daughter Hannah Clements who died 21st August 1899 aged 81 years. Also Marianne died 14th May 1913, in her 87th year.

CLOSE

[Attached to high railing.] To the memory of James Close, of Belfast, who departed this life the 10th August 1860 aged 72 years. Also his beloved wife Margaret Close who departed this life the 21st October 1868 aged 77 years. Also his grandson Charles STILWELL who died 1st May 1861 aged two weeks.

[The will of James Close, late of Belfast in the county of Antrim, grocer, who died 10 August 1860 at Belfast aforesaid, was proved at Belfast 17 October 1860 by the oaths of William Walker, rent agent, and William Knox Baker, both of said place, the executors. Effects under £1,000.]

COATES

[Cast iron tablet.] 1833. The burying place of John Coates, Belfast. [Plot purchased by William ALLEN in March 1810, and later transferred to John Coates who was the eldest brother of Mrs Allen.]

COATES

[Family name on low stone enclosure, now lost.] Coates. [This plot was bought by Charles Standfield MURPHY in April 1854.]

COATES

See McFARLAN

COBURN

Erected by William Coburn, 1853. Charles Coburn died 19th June 1864 aged 15 years.

COBURN

See DOUGHERTY

COCHRAN

[Altar-tomb, now destroyed.] To the memory of William Cochran, merchant, who died (6)th December 1821 aged 60 years.

[He was a cotton dealer of Commercial Court.]

COCHRANE

See YORK

COEY

[In entablature secured to south wall.] Erected by James Coey, Donegall Place, to the memory of his beloved wife Margaret who died 22nd August 1844 aged 43 years. Also his daughter Mary, wife of James McCARTER, of Londonderry, died Feby 16th 1854 aged 20 years. Likewise her infant son Robert Alexr aged 15 weeks. Also his son William who died at Demerara, 22nd Jany 18(5)2 in his 19th year. Also the above named James Coey died 22nd January 1860 aged 60 years.

[James Coey owned the Northern Boot and Shoe house, 12 Donegall Place.

The will of James Coey late of Knock in the county of Down, gentleman, who died 22 January 1860 at Knock aforesaid was proved at Belfast 25 July 1860 by the oaths of Edward Coey of Mervale in the county of Antrim and James Coey of Liverpool, merchants, the executors. Effects under £4,000.]

COFFEY

[Now missing from lower ground.] Erected in memory of Captain Hugh Coffey, of this port, who died at sea 29th March 184(0) aged 27 years. Also his brother Robert Coffey M.D., who died 5th January 1847.

[Robert Coffey obtained the L.R.C.S of Edinburgh in 1819, was elected to the Belfast Medical Society in 1822, was appointed to the hospital committee in 1823 and appointed attending surgeon on 15 May 1827. He obtained a M.D. of Glasgow University in 1833. When the R.B.A.I. established a Chair in Surgery in 1835 they made two false starts with Dr John McDonnell and Dr Thomas Ferrar, but Dr Coffey was effectively the first Professor of Surgery and, in spite of objections presumably because of Arian views, he held the chair from January 1837 until his death. He married on 22 May 1820 (by the Rev. Henry Montgomery) Miss Blackwood "both of this town" (*BNL*). See Fisher and Robb: *The Royal Belfast Academical Institution, Centenary Volume* (1913); Allison: *The Seeds of Time* (1972); Calwell: *Andrew Malcolm of Belfast* (1977); Logan J. S., personal communication.]

COLEMAN

[Flaking and undated stone of c.1820, now lost.] (Erected) by James Coleman. [Plot purchased by Isabella MUNN, in December 1817 and subsequently transferred to Thomas Coleman.]

COLEMAN

See McCABE

COLLINS

[Mostly copied from Society's Inscription book, now lost. Very worn marble tablet in pedestal of an obelisk bearing carving of three field guns and two crossed barrels in ellipse.] (Erected by the Officers, non-commissioned Officers .... of the Queen's Royal Rifles to the memory of ..) James (Collins) late ban(d Master) of the (Royal Artillery died) at Belfast (3rd Jany 1865) aged 4(6) years.

COMYNS

[Horizontal slab in "Cholera Ground".] Beneath this stone are deposited the remains of Sarah, wife of Joseph Comyns Esq., of the Customs Service, Belfast, who died the 24th Novr 1837 aged 56 years. This tribute of respect is erected to her memory by their sons, Alexander, William, Joseph and Robert Comyns. Here also lie the remains of William, brother of said Joseph Comyns, who died 12th March 1838 aged 69 years.

CONIN..HSE.

See LENNOX

CONNELL

[Worn and bulging tablet in surround attached to north wall (now lost), in enclosure that was formerly high-railed. Crest: Castle tower with plumes. Motto: ...] The family burying place of Charles Connell, shipbuilder, Belfast. His daughter Mrs Ann NICHOLSON died 2nd March 1828 aged 23 years. Also his daughter Mrs Jessie AGNEW died 19th Novr 1836 aged 27 years. Likewise the above named Charles Connell died 27th July 1844 aged (72) years, (who lived beloved and died lamented). Charles Connell, junr died 2nd June 1846 aged (49) years. Ann Connell died 26th Novr 18(5)1 aged 80 years. James Connell who died at Wellington, New Zealand (26th May) 1882 aged 61 years. Also his wife Mary Connell who died 24th Jany 18(63) aged (45) years.

[When William Ritchie (1756-1834) retired from shipbuilding in 1828, Charles Connell, senr, took over the famous yard at Ritchie's Dock which is now covered by Corporation Square, and ran it until 1843 when he surrendered the lease. His son Charles, junr was also a ship-builder.]

CONNOR

[Laid flat.] Erected by Eliza Connor in memory of her husband Henry Connor who departed this life 23rd of September 1838 aged 64 years. Also her son William Connor who departed this life 7th of April 1841 aged 30 years. Also her son Robert Connor who departed this life 28th Feb. 1856 aged 50 years. And his daughter Sarah E. Connor who departed this life 27th Dec. 1868 aged 17 yers.

Her sickness she with patience bore,
She is not lost, but gone before.

CONNOR

See MOLYNEUX and SKELTON

COOPER

[Slate tablet with pedimented entablature secured to west wall.] Erected to the memory of James Cooper, of Belfast, by his heirs, who departed this life the 24th Septr 1799 aged 67 years. Also his wife Margaret Cooper who departed this life the 16th of February 1806 aged 76 years. Also Jane BLACK who departed this life on the 7th of April 1814 aged 16 years.

In early life she wisely sought her God,
And in the paths of pure religion trod,
She found in this what nothing else can give,
And learn'd to die ere others learn'd to live.

And the body of John Cooper who departed this life the 27th of June 1837 aged 82 years. And Isabella his wife who departed this life the 27th of May 1854 aged 83 years.

[John Cooper was a merchant of Great George's Street.]

COPLAND

See THOMSON

CORBITT

[Worn marble with pedimented entablature (now lost) in low-walled enclosure formerly with high rails.] To the memory of Thomas Corbitt, merchant, Belfast, who died 27th May 18(54) aged 7(5) years. And also Margaret ANDREWS who died 2(7)th March 18(14) aged (29) years. And their son Michael who died 25th July 18(13) aged 3 months. Also Elizabeth THOMPSON, his wife who died 4th October 1878 aged 93 years.

[The will of Elizabeth Corbitt, late of Clarendon Place, Belfast, widow, deceased who died 4 October 1878 at same place, was proved at Belfast 28 October 1878 by the oaths of William Thompson of Lisburn, medical doctor, and Francis Thompson of Clarendon Place, Belfast, esquire, both in county Antrim and John Borthwick of Prospect House, near Carrickfergus, esquire, their executors. Effects under £40,000.

Thomas Corbitt was a prosperous timber merchant whose yard was in Great George's Street.]

CORDUKES

[Horizontal slab on the ground.] Sacred to the memory of John Cordukes who departed this life 7th July 1834 aged 38 years. Also of his daughter Mary Ann Cordukes who died 1st November 1823 aged 2 years, and Jemima Cordukes who died in infancy. And of his son Thomas Shaw Cordukes who died 7th June 1828 aged 4 years and 10 months. And also his wife Charlotte Jemima who died 19th June 1869. And her sister Mary Anne SHAW who died 2nd April 1878.

[The Cordukes family were provision merchants and lived in the York Road and Skegoniel area. Part of York Street was for a time called Corduke's Place.]

CORDUKES

[Flaking.] Sacred to the memory of Thomas Cordukes who died October 24th 1825 aged 28 years.

In silent anguish, Oh, my spouse,
When I recally thy worth;
Thy (lovely) lifetime's early end,
I feel estranged from earth;
My soul desires with thine to rest,
Supremely and for ev(er b)lest.

CORDUKES

[Badly damaged stone formerly with above two but now lost.] Erected in memory of Mrs Anna Cordukes, late wife of Mr .... Cordukes, of Belfast, ... merchant who departed) this l(ife 31st January .... aged 60. And of her .... Cordukes, who died ....)

CORRY

See HUGHES, and ROGERS

COULTER

See SMITH

COWAN

[Now removed.] Sacred to the memory of Isabella Cowan who departed this life Sep. 19th 1847 aged 87 years.

COWAN

[Railed enclosure with cast-iron tablet and polished granite stone now laid flat.] Erected by John Cowan, master mariner, Belfast, 1840.

[Modern stone] In loving memory of John Cowan, master mariner, who died 24th May 1852 aged 56 years. And of his wife Mary Cowan died 23rd November 1879 aged 80 years. And of their children: Alexander, Jane, Mary and William who all died in childhood. And of James Cowan, master mariner, who died 18th May 1845 aged 64 years. And of Margaret Eliza Cowan, eldest daughter of the above John and Mary Cowan, died 19th September 1908. Samuel H. Cowan departed this life 28th Octr 1912. Micah VI, 8. Also Mary Cowan, died 12th March 1924 aged 84 years. "The memory of the just is blessed."

CRABB

Sacred to the memory of Anne NICHOLLS, wife of Charles T. Crabb, who died the 30th of April 1848 AE 28 years.

CRAIG

[Badly flaking near the top.] Erected to the memory of Mary Craig who departed this life on the (4th) of May Anno Domini 1828 in the 74th year of her age. And also of her husband Stewart B. Craig who died on the 12th of the same month aged 78 years. Also their daughter Mary BURROWS who died on the 29th of February, 1864 in the 73rd year of her age. Also Martha Craig died 6th May 1879 aged 92 years.

[The will of Martha Craig, late of Great Victoria Street, Belfast, spinster, who died 6 May 1879 at same place, was proved at Belfast 28 May 1879 by the oaths of James Ferguson of Holestone, Doagh, county Antrim, farmer, John Wylie of 6 Cromac Park Terrace, Ormeau Road, Belfast, and Henry McClury of Park Place, Ormeau Road, Belfast, rent agent, the executors. Effects under £6,000.]

CRAIG

[Now lost.] (Erected by Helen) Craig (to the memory of her affectionate and beloved husband Ric)hard Craig (who died 28th) March (1850) aged (37) years.

CRAIG

[With initials "A.W.C." at top and date MDCCCLIV.) Erected by John Craig in memory of his brother Abraham Walter Craig, proprietor of the Falls Factory, Belfast, who died 29th September 1854 aged 41 years.

[Abraham Walker Craig's flax-spinning works on the Falls Road was the first in Belfast to weave linen successfully by mechanised power. Craig Street, nearby, is named after the family.]

CRAIG

[Undated polished granite headstone in enclosure, against east wall - looks of c.1880-1910.] The family burying ground of John Craig. [The plot was bought by John Craig in August 1845.]

CRAIG

See BENN and WOODS

CRAMER
[Very badly flaked and now lost.] Erected (by) Charles (C)ramer in memory of his wife Mary (Ann) who departed this life 14th (Ma)rch (1828) aged (26 years).

CRAMSIE
[Worn marble shield formerly with motto beneath and on sandstone headstone, now laid flat.] In memory of John Cramsie who died August 2(2nd) 18(47) aged 6(0) years. Also his daughter Jane, who died September 21st 185(1) aged (30) years. John Crossley Cramsie, eldest son of the above died November 1st 18(79).

[John Cramsie senr. was a wine merchant and notary public with an office in Waring Street.]

CRANSTON
See ALEXANDER

CRAWFORD
[Very badly flaked and now lost.] Erected by Margaret Crawford in memory of her hus(band Walter) Crawford, of Belfast, (merchant who departed this) life the (1st day of) May 18(12 in the 57th year of his age. Also the above-named Margaret) Crawford who departed (this life) on the 22nd day of April (1841 aged 73 years.)

CRAWFORD
[Headstone in upper ground and no longer extant. In 1907 it was broken in two, the lower half being missing at that time.] Erected to the memory of Isabella Crawford, of Belfast, who died Feby 12th 1814 aged 84 years. Also to the memory of Daniel TOLEN of Belfast, who died 6th Novr. 1814 aged ...

CRAWFORD
[Large slate tablet in surround secured to dividing wall in low-railed enclosure.] Erected to the memory of Arthur Crawford, formerly of Bloomfield, in the County of Down, who departed this life on the 2nd of June 1833 aged 84 years. Also his grandson John Stevenson Ferguson, second son of James Crawford, who departed this life 12th of February 1839 aged 12 years. Also of Theodosia, relict of the late Arthur Crawford who departed this life 15th of April 1849 aged 76 years. Also of James Crawford, of Donegall Place, Belfast, who departed this life 25th of August 1860 aged 65 years. Also of Ellen, relict of the late James Crawford, who departed this life 19th of May 1880 aged 82 years.

[The will of James Crawford, late of Dooneen, Donegall Place, Belfast in the county of Antrim, esquire, who died 25 August 1860 at Donegall Place aforesaid, was proved at Belfast 18 October 1860 of the oath of Henry Crawford of same place, solicitor, one of the executors. Effects under £18,000.

James Crawford was a well-known wine merchant whose business premises were in Callendar Street. He also took an active part in the civic life of the town, being one of the first Councillors of the reformed Belfast Corporation which was elected in 1842. His widow was one of the last private residents of Donegall Place, she remaining there till her death. Her house was demolished to make way for Robinson and Cleaver's department store.]

CRAWFORD

[Large monument, formerly topped by a draped urn, and containing three tablets, attached to east wall.] In memory of Arthur Crawford who died 14th December 1852 aged 58 years. Jane, relict of Arthur Crawford, who died 11th January 1885.

In memory of Arthur REID, who died 2nd January 1854 aged 66 years. Ellen, relict of Arthur Reid, who died 19th November 1867. Also Arthur Reid their son, who died 25th March 1879. Also Andrew Reid, their eldest and last surviving son who died 11th August 1893. Also Isabella Reid their youngest daughter who died 3rd March 1905. Also Ellen Reid their last surviving daughter who died 10th June 1910.

In memory of James Reid who died 3rd March 1872. Also his wife Selina who died 25th May 1865. Arthur his son who died 21st July 1866, Annie Selina, his eldest daughter who died 3rd November 1926.

[The will together with the document marked "B" of Jane Crawford, late of Albert Villa, Crumlin Road, Belfast, widow, who died 11 January 1885 at same place, was proved at Belfast 18 March 1885 by Brereton John Newell of 67 High Street, Belfast, stockbroker, the sole executor. Effects £4,608 5s.3d.

Arthur Crawford was a woollen draper and lived at New Lodge. Arthur Reid, senior, was a farmer at Old Park.]

CRAWFORD

See JONES

CROMBIE

[Badly flaking stone, now lost.] Here lieth (the) body of El(len Cro)mbie who d(eparted this) life Novr 25th, 180(.) aged 70 years.

CROOKSHANK

[Marble headstone in low-railed enclosure.] Erected to the memory of Alexander Crookshank, who entered into rest February 28th 1845 aged 69 years. His daughter Jane

Johnston Crookshank, February 28th 1848 aged 5 years. His widow Jane Millar Crookshank, August 20th 1896 aged 93 years. Also Elizabeth the dearly beloved wife of Robert A Crookshank, who entered into rest, 17th March 1907. And Robert Alexander Crookshank who entered into rest 25th April 1909 aged 75 years.

[Probate of the will of Robert Alexander Crookshank, late of Richmond, Marlborough Park, Belfast, warehouse assistant, who died 25 April 1909 granted at Belfast 11 June 1909 to Reverend Charles H. Crookshank, clergyman and Charles Kevin M.D. Effects £2,513 6s.1d.

Alexander Crookshank, senr was a prosperous solicitor with a practice in Donegall Street, Belfast where he lived and in Upper Rutland Street, Dublin.]

CROSSEN
[Flaking slightly.] Sacred to the memory of James Crossen, Belfast, muslin manufacturer, who died 27th April 1813 aged 28 years. Also two of Wm Crossen's children, Wm John aged 1 year and 9 months, and Ann, 3 months.

CUDDY
[Headstone in upper ground which has disappeared since 1907.] John Cuddy, Belfast.

[The lot was purchased by John Cuddy in December 1805. He was a glazier and a dealer in paints, oils and glass in Church Lane. Later his business expanded and he became a ship-owner as well. He was a Councillor for St George's Ward from 1842 to 1860, and occupied Gasfield House on the Ormeau Road for a short time before acquiring a residence in College Square East and at Summerhill, Co. Down.]

CULLEN
See CARLISLE

CULLODEN
See PINKERTON

CULTON
See DUNN

CUMINE
[Beginning to flake.] Milicent Cumine departed this life the 17th August 1820 aged 76 years.

CUMMING
[Undated marble in surround, similar to and beside Robert J. Dickey's, now lost.] The family burying place of Samuel Cumming, merchant, Belfast.

[The plot was purchased Robert J. Dickey in May, 1816.]

CUMMINGS
See KENNEDY

CUNNINGHAM
[Tablet secured to east wall of upper graveyard in same low-stone enclosure as Miller tablets.] Erected to the memory of Robt Cunningham, son of John Cunningham, Macedon, who departed this life at Warrenpoint the 16th Octr 1823 aged 42 years. Edwin BLOW, 17th July 1849 aged 49 years. Willm Blow, 17th July 1849 aged (1)6 years.

[Robert Cunningham's father was a noted linen merchant who bought Macedon in 1813 which, incidentally, had been in Cunningham Greg's possession for a few years in the previous decade. Robert's brother, also called John, was one of the six original founders of the Belfast Commercial Bank in 1809. A grand-daughter of John, senr married James Thompson J.P. who eventually obtained possession of Macedon and whose brother was William Thompson, the distinguished naturalist. Edwin and William Blow were grandson and great-grandson of Daniel Blow (1718-1810), the well-known Belfast printer whose father James printed in 1751 the famous Blow Bible, at one time believed to be the first printed in Ireland. In the opening years of the nineteenth century, the Joy family sold the Cromac Paper Mills to the firm of Blow, Ward and Greenfield, on the dissolution of which partnership the firm became Edwin and William Blow who worked the mills until 1842, these two being brothers.

For family connections, see under MILLER.]

CUNNINGHAM
[Broken and laid flat.] Erected by James Cunningham to the memory of his beloved children, viz: his son James who departed this life the 26th Feby 1830 aged 9 years. Also his daughter Mary who departed this life the 10th Nov. 1834 aged 9 years. Also his son John who departed this life the 23rd July 1836 aged 13 years. Likewise his beloved wife Catherine Cunningham who departed this life the 28th October 1847 aged 50 years.

CUNNINGHAM
[Very badly flaked.] Erected (by) A. Cunningham, (to) the memory of (his dear)ly beloved wife Mary Ann Cunningham who departed (this life the 5)th of (April), 1835 aged (38) years. Also their son Ezekiel Cunningham who departed this life 14th May 1856 aged 26 years. Also of the above named Archibald Cunningham who departed this life 13th Nov. 1862 aged 64 years.

[The will of Archibald Cunningham, late of Belfast in the county of Antrim, publican, who died 13 November 1862 at same place, was proved at Belfast 23 December 1862 by the oaths of Ralph Stockman, nail manufacturer and Hugh McMullen, baker, both of Belfast aforesaid, the executors. Effects under £600.]

CUNNINGHAM
[Capstone missing.] (Erected by Ruth Cunningham), to the memory of her beloved husband James Cunningham, of Belfast, who departed this life 7th May 1847 aged 56 years. Also the above Ruth Cunningham who departed this life 22nd April 185(9 aged 76) years.

[In the burial register, James Cunningham is described as a gentleman with a residence in Tomb Street.]

CUNNINGHAM
To the memory of Mary, daughter of the late Josias Cunningham Esqr, who departed this life on the 12th August 1853 aged 26 years. Eliza, relict of the said Josias Cunningham Esqr, died 21st September 1853 aged 56 years.

[Josias Cunningham was a prosperous wholesale and retail tobacconist at 15, Rosemary Street.]

CUNNINGHAM
[Iron plaque, now detached from support, of c.1860-1900.] Erected by John Cunningham of Belfast. [The ground was bought by John Cunningham in November 1815.]

CUNNINGHAM
See MILLER

CURLEY

[White limestone, now lost.] In memory of Elizabeth Curley, died 10th March 1879 aged 68 years. "A faithful wife, a loving mother and a sincere friend". John A. KENNEDY, born 14th July 1869, died 12th February 1875 aged 5 years and 7 months.

CURRAN

[Broken down the middle and lying flat.] I.H.S. Sacred to the memory of Capn Henry Curran who departed this life 23rd June 1844 aged 62 years. Also his daughter Margaret Curran who departed this life 28th June 1847 aged 26 years. Also in memory of Margaret the beloved wife of Captain Henry Curran, the second daughter of Captain Thomas BELL, who departed this life 2nd August 1850 aged 58 years. "Requiescant in pace".

[Capt. Henry Curran was Harbour Master for the south side of the Port of Belfast in the early 1840s.]

CURRELL

[Large headstone bearing tablet, now lost.] The family burying ground of John Currell, who died November 9th 1864 aged 80 years. His wife Elizabeth GIHON who died July 30th 1864 aged 79 years. Their daughters: Mary Ann who died August 28th 1882 aged 58 years, and Jane who died January 20th 1904 aged 83 years.

[The will of Mary Currell, late of Abbeyhill, Whitehouse, county Antrim, spinster, who died 28 August 1882 at same place, was proved 20 April 1883 at Belfast by Jane Currell of Abbeyhill, spinster, the sole executrix. Effects £57.

John Currell and Son were linen merchants with offices in the White Linen Hall. John lived at 4 College Square East before moving out to Whiteabbey.]

CURRIE

[White limestone, now lost.] In memory of James Currie, died 21st December 18(51) aged (54) years. Elizabeth MARTIN his wife died (..) September 18(3)9 aged (41) years. John Robert their son died (25th May 1827) aged (6) years. Mary Currie (their daughter died 31st March 1835 aged 17 months). This stone (was) erected (by their surviving) children March 18(35).

[In the admon. of James Currie died 21 Dec 1851 intestate. Alex Currie (son) of Greenwich in Scotland, merchant, maketh oath and saith that letters of admon. of the goods, chattels and credits of James Currie, late of Belfast in the county of Antrim, were granted to this deponent by the diocesan court of the Bishop of Down and Connor on the 4th day of January 1852, sworn under the value of £450, whereas it should have been valued £450 less than £600. Sworn before me at Glasgow in the county of Lanarkshire 31st day of August 1855, by virtue of a commission to me directed forth of the High Court of Chancery in Ireland and I know the depondent A. P. Henderson. From testamentary papers 1855. Effects less than £600.]

DALTON

[Laid flat.] In loving memory of William James Dalton, died 2nd January 1972 aged 86 yrs. His beloved wife Elizabeth Madeline died

9th June 1984 aged 90 yrs.

[These are the most recent burials in the graveyard and it is highly unlikely there will be any more.]

DALE

[Memorial now missing from lower ground.] The family burial place of William Dale, Belfast, 18(6)1.

DAN

See HAMILTON

DAVIDSON

[Top part worn away.] A.D. 1809. Captain Alexander Davidson. Elizabeth Davidson departed this life on the 27th Dec. 181(0) aged 5(0) years. Margaret Davidson departed this life on the 21st March 1823 aged 77 years. Here also lie the remains of Captain Alexander Davidson who departed this life on the 12th Feb. 1836 aged 86 years. Also Rachael Davidson who departed this life on the 11 May 183(0) aged 81 years.

DAVIDSON

See ECCLES, HOWARD and PINKERTON

DAVIS

[Undated flat slab, of c.1800-1820.] Here lies the body of Jane Davis. [The plot was purchased by James Cowan of Carrickfergus in June 1813.]

DAVIS

[Laid flat.] Beneath this stone lie the remains of Robert Davis Esqr. of uniform excellent integrity, alike in public and in private life, liberal as a companion, faithful as a friend, he added to the manners which conciliate attachment, the principles which merit respect and he obtained the esteem and confidence of those who best knew and were best able to estimate the virtues by which his character was distinguished and adorned. He died at the age of 54 on the 27th January 1817.

DAVIS

[Flaking and now removed.] Erected in memory of James Davis, late of Belfast, merchant, who departed this life 30th May 1836, aged 50 years.

DAVIS

[Now lost.] Erected by Margaret Davis in memory of her beloved husband James Davis who died 7th Jan. 1883 aged 50 years. Also his mother Elizabeth Davis died 26th May 1861 aged 60 years. Also his sister Jane SPRATT died 8th Nov. 1862 aged 32 years. Also the above named Margaret Davis who fell asleep in Jesus, 17th February 1915.

They are now sweetly sleeping,
Their spirits rest with thee,
And though their friends are weeping,
Their song is victory.

DAVIS

See MOORE and WARD

DAVISON
[Masonic symbols with letter G at the top.] Erected by John Davison in memory of his father James Davison, builder, Belfast, who died the 16th of July 1832 aged 73 years. Also of his mother Esther Davison who died the 10th of May 1832 aged 66 years. Also of his sister Mary HYLTON who died the 1st of September 1850 aged 42 years. Also of her husband Captain Charles Hylton who died at sea 1st of May 1840 aged 36 years. Also 2 of their children Charles and Richard who died young.

DAVISON
[Twin marble tablets (now lost) in pedimented entablature secured to south wall.] Here lieth the remains of Stewart TORBETT who departed this life on the 14th October 1842 aged 39 years. Also of his wife Anne, daughter of the Revd John Davison, who died 16th April 1890.

Sacred to the memory of John, only son of the Rev. John Davison, who died at Liverpool on the 21st June 1844 aged 32 years. Here also lie the remains of his father, the Rev. John Davison, Presbyterian Minister of Cookstown, in the County of Tyrone for 50 years, who died at Belfast on the 22nd of Novr 1847, aged 78 years. "Blessed are the dead who die in the Lord". And Elizabeth Davison his wife who died on the 14th October 1867 aged 90 years.

[The will (with three codicils) of Elizabeth Davison, late of 31 Lower Gloucester Street, Dublin, widow, who died 14 October 1867 at same place was proved at the Principal Registry 30 October 1867 by the oaths of James Lemon of Belfast and Samuel Little of Liverpool, merchants, the executors. Effects under £8,000.

The Rev. John Davi(d)son was born near Cullybackey in 1769 and educated at King's College, Aberdeen, where he graduated M.A. in 1793. He was licensed by the Ballymena Presbytery in 1794 and ordained at First Cookstown Presbyterian Church where he remained until his retirement in 1835. He married, firstly, Elizabeth Ekenhead (vid. inf.), daughter of John Ekenhead of Lisburn and Belfast, and secondly Mrs Elizabeth Gordon. See McConnell: *Fasti of the Irish Presbyterian Church* (1951).]

DAVISON
See EKENHEAD

DAWSON
[Laid flat, broken and flaking near bottom.] Died on the 29th of March 1811, William Dawson junr. in his 21st year. On the 15th of January 1834, William Dawson Senr, in his 76th year. Also his wife Martha Dawson who departed this life 30th May 1835 aged 82 years. And his brother Samuel who died 15th March 1837 aged 75 years. Margaret, daughter of the above named William Dawson, 11th March 1863, Isabella Ellen daughter of the above named William Dawson, died 31st Jany 1871.

[The will (with 3 codicils) of Margaret Dawson, spinster, late of Hillbrook Hollywood in the county of Down, died 11 March 1863, were proved at Belfast 1st May 1863 and granted to Isabella Dawson, spinster, sister of above. Effects under £800.

Letters of administration of the personal estate of Isabella Eleanor Dawson, late of Strandtown, county Down, spinster, who died 31 January 1871 at same place, were granted at Belfast 13 March 1871 to Martha Baxter, wife of Richard Baxter of Strandtown (Belfast) aforesaid, merchant, the sister and one of the next of kin of said deceased. Effects under £3,000.]

DEMPSTER
See CAMPBELL

DEMPSY
[No longer extant.] Erected by Margaret McDONAGH to the memory of her uncle Matthew Dempsy, a native of Dublin and late of Belfast who departed this life 30th May 1822 aged 81 years.

[Matthew Dempsy was a pawnbroker in Pottinger's Entry.]

DENBIGH
See HALLIDAY

DENHAM
See HANNA

DENNISON
[Flaking stone, now removed.] Erected 1850, by Robert Dennison, Belfast, to the memory of his daughter, Margar(et) who departed this li(fe 19th April) 1850 aged 9 (years). And three children who (died in) infancy. Anna Mitchell, wife of (R.F.) Dennison died (26) August 1888. Martha, wife of above named Robert Dennison, died 25th April 1889. The above named Robert Dennison died 26th June 1889. The above Robert Ferris Dennison died 30th July 1905 aged 69 years.

[The will of Robert Dennison late of Hollywood county Down, gentleman, who died 26 June 1889 at Bangor, said county, was proved at Belfast 14 April 1890 by Robert Ferris Dennison of Bangor, bank manager, the sole executor. Effects under £50.]

DICK
[Large headstone, now lost, copied from Society's Inscription Book.] Sacred to the memory of Robert Henry, son of Dr Dick, 12th Regt., and of his wife .... born at Mauritius, 27th Jany 1847, died at Belfast, Septr 5th 1853.

DICK
See GRAHAM

DICKEY
[Badly smashed marble shield, formerly secured to south wall and now lost. Crest on top of stone backing.] In mem(ory of) James Dickey, late of Belfast, formerly of Hollybrook, County Antrim, who died on 20th (Mar. 1847) aged (5)7 years. "Exemplary in all the (relations of life) he was universally (respected) ...... and beloved by his (family)".

[James Dickey was the Post-Master, the Post Office then being situated at 65 Donegall Street.]

DICKEY

[Marble tablet with carved surround secured to east wall in high-railed enclosure. Arms: Two martlets, band, and unicorn's head, in chief. Crest: Knight's helmet surmounted by a sailing ship. Shield on draped mantle.] Erected by his children to the memory of Adam Dickey, Esq., late of Belfast, formerly of Hollybrook, County Antrim, who departed this life on the twenty sixth day of November Anno Domini MDCCCLXIV, aged seventy years. "He walked with God and God took him" (Gen. V,24). The remains were afterwards removed to the Borough Cemetery.

[Letters of administration of the personal estate of Adam Dickey, late of Donegall Street, Belfast, in the county of Antrim, gentleman, who died 26 November 1864 at Belfast, were granted at Belfast 30 June 1865 to Eleanor Dickey of Donegal Street, the widow. Effects under £100.]

DICKEY

[Undated marble in surround beside Samuel Cumming's, now lost.] The family burying place of Robert J. Dickey and John WYLIE.

[Robert John Dickey, late of Belfast, county Antrim, who died intestate 1818. Administration of his effects granted to Martha Dickey, widow, on the 6th June 1819. Effects £3,296 12s.6d.

The plot was purchased by Robert J. Dickey in May 1816.]

DICKEY

See MACAULEY

DICKSON

[Broken fragments.] Erected by Simon Dickson in memory of Jane Dickson who died 19th April 1817 AE 72. Also here lieth the body of Simon Dickson who departed this life 2nd May 1825 aged 56 years. Also in the adjoining grave lieth four of his children, viz: John, Jane, William and Violet.

DICKSON

[Headstone flaking near bottom.] Sacred to the memory of Alexander Dickson, of Belfast, who departed this life 25th May 1837 aged 74 years. Also his wife Mary Dickson, who departed this life 30th August 1826 aged 72 years. Also his daughter Elizabeth WALKER, who departed this life 1st March 1823 aged 33 years. And his son Alexander who died young. Also Sarah and Catherine Dickson, who died July 1890.

[Letters of administration of the personal estate of Sarah Dickson, late of 20 Ward Street, Belfast, spinster, who died 26 July 1891 at same place, were granted at Belfast 7 December 1891 to William Shaw of Chambers Street, warehouse manager, the attorney of the brother. Effects £23 10s.

Letters of administration (with the will annexed) of the personal estate of Catherine Dickson of 20 Ward Street, Belfast, spinster, who died 26 July 1891 at same place were granted at Belfast 7 December 1891 to William Shaw of Chambers Street, warehouse manager, the attorney of the universal legatee. Effects £23 10s.

Alexander Dickson was a chandler in Mustard Street.]

Memorial to Adam Dickey with its fine armorial bearings.

DICKSON

[Headstone in Paupers' Ground, with cross at top and flaking.] William Steel Dickson, patriot, preacher, historian, born at Carnmoney, 1744, died at Belfast, 27th Dec. 1824. "Do cum onora na h-Ereann".

[The Rev. William Steel Dickson was trained at Glasgow University and it was while he was minister of Portaferry Presbyterian Church that he joined the Irish Volunteer movement. He represented the Ards area at the Dungannon Convention of 1782. A United Irishman from his very early days, Dickson was soon Adjutant-General for County Down. He was arrested and imprisoned on the eve of the Battle of Ballynahinch in 1798 on suspicion, and after spending a year on a prison hulk in Belfast Lough and three years in Fort George, Scotland, he was released. By now penniless, he became Minister of Keady Congregation for a short time. He died a pauper on the outskirts of Belfast, his funeral attended by only eight people. His headstone was erected in the early years of this century by F.J. Bigger and the epitaph means "For the honour of Ireland".] See Latimer: *Ulster Biographies, Relating Chiefly to the Rebellion of 1798* (1897)]

DICKSON

See GAMBLE

DIGBY

[Very badly flaking and ivy-covered, now lost.] (To the memory of Cecilia wife of) John Digby who (departed this) life the (9th) of Jan. 1814 (aged) 60 years. (Also) John Digby, (husband to Cecilia who departed this life 30th Decr 1825, aged 83 years. Also their daughter Barbara who died 9th March 1836. Also Maria Susanna who died 7th March 1844). Also Margaret (who died) 16th January (1854). Also Alicia BUTLER who departed this life 16th Nov. 1868.

[The will (with four codicils) of Alicia Butler Digby, of Whitehouse, county Antrim, spinster, who died 16 November 1868, was proved at Belfast 4 December 1868 by the oath of William Johns, solicitor of one of the executors. Effects under £1,500.]

DIXON

See AGNEW and KENNEDY

DOBBIN

[With a laurel wreath on the capstone and in high-railed enclosure.] The burial place of Samuel Dobbin whose daughter Sarah died 5th January 1824 aged 17 months. His sister-in-law Elizabeth Dobbin who died 23rd September 1843 aged 73 years. His son John who died 17th March 1845 aged 26 years. Samuel Dobbin died 13th April 1867 aged 83 years. Margaret Dobbin his wife died 2nd December 1879 aged 95 years. Samuel Dobbin, youngest son of the above mentioned died 23rd April 1909 aged 84 years.

[John Dobbin was a partner in the firm of W. & J. Dobbin, druggists, oil and colour merchants at 20 North Street.]

DOBBIN
[Worn in the middle, now lost.] Alithea Maria, daughter of Leonard Dobbin, Botanic View, Belfast, died 4th January 1850 aged 11 months. Marion WETHERED, widow of the late Dr Wethered, of Lisburn, died 9th February 1864 aged 87 years.

DOE
[Very badly weathered sandstone.] Erected to the (memory of) Jane Doe of Belfast, who died (22nd Aug)ust 18(46) aged (66) years. Also (her sister) Frances YOUNG, who departed this life July (6th) 18(47) aged (5)8 years.

D'OISY
[Very badly flaked stone, now lost.] Sacred to the memory of Elizabeth (D'O)isy (who) departed (this life 23rd June) 1826 aged (6.) years.

[Her husband was Adelbert D'Oisy, Master of the French Department in the Royal Belfast Academical Institution from 1818 to 1837.]

DOLAN
See CHAPMAN

DONALDSON
[Formerly in lower ground, but now missing.] The burying place of William Donaldson, Belfast, 1859.

DONNAN
[Badly worn and now lost.] Erected by Eliza Donnan, to the memory of her husband Capt. John Donnan who departed this life 22nd April 1833 aged (37) years. (Also their son) James Donnan who departed this life (9th Sept. 1834 aged 1 years.) Also the above Eliza Donnan who departed this life 20th (August 1851) aged 49 years. By Eliza Donnan in memory of her beloved husband Captain David Donnan who departed this life on August 30th 1867 aged 40 years.

[The will (with one codicil) of David Donnan of Canning Street, Belfast, master-mariner, who died 30 August 1867 at the Queens Hotel, York Street, Belfast, was proved 23 September 1867 by the oaths of Eliza Donnan of Canning Street, widow, and the Rev. Charles Quin of Donegal Street, R.C. clergyman. Effects under £5,000.]

DONNELLY
See MAGEE

DOUGHERTY
[Very worn horizontal slab, no longer identifiable.] Sacred to the memory of Thomas Dougherty of Malone, who departed this life August 28th 181(2) aged (52) years.

DOUGHERTY
I.H.S. Erected by Hugh Dougherty to the memory of his brother John Dougherty who departed this life March 17th 1845 aged 23 years. Also his sister Elizabeth Dougherty aged 2 years. Also Mary Anne aged 1 year and 6 months. Also Patrick John aged 11 months. Also his nephew Hugh COBURN aged 9 months. Also his father Patrick Dougherty died 4th

Headstone of the Rev. William Steel Dickson, United Irishman.

August 1854 aged 76 years. Also his mother Margaret Dougherty died 27th February 1871 aged 94 years. "I know that my Redeemer liveth" Also Elizabeth Dougherty died 3rd November 1886 aged 74 years.

DOUGLAS

[Now lost and copied from Inscription book.] The burying place of ...... Douglas. Sacred to the memory of his mother Jane Douglas who died 13th Nov. 1849 aged 59 years. Also his son Alexander who died 20th Decr. 1859 aged 7 years.

DOUGLAS

[Worn limestone now lost.] In memoriam ..... Sacred to the memory of Mary, the beloved wife of John Douglas, of Belfast. She died suddenly at Holywood on the 14th of March 1858 aged thirty-one years. Here also beside their mother sleep the following children: Samuel Douglas, born 6th September 18.., and died 13th March 18.., Jane Orr Douglas, born 6th October 1850, and died 3rd March 1853, Helen Montgomery Douglas, born 4th February 1852, and died 8th May 1853, Emily Douglas, born 23rd September 1856, and died 26th November 1859. "Blessed are the dead which die in the Lord, from henceforth. Yea, saith the Spirit, that they may rest from their labours, and their works to follow them".

DOUGLASS

[Formerly in upper ground but now missing.] The burial place of William Douglass, and William GAMBLE, Belfast, 1847.

DOWLING

[Flaking and now lost.] Erected 1854, by James Dowling, in memory of his mother Mary Dowling, who died 5th Novr 1824 aged 46 years. Also of his father the Revd Blakely Dowling, Wesleyan Minister, who died Feby 1830 aged 65 years. And of his beloved wife Mary who died 19th Decr 1852 aged 45 years. Likewise in remembrance of his three sons: Blakely, James and Jonathan, who died in infancy, and were interred in Liverpool.

DRENNAN

[Small and worn tablet with surround topped by draped urn and secured to west wall in enclosure with Lennox and Mattear stones.] William Drennan, M.D. born May 23 1754, died Feby 5th 1820.
   Pure, just, benign: thus filial love would trace,
   The virtues hallowing this narrow space,
   The Emerald Isle may grant a wider claim,
   And link the Patriot with his Country's name.
[Dr William Drennan was born at the manse of the First Presbyterian Church in Rosemary Street where his father, the Rev. Thomas Drennan was minister. He received his medical training at Glasgow and Edinburgh where he developed the political philosophy that was to distinguish him later. Returning to this country in 1778, he set up practice, first in Belfast, then in Newry and Dublin. In the early 1780s he was advocating innoculation as a method of preventing smallpox, and in 1793 clearly sta-

ted the necessity of washing one's hands to prevent the spread of disease - in both instances he was well ahead of his time. Although a member of the Belfast Charitable Society, he never became its Physician.

He is, however, best remembered for his liberal political views and, like many young academics of the time, was fired by the ideals of the American Revolution and later the French Revolution. A well-known figure in both literary and political circles in Dublin, he was one of the founders of the Society of United Irishmen in 1791, wrote its original prospectus and was its first Chairman. After his trial and acquittal on a charge of libel in 1794, he withdrew from the more active political activities of the day, and was not directly involed in the 1798 Rebellion. His patriotism continued in the form of his writings and in one of his poems, published in 1795, he was the first person to call Ireland the "Emerald Isle".

In 1800 he married Sarah Swanwick and thereafter devoted himself to literature and medicine and was for a time President of the Belfast Medical Society. One of his greatest achievements during the latter part of his life was the prominent part he took in the founding of the Royal Belfast Academical Institution which was opened in 1814. A large collection of letters which passed between him and his sister Martha, Mrs Samuel McTier, and their mother in the 1790s and 1800s, and known as the Drennan Letters, has survived and forms an invaluable primary source of information concerning society, politics and life at that time.

They had 4 sons and 1 daughter:

1. Thomas Hamilton Drennan, born 24 March 1801, died 1811.
2. William Drennan, born 1802, entered T.C.D 1819, B.A. 1824, Irish Bar 1826.
3. Sarah Drennan, born 10 April 1807, married John Andrews of Comber, died 13 February 1902, buried Comber Churchyard.
4. John Swanwick Drennan (vid. inf.), entered T.C.D 1826, B.A. 1831; M.B. 1838; M.D. 1854.
5. Lennox Drennan.

See Fisher and Robb: *Royal Belfast Academical Institution, Centenary Volume* (1913); Chart: *The Drennan Letters* (1931); Strain: *Belfast and its Charitable Society* (1961); McNeill: *Little Tom Drennan* (1962); Clarke: *Gravestone Inscriptions, County Down*, Vol 5, 2nd ed. 1984; Collection of Drennan Letters, P.R.O.N.I. T765B.]

DRENNAN

[Cross in enclosure with above.] In loving memory of John Swanwick Drennan, M.D. physician, student, poet, born 3rd Oct 1809, died 1st Nov. 1893. "Felix qui potuit verum cognoscere causas atque metus omnes et inexorabile fatum subjecit pedibus". Emma his wife, daughter of the Rev. William HINCKS, born 1826, died 26th December 1859. "Desideratissim" And their daughter Emma Drennan, born 6th Oct. 1857, died 7th April 1863. "He shall gather the lambs with his arm".

DRENNAN

See LENNOX and MATTEAR

Portrait of Dr William Drennan, United Irishman.

DRUMMOND
See MARSHALL

DUCKE
See McCLEAN

DUDGEON
See FITZGIBBON

DUFF
[White limestone, now lost.] To the memory of William Duff who died May 1847 aged 30 years.

DUFFIELD
[Headstone now lying flat within low-railed enclosure and with next stone.] Erected to the memory of Samuel Duffield, of Belfast, who departed this life the 16th of Decr. 1821 aged (5)2 years. Also 5 of his children: viz, Hugh, died 31st May 1814 aged 19 years, Jane 1st May 1820 aged 15 years, David, Wm John, and Hugh died when infants. Also Margt. BIGGAR aged 88 years. Also his wife Jane Duffield who departed this life on the 11th day of August 1832 aged 60 years.

DUFFIELD
[Polished granite headstone in enclosure with above.] Erected to the memory of Samuel Duffield, Summer Hill, Dunmurry, who died 20th Dec. 1877 aged 75 years. Also his son Samuel who died 20th May 1872 aged 32 years. Also his sister Margaret who died 1st Feb. 1878 aged 78 years. Also his wife Anne Duffield who died 18th Nov. 1891 aged 77 years. Duffield, 1879.

[The will (with one codicil) of Samuel Duffield of Kilaston, county Antrim, farmer, who died 20 December 1877 was proved at Belfast 23 January 1878 by the oaths of Ann Duffield of Killeaton (Dunmurry), widow, Samuel Gibson of Mill Street, Belfast, merchant, William Hunter of Townsend Street, Belfast, pawnbroker, and Robert Hugh Ireland of the Falls, Belfast, farmer, all in said county, the executors. Effects under £10,000.

Samuel Duffield, senr, was a farmer, of Dunmurry, Co. Antrim.]

DUFFIELD
[Worn marblet tablet in carved entablature secured to east wall of upper graveyard in low-stone enclosure.] Sacred to the memory of William John Duffield who died 23rd December 1852 aged 43 years. William Duffield, his son, who died 7th June 1839 aged 2 months. Also his wife, Anna MONTGOMERY who died 14th August 1873, aged 66 years. Also their son Alexander William who died at Limerick 23rd March 1876 aged 3(1) years, and is interred here. "Them also which sleep in Jesus, will God bring with him".

[Letters of administration of the personal estate of Anne Montgomery Duffield, late of York Street, Belfast, widow, who died 14 August 1873 at Greenisland, were granted at Belfast 23 January 1874 to Alexander W. Duffield of 115 George Street, Limerick, provision merchant, the son of said deceased. Effects under £300.

William John Duffield was the proprietor of W.J. & A. Duffield, provision merchants in James Street, now Corporation Street.]

DUGAN

[Damaged and laid flat.] Erected by Eliza Dugan, of Belfast, in memory of her beloved husband James Dugan, who departed this life on the 11th of June 1842 aged 37 years. Also her (two) children who died young. "Blessed are the dead who die in the Lord". Here lieth also the remains of her brother Charles POLLOCK, of Belfast, who died 1st December 184(9) aged 31 years. Also his son William who died young.

DUGAN

See CAMERON

DUMMETT

See EKENHEAD

DUNCAN

[Worn and broken.] Erected by Nathaniel Duncan, of Belfast, in memory of his children, viz: his son Thomas who died 23rd March 1845 aged 17 months, also his daughter Jane who died 19th May 1845 aged 9 years, also Nathaniel died 5th July 184(5) aged 4 years and 5 months. Also his son James who died in infancy. Also the above named Nathaniel Duncan who departed this life (.)0th July 186(4) aged 52 years. Also Mary who died Septr 24th, 1870 aged 33 years.

[The will (with three codicils) of Nathaniel Duncan of Belfast, county Antrim, shopkeeper, who died 18 July 1864 at above place was proved at Belfast 19 September 1864 by the oath of Nathaniel Duncan, Barnish (Doagh) in the county of Antrim, farmer, one of the executors. Effects under £800.]

DUNLAP

[Now lost.] In memory of Jane Dunlap, widow of the late Hugh Dunlap, who died the 7th day of January 1815 aged 52 years. William Annesley BLAIR, eldest son of James Blair of .... who died the 27th day of August 1810 aged four years. Ebenezer Blair who died the 5th day of December 1811 aged twenty-three years. James Blair of .... who died the 7th day of February 1818, aged seventy-three years. Mary Hodgen Blair, youngest daughter of the said James Blair, who died the 31st day of October 1818 aged .. years. Sarah Blair, widow of the said James Blair, who died the 15th day of March 1866 aged eighty-four years.

[The will of Sarah Blair, late of Clearstream Cottage in county of Antrim, widow, who died 15 March 1866, was proved at Belfast 27 July 1866 by the oath of James Kennedy Blair of Liverpool in the county of Lancaster, England, judge of the Liverpool County Court the sole executor. Effects under £200. Re-sworn at Liverpool April 1868 under £600.]

DUNLAP

[Laid flat.] Sacred to the memory of Jane Dunlap, who departed this life on the 7th of February 1815 aged 52 years.

DUNLAP
[Broken in two and lying flat.] Erected by (Robert) Dunlap in memory of his son Alexr Dunlap who departed this life Decr 20th 1824 aged 15 years. Also his daughter Mary who departed this life Jany 4th 182(5) aged 13 years. And his wife Margart Ellen who departed this life Jany 6th 1825 aged 39 years. Also the above named Robert Dunlap departed this life Decr 20th 1829 aged 43 years. And his son-in-law Adam GILESPIE who departed this life June 18th 1847 aged 32 years. Also his grand-daughter Mary McDONALD departed this life Decr 26th 1847 aged 10 years.

DUNLOP
[In entablature, with and identical to those of Charles Kelso's mother and John Gray, formerly attached to dividing wall and now lost.] Erected by James Dunlop, of Belturbet, in memory of his daughter Helen who died on the 4th July 1828. Also to the memory of Helen BARBOUR his sister-in-law who died the 30th November 1820.

DUNLOP
[Iron plaque in low-railed enclosure.] Family burying place of Wm Dunlop, Belfast, 1850.

DUNLOP
[Small memorial formerly in lower ground and now missing.] The family burying place of James Dunlop, Carrick Hill, 1856.

DUNN
[Badly flaking and now lost.] In memory of (James) Dunn who (departed this life) the 27th June 1804 a(ged 92 years). Also his gr(andson) David Dunn who dep(arted this life) 7th October 1810 aged (6) years.

DUNN
Erected by John Dunn in memory of his son Samuel who departed this life 23rd January 1835 aged 9 years & 5 months. The above named John Dunn died 30th March 1837 aged 59 years. Also his son Thomas died 4th June 1837 aged 17 years. Martha Dunn, relict of the above named John Dunn, died 22nd March 1842 aged 59 years. And John Dunn junr, their son, and the only remaining one of the family, died 21st November 1842 aged 19 years. Also Mary CULTON who departed this life on the 29th of July 1843 aged 52 years.

DUNNE
See BENN

DUNVILLE
[Large neo-Gothic vault with wrought-iron gate, against east wall of upper graveyard.] [Inscription on outside.] Burials place of John Dunville and his family.

[Inscription around circular medallion bearing male bust in east end of vault.] William Dunville, born 25 Dec. 1812, died 18 May 1874.

[Beneath medallion.] This medallion was placed here in affectionate remembrance by his attached wife Anne Georgina.

[Twin tablets beneath above.]
"Some to its place on high".
Calm on the bosom of thy God,
Fair Spirit, rest thee now,
E'en while with ours thy footsteps trod,
His Seal was on thy brow.

Dust, to its narrow house beneath,
Soul, to its place on high,
They that have seen thy look in death,
No more may fear to die.

O sweeter than the fragrant flow
At ev'nings dewy close,
The wil united with the pow'r,
To succour human woes.

And softer than the softest strains
Of music to the ear,
The placid joy we give and gain,
By gratitude sincere.

Tis he who scatters blessings round,
Adores his Maker best,
His walk through life is mercy crowned,
His bed of death is blest.

[There is an obliterated inscription on the south wall.]

[Inscription on circular medallion bearing female bust (now lost) on south wall.] Sara Dunville, obit 24 June 1863.

[Twin marble tablets, (now lost), on either side of Sara Dunville's bust.]
Death was full urgent with thee, sister dear,
And startling in his speed,
Brief pain then langour till thine end come near,
Such was the path decreed;

The hurried road,
To lead they Soul from earth to thine own God's abode
Joy of sad hearts, and light of downcast eyes,
Dearest, thou art enshrined,

In all thy fragrance in our memories,
For we must ever find
Bare thought of thee
Freshen this weary life, while weary life shall be.

[Inscription around oval medallion bearing female bust, on north wall.] Anne Georgina Dunville, born 26 Oct. 1827, died 8 Jan. 1886.

[The following inscription was on the floor of the vault, but has disappeared since 1907.] Erected by John Dunville of Belast, 1832. To the memory of Agnes Dunville his mother who died 25th Decr. 1824, in the 68th year of her age. Also Margaret his daughter who departed this life the 8th of January 1832 aged 12 years. Also John his son who died the

15th day of April 1841 aged 26 years. And here rest the mortal remains of John Dunville who, after a long life of active usefullness, died the 21st of March 1851 aged 65 years. Also of Sarah his surviving daughter who died on the 24th June 1863 aged 45. And of his wife Anne Dunville who died on the 25th January 1865 aged 76. Also of Mary, wife of above John Dunville, jun., who died 15th March 1855 aged 39.

[Anne Georgina Dunville, late of 54 Prince's Gate, in the county of Middlesex, widow, died 8 January 1886. Probate granted at London 22 February 1886. Re-sealed at the Principal Registry, Dublin 3 April 1886. Effects in Ireland £18,433 16s.4d.

For much of the 19th century and well into the 20th, the firm of Dunville & Co. Ltd. was the leading whiskey distillery in Belfast.

John Dunville senior, a son of William Dunville of Whitehead, began his career by being apprenticed to William Napier, whose distillery was in Bank Lane, now Bank Street. In 1808 they became partners and in 1825 the firm became John Dunville & Co., trading from Calendar Street where they remained for many years. They were also one of the leading tea merchants in Ireland, but gave up that side of the business in the early 1860s, as the space was required for the whisky, the trade in the latter commodity proving to be extremely prosperous.

When William Dunville built the bonded warehouse in Franklin Street in 1867, it was widely acclaimed the finest in the United Kingdom and by this time the family was living at Richmond Lodge near Holywood. Soon afterwards they built Redburn House. From the late 19th century onwards, the family buried in the Old Priory Churchyard in Holywood. See *Burke's Landed Gentry of Ireland*, 1912 ed.; Roddie: *An Excellent Medical School*, Inaugural Lecture, Q.U.B., 1965; Clarke: *Gravestone Inscriptions, County Down*, Vol. 4 (1969).]

DU PARCO

Erected to the memory of Elizabeth Du Parco, relict of John Du Parco, Esq., of the Island of Jersey, who departed this life Feb. 27 1853 aged 70 years. Also to the memory of Adolphus William Du Parco who died 15 December 1839 aged 24 years. They rest here until the day break and the shadows flee away. "Thy dead men shall live, together with my dead body shall they arise. Awake and sing, ye that dwell in dust: for thy dew is as the dew of herbs and the earth shall cast out her dead". Isaiah 26c., 19 v. "When Christ who is our life shall appear then shall ye also appear with Him in Glory". Col. 3. This testimonial is placed here by Elizabeth Du Parco.

DYER

[Now lost.] Erected by John THOMPSON, in memory of his grandchild Susanna Dyer who departed this life the 1st May, 1835 aged 3 years. The above named John Thompson departed this life 1st Decr 1846 aged 76 years. Agnes Thompson his wife departed this life 3rd Augt 1847 aged 70 years. Isabella Dyer departed this life 11th January 1852 aged 11 years. Hugh Dyer departed this life 1st December 1860 aged 58 years. Susanna Thompson departed this life 22nd November 1862 aged

Medallion of Sarah Dunville, before re-erection.

61 years. John Dyer departed this life 10th October 1868 aged 35 years. Isabella Dyer, widow of the above named Hugh Dyer, departed this life 4th November 1884 aged 86 years. Mary Ann Dyer died 9th April 1923 aged 81 years.

[The will of Hugh Dyer, late of Belfast in the county of Antrim, grocer, who died 1 December 1860 at same place, was proved at Belfast 9 January 1861 by the oaths of Robert Potts, merchant, and Isabella Dyer, widow, both of said place, the executors. Effects under £2,000.

Letters of administration of the personal estate of John Dyer, late of North Queen Street, Belfast, county Antrim, grocer, a bachelor, who died 11 October 1868, was granted 30 October 1868 to Isabella Dyer of North Queen Street, Belfast aforesaid, widow, the mother and one of the next of kin. Effects under £1,000.

The will of Isabella Dyer of Belfast, widow, who died 4 November 1884, was proved at Belfast 26 January 1885 by Jane Rice (wife of Edward Rice) and Mary Anne Dyer, spinster, both of Lucyville, Whitehouse, county Antrim, the executrixes. Effects £200.]

D.Y.
See MUNFOAD.

EAGLE
In memory of the children of Luke Eagle and Eliza his wife, late of Manchester. Bagnall Eagle died Aug. 4th 1850 aged 3 years and 7 months, James Luke Eagle died June 6th 1862 aged 19 years. Also William Henry their last surviving child died Aug 2nd 1864, aged 19 years, and was interred at Lymm Church, Cheshire. Eliza Eagle died April 11th 1880 aged 76 years.

[Luke Eagle ran a Racket and Billiard Court in Chichester Street.]

EAGLESON
[Marble obelisk bearing crest of an eagle with obliterated motto beneath, a monogram "H.M.A.E.", and surmounted by a mayoral robe. Inscription on three sides of the base.] Erected by her daughters to the sacred memory of their dearly beloved mother Anna Maria Eagleson who died at Glynn Park, Carrickfergus, 15th June 1875, wife of the late Richard Eagleson Esqr, Belfast.

[South side.] And of Margaret Eagleson who died at Cannes, France, 18th November 1864, whose remains are here interred.

[North side.] Also of Anna Maria MOORE, wife of David Nevin Moore M.D., who died at Ballymoney, 16th October 1873.

[On plinth.] "Therefore, being justified by faith, we have peace with God through Our Lord Jesus Christ".

[Iron plaque on railing.] Erected by James McCONNELL, of Belfast.

[The will of Anna Maria Eagleson of late of Glynn Park, Carrickfergus, widow, who died 15 June 1875 at same place, was proved at Belfast 4 February 1876 by the oath of Robert MacMurray of Glynn Park, merchant, the sole executor. Effects in U.K. under £2,000.

Letters of Administration of the personal estate of Anna Maria Moore, of Charlotte Street, Ballymoney, county Antrim, who died 16 October 1873 were granted at Belfast 6 March 1874 to Anna Maria Eagleson of Glynn Park, Carrickfergus, widow, the nominee of David Nevin Moore, the husband of said deceased for his use and benefit. Effects under £100.

James McConnell bought the ground in February 1815.]

ECCLES

[Flaking and now lost.] This (burying) ground belongeth to Jane Eccles, of Belfast, Here lieth the body of Jane Eccles, daughter of William Eccles of Belfast, who departed this life April the 19th 1803 aged 9 years.

ECCLES

[Twin tablets in entablature secured to north wall in enclosure, formerly high-railed.] Erected by Mary Eccles in memory of her beloved husband William Eccles who died on the 6th of March 183(5) aged 64 years. Here lieth the remains of the above named Mary Eccles who departed this life 14th September 1855 in the 83rd year of her age. Also in memory of William Marcus HANSON who departed this life on 22nd April 1895 aged 67 years. And his wife Rosa M. Eccles who departed this life on 6th June 1874. And also their daughter Florence Kathleen who died in infancy. "Prepare to meet they God". [Continued on small slate below.] William Hughes Hanson died 18th January 1920 aged 55 years. And his wife Mary Hanson died 24th March 1925 aged 65 years.

Erected by Mary DAVIDSON to the memory of her beloved husband Samuel Davidson who died on the 17th Oct. 1835 aged 35 years. Also his daughter Mary C. Davidson who died on the 24th Octr 1834 aged 4 years. "Blessed are the dead that sleep in Jesus".

[Letters of administration of the personal estate of Rosa Hanson of Balmoral Terrace, Belfast, who died 6 June 1874 were granted at Belfast 28 June 1874 to William Marcus Hanson, a draper, the husband. Effects under £300.

Letters of administration of William Hugh Hanson granted at Belfast on 18 February 1920.

Mary Hanson of 18 Holland Park Knock, Belfast, widow, died 24 March 1925 at Somerset Nursing Home, University Street. Administration granted 19 June 1925 to William Marcus Hanson, linen merchant. Effects £1,160.

William Marcus Hanson, originally from Coleraine was a merchant tailor and outfitter in High Street, and lived at 68, Wellington Park.]

ECHLIN

[Missing.] The burying place of Peter Echlin, Belfast, 1854.

[The will (with one codicil) of Peter Echlin, late of the Commercial Hotel, Waring Street, Belfast, county Antrim, hotel-keeper who died 17 July 1863 at Belfast, was proved at Belfast 26 August 1863 by the oaths of William Saunderson of Newtownards, county Down, hotel-keeper and James Lipsey of Anne Street, wine merchant, the executors. Effects under £4,000.

He was the proprietor of the Commercial Hotel in the Commercial Buildings, Waring Street.]

EDGAR
[Polished granite in low-railed enclosure.] In memory of Samuel Edgar, of Arthur Square, who died 3rd January 1864 aged 53 years. "But go thou thy way till the end be; for thou shalt rest and stand in thy lot at the end of the days". Dan. XII.13. Also of his three sons, John who died 22nd March 1839 aged 13 months, Samuel, who died 6th November 1851 aged 11 months, and David who died 17th September 1857, in his twenty-second year. "He being dead, yet speaketh". Heb.XI.4. Also of Agnes his wife who died 10th January 1891, aged 87 years. "After she had served her own generation, by the Will of God she fell on sleep". Also their daughter Agnes Edgar died 9th August 1937 aged 93 years.

[The will of Samuel Edgar of Belfast in the county of Antrim, draper and haberdasher who died 3 January 1864 at Farnham House in the city of Dublin, was proved at Belfast 22 February 1864 by the oaths of Agnes Edgar of Antrim Road, widow, William Edgar of Arthur Square, woollen draper and Robert M'Cheyne Edgar of Antrim Road, theological student, all in Belfast, the executors. Effects under £9,000.

The will of Agnes Edgar of 2 Lincoln Avenue, Antrim Road, Belfast, widow, who died 10 January 1891, was proved at the Principal Registry 2 February 1891 by the Reverend Robert McCheyne Edgar of 16 Northbrook Road, in the county of Dublin, Presbyterian clergyman, and Agnes Edgar of 2 Lincoln Avenue, spinster, the executors. Effects £3,389 16s.7d.

Edgar, Agnes, of 2 Lincoln Avenue, Belfast, spinster, died 9 August 1937. Probate granted Belfast 1 November 1937 to Herbert Morrison, factory manager, and Robert Maxwell, estate agent. Effects £1,691 16s.2d.

Samuel Edgar & Son were woollen-drapers in Arthur Square.]

EDGAR
[Polished granite secured to north wall.] In affectionate remembrance of Isaac Edgar died 25th Feby 1842 aged 30 years. Margaret Carmichael his wife died 17th September 1898 aged 87 years. James Gibson, 2nd son died 21st June 1865 aged 27 years. Richard, 3rd son died 26th May 1870 aged 30 years. Walter Moffat, 4th son died 11th March, 1880 aged 38 years. Also John Edgar, grandson, M.R.C.S., L.R.C.P., of Manchester, died 8th June 1897 aged 27 years. And Elizabeth Carmichael, daughter died 29th October 1907 aged 73 years.

[The will of James Gibson Edgar, late of Lonsdale Street, Belfast, county Antrim, bank clerk, who died 21 June 1865 at Belfast, was proved at Belfast 15 December 1865 by the oaths of Robert Steen of the Royal Academical Institution Belfast, Ph.D. and David Carmichael of Millisle (Donaghadee), county Down, mill owner, the executors. Effects in Great Britain and Ireland under £600.]

EDGAR
[Very corroded iron shield in low railing no longer identifiable.] The burying ground of Alexr Edgar, 188(5).

EDMONDSON
[Very worn marble in headstone, with capstone and draped urn, now

removed.] Erected by the Presbyterian Church, Townsend St., Belfast, to the memory of Thomas Edmondson (who upwards of sixteen) years (proved himself amongst them a kind friend, a consistent Christian and an efficient Elder. He died on the 20th Sept.) 1854 aged (62 years). Frances (his wife died 21st October 1860) aged 5(0). Also their daughter (Minnie who departed this life 12th July 1865 aged 17 years.)

[He was also headmaster of the Brown Street Lancasterian School, and originally came from Stranorlar, county Donegal.]

EID

Erected by Sarah Eid, to the memory of her husband Lorenzo Eid, a native of Norway, who departed this life in the faith of the Gospel on the 23rd Decr. 1835 aged 33 years. Also to the memory of her father John LYNCH, who died 1824 aged 52 years. Her mother Ann Lynch died 1834 aged 60 years. Also are interred here her son-in-law Malcolm McGEE, who died on the 8th July 1853, AE 25, leaving a wife and two children. Lorenzo Eid died 2nd November 1857 aged 29 years, son of the above Sarah Eid. Also the above Sarah Eid who died 30th November 1885.

EKENHEAD

[Urn-topped marble altar-tomb with east panel missing, once beside next but now lost.] Erected to the memory of Elizabeth Ekenhead, late of Lisburn aged 55 years, who departed this life 5th January 1810. Also her husband John Ekenhead who died 18th August 1828 aged 78 years. Also their daughter Mary, relict of the late William DUMMETT, Esq., of Crewkerne, who died in the Lord on the 11th day of March 1879 aged 93 years. "There remaineth therefore a rest to the people of God". Heb.IV.9.

[The will (with nineteen codicils) of Mary Dummett of 25 Upper Buckingham Street, Dublin, widow, who died 11 March 1879 at same place, was proved at the Principal Registry 21 May 1879 by the oaths of Robert Thomas McGeah of Belfast, merchant, and Henry Cobbe Bloxham of 36 College Green, Dublin, esquire, two of the executors. Effects under £35,000.

John and Elizabeth Ekenhead's son was Thomas, one of the leading rope-manufacturers in Belfast in the early 19th century (see below), whilst another son Lieut. Ekenhead swam across the Hellespont with Lord Byron in 1810. Their daughter Mrs Mary Dummett founded and endowed the Ekenhead Memorial Presbyterian Church in North Queen Street, to the memory of Thomas.] This building later became St. Kevin's Church Hall and was demolished in 1990. See Benn: *A History of the Town of Belfast* Vol. II (1880).]

EKENHEAD

[North panel of urn-topped marble altar-tomb beside above.] Beneath this tomb are deposited the remains of Thomas Ekenhead, of Belfast, merchant, who, while in the vigour of life, died suddenly at Cookstown in the month of September 1832. As a citizen he will be long remembered by the people of Belfast for his public spirit, independence of mind, sound judgement and the activity by which he was distinguished as a member of its public institutions.

[Fragments of south panel, now lost.] This monument .... the relief of distress, his benevolence was difusive and disinterested as his means were (ample. And while independence of mind, true patriotism and generosity of heart shall be esteemed among men, so long shall the remembrance of his worth be cherished in the breasts of all who know him. He lived beloved and respected by his relatives and friends who deeply deplore his loss. In all the relations of private life, that kindness and genuine warmth of heart which inspired his public conduct appeared to greater advantage and made happy the domestic circle in which he moved).

[East panel.] "For yourselves know perfectly that the day of the Lord so cometh as a thief in the night". "We shall not all sleep but we shall be changed".

[West panel.] (As) a tribute of affection to the memory of a dear and valued brother, this tomb has been erected by his sisters, Elizabeth DAVISON and Mary Ekenhead, 18(33).

[For most of the first three decades of the 19th century, Thomas Ekenhead, whose family was originally from Lisburn, was the leading rope and sail manufacturer in Belfast, the works being situated at Chichester Quay where Queen's Square is now. His sister Mary later married William Dummett (see above)].

ELLIOT

[Obelisk on ornate plinth in low-stone enclosure. Inscribed on three sides - south side has a sickle and rose.] Sacred to the memory of Jane, the beloved wife of S. McDowell Elliot, died the 5. Nov. 1835 aged 27 years. Also of her two children, Anne and Francis who died in infancy. "The righteous shall inherit the Kingdom of Heaven and the pure in heart shall see God". Interred here are the remains of the above S. McDowell Elliot, who died 20 November 1852 aged 45 years.

High peace to the soul of the dead,
From the dream of this world she has gone,
On the stars, in their glory to tread,
To be bright in the blaze of the Throne,

Our weakness may weep o'er her bier,
But her spirit has gone on the wings,
To triumph for agony here,
To rejoice in the Joy of its King'.

[North side - winged hour-glass.] Here lie the remains of Robert Elliot Esq., upwards of thirty years a merchant in Belfast. He died the 25 January 1837 aged 75 years. Also Anne his widow who died the 20 November 1839 aged 59 yers. Also Major Robert P. Elliot, son of S. McDowell Elliot, born 25 June 1830, died 26 November 1880.

The sweet remembrance of the just,
Shall flourish when they sleep in dust.

[East side - crossed sycamore cuttings.] Here rest the remains of Mary Ann FISHER, widow of the late Rev. John Fisher, Carricallen, Co. Leitrim, and daughter of the late Robert Elliot, of Belfast, who died August

17th 1902 aged 90 years. "Blessed are the dead which die in the Lord".

Probate of the will of Mary Anne Fisher of Clonsilla Bangor, county Down who died 17 August 1902 granted at Belfast on the 3rd October 1902 to Sarah Elliot Fisher and Mary Elliot Fisher, spinsters. Effects £2,371 15s.

Robert Elliot, senr. was a wine and spirit merchant in Hercules Street and his son Samuel McDowell Elliot was Seneschal of Belfast and a solicitor who lived at the Lodge after which the Old and New Lodge Roads are named.

The Rev. John Fisher was born near Bailieborough, county Cavan, educated at the R.B.A.I. obtaining the General Certificate in 1832. He was licenced by the Cavan Presbytery in 1835 and ordained Minister of Carrigallen on 5 February 1836. He married in 1838 Mary Anne Elliott (vide supra) and died on 7 June 1860. See McConnell: *Fasti of the Irish Presbyterian Church* (1951.]

ELLIOTT

[Laid flat.] Here lies the body of John Elliott junr, of Belfast, who departed this life Febry 15th 1802 aged 22 years. Also the body of Jane, wife to John Elliott, senr, merchant of Belfast, who departed this life Febry 22nd 1802 aged 62 years.

[John Elliott, senr. was a well-known linen merchant in Donegall Street.]

ELLIOTT

[Sandstone headstone formerly bearing worn marble tablet which is now lost.] Erected by John Elliott, of Belfast, in memory of his mother Jane Elliott who departed this life June 7th 1833 aged 56 years. Erected by The Rev. J. Kennedy Elliott (B.A.) in loving remembrance of (his mother Ann Ferguson) Elliott who departed this life on the (24th May) 18(76) in the (59) year of her age. Also the above named John Elliott who died 23rd April 18(93) aged 81 years.

Reader, reflect thou too must die,
And in the grave forgotten lie,
Think what the future state shall be,
When Death reveals Eternity.

[John Elliott was a builder and lived in Trinity Street].

ENGLESBY

[Formerly flaking and broken, now lost.] Erected by Jane Englesby in memory of her husband John Englesby who departed this life the 29th September 1835 aged 54 years. Also her son William who departed this life the 5th March 1837 aged 25 years. Also her daughter Isabella who departed this life the 16th Jany 1842 aged 19 years.

ERWIN

[White limestone, laid flat.] John Erwin died 31st March 1888, Elizabeth, wife of John Erwin, died 14th April 1906. Also interred here his brother Thomas who died July 1858. And his wife Margaret Scott died 25th April 1913. The Rev. John Erwin B.A., son of above John Erwin, died 3rd March 1917. A man greatly loved.

Administration of the estate of the Reverend John Erwin of 43 Kansas Avenue, Belfast, Presbyterian Minister, who died 3 March 1917, granted at Dublin 4th October 1917 to James Erwin, manager. Effects £721 10s. (limited).

The Rev. John Erwin was educated at Queen's College, Belfast, graduating B.A. in 1891. He was ordained at Cambridge as a missionary to New Zealand in March 1899 and was minister of Dunedin 1904-12 and Limestone Plains from 1912. He married on 26 June 1907 Emily Acheson, daughter of John Acheson of Portadown. See Barkley: *Fasti of the General Assembly ... 1891-1910* (1987).]

EVANS

Erected by Grace Evans to the memory of her beloved son John Waugh who died 29th December 1839 aged 16 years and 5 months. Also her infant daughter Margaret Evans who died 7th March 1838.

EWART

[Large horizontal slab, broken across the middle.] Erected to the memory of James Ewart who departed this life 1st Jany 1829 aged (4)0 years. Also his daughter Sarah aged 5 months. Also his daughter Eliza Ewart who departed this life 9th of May 18(35) aged 15 years. Also his beloved wife Jane who departed this life 8th September 1848 aged 59 years. Also his daughter Mary KING who departed this life on the 16th day of November 1852 aged 34 years. Likewise his son-in-law Thomas SLOAN who departed this life on the 16th day of May 1854 aged 38 years. [Sarah Ewart (see below) was also buried in this plot.]

EWART

[Large and handsome monument, bearing twin slate tablets divided by three classical pillars, in low-stone enclosure and attached to dividing wall.] William Ewart, ob.24th Nov. 1851 AE 93 yrs., Sarah his wife, ob.12th May 1833 AE 72 yrs interred in James Ewart's ground. William Ewart, of Glenbank, his son, ob.22nd Sept. 1873 AE 83 yrs. Marianne his wife ob.4th May 1856 AE 68 yrs. Robert James his son, ob.15th July 1833 AE 11 weeks. Mary Anne his daughter ob.6th Dec. 1837 AE 16 yrs. George Henry his son, ob.7th Feb. 1843 AE 18 yrs. Mary MAGUIRE his grand-daughter ob.[left blank] 1851 AE 1 week. William Ewart Maguire his grandson, ob.28th Feb. 1856 AE 3 mths. Sarah Jane Maguire his daughter, ob.14th May 1856 AE 29 yrs. Marian Maguire his grand-daughter, ob.11th Aug 1870 AE 20 yrs. Interred at Dunluce. Eliza BARTER his daughter, ob.11th Dec. 1867 AE 39 yrs, interred at Nice. Maria his second wife, ob. 7th May 1884 AE 89 yrs. Sir William Ewart, his son, 1st Bart. ob.1st Aug. 1889 AE 71 yrs. George Henry his son, ob.19th Feb. 1855 AE 5 yrs. Rosabel his daughter ob.31st Aug. 1857 AE 20 mths. Isabella KELSO his daughter, ob.2nd Jan. 1859 AE 11 yrs. Harold Octavius his son, ob.21st Oct. 1859 AE 3 days. Charles his son ob.1st Feb. 1862 AE 1 mth. Martin Luther McCREADY his grandson ob.2nd July 1875 AE 4 mths. Wilfred Richard, son of Lavens M. Ewart, ob.28th May 1875 AE 14 mths. James Mathewson Ewart his son ob.7th Aug. 1898 AE 44 yrs. Interred at Somerville, New Jersey, U.S.A. Lavens Mathewson Ewart his son ob.13th Dec. 1898 AE 53 yrs. William Quintus Ewart, eldest son of Sir William Quartus Ewart, 2nd Bart. ob.25th Jan. 1900 AE 22 yrs. Clement Clarendon Ewart, third son of Lavens Mathewson Ewart, ob.20th Dec. 1903 AE 23 yrs. Isabella Kelso, widow of Sir William Ewart, 1st Bart. ob.8th Jan. 1905 AE 84 yrs. Ernest St. John Ewart, second son of Lavens Mathewson Ewart ob.11th Oct 1907 AE 29 yrs. Mary Elizabeth, widow of Lavens Mathewson Ewart, ob.9th Dec. 1908 AE 54 yrs. Cecil Frederick Kelso Ewart, Captain 11th Royal Irish Rifles, son of Frederick William Ewart, killed at Thiepval, 1st July 1916 AE 28 yrs, burial place unknown. Sir William Quartus Ewart, 2nd Bart., eldest son of Sir William Ewart, 1st Bart., ob.17th Oct. 1919 AE 75 yrs.

William Basil Ewart, Major, 15th Royal Irish Rifles, son of Frederick William Ewart, ob.13th Feb. 1920, of illness contracted on active service in France AE 29 yrs. Mary Anne Elizabeth, wife of Frederick William Ewart, ob.31st Dec. 1922 AE 66 yrs. George Herbert Ewart, son of Sir William Ewart, 1st Bart, ob.26th March 1924 AE 67 yrs. Mary WARREN, widow of Sir William Quartus Ewart, ob.26th Feb. 1929 AE 79 yrs. Frederick William Ewart, son of Sir William Ewart, 1st Bart., ob.7th March 1934 AE 75 yrs. Charlotte Hope HARDING, eldest daughter of Sir William Quartus Ewart, Bart., ob.20th June 1934 AE. 52 yrs. Gerald Valentine Ewart, Major R.A.S.C. (retired), eldest son of Frederick William Ewart ob.20th April 1936 AE 52 yrs. Charles Gordon Ewart, youngest son of Sir William Quartus Ewart, Bart., ob.4th Aug. 1936 AE 51 yrs. Sir Robert Heard Ewart, 3rd Bart., second son of Sir William Quartus Ewart, Bart., ob.12th Aug. 1939 AE 59 yrs. Sir Lavens Mathewson Ewart, 4th Bart., youngest son of Lavens Mathewson Ewart, ob.21st Sept. 1939 AE 54 yrs. Rebe Annette, widow of Major William Basil Ewart, ob. 3rd Nov. 1939 AE 48 yrs. Alice Flora, widow of George Herbert Ewart ob.18th Aug. 1945, AE 83 yrs.

[The will (with four codicils) of William Ewart senior of Belfast, county Antrim and of Sydenham Park, county Down, merchant, who died 22nd September 1873 at latter place, was proved at Belfast 25 February 1874 by the oaths of William Ewart and William Quartus Ewart, merchants, and Robert Kelso Mathewson, book-keeper, all of Belfast aforesaid, the executors. Effects under £120,000.

Letters of administration of the personal estate of Maria Ewart of 24 Belvoir Terrace, University Street, Belfast, who died 7th May 1884 at same place, were granted at Belfast on the 1st December 1884 to Anna Maria Eves of Luton, Bedfordshire, England, spinster, a grandchild. Effects £314 13s.9d.

The will of Sir William Ewart of Glenmachan House, Strandtown, county Down and Belfast, Baronet, M.D. who died 1 August 1889 at London, was proved at Belfast 22 August 1889 by Sir William Quartus Ewart, Baronet, Lavens Mathewson Ewart esquire and George Herbert Ewart esquire, all of Belfast, the executors. Effects £313,126 13s.1d.

Probate of the will of James Mathewson Ewart of Broadway, New York, U.S.A., esquire, who died 8th August 1898 granted at Dublin 27th October 1898 to Sir William Q. Ewart, Baronet and George H Ewart, esquire, both of 9 Bedford Street, Belfast. Effects £14,708 13s.8d.

Probate of the will of Lavens Mathewson Ewart of Glenbank House, Ballysillan, Belfast, merchant, who died 13 December 1898 at London, granted at Belfast 10th March 1899 to Sir William Q. Ewart, Baronet, and Frederick W. Ewart, esquire, both of Bedford Street, Belfast. Effects £88,351 16s.3d.

Probate of the will of Clement Clarendon Ewart of Glenbank House, Ballysillan, Belfast, who died 20 December 1903, granted at Belfast 24 February 1904 to Ernest St. John Ewart, gentleman. Effects £1,331 10s.

Administration of the estate of Lady Isabella Kelso Ewart of Schomberg, Strandtown, Belfast, who died 8 January 1905, granted at Dublin, 15th March 1905 to George H. Ewart, merchant. Effects £1,250 12s.11d.

Probate of the will of Ernest St. John Ewart of Glenbank House, Ballysillan, county Antrim, gentleman, who died 11 October 1907 granted at Belfast 21 February 1908 to Charles Owen Slacke, merchant. Effects £2,336 2s.10d. Resworn £1,812 2s.10d and £3,666 4s.4d.

Probate of the will of Mary Elizabeth Ewart of Glenbank House, Ligoniel, Belfast, who died 9 December 1908, granted at Belfast 15th March 1909 to the Reverend Thomas William Clarendon, clerk. Effects £3,202 8s.8d.

Administration of the estate of Cecil Frederick Kelso Ewart of Derryvolgie, Lisburn, county Antrim, Captain Royal Irish Rifles, killed in action 1 July 1916 in France, granted at Belfast on the 28 August 1916 to Frederick W. Ewart esquire. Effects £4,508 5s.9d.

William Basil Ewart of Mount Donarel, Lisburn, county Antrim, died 13 February 1920. Probate Belfast 9 June 1920 to Gerald Valentine Ewart, linen merchant, and Wycliff McCready, Opthalimic Surgeon. Effects £5,723 15s.10d.

Mary Anne Elizabeth Ewart of Derryvolgie, Lisburn, county Antrim (wife of Frederick William Ewart) died 31 December 1922. Administration Belfast 21 February 1923 to the said Frederick William Ewart, merchant. Effects £886 13s.2d.

Lady Mary Warren Ewart of Glenmachan, Strandtown, Belfast, died 26 February 1929. Probate Belfast 24 May 1929 to Sir Robert Heard Ewart, baronet, and Charles Gordon Ewart, esquire. Effects £9,504 11s.

Charlotte Hope Harding of Nore View, Mountrath, Queen's County, and of Tulach Nore, Borris-in-Ossory, Leix, married woman, died 20 June 1934 at Richmond Hospital, Dublin. Probate Belfast 1 November 1934 to George Harding, Colonel H.M. army. Effects £352 16s.10d.

Gerald Valentine Ewart of 17 Bedford Street, Belfast, and of Derryvolgie, Lisburn, county Antrim, Major (retired) H.M. Army, D.L., died 20 April 1936 at 7 Upper Crescent, Belfast. Probate Belfast 26 November 1936 to Victor Frederick Clarendon, director, and Eileen Geraldine Ewart, spinster. Effects £16,799 2d.

Charles Gordon Ewart of Schomberg, Belmont Road, Belfast, gentleman, died 4th August 1936. Probate Belfast 4 May 1937 to Sir Robert Heard Ewart, baronet, and Hugh Latimer McCready D.L., director. Effects £65,368 14s.1d.

Sir Robert Heard Ewart of Glenmachan, Strandtown, Belfast, baronet, died 12 August 1939 (with four duplicates) Belfast 22 January 1940 to Victor Frederick Clarendon, director. Effects £173,090 6s.6d.

Sir Lavens Mathewson Ewart, baronet, of The Banks, Ballyholme, Bangor, county Down, died 21 September 1939 at Private Nursing Home, 35 Wellington Park, Belfast. Administration Belfast 24 November 1939 to Violet Villiers Lutwyche, married woman. Effects £1,576 2s.1d.

Rebe Annette Ewart of Derryvolgie, Lisburn, county Antrim, widow died 3 November 1939 at 7 Upper Crescent, Belfast. Administration to Ethel Elizabeth Isabella Corkey, married woman. Effects £837 7s.5d. Unadministered Grant 16 October 1940.

Rebe Annette Ewart of Derryvolgie, Lisburn, county Antrim, died 3 November 1939. Administration Belfast 16 October 1940 to William Ivan Cecil Ewart, Sub-lieutenant. Unadministered Effects (if any) Nil. Former Grant Belfast 19 March 1940.

Alice Flora Ewart of Ridgemount, Greenisland county Antrim, and of 12 Cleaver Avenue, Belfast, died 18 August 1945 at latter place. Probate Belfast 24 October 1945 to Hugh Latimer McCready, director. Effects £9,958 4s.11d.

The firm of William Ewart & Son was undoubtedly the most extensive concern of flax spinners and linen manufacturers that Belfast has known.

William Ewart, who died in 1873, started as a fancy muslin manufacturer in Rosemary Street about 1820. It was he who built up the family fortunes, and by the 1840s the firm was manufacturing linen and cotton as well as sewed muslin, the offices being in Donegall Street. In 1842, William Ewart became one of the first Aldermen in the re-formed town council. By 1850 the famous mills on the Crumlin Road had been built.

The family by this time lived at Glenbank at Ballysillan, and in the 1880s William's son, also called William was created a baronet. He lived at Glenmachan House, Strandtown and was M.P. for the Borough of Belfast, whilst his eldest son William Quartus lived nearby at Clonaver. His second son, Lavens Mathewson Ewart, of Glenbank, was a noted antiquarian and an authority on Belfast maps, a valuable discovery of his being a hitherto unknown map of Belfast in 1757.

By the latter part of the nineteenth century the firm had offices, factories and mills in Bedford Street, the Crumlin Road and Ligoniel as well as offices in Manchester, London and New York.

Sir William Quartus Ewart, 2nd Baronet, was a Deputy Lieutenant for County Down and amongst other positions held that of Chairman of the Board of Directors of the Great Northern Railway Company. He lived at Glenmachan House after his father died.

In 1920, the firm gave Glenbank House and its grounds to the Belfast Corporation as a small park, and in the 1960s the firm closed down. See Young and Pike: *Belfast and the Province of Ulster* (1909); *Burke's Peerage and Baronetage*, 1978 ed.]

EWART

See GILLIS and TILLEY.

Photograph of Sir William Quartus Ewart, 2nd Baronet.

EWING

[Very badly flaked headstone, now lost.] Erected (by) Sa(muel Ew)ing, in memory (of his) daughter (Elizabeth) who depar(ted this life 20th Aug 1834 aged (8 years and 5 months). Also (his wife Eliza who died on the 29th day of May 1872 aged 74 years.)

[Letters of administration of the personal estate of Eliza Ewing late of Great Georges Street, Belfast who died 29 May 1872 at Belfast aforesaid, were granted at Belfast 29 January 1873 to Samuel Ewing of Great Georges Street, Belfast aforesaid, gentleman, the husband of said deceased. Effects under £300.]

FAINT
See STEPHEN

FALOON

[Weathered sandstone headstone in low-railed enclosure.] Erected by Wm Faloon in memor(y of h)is father Wm Faloon, (late) of Belfast, (who) departed (this life) 28th Feb. 1803 in the 70th (year of) his age. Margaret Eliza SELBY, great-grand-daughter of the above, died 11th (February) 1898.

[The members of the Faloon family commemorated on this and the next two stones were tavern-keepers in the Sugar-house Entry, Waring Street and Hanover Quay area of the town.]

FALOON

[In upper ground, but no longer extant.] Erected to the memory of Elizabeth Faloon who departed this life on the 13th of June 18(1)5, aged 31 years. Also her husband James Faloon who died on the 5th of October 18(1)5 aged 44 years.

FALOON

[Flaking sandstone headstone.] This stone is erected to the memory of William Faloon, of Belfast, who departed this life on the eighteenth day of July 1828. And of his wife Margaret who died on the 9th day of April 1866.

FALOON
See BELL

FEE

[Large headstone formerly surmounted by a draped urn in a high-railed enclosure.] Erected by David Fee, of Belfast, in memory of his brother James who died 9th February 1834 aged 19 years. Also his father James who died 23rd April 1836 aged 61 years. Also his mother Jane who died 21st December 1848 aged 73 years. Also the above named David Fee who died 31st October 1853 aged 51 years. Also his brother William who died 14th February 1854 aged 53 years. Also his sister-in-law Ann who died 20th February 1854 aged 47 years. Also William, son of the above William Fee who died 10th June 1858 aged 27 years. Also his sister Jane Fee who died 22nd March 1874 aged 56 years. And Martha Fee who died 4th September 1883 aged 65 years. Sarah Jane Fee died 20th July 1913, wife of Thomas Fee, nephew of above

David Fee. Also Thos. Walter Fee, son of above T. Fee, died 28th June 1918 aged 33 years. [continued on plaque on enclosure.] Also Thomas Fee, Peeble Lodge, Holywood, who died 4th April 1921.

[Inscription on the back.] Fee family vault.

[The will of William Fee of Belfast in the county of Antrim, stone cutter, who died 10 June 1858 at same place, was proved at Belfast 6 July 1858 by the oaths of Martha Fee and Jane Fee, both of Ann Street in the town of Belfast aforesaid, spinster, the executrixes. Effects under £200.

The will of Jane Fee of Ann Street, Belfast, county Antrim, spinster, who died 22 March 1874 at same place, was proved at Belfast on 10 April 1874 by the oaths of Martha Fee of Ann Street, spinster, and Samuel Fee of Old Lodge Road, pawnbroker, both in Belfast, the executors. Effects under £4,000.

The will of Martha Fee of 102 Ann Street, Belfast, spinster who died 4 September 1883 at same place was proved at Belfast on 21 September 1883 by Samuel Fee of 72 Eglinton Street, Belfast, rent agent and Thomas Fee of 102 Ann Street, Belfast, gentleman, the executors. Effects £8,855 5s.6d.

David Fee was a ship-owner and publican at 130, Ann Street and his sister Jane continued as a publican after his death.]

FEE

[Slate in large headstone, now removed.] Erected by Thomas Fee, Belfast, in memory of his beloved wife Sarah who died 1st August 1858 aged 36 years. Also the above Thomas Fee who died 22nd Sept. 1874 aged 54 years, grandparents of D.A. Fee J.P., County Down, who died 17th January 1934.

[Thomas Fee was a spirit-dealer of Marlborough Street. David A. Fee was a magistrate and lived at Stanley House, Holywood.]

FENWICK
See SHERIDAN

FERGUSON

[Monument (now lost) with elegantly carved surround secured to west wall.] Here lie the remains of Mrs Ferguson, relict of the late Doctor Ferguson who died 24th Jany 1804 aged 83 years. Also two of her grandchildren Elizabeth and Alexander who died infants and her grandson James Ferguson who died 26th Octr 1816 aged 26 years. Also his son John Stephenson Ferguson who died 20th Decr 1816 aged 3 years. Also of John Stephenson Ferguson Esqr. who died 3rd March 1833 in his 70th year. Also his widow Mrs Ellen Ferguson who died on the 29th March 1837, in her 70th year. Also Colonel George Ferguson, youngest son of the above John S. Ferguson Esqr who died in Paris on the 30th day of April 1878 in his 75 years. Also John Francis Ferguson D.L., J.P., who died 17th Sept 1879 aged 78 years.

[The will of John Francis Ferguson of Belfast, Esq. J.P. D.L., died 17 September 1879 at same place, was proved at Belfast on the 15 October 1879 by the oaths of William Crawford, Thomas Douglas Crawford and Thomas Montgomery, all of Belfast, esquires, the executors. Effects in U.K. under £100,000.

The Ferguson family was one of the longest established in Belfast, the first member here probably being Dr. Victor Ferguson who arrived with William III's army as a surgeon. His son was Dr. Ferguson, mentioned above, who, as well as being a doctor, was a linen merchant. His son John Stephenson Ferguson was also a linen merchant and founded the extensive firm of J. S. Ferguson and Co. whose offices were in the White Linen Hall. In the early years of the 19th century he owned large bleach greens at Ballysillan and a paper mill at Antrim. He was President of the Belfast Chamber of Commerce from 1821 to 1832. He was a member of the committee of the Belfast Charitable Society and in the latter part of the previous century had been a Volunteer. He also helped to found the Linenhall Library.

His son John Francis Ferguson continued the firm and for many years was a Deputy Lieutenant for Co. Antrim. Like his father before him, he lived in Donegall Place in a house whose site was later occupied by Robinson and Cleaver's department store, and at the time of his death in 1879 was one of the last private residents in that thoroughfare.

The firm continued as handkerchief and fancy linen manufacturers until well into the 20th century, with premises in Linenhall Street West.

See Benn: *A History of the Town of Belfast*, Vol. II, 1880.]

FERGUSON

[Triangular-topped stone with obliterated coat-of-arms on south side and inscription on north side.] This stone is placed here by her children in loving memory of Matilda, wife of John Ferguson, who died 19th January 1853, whose remains together with those of her sister Margaret, wife of George McCULLOCH, who died February 1855, also her father Charles O'DONNELL who died 19th October 1825, and her mother Mary, rest beneath.

[Matilda Ferguson and Margaret, widow of George McCulloch were both resident at Comber, county Down at the time of their deaths.]

FERGUSON

[Marble tablet in surround, secured to south wall in railed enclosure.] Erected by James B. Ferguson in memory of his beloved mother Bell Ferguson who departed this life 11th Feb. 1855, in the 82nd year of her age. Here also lie the remains of Thomasina and James his children who died in infancy. William McMURRAY, his nephew who died 21st May 1848 aged 15. Isabella HARDCASTLE his niece, who died 5th Dec. 1855 aged 26. Captain W.A. Hardcastle his brother-in-law, who died 2nd Feby 1858. Helen E. Ferguson his daughter who died 11th March 1868. Margaret Ferguson his wife who died 30th Aug. 1868. James Baxter Ferguson who died 29th Sept 1877. Jane Ferguson, his daughter-in-law who died 13th Feby 1910. James Hyndman Ferguson, her husband who died 16th Feby 1921 aged 80 years. And of Margaret Ferguson daughter of James B. Ferguson, who died 17th August 1923 aged 81 years.

[Continued on polished granite slab at the base.] In memory of 2nd Lt James Ernest Ferguson, 10th Batt. Royal Dublin Fusiliers, who was killed in France on 20th April 1917, while leading the company and buried near Gavrelle, only son of James Hyndman and Jane Ferguson.

[The will of William Augustus Hardcastle of Belfast in the county of Antrim, half-pay Lieutenant in Her Majesty's 75th Regiment, who died 30 January 1858 at Belfast aforesaid, was proved at Belfast on the 3 March 1858 by the oaths of James Baxter Ferguson of same place merchant, the sole executor. Effects under £300.

James B. Ferguson was a starch manufacturer with works in Unity Street, the firm being Molyneaux and Ferguson. Formerly, in the 1840s and 1850s, it was known as the Belfast Starch Works at 79 Donegall Street.]

FERGUSON
[Slightly flaking and now lost.] Erected by David Ferguson of Girvan, who died at Belfast, 11th Novr. 1851 aged 56 years.

FERGUSON
See STEPHENS

FERRIS
[Small memorial now missing from lower ground. The plot was bought by John McLean in November 1847.] The family burying ground of Robert Ferris.

FETHERSTON
[Now lost.] Erected by John Fetherston in memory of his beloved wife Harriet who departed this life on the 19th December 1844 aged 48 years.

FINLAY
[Flaking and bottom lines buried.] Erected by Usher Finlay, of Belfast to the memory of his son John who departed this life on the 24th August 1825 in the 27th year of his age. "The relative duties of son and brother he discharged in the most affectionate and exemplary manner, while his modest demeanour, amiable disposition, and strict integrity had gained him many friends". Also to his daughter Elenor who died on the 10th April 1819, aged 27 years. His wife Jane Finlay who departed this life on the 28th June 1829 aged 64 years. And the above named Usher Finlay, who (sic) husband of Jane Finlay, who departed this life on the 10th July 1829.

FINLAY
[Badly damaged by ivy and now lost.] Martha Finlay, born 26th Septr 1750, died (..) Septr 1825. William Finlay departed this life 17th D(ecem)ber 18(27) aged 72 years. Alexr Finlay (died 28th) March 1832, a(ged 48 years.)

FINLAY
[In upper ground and no longer extant.] Erected by Alexr. Finlay of Belfast, in memory of his son Thomas who departed this life (..) July (....) aged (..) years. Also his wife Isabella who departed this life 9th Jan. 1848 aged (39) years. Also his son Robert who died (..) April 1841 aged 24 years. Also his brother John who died 10th July 1844 aged (..) years. Also James Finlay who died 30th May 1849 aged 59 years. Also Anne, wife of Charles Finlay. Alexr Finlay died 13th May 1863 aged 39 years.

FINLAY

[Worn marble tablet with surround surmounted by a casket secured to east wall, in high-railed enclosure, now removed.] The remains of Francis Dalzell Finlay, the founder of *The Northern Whig*, born 12th July 1793, died 10th Sept 1857 aged 64 years. And of Marianne his wife who died October 24th 1866 aged 58 years. Also of their children: Sinclair Finlay, who died (March 9th) 1840 aged 21 months. George (Washington) Finlay who died 184(.) aged 17 months. Mary Georgina Finlay who died Nov 16th 18(5)2 aged 10 years. [Francis Dalzell Finlay was born at Newtownards and began his career as a master printer in Joy's Entry. He was later a printer and book publisher at 1, Corn Market and it was there that he founded *The Northern Whig* on 1st January 1824. A staunch liberal, he was a man who adhered rigidly to his principles and at one time was sent to prison for three months for refusing to reveal the identity of the author of an allegedly libellous letter.

The Northern Whig was, in its early life at least, a largely literary paper, and boasted a distinguished line of editors, among them John Morgan who later founded the *Newry Examiner* and James Simms who founded the *Belfast Mercury*. *The Northern Whig* ceased publication in 1960.]

FINLAY
See CHAMBERS

FISHER

[Polished granite tablet, of c.1870, secured to dividing wall, in low-stone enclosure.] Burial place of John Fisher, of Glengall Place, and of Jane his wife. Also of all their children: Fanny, Anna, John, Hester, Lydia, Mary.

[John Fisher bought this plot in March 1836. He was the proprietor of the flax-spinning firm of John Fisher & Co. whose mill was situated in Francis Street close to the site of Capt. John McCracken's cotton mill which had been the first of its kind in Belfast.]

FISHER
See ELLIOTT and MONTGOMERY

FITZGIBBON

[Formerly pedimented archway over large plinth bearing marble tablet. This is now a simple box tomb, without arms. Arms: Saltire, three annulets in chief. Cornstocks? in angles of saltire. Motto: "Nil admirari"] To the memory of Elizabeth Fitzgibbon, relict of Philip Fitzgibbon Esqr, Lieut R.N., formerly of Castle Grace, County Tipperary, who departed this life 13th Feby 1846 aged 57 years. Also to Maryanne her daughter, widow of the late Samuel DUDGEON Esqr, St. Doulough's Hill, Co. Dublin, who departed this life September 19th 1873 aged 53 years.

[Philip Fitzgibbon, R.N., of Castle Grace, county Tipperary, and Mount Eagle, Kilworth, county Cork, was descended from Maurice Fitzgibbon (Kt. 1333) of Ballynahinch, county Limerick. He married Elizabeth Coates (vid. sup.), daughter of Abraham Coates of Killinure, county Wicklow and died in 1826. They had 2 sons and 2 daughters, including Elizabeth Dudgeon mentioned above. See Burke's *Irish Family Records* (1976).]

FLETCHER
[Large stone, very worn, but recorded in Society's Inscription book.] Frederick Fletcher died May 1858, AE 58. Jane Fletcher his wife died June 1866 AE 64. Isabella F. Fletcher, their daughter died March 1858 AE 34. Also William, Emily & Charles who died young. [Frederick Fletcher and his daughter Isabella were both music teachers, first in Joy Street, then in Catherine Street North. Frederick Fletcher had a music shop at 5 Castle Place.]

FOLINGSBY
[Memorial formerly attached to east wall of lower ground. It is no longer extant.] Sacred to the memory of Thomas Grueber Folingsby, of Belfast, merchant, who departed this life 19th of March 1871 aged 78 years. And of his wife Christian CATTO who departed this life 29th July 1839 aged 32 years. Also of his mother Margaret Folingsby who died 4th December 1837. His son Robert Catto died at Aberdeen 17th August 1851 aged 13 years. And his daughter Christian Catto at same place, 13th June 1871 aged 31 years. Also his son George Folingsby died 17th October 1880 aged 44 years. Also his wife Jane REID died 17th August 1883 aged 78 years.

[T.G. Folingsby, & Son & Co. were general merchants and shipbrokers with offices in Victoria Street. Formerly the firm had been at Donegall Quay.]

FORDE
See ANDREWS

FORDYCE
[Worn marble tablet in plinth of obelisk.] Sacred to the memory of Eliza Fordyce who died 11th Novr 1845 aged 33 years. Also her husband James Millar Fordyce who died 20th March 18(5)7 aged 44 years. Also their youngest son Charles ... Fordyce who died 4th Feby. 1868 aged (2)4 years.

[James Millar Fordyce ran the Cromac Brewery in Cromac Street.]

FORRESTER
[Celtic cross now smashed, inscribed around the plinth in Gothic characters, and in low railing. Arms: Three bugle- horns, stringed. Crest: bugle-horn.] The family burial place of Alexander Forrester, 1835. In memoriam, Alex. Forrester, obt. 6th Ap. 1860. Margt Forrester, obt. 13th Oct. 1868. Mary, wife of (J.W.) Forrester, obt. 19th Dec. 1901. John William Forrester, obt. 26th Jan. 1907.

[West side.] Elizabeth C. BROWN, obt. 30th Jan. 1846.

[East side.] Alex. T. Forrester obt. 18th Aug. 1856.

[Letters of administration, with the will annexed, of the personal estate of Margaret Forrester of Ratcliff Street, Belfast, county Antrim, who died 13 October 1868 at Belfast aforesaid, were granted at Belfast on the 23 December 1868 to Eliza Corry Forrester of 8 Windsor Terrace, Belfast aforesaid, spinster, the daughter one of the next of kin of deceased and the sole legatee. Effects under £300.

Alex. Forrester, senr was a merchant in the firm of T.G. Folingsby, ship-brokers, etc and the family resided at 107, Donegall Street.]

FORRESTER

[Flat stone beside above.] Elizabeth Margaret, eldest child of John William & Mary Adam Forrester obt 30th Jany 1870, Elizabeth NOTT obit 12th May 1897.

[Administration of the estate of Mary Adams Forrester of 23 Charleville Road, Rathmines, county Dublin, who died 19 December 1901 granted at Dublin on the 14 February 1902 to John W. Forester, esquire. Effects £453 11s.9d.

Administration of the estate of John William Forrester of 206 Clonliffe Road Dublin retired agent who died 26 January 1907 granted at Dublin on the 12 June 1907 to the Reverend John C. Forrester, Clerk. Effects £35 16s.7d.

The above were not buried here, presumably because they moved to Dublin, and the administration records are included only for interest.]

FORSYTH

[With capstone missing.] (Erected by Catherine Forsyth), in memory of her beloved husband Archibald Forsyth who departed this life 27th November 1851 aged 45 years.

FOSTER

[Worn sandstone with surround, secured to east wall of upper graveyard.] (To the) memory of Roseann, wife to James Foster, who departed this life 6th Decr 1827 aged 51 years.

FOSTER

[Laid flat.] The family burial place of the late William Foster, 1855.

FOSTER

[Laid flat.] Erected to the memory of William Foster, who died 25th July 1855 aged 72 years. Margaret his wife died 15th Nov. 1854 aged 72. Also two of their children, Margaret and Simpson who died in youth. Also their great-grandson William Foster McCLELLAND, who died 6th July 1883 aged 14 months. Also their daughter Louisa, beloved wife of Henry McClelland who died 26th March 1886 aged 68 years. Also the above Henry McClelland who died at Stranmillis Park, Belfast, 12th August 1893. "Till he come".

[The will of Henry McClelland of Great Victoria Street and Garden Cottage and of 2 Stranmillis Park, all in Belfast, warehouse manager, who died 12 August 1893 at latter place, was proved at Belfast on the 30 August 1893 by Anne Ada McClelland of 2 Stranmillis Park, widow, the sole executrix. Effects £1,075 16s.

William Foster who lived in High Street, Holywood was a shipbroker and emigration agent, with offices at Chichester Quay. His son-in-law Henry McClelland was a linen merchant with the firm of F.B. Lecky & Co,. Donegall Square North.]

FOWLER
See TROTTER

FRAZER
[Badly flaked and now removed.] Erected (by) Joseph Frazer, (to) the mem(ory of) his daug(ht)er Ma(rgaret), who departed (this life 18th February) 1807 (aged 9 years). Also his dau(ghter) Ann, (wife of) Captain W(ill)iam CAVA(N) . who) dep(arted this life 24th July 1855 aged 62 years. "Blessed are the dead which die in the Lord".)

FRAZER
[White limestone in the shape of a decorated shield, laid flat.] Sacred to the memory of Thomas Frazer whose remains are deposited in this place. He was born in St. Andrew, Scotland, and died at Belfast on the 25th Feb. 1849 in the 34th year of his age. Also in memory of his infant son Thomas Sanderson who died on the 30th of May 1846 aged 6 months. Here lieth the body of his father Hugh Frazer who died on the 8th December 1859 aged 88 years.

[Thomas Frazer was proprietor of the Shakespeare Hotel, 21, Castle Lane, and lived in Donegall Place.]

FRAZER
See MALCOMSON

FRYER
[Slightly pitted.] Erected by Thomas Fryer of Belfast, to the memory of his beloved daughter Margaret Ann Fryer who departed this life April the 25th 1840 aged 24 years. Also the above Thomas Fryer who departed this life 17th February 1845 aged 77 years. Also James McCleery BRO.., grandson of the above who departed this life 25th Sept 1868 aged 24 years. "He sleeps in Jesus".

FRYER
[Horizontal slab with the first part of the inscription missing and copied from Society's records.] In memory of Thomas William Fryer who departed this life 24th December 1866. Also his two eldest children: Anne Cecil, and Thomas Henry Fryer who died in childhood. "For what is your life? It is even a vapour that appeareth for a little time and then vanisheth away".

FULTON
See MOLYNEUX

GALWAY
[Very badly flaked headstone, broken in two and lying flat.] Erected (by) Art(hur Galway) in memory (of his two) children who died (in inf)ancy. (Also) Jane Ann the beloved wife of Thomas GILMORE who departed (this) life 16th January 18(64). "The memory of the Just is Blessed" Prov. X 7.

GALWAY
See JENKINS and SHAW

GAMBLE/GAMBLES

[Low-set slab, broken in several pieces, now lost.] Sacred to the memory of Robert Gamble, son of Robert Gambles, of Ballymoney, who departed this life the 15th of July 18(..), in the 22nd year of his age. [This ground was bought by Robert Gamble in July 1816.]

GAMBLE

[Two painted tablets in pedimented entablature secured to east wall of the upper graveyard in a high-railed, low-stone enclosure.] Erected by Arthur Gamble, in memory of his wife Margaret who died 27th Octr 1821 aged 46. Also his child John who died 13th Decr 1815 aged 6 months. And his son Benjamin, who died 1st December 1835 aged 28 years.

In memory of Arthur Gamble who died on the 27th June 1841 aged 70 years. And his son Arthur who died 6th February 1871. Also Charlotte, wife of Robert Gamble, who died 13th July 1876.

[The will of Charlotte Gamble of 3 Abercorn Street, Belfast, widow, who died 13 July 1876, was proved at Belfast 31st July 1876 by the oath of James Gamble, gentleman, and James Neill, merchant, both of Belfast, the executors. Effects under £1,000.]

GAMBLE

[Twin marble tablets in a monument attached to dividing wall and in a high-railed enclosure.] Sacred to the memory of Robert Gamble died 25th Jany 1836 aged 60 years. Eliza his daughter died 7th Aug. 1828 aged 21 years. John his son died at New Orleans 22nd Decr 1828 aged 19 years. Hamilton V., his son died at New Orleans 29th Sept 1839 aged 19 years. Anne his wife died 17th Decr 1836 aged 73 years. Mary his daughter who is here buried died 17th May 1879 aged 64 years.

Erected by Margaret Gamble to the memory of her husband William Gamble youngest son of Robert Gamble, of Belfast, who was born February 12th 1824, and died May 14th 1862. Also in memory of the above named Margaret Gamble, born 12th May 1833, died 8th Nov. 1904, buried at Highgate, London. Also their son Robert Samuel Gamble, died 30th Sept 1928, buried in Jamaica, B.W.I.

[The will of William Gamble of Hollywood in the county of Down, merchant, and of Corporation Street, Belfast, county Antrim, who died 14 May 1862, was proved at Belfast 13 November 1862 by the oaths of James Gamble of Carrickfergus, merchant and Thomas Boyle Johnson of Waring Street, solicitor, the executors. Effects under £5,000.

Robert Gamble and his son William were commission merchants in Waring Street. Robert Gamble purchased the plot in May 1829.]

GAMBLE

[Monument, secured to south wall in railed enclosure, with the next.] Sacred to the memory of Helena, wife of Benjamin Adair Gamble, who died 3rd February 1849 aged 3(3) years. Robert, son of Benjamin Adair Gamble, who died 21st July 1849 aged 8 years and (3) months. And of Benjamin Adair Gamble, above named, who died at sea, March 1854 aged 41 years. Also his daughter Eliza Gamble who died 12th January

1856 aged nearly three years.

[B.A. Gamble owned a linen warehouse in Donegall Street Place.]

GAMBLE

[Monument, topped by an urn, containing twin marble tablets of which one is uninscribed, secured to south wall in enclosure with the above.] In memory of Mary DICKSON, wife of Robert Gamble, of New Orleans, who died 10th August 1851 aged 47 years. Also of Robert Gamble who died at Bunker's Hill, Illinois, 11th November 1867 aged 61 years.

GAMBLE

See DOUGLASS, HOW and McKIBBIN

GARDNER

[Three identical marble tablets with lead letters, in large sandstone monument, secured to dividing wall, in high-railed enclosure, now destroyed and removed.] Family burying (place of James) Gardner, Belfast.

Here rest the remains of Thomas Gardner, brother of the above-named James Gardner, died 28th February 1835 aged 44 years. Also of Thomas Brown Gardner, son of James Gardner died 23rd April 1839 aged 20 years. Also of George McHENRY, grandson of James Gardner, died 28th September 1848 aged 10 months.

Here also rest the remains of the daughters of said James Gardner, namely of Roseanna, who died 16th April 1840 aged 13 years, and of Eliza who died 18th November 1859 aged 31 years. Also of his daughter Harriet Alicia GRAY who died 5th August 1907 aged 66 years.

Here also rest the remains of the said James Gardner who died 22nd September 1854 aged 68 years. Also of his wife Eliza who died 9th February 1875 aged 77 years.

[Administration of the estate of Harriett Alicia Gray of 6 Cowper Road, county Dublin, widow, who died 5 August 1907 at Farnham House Hospital, Dublin, was granted at Dublin 3 January 1908 to Campbell Gardner, insurance inspector. Effects £1,933 2s.0d.

The will (with 2 codicils) of Elizabeth Gardner of Dunedin, Belfast, widow, who died 9 February 1875, was proved at Belfast 12 April 1875 by the oaths of James Gardner and Campbell Gardner, both of Belfast, merchants, the executors. Effects under £100.

James and Thomas Gardner started as grocers in North Street. Later they were ship-owners and provision merchants with premises in York Lane. Finally James was a starch manufacturer at 10, York Lane.]

GARDNER

[Corroded iron shield.] The family burying place of Thos Gardner, Belfast, 18(6)0.

[Letters of administration (with the will annexed) of the personal estate of Thomas Gardner of Queen's Square, Belfast, in the county of Antrim, tallow chandler, who died 23 August 1860 at Queen's Square aforesaid, were granted at Belfast 10 September 1860 to Isabella Gardner of same place, widow of the deceased, the universal legatee. Effects under £5,000.

GARDNER
See LAW

GARLAND
[Now lost.] Erected by John Garland of Belfast, in memory of his beloved wife Margaret Garland, who departed this life on the first of March 1840 aged 50 years. "In early morn, the sun doth show my best beloved lies below". Also his grand-daughter Sarah REID aged 5 years. The above named John Garland aged 75 years. His son William Thomas aged 44 years. His son Edmund aged 33 years. And his son-in-law William STERNE, who died 31st October 1879 aged 64 years.

GARRETT
[Slate tablet on carved mounting secured to south wall in a low-railed, low-walled enclosure.] Sacred to the memory of Thomas Garrett, of Belfast, solicitor, born 25 Aug. 1774, died 5 March 1837. His wife Anne NEILSON, born 28 March 1782, died 26 July 1857. And their children: Henry Garrett, of Belfast, solicitor, born 4 June 1812, died 14 Feb. 1859, John Neilson Garrett, born 1816, died 1832, Thomas Garrett, of Belfast, solicitor, born 28 April 1820, died 20 Oct. 1861, Robert Garrett, of London, civil engineer, born 8 June 1823, killed at Cawnpore, East Indies in the year 1857, about the 6 June. Also Emma Frances GRIMSHAW, wife of said Henry Garrett, born in 1812, and died 24 Feb 1862. And their daughter Anne Garrett, born in 1849, and died in 1857.

[Letters of administration (with the will annexed) of the personal estate of Anne Garrett of Belfast in the county of Antrim, widow, who died 26 July 1857 were granted at Belfast 24 April 1858 to Thomas Garrett, solicitor, the son, and one of the residuary legatees. Effects under £800.

Letters of administration of the personal estate of Thomas Garrett of Dunesk, near Belfast and in the county of Antrim, solicitor, who died 20 October 1861, were granted at Belfast 18 November 1861 to Mary Garrett alias Burden of Dunesk the widow of said deceased. Effects under £9,000.

Thomas Garrett, senr. was an attorney and lived in York Street. His sons were solicitors, the firm being known as H.J.& T. Garrett with offices first in Castle Lane and later in Donegall Square. They also had offices in Dublin.]

GARRETT
[Raised flat stone, now lost.] Sacred to the memory of James Ramsey Garrett, of Belfast, solicitor, born 10 Decr 1817, died 10 April 1855. And his wife Mary HIGGINSON born 1821, died 31 March 1852.

[He was a brother of Henry Garrett (see above) and was in partnership with him in the 1840s when the firm was in Castle Lane.]

GARRETT
[Polished granite, now lost.] In loving memory of Thomas Garrett, elder son of the late James R. Garrett, who died 16th May 1883 aged 37 years.

[Letters of administration of the personal estate of Thomas Garrett, formerly of Belfast but late of Morningside, Edinburgh, gentleman, who died 16 May 1883 were granted at the Principal Registry 26 September 1883 to Mary Higginson Phillips (wife of George Arthur Phillips, surgeon) of 1 Bermingham Road, Walsall, in the county of Stafford, the sister. Effects £5,773 1s.8d.]

GAUSSEN

[Now lost.] Jeanette Gaussen died 29th August 1883. "Them which sleep in Jesus will God bring with him". Thess. IV,.14.

[The will of Jeannette Anne otherwise Jeannette Gaussen, late of Ballyholme, Bangor, county Down, spinster, who died 29 August 1883 was proved at Belfast 12 October 1883 by William Lovett Gaussen of Holywood in said county, merchant, one of the executors. Effects £1,096 11s.3d.

She was a member of the well-known merchant family which at one time owned Bankmore House. She died at Ballyholme, Bangor, aged 54.]

GAVIN

[Undated granite stone in low enclosure, with family name and looking of c.1900-1930.] Gavin.

GEDDIS

[Bottom lines buried.] Erected by Adam Geddis to the memory of his son Robert who departed this life 19th February 1825 aged 32 years. Also his son David who departed this life the 16th February 1829 aged 25 years. Also interred here the above named Adam Geddis who departed this life 26th August 1835 aged 64 years. His grandson Robert Geddis died 10th Jany 1871 aged 47 years. Eliza, wife of Robert Geddis died 15th April 1888 aged 70 years.

GEDDIS

See KENNEDY

GELSTON

[Next to wall in upper portion of graveyard. It has disappeared since 1907, but was recorded in Society's Inscription book. *M.D.*XI,1.] Thomas Gelston, of Belfast, surgeon who died in 1801, and Agnes GUNNING his widow who died in 1810, are buried here. Their only daughter Anna Maria, wife of Thomas McL...... of ....., the County of Down, died at ...... the 11th October 18(4)6, aged (5)0 years, and was buried in the churchyard of the Parish of St. David of the City of ....

[Thomas Gelston was one of the founding members of the Belfast Library and Society for Promoting Knowledge, now known as the Linenhall Library.]

GEMMILL

[Large slab tablet with sandstone entablature topped with three urns secured to north wall, together with next two memorials in high-railed enclosure.] Dedicated by the disconsolate widow and mourning family to the memory of Robert Gemmill who departed this life on the 30th May 1808 aged 64 years. "The memory of the just is blessed. I know that my Redeemer liveth and that he shall stand at the latter day upon the earth and though after my skin worms destroy this body, yet in my flesh I shall see God". Here are deposited the remains of his son Robert, who departed this life on the 30th August 1822 aged 21 years. Here also are deposited the remains of his wife Elizabeth Gemmill who departed this life on 12th August 1828 aged 67 years.

[Robert Gemmill, a native of Scotland, was a muslin manufacturer in Donegall Street and engaged in the shipping trade. He was killed when he fell between the quay and a ship. His son-in-law was the Rev. Samuel Hanna D.D., for many years Professor of Divinity at R.B.A.I. and minister of the Third Presbyterian Church, Rosemary Street.]

GEMMILL

[Marble tablet in sandstone surround secured to north wall.] Erected by Mary E.C. JOHNSTON in memory of her dear mother Agnes Gemmill who fell asleep in Jesus 12th June 1845. Mary E.C. Johnston, the beloved wife of Surgeon J. Milford BARNETT M.D. H.M. Indian Army, died at Croft House, Holywood 16th Feby 1875 AE 44. "Blessed are the dead who die in the Lord" Rev.XIV.13. Interred by her bereaved husband.

GEMMILL

[Large sloping granite block with Maltese cross in high-railed enclosure with above two monuments.] Here sleeps in Jesus, John Gemmill, of Westbourne Terrace, London; born March 19th 1803, died July 29th 1865. "If we believe that Jesus died and rose again, even so them also, which sleep in Jesus, will God bring with him".

GEMMILL
See HOW

GEORGE

[Now lost.] Erected by Margaret George in memory of her beloved husband Thomas George who died 19th January 1864 aged 51 years. Also of their children, James died 19th April 1863 aged 19 years, Archibald K. died 7th July 1863 aged 21 years, Margaret Frances, died 12th May 1864 aged 11 years, Sarah Eliza died 25th March 1867 aged 21 years, John K. died on his passage to New Zealand, 29th November 1867 aged 19 years, Nannie died 22nd September 1870 aged 30 years. Also 2 children who died in infancy. The above named Margaret George died 4th July 1888 aged 78 years.

GETTY

[Wall plot in upper portion of burial ground. It was purchased by William Getty in May 1823. Both tablets have disappeared, but are recorded in the Society's Inscription books.] (a) In memory of William Getty of the ..... died March ... aged ...

(b) Erected by William Getty in memory of his beloved daughter Margaret who died 29th Decr (1838) aged (21). Also of his daughter Elizabeth who died in infancy. Here also is interred his beloved son Robert who died 26th February 1842 aged (21) years.

[William Getty was a merchant of Donegall Street.]

GETTY

[Carved limestone with lead letters.] 1888. In memory of Mary Getty, died 27th Nov. 1858. Her son James died 26th March 1862. And her daughter Jane SMYTH, died 27th April 1888.

[The will of Jane Smyth of Denmark Street, Belfast, widow, who died 27 April 1888, was proved at Belfast 16 May 1888 by James Fielding Smyth, mechanical engineer, and Henry Greer, accountant, both executors. Effects £239 10s.4d.]

GETTY
See LUKE

GETWOOD
[Formerly in upper ground and no longer extant.] Erected by Thomas Getwood of Belfast to the memory of his beloved father .... Getwood who .... 1828 aged .. years.

GIBBS
[Broken and badly worn marble tablet formerly secured to north wall but now lost — mostly copied from Inscription Book.] Erected (by Henry Gibbs in memory of his father Thomas) Gibbs who died on (the 27th Nov. 1836 aged 61 years. Also his mother Sarah Gibbs who died on the) 17th (April 1840 aged 50 years. Likewise his sister Caroline GILBERT who died on the 27th Feb. 1843 aged 17 years. Also Henry CHEW who died on the 15th May 1841 aged 1 year and 10 months. And Mary Ann Chew, who died on the 21st Feb. 1843 aged 3 years and 4 months. Charles Davies Chew died on 14th Feb. 1851 aged 7 months. Elizabeth Chew died on the 24th May 1851 aged 8 years and 6 months. And James Chew aged 11 years and 8 months. And John BEGGS aged 15 years, who were drowned on the 26th Feby) 1864 (Also of) Margaret (HAY), widow of (Lt. General John) MACKENZIE, (of Belmaduthie) Rosshire who died at Belfast on the (7th Oct 1865) aged 86 years. (Elizabeth Chew, beloved wife of Quarterm)aster Wm (Chew, died 4th July 1866) aged (53) years.

[Quartermaster William Chew was attached to the Royal Antrim Rifles and lived in Eglinton Street.]

GIBSON
[Badly flaked and bottom lines buried. First part is therefore copied from Society's Inscription Book.] (Erected by William Gibson of Belfast in memory of his mother Sarah Elizabeth Gibson who departed this life on the 23rd February 1825 aged 63 years. "She was pious and edifying in her entire conduct and finished her) course in perfect recognition to the Divine Will". Here also lyes interred the remains of John Gibson, husband to the above Sarah Elizabeth Gibson who departed this life 19th November 1827 aged 58 years.

GIBSON
[Flaked in the middle.] Erected (by) Margret (Gibson), of Belfast, in memory of (her belo)ved husband William Gib)son, who departed t(his life 1)0th August 1832 aged (38) years. Also the above (named) Margret Gibson who departed this (life on) the 13th Decr 1847 aged (47) years.

Also her daughter (Mar)y Wallace, who departed this life on the 30th Novr 1844 aged 3 years and 9 months.

GIBSON
[Laid flat.] This stone was erected by Rachel Maria Gibson to the memory of her father Andrew Gibson who departed this life the 2 of December 1833 aged 57 years.
[He was proprietor of the "Wheat Sheaf" public house at 1, May Street.]

GIBSON
[Twin broken marble tablets, one of which has no longer any trace of inscription, and the other has recently been destroyed, formerly secured to north wall, in high-railed enclosure.] Erected by Samuel Gibson in memory of Mary his wife who died 12th August 1842 aged 36 years. Sarah his daughter who died 22nd May 18(58) aged 26 years. Mary, h(is daught)er who died 10th (May 1835 aged 6 months. A son) who died 16th (Sep 1837, the day of his birth. Elizabeth his daughter, widow of Samuel ALLEN M.D., who died 23rd May 1884 aged 54 years).

GIBSON
[Flaked in the middle and now lost.] I.H.S. Sacred to the memo(ry of Will)iam Gibson, who departed (this life in) the full hope of a glorious (immortality) on the 16th day of October (1851 aged) 72 years. Also Margaret, the beloved and affectionate wife of the above named William Gibson, who died on the 16th day of March 18(5)7 aged 66 years. "Lovely and pleasant in their lives, in their death they were not divided."

GIBSON
[Tablet formerly attached to north wall of lower ground, but now obliterated.] James Gibson, barrister, born 1804, died 1880.
[The will of James Gibson, late of 35 Mountjoy Square, Dublin, barrister-at-law, who died 5 February 1880, was proved at the Principal Registry 23 June 1880 by the oath of Samuel Gibson of 250 Tooley Street, London, merchant, one of the executors (by decree). Effects under £8,000.]

GIBSON
See BARNETT, CAVART and SINCLAIR

GIFFORD
[Capstone broken off the top.] Erected by N.B. Gifford to the memory of his father John Gifford who departed this life on the 26th of April 1834 aged 58 years. "We die for Adam sinned, we live, for Jesus died". Also his aunt Norminda O'NEILL who departed this life on the 17th March 1843 aged 70 years. His sister Cordelia Gifford who departed this life on the 7th May 1845 aged 35 years. His aunt Elizabeth SHEKLETON who departed this life on the 17th April 1847 aged 80 years. His son William John Gifford who departed this life on the 13th Novr 1847 aged 10 years. And three of his sons who died in infancy fell asleep in their Redeemer. Likewise his mother Mary-Ann Gifford who died 17th March 1853 aged 82 years. Also his dear daughter Henrietta Amelia who died 25th May 1857, in her 10th year. Also his beloved wife Susan Netterville Gifford

who departed this life 21st June 1878 aged 72 years. And above named Norman B. Gifford who died 23rd July 1879 aged 76 years.

[Letters of administration (with the will annexed) of the personal estate of Norman Brabazon Gifford of 13 Spencer Street, Belfast, accountant, who died 22 July 1879, were granted at Belfast 5 March 1880 to Elizabeth Garston Harvey (wife of James Thompson Harvey of Atlantic House, Limestone Road, Belfast, ship broker) the child and a legatee. Effects under £100.]

GIHON

[Flaking and now lost.] 1837. Sacred to the memory of Mary Anne Gihon, who departed this life the 3rd of August 1837 aged 68 years. Erected by her daughter Jane Gihon.

GIHON

See CURRELL

GILBERT

[Twin slate tablets in carved entablature, against south wall in railed enclosure.] William Gilbert, Belfast. Sacred to the memory of my beloved wife Martha who departed this life on the 3rd of January 1848 in the fortieth year of her age. Also five of our children who died young. Also to his 3rd daughter Emma the beloved wife of Hugh MACK, who died 6th January 1866 aged 26 years. "Blessed are the dead which die in the Lord". William Gilbert fell asleep 19th September 1890 aged 85 years.

Also in memory of his mother Sarah Gilbert who died 13th November 1865 aged 84 years. And of his eldest son Matthew Gilbert who departed this life 10th March 1866 aged 42 years. Also his son-in-law the Revd Samuel MATEER who died 30th July 1889 aged 69 years. "The memory of the just is blessed". Also his daughter Sarah, wife of the Revd Samuel Mateer, who died 2nd December 1910 aged 82 years. "He giveth his beloved sleep".

[The will of William Gilbert of Windsor Park, Belfast, gentleman, who died 19 September 1890 was proved at Belfast 13 October 1890 by Elizabeth Mathews of 25 Christ Church Road, Brondesbury, London (wife of the Rev. Dr Mathews), one of the surviving executors. Effects £10,882 18s.8d.

The will of the Reverend Samuel Mateer of Mossbank, Comber, county Down, Presbyterian minister, who died on 30 July 1889, was proved at Belfast 11 September 1889 by Sarah Mateer, widow, and Henry Mateer, farmer, both of Mossbank, Comber, and William Mateer of 7 Eglantine Avenue, Belfast, salesman, the executors. Effects £3,083 15s.7d.

Administration (with the will) of the estate of Sarah Mateer of Bessmount, Dundonald, county Down, widow, who died 2 December 1910 granted at Belfast 16 January 1911 to Henry Mateer, farmer. Effects £345 3s.8d.

William Gilbert was proprietor of William Gilbert & Son, a large firm of jewellers and watch-makers with premises at 15 High Street and 3 Donegall Square South.

Hugh Mack was a partner in McGonigal & Mack, wholesale haberdashers in High Street.

The Rev. Samuel Mateer was born in 1821, the son of Alexander

Mateer of Boardmills. He was educated at the Royal Belfast Academical Institution from 1838, obtaining the General Certificate in 1841, was licensed for Down in May 1846 and was Minister of Mourne Congregation from 1849 until he retired in 1881. He opened a classical school beside the church and scholars paid one penny a week. He married in 1854 Sarah Gilbert and died at Mossbank, Comber. See Fisher and Robb: *Royal Belfast Academical Institution, Centenary Volume*, 1810-1910 (1913); Bailie: *A History of Congregations* (1982); Barkley: *Fasti of the Presbyterian Church*, 1840-70 (1986).]

GILBERT

[Tablet in a large headstone, now lost.] Sacred to the memory of my beloved husband Edward Gilbert who died 7th March 1853 aged 38 years. Also our only son Edward Gilbert who died 27th March 1868 aged 16 years. And Eliza MAY, nee Gilbert who died on the 26th October 1895 aged 70 years.

[The will of Eliza May of Alexandra Park, Holywood, county Down widow, who died 26 October 1895, was proved at Belfast 4 December 1895 by George T. Armstrong of Windsor Park, Malone, county Antrim, esquire, the sole executor. Effects £1,582 7s.3d.

Edward Gilbert was a jeweller, watchmaker and silversmith at 43, High Street.]

GILBERT
See GIBBS

GILESPIE
See DUNLAP

GILL
[Laid flat.] Jemima Gill ob. Feb. 1887. Martha Gill, ob. Dec. 1876. Erected by Dr & Mrs BUSBY.

GILLESPIE
See CINNAMOND

GILLILAN

[Once surmounted by a floreated cross, now broken and flaking in Gothic characters.] Erected by his children in memory of their revered (and beloved) William (Gillilan) who died Jany Xth mdccclvii aged lxxix years, and Clara G(illil)and who died May xx (vii), mdccclxviii aged lxxxv years. Here also are interred (their) children, William who died Octr xviith mdcccxxxiii aged (xvi) years, John who died June xxth mdcccxlix aged xxix years, Hugh who died July xiith mdccclviii aged liii years. "God, forbid that I should Glory, save in .. the Cross of Our Lord Jesus Christ". Gal. xxv. "The dead shall be raised incorruptible, and (we) shall be changed". 1.Cor.xv(lii).

[William Gillilan was a linen merchant who lived in Wellington Place and had offices in the White Linen Hall.]

GILLILAND

[Polished granite.] Erected in memory of Joseph Gilliland, for five years

WILLIAM GILBERT,
JEWELLER, SILVERSMITH,
AND WATCHMAKER,
15 HIGH-STREET, BELFAST,

Importer of Geneva Watches, Clocks, Music-Boxes, Accordions, &c.

BEST LONDON MADE WATCHES.

Bardin's GLOBES.

Superior SHEFFIELD Plate,

FINEST STEEL RAZORS.

Optical, Mathematical,
AND
PHILOSOPHICAL INSTRUMENTS;
TABLE AND OTHER CUTLERY.

W. G. respectfully informs the Nobility, Gentry, and Inhabitants of the North of Ireland generally, that he has opened the above Concern with an assortment of Articles of FIRST-RATE QUALITY, and NEWEST FASHION, employing Workmen of Superior Talents, and sparing no expense to make his Establishment EQUAL to any in the Three Kingdoms. Having purchased his entire Stock for CASH, and being determined to sell for a MODERATE PROFIT, he respectfully solicits a share of Public Support.

Advertisement of William Gilbert (1805-1890), jeweller, etc., in the Belfast Post Office Directory for 1843.

a member of the Literary Staff of the Belfast News-letter, by the proprietor, his fellow journalists and other friends by whom he was beloved and respected. He died on December 28th 1878 in the twenty-first year of his age. "A life of promise cut short".

GILLILAND
See HARRISON and HOWARD

GILLIS
[Wall side grave in upper ground, but now missing.] Erected by Mary Jane EWART, of Belfast, in memory of her father James Gillis who died 29th May 1831 aged 56 years. Her mother Jane Ormiston Gillis who died 25th January 1846 aged 64 years. Her sister Eliza Gillis who died 29th August 1846 aged 24 years. Her sister Matilda MAHON who died 25th October 1850 aged 26 years. Her brother Hugh Gillis who died 11th December 1851 aged 30 years. Her nephew George James Mahon, son of above-named Matilda Mahon, who died 1st February 1852 aged 3 years and 3 months. Here also are interred the remains of the above Mary Jane Ewart, wife of Thos. Ewart, Belfast, who departed this life on the 2nd day of February 1861 aged 44 years.

[The will of Mary Jane Ewart alias Gillis of York Street, Belfast, county Antrim, who died 2 February 1861, was proved at Belfast 3 April 1861 by the oath of Thomas Ewart of Holywood in the county of Down, commission merchant, the husband and sole executor. Effects under £100.

Thomas Ewart was a Commission merchant and ship owner in York Street, and lived at 214 York Road at the time of his wife's death.]

GILMOR
[In upper ground and now missing. The plot was purchased by Joseph Gilmor in December 1805.] Erected by Joseph Gilmor, Belfast, in memory of his wife Agnes Gilmor, alias .... who departed this life the 16th of .... in the xxviiith year of her age .... Also three of his children. Likewise his son Andrew, a child.

GILMORE
[Marble headstone with surround in a low-railed enclosure.] Sacred to the memory of Charlotte, wife of Robert Gilmore, died Sept. 1864.

GILMORE
See GALWAY

GILPIN
[Slate tablet which may have belonged to broken headstone, now lost.] Here repose the remains of Thomas W. Gilpin, of Philadelphia, who died at Belfast, Consul of United States of America, 4th January 1848 aged 42 years. This simple tribute to his memory is raised by a few sorrowing friends.

GLENDINNING
[Small iron shield attached to north wall with a polished granite tablet above, and in high-railed enclosure.] The family burying place of Wm Glendinning, Belfast, 1833.

1833. Glendinning. The family burying ground of William Glendinning, died 1859, and his wife Mary Ann MARSHALL, died 1853, who rest here together with the following members of their family, the others being interred in various cemeteries throughout the Empire: Andrew died 1884. His wife Martha died 1892. Their daughter Margaretta died 1909, Jane died 1887. William M., died 1872. His wife Margaret died 1889. Their children, Charles B., died 1869, Annie died 1889, William died 1914. John died 1858. His wife Anna died 1888. George died 1860. Dorothea McKNIGHT died 1904. Her daughter Matilda died 1890.

[Although their burial place is ostentatious, the family appears to have been from a comparatively humble walk of life. William Glendinning (d.1859) was a clerk living in Lindsay's Place, off the Ormeau Road.]

GLENDINNING

[Tablet formerly attached to north wall of lower ground. No longer extant.] The family burial ground of William Glendinning and his wife Mary Ann Marshall who rest here with their family. George and Dorothea ...... and his wife, Martha William and his wife Margaret and their son William died 8th May 1914. John and his wife Ann.

GLENFIELD

See MILLIKEN

GORDON

[Very badly weathered headstone, now lost.] (Erected by) James (Gordon of Belfast in memory of his son William John Gordon who died 26th) March (1814) aged (2) years. (Sarah Jane) McCAVANA (died 6th Aug 1855 aged 8 months). Elizabeth McCavana (died 18th Feby) 1866 aged 2 years.

GORDON

[Flaking and now lost.] 1817. Erected by John Gordon. In loving memory of my dear husband John Gordon BEATTY, died (26) June 1891.

[Letters of administration of the personal estate of John Gordon Beatty of No. 22 Deramore Avenue, Belfast, book-keeper, who died 26 June 1891, were granted at Belfast 3 August 1891 to Charlotte Beatty of No. 22 Deramore Avenue, the widow. Effects £106 3s.

According to the Society's records, the inscription reads: "Erected by John Gordon in loving memory of John Gordon Beatty who departed this life June 26th 1891 aged 54 years". The plot was originally bought by John Gordon in 1837 and later transferred to John Gordon Beatty.]

GORDON

[Two iron plaques formerly on low-railing but now lost - Samuel Wilson looks of c.1850.] (a) John Gordon, 1828.

(b) The family burying ground of Samuel WILSON, Belfast

[Letters of administration of the personal estate of Samuel Wilson of Farranshane, county Antrim, formerly a farmer, who died 28 March 1873, were granted at the Principal Registry to Jane Wilson of Greenmount, North Queen Street, Belfast, the widow. Effects under £200.]

GORDON
See ANDERSON

GOURLEY
[In lower ground and no longer extant.] In memory of Elizabeth Gourley died 10th March 1879 aged 68 years. A faithful wife, a loving mother and a sincere friend. John A. KENNEDY, born 14th July 1869, died 12th February 1875 aged 5 years and 7 months.

GOWAN
[Polished granite headstone in railed enclosure with iron plaque, both now lost.] In loving memory of John Gowan, master mariner, who died 24th May 1852 aged 56 years. And of his wife Mary Gowan who died 23rd November 1872 aged 80 years. Also of their children: Alexander, Jane, Mary and William, who all died in childhood. And of James Gowan, master mariner, who died 18th May 1845 aged 64 years. And of Margaret Eliza Gowan, eldest daughter of the above John and Mary Gowan died 19th September 1908. Samuel H. Gowan departed this life 28th Octr 1912. Micah,VI.8. Also Mary Gowan, died 12th March 1924 aged 84 years. "The memory of the just is blessed".

[Iron plaque.] Erected by John Gowan, master mariner, Belfast, 1840.

[Probate of the will of Margaret Eliza Gowan of Ben Madigan, Alexandra Gardens, Belfast, spinster, who died 19 September 1908 were granted at Belfast 6 November 1908 to Samuel Hoy Gowan, gentleman, Mary Gowan, spinster and Henry Gowan, shipping agent. Effects £1,747 12s.4d.

Probate of the will with two codicils of Samuel Hoy Gowan, formerly of 9 Duncairn Terrace and late of Ben Madigan, Alexandra Gardens, Belfast, shipping agent (retired), who died 28 October 1912 were granted at Belfast, 13 January 1913 to Mary Gowan, spinster, Robert McFadden, merchant, and Nicholas Fitzsimmons, architect. Effects £5,694 14s.8d.

Mary Gowan of Ben Madigan, Alexandra Gardens, Belfast, spinster, died 12 March 1924. Probate granted at Belfast 2 June 1924 to Samuel Gowan, retired captain in the mercantile marine, James Tedford, shipping agent, John Cunningham McClung, retired managing director, and Alexander Stewart Merrick, solicitor. Effects £7,149 10s.6d.]

GOWDY
[Flaking badly.] Erected by James Gowdy, of Belfast, to the memory of his wife Mary who departed this life on the 14th July 1810 aged 3(3) years. Also two of his children. Also his son John who (de)parted this life on the 23rd January 1835 aged 33 years.

GOWDY
[Missing from lower ground. Copied from Society's Inscription Book.] The family burying place of James Gowdy, Rosemary St. 1852.

[James Gowdy was a bookseller and owned the Unitarian tract repository at 28, Rosemary Street.]

GOYER
[Modern small granite in cement floored enclosure.] Goyer, 1801.

[This plot was bought by William Goyer on 29th February 1801. He was a very early member of the Belfast Library and Society for Promoting Knowledge, now called the Linenhall Library.]

GRACEY
See MORRISON

GRAHAM
[Very worn and badly flaking sandstone formerly against north wall but now lost.] The burying ground of John Graham (who) died (11th) Oct. 1806. His (mother) Mary Graham (who died 7th Oct.) 1807. (His wife Mary DICK) who died (Jany 1808). His nephew Hugh CAIRD, who died .... 18.. (His sister Elizabeth Caird) ... died .... Her husband John Caird, (who) died 8th J(uly) 1837. Elizabeth THOMPSON, aunt of Jo(hn G)raham (who) died 2nd (Novr) 1837.

[Inscription Book states "and of John Graham" and not "aunt".]

GRAHAM
[Flaking headstone lying flat.] Erected by Robert Graham, of Belf(ast, in memory) of his daughter Jane who departed this life the 30th of September 181(3) aged 6 years. Also his his mother Jane Graham who departed this life the 18th of July 1814 aged 75 years. Also Robert Graham who died on the (..) of December 1827 aged 46 years.

GRAHAM
[Very worn and now lost.] .... Graham, merchant of High St, Belfast, to the memory of his son Robert Allen Graham, who departed this life 6th Decr 18(15), aged (3) years.

GRAHAM
[East side of tall obelisk of polished granite in low-railed enclosure.] The burying ground of Campbell Graham who died 30th June 1834 aged 56 years. Here also are buried: Dorothea Blair Graham, his daughter who died 22nd May 1812 aged 1 year and 9 months, Dorothea Blair Graham, his daughter who died 8th February 1821 aged 8 years and 6 months, Elizabeth Ogilvie Graham his daughter who died 26th February 1840 aged 24 years. Erected in filial remembrance by Ogilvie Blair Graham, Larchfield, Co. Down.

[West side.] Campbell Graham, junr who died 10th September 1851 aged 27 years. Helen Jemima OGILVIE, wife of Campbell Graham senr, who died 26th April 1852 aged 71 years. Dora Blair Graham their daughter who died 16th April 1862 aged 41 years.

[Campbell Graham, senr, was a wine and spirit merchant in Ann Street, and at the time of his death resided at Broomhill.]

GRAHAM
[Polished granite broken and laid flat in low-stone enclosure.] Erected by Ann KNOX, in loving memory of her father William Graham who died 18th June 1845 aged 77 years. Also her mother Ellen Graham died 10th October 1840 aged 77 years. Her brother and sister, Charles & Jane Graham. Her husband Robert Knox died 4th June 1860 aged

62 years. Her son Charles died 7th October 1855 aged 1 year. Her son Robert died 11th March 1866 aged 14 years. Her daughter Ann Jane Graham Knox died 7th December 1867 aged 18 years. Also her daughter Ellen Crawford Knox died 5th April 1890 aged 32 years. The above Ann Knox died 31st December 1890. Also her son William John died December 1905. And his wife Isabelle MENOWNE, died 8th November 1899. "They fell asleep in Jesus".

GRANT

[Horizontal slab, broken across the middle and now lost.] Sacred to the memory of Catharine Grant, wife of Alexander Grant, of Belfast, who departed this life April the 25th 1815 aged 34 years. Also three of her children ....., (Ca)tharine and H..e who died young.

GRANT

See SKILLEN

GRATTAN

[Worn marble in a large headstone in low railing but now lost.] Here lie interred the remains of Mary Grattan, died Dec. 15th 1832 aged 9 months. Harriet Grattan died Feb. 16th 1836 aged 7 years. John Grattan (PRING) died Feb. 28th 1855 aged 17 months. Harriet Grattan senr, died May 8th (1864) aged 7(6) years. John Grattan, died April 2(8)th 187(1) aged (70) years. Eliza (Caroline WILKINS) died 1st (October 1880) aged (86 years and 4 months). Mary (Shawe Grattan died (December 1st 1893) aged 5(8) years. (Anne Jane Grattan died November 24th 1898) aged (71 years. "There remaineth a rest to the people of God".)

[The will (with one codicil) of John Grattan of Belfast county Antrim, apothecary, who died 24 April 1871 at Coolgreaney, Fortwilliam Park near Belfast, was proved at Belfast, 21 July 1871 by the oaths of Anne Jane Grattan, spinster, the Rev. John Thomas Willis of Forest Hill, London, clerk and James White of Muckamore, flour miller, the executors. Effects under £12,000. Re-sworn at Belfast February 1872, Effects under £14,000.

The will of Mary Shawe Grattan of Coolgreaney, Belfast, spinster, who died 1 December 1893, was proved at Belfast 23 December 1893 by Anne Jane Grattan of Coolgreaney, Fortwilliam Park, spinster, the sole executrix. Effects £2,888 13s.4d.

Probate of the will of Anne Jane Grattan of Coolgreaney, Fortwilliam Park, Belfast, spinster, who died 24 November 1898, were granted at Belfast, 12 December 1898 to Bowman Malcolm of Antrim Road, engineer, Robert W. Murray of Fortwilliam Park and Charlotte de Castro Willis of Coolgreaney, spinster. Effects £6,305 14s.8d.

John Grattan founded Grattan & Company, the well-known chemists and apothecaries, and aerated water manufacturers. For many years their medical hall was in Corn Market and at the present day the business is in existence in University Road. He was President of the Belfast Literary Society in 1843. See *Belfast Literary Society 1801-1901* and Deane: *Belfast Natural History and Philosophical Society, Centenary Volume* (1924).]

The New Burying Ground

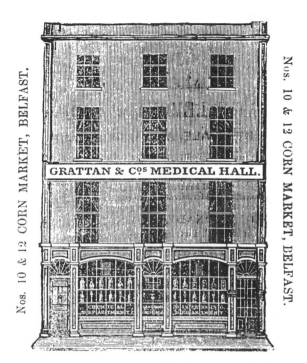

Un ler the personal superintendence of Mr. GRATTAN, and his Son-in-Law, Mr. R. W. PRING.

EMBRACES in its arrangements every medicinal preparation requisite for *dispensing*, as well as all those *auxiliary appliances* so essential to the comfort and convenience of the invalid; and continues to be watched over with the same unremitting care which has characterised it for the last *nine-and-twenty years*. Messrs. G. & Co., *by wholly abstaining from medical practice*, being enabled to devote their *undivided* attention to the sufficiently onerous and responsible duties of their *own profession*—duties which affect, and to no inconsiderable extent, the usefulness and reputation of the Physician, as well as the health and safety of the patient.

THE DRUG AND CHEMICAL DEPARTMENT

Is kept constantly supplied with medicines of the *freshest* and *purest* description.

THE SODA AND MINERAL WATER DEPARTMENT

Comprises the GENUINE MINERAL WATERS and CRYSTALLIZED MINERAL SALTS, direct from their respective Springs, as well as the various artificial AERATED WATERS in general demand.

PURE CHEMICALS, FOR PHOTOGRAPHIC PURPOSES.
VETERINARY PREPARATIONS, AND EVERY PATENT MEDICINE,

MUCH IN DEMAND, OR OF ESTABLISHED REPUTATION.

AGENTS FOR MR. JEFFREY'S RESPIRATOR.

An inimitably simple, complete, and scientific contrivance for protecting the lungs of delicate persons from the ill effects of our inclement and variable climate.

☞ The Public will please to observe, that every article sold by them bears the name of "GRATTAN & Co." on the label.

Full-page advertisement placed in the Belfast and Ulster Directory for 1854 by Grattan & Co. of Corn Market.

GRAY

[Flaking near the bottom and in low-railed enclosure.] Erected by William Gray, of Belfast, in memory of two of his children: viz, Maryann and Eliza. Also William who departed this life 23rd June 1827 in the 25 year of his age. Also Alexr Gray who died June 23rd 1840 aged 35 years. Also the aforesaid William Gray who died July 12th 1841 aged 79 years. And also on the 9th Decr 1846 in her 75th year Maria Gray, relict of the said William Gray, And also their son Robert Gray who died 13th February 1875 in the 81 year of his age. Anne Charters Gray, relict of last mentioned Robt Gray, died 9th April 18(84) aged 61 years. Maria Gray, olny (sic) daughter of Alexander and Jane Gray, died 4th February 1920.

[The will (with one codicil) of Robert Gray of 4 College Square East, Belfast, gentleman, who died 13 February 1875, was proved at Belfast 25 March 1875 by the oaths of Anne Charters Gray of 4 College Square East, widow, and John Patterson of Craighdarragh, Holywood, county Down, merchant, the executors. Effects under £6,000.

The will (with one codicil) of Anne Charters Gray of 3 College Square North, Belfast, widow, who died 9 April 1884 was proved at Belfast 29 August 1884 by Eleanor Greer, widow, one of the executors. Effects £8,041 13s.

The will of Maria Gray was probated at Belfast on the 26 March 1920 having died on 4 February 1920 at 5 University Square, Belfast, a spinster, aged 80, the sole remaining executor being William Henry Phillips of Craigower, Malone Road, Belfast, manufacturer. Effects £745 3s.10d.]

GRAY

[Broken tablet in entablature, formerly beside and identical to those of Charles Kelso's mother and James Dunlop, and secured to the dividing wall, now removed.] Erected by Charles KELSO, of Belfast, in memory of John Gray, of High Street, who died the 18th of November 1832, in the 68th year of his age.

GRAY

[Polished granite, formerly in low-stone enclosure, now lying flat.] Sacred to the memory of John Gray, died 5th Feb. 1860 aged 68 years. Sarah Gray his wife died 27th June 1860 aged 64 years. Robert Gray, their son died 28th April 1828 aged 11 months. Isabella Gray, their daughter died 13th May 1838 aged 9 years. John Caughey Gray their son, Assistant Surgeon, in the 44th Regiment of Foot, died of cholera, in Malta, 14th July 1850 aged 25 years. William Gray their son died 16th October 1854 aged 31 years, Agnes Gray, wife of the above died 28th October 1860 aged 37 years. Jane Gray, their daughter died 17th March 1852 aged 10 months. Agnes Gray their daughter died 14 June 1873 aged 19 years.

[The will of John Gray, of Castle Place, Belfast, county Antrim, watchmaker, who died 5 February 1860 at Belfast, was proved at Belfast 25 April 1860 by the oaths of Robert Gray of College Square East, gentleman, and William Hartley of the Castle, Belfast, accountant, and John

Patterson of Sydenham, county Down, the executors. Effects under £5,000. Resworn at Belfast October 1860 under £6,000.

John Gray and his son William were manufacturing jewellers, watchmakers and silversmiths at 18, Castle Place.]

GRAY
See GARDNER

(GREER)
[Badly flaked and now lost.]
The dew drop that falls tho' in silence it rolls,
Shall long keep her memory green in our soul(s).
Beneath this stone are shrouded the remains of Dorothy, wife of James (Greer) who died the 30th day of (Oct)ober ... 18(23) aged 54 years. To perpetuate the (remembrance of her fidelity and attachment to her husband, her ardous love and affectionate tenderness to her children this stone was erected by her son Henry Greer.)

GREER
[Small iron plate attached to railing with that of Eleanor Greer. Now missing.] The family burying ground of Henry Greer, bookseller, Belfast, 1840.

[Henry Greer founded the family firm in North Street about the year 1815. By the middle of the century, they were in High Street and had expanded considerably, being one of the leading booksellers and stationers of the town. They were also printers and publishers, with a high standard of workmanship. The firm remained in the Smithfield area until the 1970's at which time they removed to Bangor.]

GREER
[Entablature in a high-railed enclosure, now without tablet.] 1848. The family burying place of Henry Greer, King Street. [He was a book-binder.]

GREER
[Small marble plaque laid flat.] Eleanor, widow of the late Henry Greer, ob. 15 Dec. 18(9)0, AE. 90.

[The will (with one codicil) of Eleanor Greer of 3 College Square North, Belfast, widow, who died 15 December 1890 was proved at Belfast 2 February 1891 by Samuel Mackay McGee of 51 University Square, esquire, and James McGee of High Street, the executors. Effects £1,449 18s.7d.

GREGG
[Monument secured to west wall.] Sacred to the memory of John Gregg Esq., of Belfast, who departed this life on 26th Novr 1825 aged 72 years. "The memory of the just is blessed" Also of his beloved wife Martha Gregg who died 6th December 1834 aged 77 years. "Blessed are the dead who died in the Lord". Fortesque Gregg Esq., son of the above John Gregg who died 5th Sept. 1846 aged 58 years. Here lie also the bodies of his three children, Nathan who died 16th Feb. 1837 aged one month, Catherine Jane who died 16th June 1843 aged 3 years, Henry Robert Felix who died 16th Octr 1843 aged 3 days. Here also lie the remains of Miss Jane Gregg, daughter of the above John Gregg

Esq. who died 25th Novr 1852 aged 57 years.

[John Gregg was of a very old Belfast family and was the last Assistant Clerk to the Irish House of Lords. He was involved with several of the public bodies of the town and was one of the founders of the Belfast Library and Society for Promoting Knowledge. He was also an early Committee member. A wealthy merchant, he is reputed to have contributed £1,000 at a charity sermon preached in Rosemary Street Presbyterian Church in 1820. See Anderson: *History of the Belfast Library*... Belfast, 1888.

The family were partners in Gregg & Boyd's Vitriol Works near the site of the present-day Albert Bridge in Ballymacarret. About the year 1815 Fortesque Gregg started salt works near Bridge End in Ballymacarret.

So far as is known, this family was not related to that of Thomas Greg or his son Cunningham.]

GRIBBIN
See WIRLING

GRIFFITH

[Badly flaking.] I.H.S. Erected in memory of John Griffith who departed this (life 4th) July 1826 aged 54 years. Also in memory of three of his children who died in infancy. Also his wife Hannah who departed this life 7th Febry 1833 aged 49 years. And of her son Samuel Griffith who died 27th October 1834 aged 27 years.

GRIMSHAW

[Worn marble in large headstone, now lost.] The family burying place of C.B. Grimshaw. Conway B. Grimshaw, born (February 1789), died (11th December 1869). Mary his wife, born 1797, died Jan 1863. Osborne born (6th Sept 1821) died (February 1860). Henry Tif born 23rd March 1823 died (16th June 1848). Robert Conway born 5th Feby 1828 died (18th Jany 1847,......... Margaret Emma, born 5th (Feby. 1828) died 3rd December 18(3)9,. (Mary Osborne, born 1764, died 6th May 1846. Margaret Osborne (born 1788) .. died 20th March 1863. Mary Arabella Grimshaw, born 8th April 1826, died 2nd August 1852.

[The will of Conway Blizard Grimshaw of Sydenham, county Down, esquire, who died 18 December 1869, was proved at Belfast 4 February 1870 by the oaths of O'Donnell Grimshaw of Mertown Hall, county Down, and Nicholas William Grimshaw of Cloona, county Antrim, merchants, the executors. Effects under £16,000.

This stone and the next commemorate the family which was in partnership with J. Murphy & Co., flax-spinners at Linfield Mill. Conway B. Grimshaw who assisted in building the mill, lived in Linfield House nearby. Later he lived in Sydenham House.

It was their ancestor, Nicholas Grimshaw (1748-1805), a Lancashire man, who together with Robert Joy introduced the manufacture of cotton to this country, the first looms being in the old Poor House, now Clifton House. That was in about 1778. He built Longwood, Whitehouse, as well as improving the village and building the original cotton mills there. He had a family of seven sons and two daughters, one of whom was the mother of Edmund Getty, the noted antiquarian and an outstanding Ballast Master of Belfast Harbour. One of Nicholas's grandsons, James, married into the Templeton family of Malone.

Robert Grimshaw formed a partnership with William Murphy who married his sister, and as the firm of Grimshaw and Murphy they provided the requirements of cotton-spinners. The building of Linfield Mill came a little later, in the 1850s. See Benn: *A History of the Town of Belfast*, Vol II (1880). Strain: *Belfast and its Charitable Society* (1961).]

GRIMSHAW

[Shield-shaped tablet formerly in enclosure with C.B. Grimshaw's stone, but now lost.] Ella Osborne Grimshaw, born 1st February 1863, died 23rd August 1863. Ramsey Newsam Grimshaw, born 5th September 1866, died 11th August 1867, children of Nicholas W. Grimshaw. "Of such is the Kingdom of Heaven".

GRIMSHAW

See GARRETT

GROGAN

[Altar-tomb, inscribed on south panel only] In memory of John Grogan who died 7th October 1832 aged 64. Jane his wife, who died 7th October 1852 aged 72. And of their children: Edward who died 5th October 1847 aged 24, John who died 17th August 18(5)2 aged 49, Eliza who died 29th (October 1855.) aged 39, William who died 10th (January 1873) aged (71).

[The will of William Grogan of Wellington Place and late of 15 Mount Charles, Belfast, county Antrim, merchant, who died 10 January 1873 was proved at Belfast 16 January 1873 by the oaths of Alexander Brice Grogan of corner of Sansome and Jackson Streets, San Francisco, California, merchant and Foster Connor of the Linen Hall Belfast, merchant, the executors. Effects in U.K. under £18,000.

The Grogan family were linen merchants, John senr. living at Glenbank, Ballygomartin. William lived in Wellington Place, then later at Mount Charles and was a linen merchant with the firm of S.G. Fenton & Co., whose offices were in the White Linen Hall.]

GUNNING

See GELSTON

GUTHRIE

[Marble tablet in surround, formerly attached to south wall but now lost.] In memory of Anne Hunter, second daughter of James Guthrie Esq., of Belfast, died July 7th 1854 aged 16 years. And of James Guthrie, for many years Town Clerk of Belfast, died at Rostrevor, April 21st 1878 aged 80 years. And of Jane his wife who died 26th December 1882 aged 83 years. And of James, their eldest son who died 19th August 1877, and was interred at Southend. Jane their eldest daughter died 10th March 1895. Charity, sister of James Guthrie, died 31st March 1887. "Them that sleep in Jesus will God bring with him".

[The will of James Guthrie of 10 University Square, Belfast, town clerk of the borough of Belfast, who died 21 April 1878 at Rostrevor, county Down, was proved at Belfast 31 May 1878 by the oath of Jane Guthrie of 10 University Square, Belfast, widow, the executrix. Effects under £4,000.

The will of Jane Guthrie, formerly of 10 University Square, Belfast, and late of Wilmont Terrace, widow, who died 26 December 1882, was proved at Belfast 5 February 1883 by Jane Guthrie of 9 Wilmore Terrace, Belfast, spinster, the sole executrix. Effects £84 13s.11d.

Probate of the will of Jane Guthrie of Belfast and late of 22 Belgrave Road, Rathmines, county Dublin, spinster, who died 10 March 1895, was granted at Belfast 27 April 1895 to John F. O. Guthrie of 22 Belgrave Road, piano tuner and Alpin J. Guthrie of 82 Eglantine Avenue, Belfast, mercantile assistant. Effects £3,201 9s.1d.]

HAINEN

[Broken fragments.] Sacred to the memory of Hugh Hainen who departed this life Octr. 11th A.D. 1806, aged 54 years. Also lieth here four of his grandchildren. Likewise Thoebe [sic] Hainen died 27th Nov. 1841 aged 70. And William Hainen died 27th Jan. 1847 aged 71.

HALIDAY

[Twin bulging marble tablets in large carved and pedimented entablature secured to south wall in low-stone enclosure. Arms: Crescent and sword in chief, with two crossed maces. Crest: Boar's head on wreath.] The family burial place of Robert Haliday, Belfast.

Sacred to the memory of Robert Haliday who died 26th April 1838 aged 63 years. Also Anne Haliday his wife who died 15th November 1852 aged 70 years. Likewise his son Robert Haliday who died 17th Novr 1856 aged 34 years.

[Second tablet now lost.] Sacred to the memory of Johnson Haliday who died 26th September 1853 aged 32 years. Also his son John Henry Haliday who died 12th September 1873 aged 23 years. Also his son Lascelles Rogers Haliday who died at Auckland, New Zealand, 27th May 1875 aged 24 years. Also his son Robert Haliday who died at Tamworth, Australia, 1879 aged 33 years. Also his wife Elizabeth Haliday, who died 3rd April 1894 aged 66 years.

[The will of John Henry Haliday of Strawberry Hill, near Lisburn, county Down, gentlemen, who died 12 September 1873 at same place, was proved at Belfast on the 17 November 1873 by the oath of George Haliday of Strawberry Hill, near Lisburn aforesaid, farmer the sole executor. Effects under £450.

The will of Lascelles Rodgers Haliday of Strawberry Hill near Lisburn, county Down in Ireland, and of the Hermitage Grafton Road, Auckland in New Zealand, gentleman, who died 27 May 1875 at Auckland, was proved at the Principal Registry on the 26 April 1876 by the oaths of George Haliday of Strawberry Hill gentleman, the brother, and Samuel Vance of Belfast, county Antrim, secretary to the Chamber of Commerce, the executors. Effects under £1,000.

The Haliday vault before its destruction (photograph R.W.M. Strain).

The famous Dr Alexander Henry Haliday (1727-1802) and his nephew Dr William Haliday were of this family and are buried in an unnamed vault nearby. Dr Alexander Haliday, the son of the Rev. Samuel Haliday of the First Presbyterian Church, Rosemary Street, was the most distinguished physician in Ulster for much of the latter part of the eighteenth century. He played a key role in bringing peace when the Hearts of Steel attacked the barracks in Belfast in 1770, and later he joined the Volunteer movement. A man of keen literary tastes, he was the first President of the Belfast Library and Society for Promoting Knowledge. He was also closely connected with the Belfast Charitable Society.

Dr William Haliday was also connected with the Belfast Charitable Society and was an early President of the Belfast Medical Society. Like his uncle, he was of a strong literary disposition.

Robert Haliday was a woollen draper and haberdasher at 2, Donegall Street.

See Strain: *Belfast and its Charitable Society* (1961); Benn: *A History of the Town of Belfast*, Vol. I (1877).]

HALL

[Laid flat.] I.H.S. Erected by Joseph Hall in memory of his wife Rebecca who departed this life on the 24th of April 1821 aged 32 years. Also three of their children viz| Judith, on the 22nd of May 1819 aged 7 years, and two in infancy. Likewise Judith aged 5 months. Also the above named Joseph Hall who died 1st Oct 1825 aged 46 years.

HALL

[Polished granite in low-railed enclosure.] In memory of Henry Hall who died 30th January 1830, Also of his wife Sarah. "For ever with the Lord". In loving memory of Maria Hall, born May 12th 1823, died May 4th 1891. Also of her husband Henry, son of the above Henry Hall, born January 21st 1821, died April 11th 1892. "The salvation of the righteous is of the Lord. He is their strength in the time of trouble".

[Letters of administration of the personal estate of Maria Hall of 99 South Parade, Ormeau Road, Belfast, who died 4 May 1891 at same place, were granted at Belfast on the 25 May 1891 to Henry Hall of 99 South Parade, gentleman, the husband. Effects £247 10s.

The will of Henry Hall of 99 South Parade, Ormeau Road, Belfast, gentleman, who died 11 April 1892 at same place, was proved at Belfast on the 24 October 1892 by Mary Grace Davis of Saint Jude's Avenue, Ballynafeigh, county Down (wife of the Reverend W. H. Davis), the sole executrix. Effects £150.]

HALL

[Small and worn sandstone cube, formerly surmounted by an urn.] Sacred to the memory of Sarah Hall, obit April 17th 18(4.).

HALL

[Large headstone, formerly in lower ground and now missing.] Erected by George Hall of Belfast to the memory of his beloved wife Margaret

Hall who departed this life the 28th of June 1847 aged 60 years. Also John Hall died 23rd August 1853 aged 41 years. The above George Hall died 7th February 1857 aged 69 years. "Them also which sleep in Jesus, will God bring with Him". Sarah, beloved wife of James Hall died 17th June 1894 aged 63 years. "Thy Will be done". James, husband of Sarah Hall, died 20th Feby 1897 aged 72 years. Francis, grandson of James and Sarah Hall, died 6th Jany 1900 aged 40 years. "Severed only till He come". Dedicated by James Hall.

[Administration of the estate of James Hall of 52 Bentinck Street, Belfast, stone mason, who died 20 February 1897, granted at Belfast on the 19 March 1897 to Francis Hall of 52 Bentinck Street, compositor, the son. Effects £215.]

HALL

[Laid flat.] Family burying ground of George and James Hall. [The ground was bought by George Hall in June 1847.]

HALL

See HILL

HALLIDAY

[Worn marble tablet formerly secured to dividing wall but now lost.] Sacred to the memory of Maxwell Halliday died 6th Octr 1829 aged (57) years. Also his (wife) Elizabeth died (10th March 1842) aged (67) years. (Also their eldest son James died 2nd Jan. 1843 aged 36 years.)

[Maxwell Halliday was proprietor of the "Coach and Horses" public house at 26 Cornmrket.]

HALLIDAY

[Tablet in carved entablature, bearing draped urn, in high-railed enclosure and secured to dividing wall.] Erected to the memory of Hugh Halliday, merchant of Belfast, died 10th April 1852 aged 56 years. Died also his wife Ellen Halliday at Bangor, on the 14th day of November 1860 aged 38 years. Also their son John Halliday, M.I.C.E., Engineer-in-Chief to Melbourne Harbour Trust, until his death 16th July 1912 aged 61 years. And their daughter Mary, widow of John DENBIGH, of Leeds, died in New York, 29th April 1916 aged 70 years.

[Hugh Halliday was a flour merchant of York Street and and was elected one of the first Town Councillors of the re-formed Belfast Corporation in 1842, representing Dock Ward. He purchased the plot in December 1840.]

HALLIDAY

See McFADDEN

HAMILTON

[Polished granite headstone against north wall.] Sacred to the memory of Mary Hamilton wife of Hill Hamilton, Sen. died 19th September 1820. The above named Hill Hamilton died 16th December 1832. Mary HARDY, their daughter, the wife of Isaac Hardy, died 28th January 1836, Elizabeth Hamilton, their daughter died 4th January 1869. Hill

Hamilton, their son, died 31st May 1872. Margaret BARRETT, their grand-daughter, died 28th June 1886, Ellen Hamilton, their daughter, died 8th April 1887. Mary Barrett, their grand-daughter, died 29th May 1887. The burial place of Hill Hamilton, of Mountvernon.

[Letters of administration of the personal estate of Elizabeth Hamilton of Mountvernon, Belfast, county Antrim, spinster, who died 5 January 1869 at same place, were granted at Belfast on the 22 February 1869 to Hill Hamilton of Mountvernon, Belfast aforesaid, esquire, the brother and one of the next of kin of said deceased. Effects under £5,000.

Letters of administration of the personal estate of Hill Hamilton of Mountvernon, Belfast, county Antrim, esquire, a bachelor, who died 31 May 1872 at same place, were granted at Belfast on the 1 July 1872 to Ellen Hamilton of Mountvernon, Belfast aforesaid, spinster, a sister and one of the next of kin of said deceased. (Deceased died domiciled in Ireland). Effects in U.K. under £250,000.

The will with one codicil of Margaret Barrett, formerly of Stirling, Scotland, and of Mountvernon near Belfast, spinster, who died 28 June 1886 at same place, was proved at Belfast on the 16 August 1886 by Mary Barrett of Mountvernon, near Belfast, spinster, one of the executors. Effects £17,785 7s.1d.

The will with two codicils of Ellen Hamilton of Mountvernon, county Antrim, spinster, who died 8 April 1887 at same place, was proved at Belfast on the 6 May 1887 by John Coates of Bangor, county Down, esquire, and Richard Ross of Wellington Place, Belfast, M.D., the surviving executors. Effects £6,719 1s.8d.

The will with one codicil of Mary Barrett of Mountvernon, county Antrim, spinster, who died 29 May 1887 at Glenageary, county Dublin, was proved at Belfast on 22 June 1887 by Jessie Barrett of Eglinton Crescent, Edinburgh, widow and John Campbell White of Crosslett, Dumbarton, esquire, both in Scotland, the executors. Effects £15,442 1s.7d.

Hill Hamilton, senr. began his career as a hawker, peddling small items from a basket in Smithfield. He succeeded in attracting customers and soon progressed to a haberdashery stall and then to a warehouse. From this he turned his attention to property and became the owner of many streets and alleys. The fortune so amassed enabled the family to move out to Mount Vernon on the Shore Road.

It is said that his son Hill Hamilton, junr. received £7,000 per annum in house rents.]

HAMILTON
[Pedimented entablature, with carving of inverted torches, bearing broken marble tablet, secured to south wall.] Erected by John Hamilton, Hamilton Place, Belfast. Beneath are interred the mortal remains of his beloved wife Jane Hamilton who died 22nd July 1838 aged 68 years. Also the above named John Hamilton, who died 5th October 1851 aged 91 years.

HAMILTON
[Very worn marble in ornate headstone, and nearly all copied from

Society's Inscription book, now removed.] Erected by Richard Hamilton to) the (memory of his beloved wife Eliza who died 24th Decr 1849 aged 25 years. Also their son Richard who died 23rd October 1852 aged 4 years. Also his mother Mary Hamilton, who died 20th Decr 1860 aged 65 years. Also the) above (named Richard Hamilton died Dec. 15th 1891 aged 74 years. "Blessed are the dead who die in the Lord".

HAMILTON
[Large marble monument in low-railed enclosure.] Sacred to the memory of Rev. David Hamilton, for 10 years the faithful Minister of Connor, for 20 years the beloved Pastor of the York St., Presbyterian Church, Belfast, who died on the 13th Jan. 1860 aged 54 years. "The memory of the just is blessed". Also his children Thomas, who died 23rd December 1840, aged 1 year, David who died 21st October 1851 aged 5 months, Margaret Henry, who died 29th March 1854 aged 15 years. Henry Henry who died 17th May 1854 aged 17 years. Jane WEIR, who died 18th October 1861 aged 25 years. And his wife Eliza Weir who died 16th October 1881. Also Solomon DAN a Prussian, the first fruit of the Irish Assembly's Jewish Mission at Bonn, who died 20th November 1856 aged 26 years. William Weir Hamilton M.A., L.L.D., died 26th February 1913 aged 67 years. Annie Hamilton who died 8th January 1924. Erected by the members of the York St Presbyterian Church.

[Letters of administration of the personal estate of the Rev. David Hamilton of Belfast in the county of Antrim, Presbyterian Minister, who died 13 January 1860 at same place, were granted at Belfast on the 2 April 1860 to Eliza Hamilton of Belfast aforesaid, the widow of said deceased. Effects under £1,500.

Letters of administration of the personal estate of Eliza Weir Hamilton of Belfast, widow, died 16 October 1881 at same place, were granted at Belfast on the 14 November 1881 to the Reverend Thomas Hamilton of Brookvale House, Cliftonville, Belfast, Presbyterian Minister, a child. Effects £1,647 5s.6d.

Administration of the estate of the Reverend William Weir Hamilton of 15 Rutland Street Belfast clergymen (retired) who died 25 February 1913, granted at Belfast on the 9 April 1913 to Thomas Hamilton, Vice-Chancellor. Effects £1,331 13s.3d. Re-sworn £1,456 15s.3d.

The Rev. David Hamilton was born on 22 April 1805, son of Thomas Hamilton, farmer, of Upper Ballykine, Ballynahinch. He was educated at the Old College, Belfast, obtaining the General Certificate in 1835. He was licensed by the Dromore Presbytery in 1829 [sic] and ordained Presbyterian Minister of Connor in September 1829. He resigned in 1840 and was Minister of York Street, Belfast from 1840 until his death. He was Moderator of the General Assembly 1854-55. He married Elizabeth Weir, daughter of Henry Weir of Banbridge and had, as well as four children mentioned above, three sons:

    1. The Rev. Thomas Hamilton was born on 28 August 1842, was minister of York Street Presbyterian Church, Belfast and eventually President and Vice-Chancellor of Queen's University. He died on 18

May 1925.

2. The Rev. David Hamilton went as a missionary to New Zealand in 1871 and died of exposure in Manukan Forest in 1873.

3. The Rev. William Weir Hamilton was educated at Queen's College, Belfast and the Assembly's College, graduating M.A. in 1869, LL.B. in 1871 and LL.D. in 1882. He was licenced in 1872 and was minister of Shore Street, Donaghadee 1876-93.

See McConnell: *Fasti of the Irish Presbyterian Church* (1951); Barkley: *Fasti of the General Assembly*, 1871-90 (1987).

HAMILTON
[No longer to be seen.] The burying place of Hugh Hamilton, Belfast, 1853.

HA(MILTON)?
[Very badly worn tablet of c.1880 formerly attached to north wall, but now removed.] .... by Robert (Hamilton) ..... his wife and family.

HAMILTON
See LENNOX, LINDSAY, MOORE and THOMPSON

HANLON
See MOORE

HANNA
[Twin polished granite tablets in large monument bearing words: "The family burial place of the (Rev Dr Hanna)", secured to dividing wall and in low-stone enclosure.] Sacred to the memory of the Rev. Dr Hanna who died April 1852, and of Martha his wife who died 1860. And of their children: Martha, Matilda, Robert and John. Also of Eliza DENHAM, wife of the Rev. Dr. Denham.

[Broken and laid flat.] Sacred to the memory of Murray SUFFERN, son-in-law of the Rev. Dr Hanna, who died 8th Decr 1864 aged 74 years. "Mark the perfect man and behold his ways, for the end of that man is peace". And of Jane Hanna, widow of Murray Suffern who died 16th Novr 1868 aged 66 years. "Whosoever liveth and believeth in Me shall never die".

[The will (with one codicil) of Murray Suffern of Howard Street, Belfast, in the county of Antrim, esquire, who died 8 December 1864 at same place, was proved at Belfast on the 11 January 1865 by the oath of Reverend James Denham of the city and county of Londonderry, Doctor of Divinity, and Reverend William Hanna of the city of Edinburgh in Scotland, Doctor of Laws, the executors. Effects under £18,000.

The Rev. Samuel Hanna was born in 1771, 5th son of Robert Hanna, merchant, of Kellswater. He entered Glasgow University in 1784, graduating M.A. in 1789 and D.D. in 1818. He was licensed in 1790, was minister of Drumbo 1795-99 and of Rosemary Street 1799-1852. He was Professor of Divinity for the Synod of Ulster 1817-40 at the Royal Belfast Academical Institution and for the General Assembly 1840-52,

Moderator of the General Synod 1809-10 and first Moderator of the General Assembly 1840-1. He married in 1800 Martha, daughter of Robert Gemmil (q.v.), cotton manufacturer. He purchased the two plots

Portrait of Hill Hamilton, Junior, (died 1872) (photograph P.R.O.N.I.).

here in August 1830 and December 1831 and died on 20 or 23 April 1852 in Londonderry. As well as the above children he had a son, the Rev. William Hanna, M.A., LL.D. and D.D. who was minister in Scotland. See Addison: *The Matriculation Albums of the University of Glasgow* (1913); McConnell: *Fasti of the Irish Presbyterian Church* (1951).

Murray Suffern was a merchant and gentleman and lived at 2, Howard Street.]

HANNA
[Corroded iron shield.] The family burying place of Samuel Hanna, Belfast, 18(53).

HANNA
[Formerly in lower ground and now missing.] The family burying ground of Hugh Hanna, C.E., Belfast, 1854.

HANNA
[Now removed.] Erected by Sarah Hanna in memory of her son Henry who died 10th October 1903 aged 30 years. Also of a grandson who died in infancy. Also our dear mother, the above named Sarah Hanna who died 1st July 1921. "In God's Keeping".

HANNA
See BOYD

HANNAN
Erected by Anthony Hannan in memory of his wife Ann Hannan who departed this life on the 13th of January 1836 aged 67 years. Also his son Robert B. Hannan who died 29th Sept 1840 aged 7 months. Also the above named Anthony Hannan who departed this life 9th January 1843 aged 69 years. Also two of his children Mary and Anne who died in infancy.

HANNAY
[Three marble tablets, two of which had largely disintegrated, in a neo-Gothic castellated entablature secured to west wall. All have now gone. Arms: Three horses' heads in chief. Crest: wreath with crescent and surmounted by cross. Motto: "Per ardua ad alta". Portions in brackets copied from Inscription Book.]

(a) Sacred to the memory of Nancy, daughter of Robert H. Hannay, of Belfast who (died 4th April 1840 aged 3 months.)

(b) (Sacred to the memory of James Hannay who departed this life on the 18th May 1823 aged 43) years. (Also his wife Mary who departed this life the 24th) January (1840 aged 56 years. And their son Hugh Haliday) Hannay (who died 9th September) 1873 (aged 67 years. Also his children: Robert Haliday) Hannay (who died on the 12th July) 1847 (aged 4 months. And Margaret Anne) Hannay (who died on the 24 May) 1856 (aged 4 years. Campbell Hannay died at New York on the 18th July) 1892 (aged 48 years. Agnes CAMPBELL, wife of Hugh Haliday Hannay who died at Newton Stewart N.B. on 23rd) April 1904 (aged 79 years), George Ha(nnay) eldest son of the above James Hannay, died 6th August 1854. George Haliday Hannay the elder son of George Hannay, died 31st

March 1866. Also the younger son John Young Hannay, died 23rd November 1879.

(c) Sacred to the memory of Elizabeth wife of John Hannay, of Belfast, who departed this life on the 22nd of March 1841 aged 28 years. Likewise Nancy their daughter who departed this life on the 24th April 1841 aged 11 months. John Hannay died 31st January 1847 aged 38 years.

[Inscription at base of entablature.] (The) burying ground (of James) Hannay, late of Bangor.

[Hugh Haliday Hannay was the owner of a wholesale woollen and haberdashery warehouse in Donegall Street and at one time lived in Haliday's Buildings, York Street. His brother George was a broker in York Street.]

HANSON
See ECCLES

HARDCASTLE
See FERGUSON

HARDING
See EWART

HARDY

[Twin tablets in entablature formerly secured to north wall. There are now only scattered fragments left.] Erected by Freeman Hardy, of Belfast, in memory of his beloved child Sarah Anne who departed this life Jan. 23rd 1828 aged 2 years. The above Freeman Hardy died 22nd March 1863 aged 64 years. And his beloved wife Mary who died on the 11th Novr 1866 aged 64 years. "The memory of the just is blessed". Freeman B. Hardy, nephew of Thomas and Freeman Hardy, born 1 January 1818, died 26th July 1851. Also Gardiner Hardy, son of the above Freeman and Mary Hardy, died June the 8th 1909. [contd. on slate plaque.] Also Cordelia Hardy, 4th daughter of the above Freeman and Mary Hardy, died 14th November 1926 in her 92nd year.

Erected by Thos Hardy, of Belfast, in memory of Thomas his son who died an infant, January 1829, Also Sarah his daughter who departed this life the 10th Decr 1831 AE 10 years and 5 months. Also Anne his beloved wife who departed this life June 4th 1836 aged 42 years. The above Thomas Hardy who died 19th March 1877 aged 84 years.

[The will of Mary Hardy of Mount Pottinger, county Antrim, widow, who died 11 November 1866 at same place, was proved at the Principal Registry on the 3 January 1867 by the oath of John Gardiner of Lemington Priars, Warwickshire, gentlemen, the sole executor. Effects under £600.

Probate of the will of Gardiner Hardy of 5 Wellington Park, Belfast, commission agent, who died 8 June 1909 at Ballyholme, Bangor, county Down, granted at Belfast 13 August 1909 to Cordelia Hardy, spinster. Effects £831 0s.11d.

Cordelia Hardy of 5 Wellington Park, Belfast, spinster, died 14 November 1926. Probate Belfast 14 January 1927 to Robert Maitland

Beath M.D. Effects £42 16s.3d.

Thomas and Freeman Hardy were proprietors of a large and well-known firm of woollendrapers, haberdashers and house furnishers at 33-37 High Street for many years. After about 1850, the firm continued under Thomas Hardy.]

HARDY
See HAMILTON and PRETTY

HARKNESS
[Undated iron shield in low-railing of c.1850.] The burying ground of James Harkness.

HARPER
[Marble tablet formerly secured to east wall of upper graveyard. Only the top survives.] The burying ground of James Harper, of Belfast, builder. Sacred to the memory of his wife Elizabeth, who died 6th June 1799 aged 41 years, whose remains moulders at the Knock. Also the above James Harper, who died 31st Decr.1820 aged 80 years. Here also lieth the remains of four of their children viz; James Harper, who died 19th April 1821 aged 29 years. William Harper who died 12th Decr. 1826 aged 36 years. Hugh Harper, who died 16th January 1837 aged 43 years. John Harper, who died 4th Decr. 1838 aged 50 years. Also Margaret CLARK, wife of John Harper, who died 17th Novr. 1870 aged 69 years. And Mary, wife of Hugh Harper, who died 11th Sept. 1871 aged 76 years.

[In street directories of the 1800s, James Harper is described as a master joiner of Mill Street, which thoroughfare now forms part of Castle Street.]

HARPER
[Very badly weathered, sandstone, now lost.] Erected (by) William (H)arper in memory of his ... father William H(arp)er who died 27th (August) (1853) aged (52) years. Also (his brother) Henry COOKE (Harper) who died at (Calcutta) .... March 17th 18(57) aged (15 years). Also his sister Charlotte McSORLY who died (6)th April 1877 aged (3)7 years.

HARPER
See PRICE

HARRISON
[Broken in two and very badly weathered, now lost.] Erected (to the memory of Letitia Ireland Harris)on, daugh(ter of George Harri)son senr. who di(ed 18th June 1833 aged 2 years.) Also his d(aughter Leah Harrison) who died 11th (January 18)39 aged 19 years. Also Jane Eliza (Harrison his beloved wife died 31st (May) 1839 (aged 44 year)s. (His son George Harrison junr who died Sep. 29th 1849 aged 23 years. The) above-named George Harrison senr died) 10th Nov 1855 aged (65) years. Edward Harrison, brother of the above named George (Harrison) who died in 1862 aged 78 years. George Harrison GILLILAND, (grand)son of the above named George Harrison who died 1st December 1887 aged 20 years.

[George Harrison, senr, was a well-known stationer and book-binder in

Pottinger's Entry. He died at his residence in Holywood.]

HARRISON
[Laid flat.] Here lieth the remains of Susannah Harrison, who departed this life 20th December 1842 aged 83 years. Died 30th Octr 1852, Susannah, 9th June 1858, Judith, 11th May 1861, Mary. Also Anne Harrison who died 2nd January 1876.

HARRISON
[Worn tablet in headstone, now lost.] Erected by Margaret Harrison, widow of the late Francis Harrison, Dublin, in memory of her beloved Francis Harrison who departed this life April (30th 1849) aged 24 years. Also her beloved daughter Mary Ann Harrison who departed this life February (22nd 1853). And also to the memory of the above Margaret Harrison who departed this life May 16th (1869) aged 69 years. [sic].

HART
[Polished granite tablet, now loose from monument.] Joseph Hart died 24th November 1874 aged 81 years.

[He owned a music and piano shop at 14 Castle Place, and in the 1870s the firm became Hart & Churchill, one of the best known music shops in Belfast.]

HART
[Missing. Robert Hart bought this plot in May 1830.] Erected by Robert Hart of Belfast.

HART
See JOHNSTON

HARVEY
See CAIRNS

HASLETT
[Very worn horizontal slab, now lost.] Erected to the memory of (Mary), wife of Alexander Haslett, (of Belfast) (merchant) who departed this life May 30th 18(19) aged (58) years. Also the said Alexander Haslett, (who) died on the (26)th May 18(28) aged (59) years.

HASTINGS
[Three tablets in entablature formerly in a high-railed enclosure, but now lost.] Erected by William Hastings, MDCCCLX.

(a) William Hastings died (1st) January 18(3)1 aged (53) years. Elizabeth YOUNG his wife died 3rd January 1847 aged 6(9) years. His children: Margaret died (..)th March 1812 aged (1) year, William died 10th June 1813 aged (..) months, Joseph died 12th January 1840 aged (34) years, Isabella died 26th December 1849 aged 32 years, Elizabeth died 31st August 1880 aged 61 years.

(b) Ebenezer Hastings died at Fort George, N.B., 25th January 1860 aged (53) years, and is interred here. Deborah HOLDEN, wife of Ebenezer Hastings, died 2nd April 1876. Martha HILLYARD, sister of Deborah Hastings, died 25th December 1868. Their daughter Elizabeth

Jane Hastings, died 22nd July 1925 aged 79 years.

(c) Eliza Hall Hastings, died 20th April 1860 aged 13 months.

[Letters of administration of the personal estate of Deborah Holden, otherwise Hastings, who died 25 January 1860. Grant Scotch Intestate herein from Commissary Court of Inverness dated 30 April 1860. Re-sealed at Principal Registry Dublin 24 May 1860 (compared copy lodged same day). Effects under £1,727 5s.

William Hastings was an architect and lived in Academy Street.]

HAUGHTON

[This stone was formerly in the upper portion of the graveyard, but has now disappeared.] Helena Haughton died 3rd February 1879 aged 74 years.

HAVEN

[In upper ground and no longer extant.] Sacred to the memory of Margery Haven, wife of William Haven Esqr., of Belfast, who departed this life in January 1807 aged 70 years. Also to that of Catherine ...... who departed this life January 1821 aged 80 years. Also to that of Grace Haven, daughter of Margery and William Haven who departed this life June .... aged 66 years. Also to that of Arminella Haven, daughter of Margery and William Haven who departed this life on 17th December .... aged 71 years.

HAY

See GIBBS and McCLEERY

HEATHER

[Slightly flaking.] In memory of George Heather who departed this life 21st of January 1820 aged 22 years. Also his father Edward Heather who departed this life 23rd of July 1823 aged 51 years. Sarah, relict of the late Edward Heather who departed this life 27th Feby 1834 aged 62 years.

HENDERSON

Here lieth the remains of Mrs Grizzele ["izz" in rectangle] Henderson aged 77 years, relict of Jno Henderson of Belfast, merchant, who departed this life 2 July 1815.

HENDERSON

[Polished granite tablet secured to east wall in high-railed enclosure.] The burying place of Robert Henderson, Belfast. James Kennedy, his infant son died 27th Feby 1840 aged 10 months. Elizabeth Salmon his second daughter died 25th June 1844 aged 3 yers and 7 months. Minnie Kennedy died 17th Jany 1874 aged 5 weeks, Charlotte Kennedy, died 4th Feby 1874 aged 7 weeks, infant twin daughters of Robert Henderson.

[Robert Henderson was a corn factor and shipping agent for the Fleetwood, Isle of Man, Whitehaven and Stranraer steamers, with offices on Donegall Quay.]

HENDERSON

[Flaking near the bottom.] The burial place of W.D. Henderson. In memory of Sophia PORTER, his wife who died the 22nd of April 1853 aged 54 years. Jane, his daughter wife of the Rev. Joseph WOOD, (died ..) August 14th

1856 aged 23 years. Also of the above named W.D. Henderson (who died 26th July 1864 aged 66 years. Also of his son W.D. Henderson who died March 13th 1882 aged 4)5 years. (And of his daughter Anna Sophia Henderson who died on the 18th November 1895.)

[Letters of administration of the personal estate of William Dickey Henderson of Belfast, merchant, who died 13 March 1882 at London, were granted at Belfast on the 6 April 1882 to James Porter Henderson of Cheltenham, county Gloucester, in England, merchant, the brother. Effects £12,034 17s.7d.

The will (with one codicil) of Anna Sophia Henderson of 1 Castleton Terrace, Bangor, county Down, spinster, who died 18 November 1895, was proved at Belfast on the 31 January 1896 by John McKee of 100 High Street, Belfast, stock and share broker, the sole executor. Effects £2,098 7s.8d. Resworn £2,768 11s.8d.

William D. Henderson & Sons were grain merchants, commission merchants and insurance agents with offices in Waring Street, and then in Corporation Street.]

HENDERSON

[Polished granite in low railing.] Erected in loving remembrance of John Henderson who died February 14, 1866 aged 53 years. Catherine his wife who died December 5, 1873 aged 63 years. Mary their daughter who died August 24, 1862 aged 27 years. James their son who died July 9, 1850 aged 7 years.

No prayers, no tears, their flight could stay,
Twas Jesus called their souls away.

[The will of John Henderson of Castle Place, Belfast, in the county of Antrim, bookseller, who died 14 February 1866 at same place, was proved at Belfast on the 14 June 1866 by the oath of Catherine Henderson of Castle Place, Belfast aforesaid, widow, the sole executrix. Effects under £2,000.

The will of Catherine Henderson of 13 Castle Place and of Cromac Park Terrace, Ormeau Road, both in Belfast, county Antrim, widow, who died 5 December 1873 at Cromac Park Terrace, Ormeau Road aforesaid, was proved at Belfast on the 23 January 1874 by the oath of Annabella Henderson of No. 13 Castle Place, Belfast aforesaid, spinster, one of the executrixes. Effects under £1,500.]

HENESSEY

[Polished granite.] The burying place of Edward Henessey, Belfast, 1851.

HENRY

[Top is broken off.] Erected by Andrew Henry, of Belfast, in memory of his wife and children. Also the above Andrew Henry who departed this life Augt the 4th 1825 aged 78 years.

HENRY

[Badly weathered in the middle and now removed.] Erected by John Henry, of Belfast, in (memory) of his father William Henry (who de)parted this life 10th March .... aged 55 years. Also his bel(oved) daughter Sarah (who) died (11th July 1843) aged 11 months.

HEPBURN
See BOUCHER

HERDMAN
[Twin tablets formerly in carved entablature with ornate pediment, in high-railed enclosure, now laid flat and broken.] Erected by Thomas Herdman, of Belfast, in memory of his children: Alexander who died 29th Nov. 1807 aged 35 years, Sarah who died 18th July 1812 aged 25 years, Agnes, wife of Thomas Herdman who died 15th July 1817 aged 74 years. Ann REFORD, grandchild died 6th Nov 1817 aged 2 years. Here also is interred the remains of the above named Thomas Herdman who died 23rd September 1833 aged 92 years. And Frederick Septimus his grand-nephew and son of the late John Herdman Esq. died 18th January 1919 aged 71 years. Also his only daughter Mary Aline Herdman died in London, Christmas Day 1920 aged 32 years.

Erected in memory of William Herdman Esq., of Belfast, by his devoted sister Agnes Herdman. He died 19th June 1855 aged 78 years. "Mark the perfect man and behold the upright, for the end of that man is peace". Here also are interred his two beloved nieces; Anna Sarah Reford who died 8th October 1836 aged 17 years, Charlotte Mary Reford who died 24th March 1841 aged 18 years, "They were lovely and pleasant in their lives and in death they are not divided". And also the remains of the said Agnes Herdman who died Sept 5th 1865, aged 85 years. "Blessed are the dead which die in the Lord; they rest from their labours and their works do follow them".

[The will (with one codicil) of Agnes Herdman of Cliftonville, Belfast, in the county of Antrim, who died 5 September 1865 at same place, was proved at Belfast on 16 October 1865 by the oaths of James Gibson of the City of Dublin, barrister-at-law, James Herdman of Sion Mills, Strabane, in the county of Tyrone, and Alexander Finlay Herdman of Belfast in the county of Antrim, esquires, the executors. Effects under £14,000.

The Herdman family were wealthy linen merchants with mills, first in Smithfield, then later at the Brookfield Linen Co. on the Crumlin Road. They were also ship-owners and were connected with Belfast Harbour. They are closely related to the Herdman family of Sion Mills, the pedigree being in *Burke's Irish Family Records* (1976).]

HERDMAN
[Very badly flaked and now removed.] (This stone is erected by S)usannah to (the memory of) her husband John (Herd)man, of Belfast, who died the 23rd (of) July 1810 aged 39 years. (Here a)lso is interred their son John aged 2 years.

HERDMAN
[Worn.] Erected by Sarah Herdman, in memory of her husband James Herdman who departed this life May the 14th in the year of our Lord 1817 aged 36 years. And their daughter Jane who departed this life Novr 10th 1817 aged 10 years. Also two infant children.

[The above James inherited the Millfield Tannery, Belfast. His sons, James, John and George sold the tannery and bought flax spinning mills at Smithfield, Belfast and at Sion Mills, county Tyrone. The descendants of James continued to manage the Sion Mills firm. John and George and their families remained in the Belfast area. See *Burke's Irish Family Records* (1976).]

HERON

[Twin polished granite tablets with lettering picked out in gold paint, in entablature of marble Corinthian pillars and with a heron carved in the pediment, attached to east wall of upper graveyard.] (a) Erected by John Heron, Belfast, 1841, to the memory of his children, Francis, Caroline Louisa, & Charlotte, who died in infancy. Also Sarah Eliza who died 29th April 1837 aged 11 years. Also his wife Sarah Mathews Heron, who died 26th April 1867 aged 79 years. Also the above named John Heron, banker, who died at Maryfield, Holywood, 5th September 1870 aged 89 years. Mary Heron, daughter of John Heron, died 7th June 1913 aged 95 years. William Cowan Heron, D.L., third son of John Heron, who died at Maryfield, 7th June 1917 aged 97 years. John Heron, fourth son of John Heron, who died at Maryfield, 22nd July 1917 aged 87 years.

(b) Sacred to the memory of James Heron, J.P., banker, who died 1st November 1868, aged 52 years. Also to his children, John and Sarah, who died in infancy. Also his wife Nerissa Rosavo Heron, who died 7th December 1904 aged 80 years.

[The will (with one codicil) of John Heron of Maryfield, county Down, esquire, who died 5 September 1870 at same place, was proved at Belfast 12 October 1870 by the oaths of William Cowan Heron of Belfast, county Antrim, merchant, John Heron of Maryfield (Holywood) aforesaid, esquire and Francis Robert Lepper of Belfast, county Antrim, one of the Ulster Bank directors, the executors. (Deceased died domiciled in Ireland). Effects in U.K. under £35,000.

Probate of the will of Mary Heron of Maryfield, Holywood, county Down, spinster, who died 7 June 1913 at Bella Vista, Cornwallis Gardens, Hastings, Sussex, granted at Belfast on the 21 July 1913 to William Cowan Heron and John Heron, merchants. Effects £26,172 11s.7d.

Probate of the will of William Cowan Heron of Maryfield, Holywood, county Down, D.L., who died 7 June 1917, granted at Belfast on the 29 August 1917 to Francis A. Heron, esquire. Effects £75,068 13s.4d.

Probate of the will of John Heron of Maryfield, Holywood, county Down, esquire, who died 22nd July 1917, granted at Belfast on the 3 October 1917 to Francis A. Heron, esquire, and Alfred G. Brett, solicitor. Effects £434,833 5s.4d. Re-sworn £432,899 3s.5d.

The will of James Heron of Belfast, county Antrim, a director in Ulster Bank, who died 1 November 1868 at Resavo, near Holywood, county Down, was proved at Belfast 11 December 1868 by the oaths of Nerissa Heron (the widow), William Cowan Heron and John Heron the younger (merchants), all of Belfast aforesaid, the executrix and two of the executors. (Deceased died domiciled in Ireland). Effects in Great Britain and Ireland under

£14,000. Re-sworn at Belfast, 20 December 1868, under £20,000.

Probate of the will of Nerissa Rosavo Heron of The Chalet, Sydenham Hill Road, Surrey, widow, who died 7 December 1904, granted at Dublin 14 April 1905 to Francis A. T. Heron, esquire, and James M. Heron M.D. Effects £786 12s.7d.

The Heron family were West India merchants in the Donegall Quay and Albert Square area and in the late 19th century were commission merchants. John Heron, senr, was a co-founder of the Ulster Bank in 1836 and his son James (d.1868) was in his turn, a director.

The family was originally domiciled in Donegall Street before moving to Maryfield near Holywood in the 1830s.

William Cowan Heron was a magistrate and a Deputy Lieutenant for County Down.

Members of the Heron family resided in the Holywood area until the 1970s. They were closely related to the Herons who still live at Tullyveery House, Killinchy, Co. Down.]

HERRON
See MURPHY

HEYLAND
[Badly broken slab, now scattered.] Erected to the memory of Margaret, wife of John Heyland, Officer of Excise, in Belfast, who departed this life on the 16th November 1822 aged 64 years. Also Eliza Ann his daughter who departed this life the 21st Feby 1813 aged 23 years. Also the above named John Heyland who departed this life 12th March 1834 aged 79 years. Also Frances his youngest daughter who died April 24th 1835 aged 29 years.

HEYN
See PIRRIE

HIGG...
See MANSFIELD

HIGGINSON
See GARRETT and McCOY

HILL
[Flaking.] Erected by James Hill in memory of his wife Mary who departed this life the 4th of April 1821 aged 40 years. Also three of his children who died young. Also the above named James Hill who departed this life May 13th 1860 aged 74 years. Also his children; Alexander Hill aged 21 years, Thomas Hill, aged 20 years, Mary Jane Hill aged 15 years [sic], John S. Hill, aged 10 years, Clark C. Hill aged 8 years, Agnes Hill aged 7 years, James Hill aged 1 year and 8 months.

HILL
Erected by Robert Hill, in memory of his beloved wife Selena who departed this life Oct. 10th 1864 aged 37 years. "She died in Jesus" Also his daughter Frances who died 20th Dec. 1853 aged 4½ years.

Heron Monument before restoration (photograph A.C.W. Merrick).

HILL

[Cast-iron plaque, laid flat.] The burial ground of Adam Hill, late of Belfast. His wife Leonora HALL and their children.

[Adam Hill bought two lots, one in October 1832, and the other in December 1843. He was a commission merchant and public notary and lived at 10 Queen Street. Later he lived in Windsor Terrace, Lisburn Road. He was also one of the first ouncillors of the re-formed Town Council in 1842.]

HILL
See SMYTH and STEVEN

HILLYARD
See HASTINGS

HINCKS
See DRENNAN

HIND

[Badly pitted.] Sacred (to) the memory of Jane Hind, wife of James Hind, Belfast, who departed this (life on) the 16th Decr 1822 aged (..) years. Also the above named James Hind who departed this life 1st of June 18(2)4 aged (59) years.

HIND

[Three marblet tablets with lead letters, in large entablature, now completely smashed, and in large high-railed enclosure, all now removed.] In memory of Martha, daughter of E.J. HOPPER, of Cork, and wife of James Hind, of Belfast, who died the 4th May 1849 aged (25) years. "Be ye therefore ready also". Also of James Hind, died the (6) December 1885 aged (68) years. "He giveth His beloved sleep".

Sacred to (the) mem(ory) of (John Hind who died on the 26th January 1854 aged 66 years.) Also of Elizabeth his wife who died 11th June 18(64) aged 79 years. Also of Robert Joseph, son of John and Mary Jane Hind, who died at sea on the voyage from Melbourne, Australia, 2nd March 1869 aged 23 years. Also of Annie Josephine, daughter of John and Mary Hind, who died at Queenstown, 14th April 1869 aged 14 years. Also of Rachel MARSDEN, of Manchester, sister-in-law to the above named John Hind, who died 19th April 1859 aged 72 years.

In memory of Mary Jane, daughter of Robert WRIGHT, late of Fortfield, and wife of John Hind, of Dunowen, who departed this life on the 29th day of October 1861, in the 39th year of her age. Also of Margaret Elizabeth, daughter of John and Mary Jane Hind, who departed this life, in London, 10th June 1868, in the 21st year of her age, Also of Mary Lavinia, daughter of (John) and Mary Jane Hind, who departed this life in Cimes, near Nice, 24th May 1868, in the 17th year of her age. "She is not dead, but sleepeth". St Luke, VIII Chap., 52 verse.

[The will of James Hind, formerly of Lismara, Whiteabbey, county Antrim, and late of Alexandraville, Crumlin Road, Belfast, flax spinner, who died 6 December 1885 at latter place, was proved at Belfast on the 27 January 1886 by Herbert Owen Lanyon of Castleton Terrace, Antrim

Road, Belfast, merchant, one of the executors. Effects £243.

John Hind and Sons were proprietors of the Durham Street flax-spinning mill. The family lived at Dunowen and at the Lodge, both on the New Lodge Road, Cliftonville, as the area was then known.]

HINDS

[Badly weathered headstone.] Erected by Catherine Hinds inmemory of her husband Jonas Hinds who departed this life 5th June 1817 aged (3)7 years. Also Catherine the wife of the above (who...) Jan.(..) 183(8) aged 55 years.

HINDS
See THOMPSON

HODGENS

[Two broken marble tablets with lead lettering, formerly secured to east wall of upper graveyard in same enclosure as Miller tablet, now removed.]
(a) (In me)mory of (Rev. James) Hodgens, (for eight years pastor of the (Independent Church), Donegall St., Belfast (who died 13th May 1851) aged 42 years. ("Mark the perfect ma)n and behold the (upright, for the end of t)hat man is peace". (His wife Mar)y Anne, (who died 28th Feb 18)72 aged 62 years.

(b) In memory of James Hodgens WALLACE, who died 23rd April 1877 aged 6 years. Also Jane Miller Hodgens Wallace, who died 21st June 1886 aged 8 years. Jane Miller STEWART-WALLACE, elder daughter of the Rev. James Hodgens, died 15th Jan. 1934, in her 89th year. Marianne M.H. Stewart-Wallace, died 23rd August 1945 in her 76th year. Erected by John Stewart-Wallace.

[The will (with one codicil) of Mary Ann Hodgens of Antrim Place, Belfast, widow, who died 28 February 1872 at Belfast aforesaid, was proved at Belfast on the 19 April 1872 by the oath of James Blow of Whiteabbey, county Antrim, gentleman, one of the executors. Effects under £1,500.

Jane Miller Stewart-Wallace of 20 Stormont Park, Belfast, widow, died 15 January 1934. Probate Belfast 15 May 1934 to Marianne Miller Hodgens Stewart-Wallace, spinster. Effects £507 2s.3d.

Marianne Miller Hodgens Stewart-Wallace of 20 Stormont Park, Belfast, spinster, died 23 August 1945 at Westroyd Nursing Home, Bangor, county Down. Probate Belfast 8 February 1946 to Sir John Stewart Stewart-Wallace, C.B. Effects £6,639 12s.8d.

The Independent Meeting House which stood where Donegall Street Congregational Church is now, was founded in 1804.]

HODGES
See BENN and ROSS

HODGKINSON
See McNABB

HODGSON

[Badly flaking.] In memory of Robert Hodgson, late of Belfast, bookseller, who died 17th Decr 1818 aged 69 years. Isabella Hodgson, died 30th Octr.

Headstone of Robert Hodgson, bookseller (1749-1818), (photograph: A.C.W. Merrick).

aged 5 years.

[Hodgson's Entry, near Crown Entry, High Street, was named after Robert and John Hodgson who were booksellers, publishers and stationers at No. 9 High Street. After Robert's death his brother John continued this well-known firm for many years.]

HODGSON
   See McCLEERY

HOGG
   [Now lost.] 1851. Erected by William Hogg, to the memory of his beloved wife Margaret who departed this life the 11th July 1851 aged 28 years. Also his son David 29th Sept 1851 aged 2 years 10 months. The above named William Hogg died 6th Oct 1888 aged 71 years. Also his wife Susanna died 2nd July 1909 aged 93 years. Also his son John Hogg, died 30th October 1913 aged 71 years. Also his younger daughter Annabella died 3rd July 1919 aged 62 years. And in memory of his son James Hogg, died at San Francisco, 3rd March 1916 aged 70 years. And of Elizabeth, elder daughter, wife of William HOLLAND, died 16th December 1923, interred, City Cemetery, Belfast.

   [The will of William Hogg formerly of Rosetta Avenue, Ballynafeigh, county Down, and late of Windsor Park Belfast, gentleman, who died 6 October 1888 at latter place, was proved at Belfast on the 29 October

1888 by Susanna Hogg of Windsor Park, widow, John Hogg of 8 Academy Street, merchant, and William Holland merchant, of Linen Hall, all in Belfast, the executors. Effects £3,071 8s.6d.

Probate of the will of Susanna Hogg of 14 College Green, Belfast, widow, who died 2 July 1909, granted at Belfast on the 21 July 1909 to John Hogg, merchant. Effects £3,070 8s.2d.

Probate of the will of John Hogg of Academy Street and 33 Wellington Park, both Belfast, flax merchant, who died 30 October 1913 at Lisburn Road, in said city, granted at Belfast 23 December 1913 to Edward Bailey, chartered accountant, David McKee, bank director, and Lizzie Holland, widow. Effects £232,098 7s.11d. Re-sworn £232,262 5s.1d.

Administration (with the will) of the estate of James Hogg, late of The Cliff Hotel, San Francisco, California, gentleman, who died 3 March 1916, granted on the 25 October 1917 to David G. Dickson solicitor. Effects £9,001 16s. (Limited).

Elizabeth Holland of 33 Wellington Park and Highbury, Cadogan Park, both in Belfast, widow died 16 December 1923 at Highbury, Cadogan Park, Belfast, manufacturer, and Margaret Holland, spinster. Effects £1,699 0s.3d.

This family owned the large firm of John Hogg & Company, flax-merchants in Academy Street in the later part of the 19th and early 20th centuries.]

HOLCOMBE

[Now lost.] Sacred to the memory of Alexander Grant Holcombe, second son of Captain Holcombe, 13th P.A.L.I., and Louisa his wife, born Septr 28th 1847, died Octr 19th 1848.

HOLDEN

[Small memorial missing from lower ground.] The burying ground of Robert Holden, Belfast, 1843.

[He belonged to the same family as John Holden who owned a muslin manufactory in Thompson's Court, off Donegall Street.]

HOLDEN

[Small iron shield, now missing from lower ground.] The burying ground of James Holden, Belfast, 1846.

[He was a member of the firm of Holden & Pearce who ran the Phoenix Foundry in Great George's Street. Established about 1821 by Robert Holden and Samuel Pearce, this foundry was one of the leading concerns of its kind in Belfast for a long time, and one of the men trained there, Traver Forbes started the Ulster Foundry in Townsend Street.]

HOLDEN
See HASTINGS

HOLLAND
See HOGG

HOLLIS

[Top is now broken off.] Sacred to the memory of Margaret Hollis who departed this life 2nd April 1837 aged 75 years. Also Thomas Hollis, Divinity Student, who departed this life 21st April A.D. 1839 aged 19 years.

HOLMES
[Laid flat.] Erected by John Holmes, in memory of his brother William Holmes who departed this life 1st June 1834 aged 25 years. The above named John Holmes died 2nd July 1840 aged 23 years. Also their father Robert Holmes died 21st February 1842 aged 62 years. Eliza BELL, died 28th October 1844 aged 32 years. Margaret Bell died 1st August, 1887 aged 66 years, daughter of Robert Holmes.

HOLMES
See JOY

HOPPER
See HIND

HORNER
[Formerly lying flat, and capstone missing but all now lost.] Erected to the memory of Susanna the beloved wife of Archd Horner, late of Ballibay, who departed this life the 13th of July 1843 aged 60 years.

HORNER
See JOHNSON

HOSSACK
See CLAYTON

HOUGHTON
See STEWART

HOUSTON
[Now lost and copied from Society's Inscription book.] Erected by Rachel Houston in memory of her son John who died 21st Decr 1842 aged (1)0 years.

HOW
[Twin painted tablets in entablature secured to east wall of upper graveyard and in high-railed enclosure. The left hand tablet is now largely lost.] The family burial place of Thomas How, Belfast. (a) (Sacred to the memory of Jane GEMMILL, wife of Thos How, who died in the year 1822 and Thomas How who died June 22nd 1838. Also five of their children who died previously, namely: Eliza, Mary, John and two infants. Robert Gemmill How who died 8th September 1851, aged 34 years.) Jane How who died 29th May 1923.

(b) Sacred to the memory of Arthur GAMBLE, eldest son of James Gamble and grandson of Thomas How who died 26th June 1855 aged 9 years. Sarah Maxwell Gamble who died 8th January 1868 aged 15 years. James Gamble who died 25th February 1878 aged 64 years. Margaret Gemmill, wife of James Gamble who died 19th July 1904 aged 86 years.

[Jane How of 5 Royal Terrace, Belfast, and of Lorne Craigavad, county Down, spinster, died 30 May 1923. Probate Belfast 3 September 1923 to

Jane Gamble, spinster. Effects £11,204 16s.1d.

Thomas How was a muslin and cotton manufacturer whose works were in Long Lane. His wife Jane was the third daughter of Robert Gemmill (q.v.), himself a cotton manufacturer, whose eldest daughter Martha was married to the Rev. Dr Samuel Hanna of Rosemary Street Third Presbyterian Church.]

HOWARD

[Now lying flat, with top missing.] Sacred to the memory of John Howard who died 2nd June 1848 aged 57 years. Also his father-in-law, Thomas McKELVEY, who died 12th May 1847 aged 61 years. His only child John M. Howard who died 5th March 1851 aged 2 years and 7 months. Revd Robert DAVIDSON, of Lisbellow, died 12th August 1870 aged 47 years. "What I do, thou knowest not now, but thou shall know hereafter". John XIII,7. Also Rachel GILLILAND, youngest daughter of the above Thomas McKelvey, who died 7th February 1864 aged 39 years. Julia Davidson, widow of above Revd. R. (Davidson), died 5th May (1887) aged 73 (years).

[The will of Robert Davidson of Pakenham Place, Belfast, Presbyterian Minister, who died 12 August 1870 at Belfast aforesaid was proved at Belfast on the 10 February 1871 by the oath of Julia Davidson of No. 86 Pakenham Place, Belfast aforesaid, the widow, and sole executrix. Effects under £1,500.

John Howard was an excise officer living in Eliza Street and Thomas McKelvey was a brewer in Cromac Street.

The Rev. Robert Davidson was born in county Monaghan in 1823 and educated at the Royal Belfast Academical Institution, obtaining the General Certificate in 1844. He was licenced at Monaghan and was minister of Lisbellaw 1850-69. He married in 1855 Julia McKelvey. See Barkley: *Fasti of the General Assembly* (1986).]

HOY

[Flaking raised horizontal slab, now lost.] Erected by John Hoy in memory of his mother Anne Jane Hoy, who died 11th Novr 1809 aged 34 years. His three sisters, Jane, Jane and Margaret who died in infancy. His father Samuel Hoy who died 1st May 1837 aged 65 years. And Jane Hoy who died July 1840 aged 68 years. Also his wife Margaret Hoy who died 15th January 1861 aged 51 years. John Hoy died 30th (Nov.) 1883 aged 74 years.

[Samuel Hoy was a cooper and publican in Waring Street. His son John was the proprietor of John Hoy and Company wholesale wine and spirit merchants of Victoria Street.]

HOY

Large yellow-brick mausoleum with brick obelisk on top — inscription over the bricked-up doorway. All has now been removed.] 1859. The family burying place of John Hoy, Belfast.

HUDSON

Erected by Christopher Hudson, of Mount Collyer, Esq. where lie deposited the remains of his wife Jane who died the 5th of March 1819 aged 69 years. Also the above named Christpher Hudson departed this life 17th March 1827 aged 84 years. Also his daughter Mabella, wife of Wm JOHNSON, M.D., Belfast, who died on the 24th August 1836 aged 42 years.

HUDSON
See McCOMB

HUGHES
[Tablet with polished granite surround, laid flat in a high-railed enclosure.] In memory of Thomas Hughes, late of Fisherwick, Co. Antrim, who died 15th May 1838, and their only son Thomas died 17th July 1835.

[Thomas Hughes, senr. was a Director of the Belfast Banking Company from 1833 to 1848. See Simpson: The Belfast Bank 1827-1970 (1975).]

HUGHES
[Twin tablets in neo-Egyptian entablature secured to south wall.] Erected in memory of Robert, infant son of Thomas Hughes junr, obituary 15th Augt 1842 aged 1 year and 5 months. Also his eldest son Thomas, obituary 21st July 1858 aged 18 years. Also his eldest daughter Sarah, wife of Robert W. CORRY, obituary 18th October 1867 aged 29 years. Also her youngest son Robert aged 8 years, obituary 17th April 1870.

Also Alexander Thomas Hughes, sixth son of Thomas Hughes, junr, obituary 5th October 1881 aged 31 years. Also the above named Thomas Hughes junr, obituary 20th January 1885 aged 76 years. Also of Robert James Hughes, third son of Thomas Hughes, junr, obituary 19th July 1885 aged 41 years. Also of Catharine, wife of the above named Thomas Huges junr, obituary 7th January 1893 aged 81 years.

[The will (witth one codicil) of Thomas Hughes, formerly of University Square, Belfast, and late of Fitzwilliam Place, 75 University Road, Belfast, esquire, who died 20 January 1885 at latter place, was proved at Belfast on the 11th February 1885 by Edwin Hughes of Dinnagh, Hamilton Road, Ealing, county Middlesex, merchants, the executors. Effects £3,557 16s.

The will of Catherine Hughes of Kiltubret, county Armagh, spinster, who died 7 August 1892 at same place, was proved on the 4 October 1893 at Armagh by the Reverend Charles McEvoy of Middletown, said county, P.P., the sole executor. Effects £338 2s.11d.

Robert W. Corry was of the family of James P. Corry, timber merchant and lived in Kensington House, Knock.]

HUGHES
[In lower ground and no longer extant.] The burying place of Wm. Hughes, Belfast, 1853.

HULL
See PINKERTON

HUMPHRYS
[Smashed marble tablet in broken surround, now removed.] Sacred to the memory of Joseph Humphrys who departed this life 1st Sep. 185(2)

aged 52 years. Also Elizabeth Frances mother-in-law of the above who died 5th January 1855 aged 80 years. Also Elizabeth STEELE, his sister-in-law who died on the 29th of March 1859 aged 56 years.

HUNTER
[Attached to north wall.] Sacred to the memory of John Hunter who departed this life the 28th January 1833 aged 66 years. Of Mary Ann his wife who departed this life 19th August 1833 aged 62 years. Of James their son who departed this life 8th July 1833 aged 24 years. Also their son Thomas Hunter who died ( ) Decr 1876 aged 75 years. And his wife Emily Hunter who died ( ) Septr 1877 aged 65 years. Also Lydia daughter of Thomas and Emily Hunter who died [blank] May 1880 aged 23 years.

[The plot was purchased by John Hunter in November 1828.]

HUNTER
[Iron shield.] The family burying ground of Charles Hunter, Belfast, 18(6)0.

HUNTER
[Granite headstone against the east wall of the upper graveyard and in low-stone enclosure.] Erected in 1893 by Anna Hunter in loving memory of her father and mother and other dear relations who rest here. "The memory of the just is blessed". The above named Anna Hunter, departed this life October 6th 1898, and is interred here aged 82. Her son Stewart Orr Hunter, died 6th March 1900 aged 47. Her daughter Anna Hunter died 31st October 1915 aged 70. The family burial place of William ORR, Glenalina.

[Probate of the will of Anna Hunter of 43 Cromwell Road, Belfast, widow, who died 6 October 1898, granted at Belfast on 14 November 1898 to Anna Hunter of 69 Prince's Gardens, Belfast, spinster, and Stewart Orr Hunter of Darkley House, Keady, county Armagh, mill manager. Effects £494.

Administration of the estate of Stewart Orr Hunter of Darkley House, Keady, county Armagh, mill manager, who died 5 March 1900 granted at Armagh on the 29 March 1900 at Armagh to Laurie Hunter, the widow. Effects £260 5s.1d.

Administration with the will of the estate of Anna Hunter of 4 Princess Gardens, Belfast, spinster, who died 31 October 1915, granted at Belfast on the 22 December 1915 to Katharine Payne, married woman. Effects £927 7s.9d.]

HUNTER
See MOLYNEUX and SMYTH

HURST
[Worn marble tablet in a pedestal (now lost), formerly supporting a pillar.] Erected to the memory of James David Hurst, who died Nov. 27th 1832 aged 21 years. A number of friends who admired his talent and esteemed him for his virtue have caused this monument to be

erected in testimony of their regard.

[He was a teacher at the Royal Belfast Academical Institution and lived at 11, Castle Street.]

HYLTON
See DAVISON

HYNDMAN

[Thick monument of polished granite, in enclosure.] In memory of Margaret, widow of Archibald Hyndman, of Belfast ob. 18 Decr 1800 AE 78. Her son James Hyndman, ob. 10 May 1825, AEt 64, and Cherry his widow ob. 30 Aug. 1845 AEt. 77. Also their son Hugh, ob. 29th Decr 1832, AEt. 30. Their daughter Fanny, ob. 18 Jany 1853, AEt. 60. Their son George Crawford, ob. 18 Decr 1867, AEt. 71. And Jane BAILIE, widow of Hugh, ob. 5 Novr 1885, AEt. 84.

[The will (with two codicils) of George Crawford Hyndman of Howard Street, Belfast, county Antrim, auctioneer who died 18 December 1867 at same place, was proved at Belfast on the 11 February 1868 by the oaths of Margaret Hyndman and Helena Bell Hyndman, spinsters, and Hugh Hyndman, solicitor, all of Belfast aforesaid, the executors. Effects under £5,000.

James Hyndman was a wool merchant, an auctioneer and public notary in Donegall Street. He acted for a time as Town Clerk. He was also an early Committee member of the Belfast Library and Society for Promoting Knowledge. He was one of the original Volunteers of 1778.

George Crawford Hyndman his son was born on 24 October 1796 and educated at the Belfast Academy. He entered his fathers business as an auctioneer as a young man and later became a well-known naturalist, contributing extensively to the knowledge of Irish marine fauna. He was also a founder member of the B.N.H.P.S. (1821), a President of the Belfast Literary Society (1840) and the first president of the Belfast Naturalists' Field Club (1863).

Hugh Hyndman, a well-known solicitor in Belfast during the mid-19th century, was his nephew.]

See Deane: *Belfast Natural History and Philosophical Society, Centenary Volume* (1924). Hyndman: *Article in Belfast Literary Society, 1801-1901* (1902), Chambers: *Faces of Change* (1983).

HYNDMAN

[Tablet with surround, formerly secured to the south wall with the above, but now lost.] In memory of Margaret Hyndman, relict of the late Andrew Hyndman, of Belfast, who died 31st May 183(4) aged 72 years. And of her son Archibald Hyndman who died 6th November 1815 aged 29.

HYNDMAN

[Large square monument, once topped by a statue of a dog. Statue and inscribed tablets are no longer extant.] West face — Sacred to the memory of Robert Hyndman of Portview in the County of Down who departed this life 30th August 1822 aged 72 years. Rebecca Hyndman his wife who departed this life 6th June 1830 aged 66 years.

Memorial to Robert Hyndman of Portview, Ballymacarrett, now destroyed (photograph A.C.W. Merrick).

South face — Mary Ann KYD, born 3rd April 1793, died 29th Oct. 1832. Alexander Kyd, born 4th Feb. 1796, died 21st Jan. 1820. Also Rebecca, youngest daughter of Robert Hyndman and widow of Alexander NEILL, Surgeon R.N., who died 15th November 1886.

East face — Sacred to the memory of Hugh Hyndman of Eglantinehill in the County of Antrim, who departed this life 4th January 1819, aged 67 years.

[The will of Rebecca Neill of Belfast, widow, who died 13 November 1886 at 63 Apsley Terrace, Belfast, was proved at Belfast on the 3 December 1886 by Margaret Neill and Annie Neill, both of Belfast, spinsters, the executrixes. Effects £76 6s.11d.

The monument commemorating this family is near that of James and George Crawford Hyndman (above). The two families were related.

Robert Hyndman of Portview, Ballymacarrett was High Constable of Belfast in the early 1790s and was an active member of the Belfast Charitable Society, being Treasurer and Secretary of the Water Committee in 1797.

The presence of the dog over this monument is difficult to explain as George Crawford Hyndman, to whom it would be more appropriate, is buried in a different plot (see above). See Strain: *Belfast and its Charitable Society* (1961).]

HYNDMAN
See WARD

INGLE
Erected by Ann Ingle in memory of her beloved husband John Ingle who departed this life 19th May 1849, aged 33 years. Here also are interred the remains of the above named Ann Ingle who departed this life 21st January 1891, aged 87 years.

[The will (with one codicil) of Anne Orr Ingle of 1A Pine Street, Belfast, widow, who died 21 January 1891 at same place, was proved at Belfast on the 16 April 1891 by Anne Shaw of The Parsonage, Kirkcubbin, widow, and Thomas Shaw of Kircubbin, merchant, both county Down, the executors. Effects £442 2s.8d.]

INNIS
See STEWART

IRELAND
[Very badly flaked and now lost.] Erected t(o the memory of) Sarah (Ireland daughter of Francis (Ireland who died) the 10th of May (1831, aged 1)9 (years). Also Francis Ireland, father to the above who died on the (4th) of January 1837, aged (4)9 years. [He was a painter and glazier and lived in High Street.]

(IR)ELAND
[Badly flaked near the top, now removed.] Erected by James (Ir)eland of Belfast (in memory of his mother Elizabeth (who died) 1st Jany 183(7), aged 55 years. (Also his brother) William who died (25th) Jany 1837, aged 19 years. Also his (fat)her James who died the (29th Ja)ny

1837, aged 60 years. (His sis)ter Elizabeth STEWART (who) died 4th Feb. 1866, aged 34 years. Her husband Robert Stewart who died 25th August 1872, aged 42 years. Also their son Robert Stewart died 21st July 1891 aged 36 years.

IRELAND
[Very worn headstone lying flat.] 1831. Erected by Alexander (Ire)land, of Belfast, in memory of six of his children who died in infancy. (Also) his wife (Martha) who died the (.)8th (Sepr 1844, aged ..) years. (Also the above named Alexander who died 2nd May 1847, aged 7(5) years. .... Ireland Mary (Ireland), (child)ren of D. Ireland, of Dublin.

IRELAND
[With carved entablature, formerly bearing draped urn, attached to east wall in high-railed enclosure.] In memory of Letitia, wife of Jas Ireland, died 18th January 1859. Their son who died in infancy. Robert Ireland died 24th December 1850. James Ireland died 12th November 1870, aged 84 years. Their daughter Marianne died 25th May 1884. Jane Ireland died 17th February 1895. Letitia Ireland died 2nd September 1906. Matilda Ireland died 6th September 1908. Dorothea Ireland died 19th February 1911. Elizabeth Maria Ireland, died 21st February 1912. Emily Ireland died 27th December 1913. Sarah Ireland died 2nd November 1914. Louisa Ireland died 15th March 1920.

[Letters of administration of the personal estate of Marianne Ireland of Oakley, near Holywood, county Down, spinster, who died 25 May 1884 at same place, were granted at Belfast on the 18 August 1884 to Sarah Ireland of Oakley, spinster, a sister. Effects £221 3s.

The will of Jane Ireland of Oakley, Holywood, county Down, spinster, who died 17 February 1895 at same place, was proved at Belfast on the 15 May 1895 by Sarah Ireland at Oakley, Holywood, spinster, the sole executrix. Effects £1,956 0s.10d.

Probate of the will of Letitia Ireland of Oakley, Holywood, county Down, spinster, who died 2 September 1906, granted at Belfast on the 17 July 1907 to Sarah Ireland, spinster, and John Milliken, merchant. Effects £2,016 15s.1d.

Probate of the will of Matilda Ireland of Oakley, Holywood, county Down, spinster, who died 6 September 1908 granted at Belfast on the 18 December 1908 to Dorothea Ireland, spinster. Effects £665 18s.6d.

Administration of the estate of Dorothea Ireland of Oakley, Holywood, county Down, spinster, who died 19 February 1911, granted at Belfast on the 13 September 1911 to Elizabeth Ireland, spinster. Effects £885 17s.8d.

Administration of the estate of Elizabeth Maria Ireland of Oakley, Holywood, county Down, spinster, who died 21 February 1912, granted at Belfast on the 13 June 1912 to Louisa Ireland, spinster. Effects £697 16s.8d.

Administration of the estate of Emily Ireland of Oakley, Holywood, county Down, spinster, who died 27 December 1913, granted at Belfast on 2 March 1914 to Louisa Ireland, spinster. Effects £301 16s.3d.

Administration of the estate of Sarah Ireland of Oakley, Holywood, county Down, spinster, who died 2 November 1914, granted at Belfast on the 17 February 1915 to Louisa Ireland, spinster. Effects £3,295 5s.6d. (Cancelled 15 April 1915). (Probate 28 May 1915).

Probate of the will of Sarah Ireland of Oakley, Holywood, county Down, spinster, who died 2 November 1914, granted at Belfast on the 28 May 1915 to Alexander McDowell, solicitor. Effects £3,295 5s.6d. Re-sworn £3,736 10s.8d.

Probate of the will (with two codicils) of Louisa Ireland of Oakley, Holywood, county Down, who died 15 March 1920, granted at Belfast on the 12 May 1920 to the executors and trustees, George Martin McNeill and William J. McMillen. Effects £12,249 13s.8d.

James Ireland founded the firm of Ireland and McNeill, house furnishing ironmongers, in Corn Market. He lived at Adelaide Place, then later near Holywood.]

IRELAND

[Marble, bearing lead letters, formerly in a surround with wreath and date "1859" at the top, now broken and laid flat.] In loving memory of Robert Ireland who died 6th June 1872, aged 45 years, and Jane Eliza Ireland his wife who died 11th July 1896, aged 70 years. Also their children, Anna Maria Ireland died 16th July 1880, aged 20 years. Mary Anne died 20th June 1859, aged 2 years. William Thomas died 28th Aug. 1863, aged 8 months.

[The will of Robert Ireland of Belfast, county Antrim, miller, who died 6 June 1872 at same place, was proved at Belfast on the 28 October 1872 by the oath of Jane Eliza Ireland of Belfast aforesaid, the widow, the sole executrix. Effects under £3,000.]

IRELAND

See BLAIN and McFADDEN

IRVING

See STEWART

IRWIN

[Very worn headstone, now lost.] Erected by (John) Irwin to the memory of his dau(ghter) Elizabeth Irwin who died (8th) of September 180(0), aged 6 years. And his son William Irwin died 6th Oct. 181(3), aged 19 years. Also to the above named John (Irwin died 22nd Feb. 1814), aged (50) years. (Likewise his daugh)ter Sarah B. (died 14th April 18(23) aged 26) years. Also Elizabeth his wife died 21st January 18(37) aged (73) years.

IRWIN

[Cast-iron.] The burial place of James Irwin, Wellbrooke, Co. Tyrone, died November 1833, and Caroline his wife died November 23rd 1861.

[The will of Caroline Irwin of Dundalk in the county of Louth, widow, who died 23 November 1861 at same place, was proved at Armagh on the 17 January 1862 by the oath of James Stuart of Newry in the county of Down, Major-General, one of the executors. Effects under £2,000.

Wellbrook, near Cookstown, Co. Tyrone is now a National Trust property.]

JACKSON

[Horizontal slab now almost unreadable.] To the memory of Mrs Letitia Jackson, widow of the late Hugh Jackson, of Ballibay, Esqr, who died the 11th Feby 1826 aged 65 years. And her daughter Susan Jackson who died 31st Decr 1826 aged 3(4) years. And also her daughter Isabella WINNING, relict of the late William Winning Esq., Surgeon of the Royal Navy, who died 20th May 1827 aged 37 years. Also William Winning their son who died 14th August 1878 aged 59 years.

JACKSON

Erected by Ellen Jackson, to the memory of her husband, John Jackson who departed this life 12th August 1844 aged 44 years.

Death, thou hast conquered me,
And by thy dart I'm slain,
But Christ will conquer thee,
And I shall rise again.

JACKSON

See KENNEDY and MONTGOMERY

JAMES

[Rough granite with lead letters.] In memory of William James who died 30th July 1850 aged 23 years. Robert James who died 21st Jan. 1908 aged 80 years. And his wife Anna Eliza who died 6th July 1908 aged 62 years. Also their daughter Annie, wife of John WHITMORE, who died 7th June 1918 aged 46 years.

[Administration of the estate of Robert James of 2 St. Joseph's Terrace, Marlborough Park, Belfast, gentlemen, who died 21 January 1908 at 53 Lauderdale Gardens, Hyndland Road, Glasgow granted at Belfast on the 23 March 1908 to William Sinclair James, merchant. Effects £153 15s.3d.

Probate of the will of Annie Whitmore of 25 North Parade, Belfast, married woman, who died 7 June 1918 at Belfast aforesaid, was granted at Belfast on the 25 March 1919 to John Whitmore, engineer, husband of the deceased). Effects £318 6s.8d.

JAMESON

[Worn altar-tomb, now on the ground.] In memory of Robert Jameson, of Belfast, who departed this life the 6th day of February 1821 aged 6(5) years. Also of his daughter Jane who died the 9th day of February 1807 aged 13 years. And his grand-daughter Jane PATRICK who died (5)th May 1829, Also Jane Jameson, relict of the above Robt Jameson, who died 6th Sept 1843 aged 89 years. Also in memory of John Jameson, son of the above Robert and Jane Jameson, who died 19th June 184(5) aged 65 years.

(J)AMIESON

[Almost completely flaked away and not now identifiable.] Erected by Mary (J)amieson in m(emory of her husband Hugh Jamieson), who (departed this) life on the 17th of (Augt 1840 aged 50 years. "Learn to live as you would wish to die". Mary Jamieson, died 1st October) 1869, aged (67 years).

[Hugh Jamieson, a native of Ayrshire, was the proprietor of the Belfast Brush Manufactory at 63 Smithfield for some years. At the time of his death, he resided in North Street.]

JAMISON

[Pitted.] Erected (by) William Jam(iso)n in memory of his wife (Margaret) who departed this life (29)th May 1817 aged (42) years. Also his da(ughte)r Matilda who who died 30th D(ecr) 1821 aged (..) years. Here lyeth the remains of the above named Wm Jamison who departed this life 2nd September 1824, aged 62 years. Also his daughter Jane who died 20th March 183(0) aged 21 years. Likewise his daughter Ann who died 29th Novr 1855, and his daughter Margaret who died 19th Feby 1872.

[The will of Margaret Jamison of 4 Linenhall Street, Belfast, spinster, who died 19 February 1872 at Belfast aforesaid, was proved at Belfast on the 6 January 1873 by the oath of William Edgar of Lincoln Avenue Belfast aforesaid, woollen draper, the sole executor. Effects under £450.

JAMISON

Erected by John Jamison in memory of his wife Eliza who died 25th June 1839 aged 31 years. Also 3 of her children: Margaret, who died at the age of 9 months, William aged 18 months, and James, 3 months. Underneath lies the remains of the above named John Jamison who departed this life on the 1st May 1844 aged 40 years. Also his daughter Mary Elizabeth Jamison, who died 22nd November 1875 aged 38 years.

[The will of Mary Elizabeth Jamison of 4 Linenhall Street, Belfast, spinster, who died 22 November 1875 at same place was proved at Belfast on the 12 January 1876 by the oath of John Andrew McMordie of 85 Springfield Terrace, Belfast, power-loom manager, the executor. (Deceased died domiciled in Ireland) Assets in United Kingdom sworn under £600.]

JAMISON
See RICHARDSON

JELLETT

[Small headstone, partly buried, and with the letters of the surname very close together, now lost.] William Woodward (J)ellett, born February 27th 1830, fell asleep, Ja(nuar)y 6th 1858.

JENKINS

[Sandstone entablature secured to north wall with both marble tablets missing. Most of the inscription has been copied from the Society's Inscription book.] (a) The family burying place of William Jenkins, Belfast. Sacred to the memory of his son John Jenkins aged 7 years. Also William and Radcliff who died in infancy. Rachael GALWAY who departed this life the 17th August 1828 aged 35 years. Abigail, beloved wife of William Jenkins who departed this life 8th July 1842 aged 51 years.

(b) Sacred to the memory of the above William Jenkins who departed this life 25th June 1851 aged 60 years. Margaret Jenkins who died 12th

March 1862 aged 65 years. "Not lost but gone before".

[The will of Margaret Jenkins of Belfast, in the county of Antrim, who died 12 March 1862 at same place, was proved on the 18 February 1863 at Belfast aforesaid by the oath of William John Jenkins of Belfast, muslin manufacturer, husband of the deceased, the sole executor. Effects under £100.

William Jenkins was a pawnbroker in Mill Street.]

JENKINS

[Weathered sandstone, now lost.] Erected in memory of Joseph Jenkins, late of M(ag)hera, who departed this life the 20th day of November 186(0) aged 6(1) years.

JOHNSON

[Slate tablet with sandstone entablature secured to west wall.] Precious in the sight of the Lord is the death of his saints. Psalm CXVI,15. In memory of Anna Maria Godfrey Johnson, wife to Hu. Johnson, of Belfast, who departed this life the 8th day of June 1803 aged 40 years. Also of her husband Hugh Johnson who departed this life the 2nd day of July 1840 aged 81 years. Also of their daughter Anna Maria Johnson who departed this life on the 20th January 1871 aged 73 years, and also his daughter Mary Johnson who departed this life on the 28th May 1876 aged 76 years.

[In the burial register Hugh Johnson is described as a gentleman, of College Street.]

JOHNSON

[Almost completely worn sandstone headstone, broken in two and now lost.] Here rests the body (of the Rev.) Thomas Johnson (who died 10th August 1817 aged .. years. His son-in-law Henry HORNER, died May 1860. And his wife Ellen Horner died 29th January 18(8)4 aged 73 years.)

[The Rev. Thomas Johnson is probably the Methodist minister from Coleraine who was admitted for trial in 1797 and preached all over Ireland in the following 20 years. He was a zealous supporter of the dispensing of the sacraments by Methodist ministers, which split the church at that time. He died of fever in Belfast.]

JOHNSON
    See HUDSON

JOHNSTON

[Very worn, raised horizontal stone, now lost - largely copied from Society's Inscription book.] (Erected to the memory of) Anna Johnston, wife of John Johnston, (merchant), Belfast. She died on the (3rd) of May 18(30) aged (31) years. Also (Margaret their beloved daughter.) She died (on 10th July 1821) aged (5) years. Also (the body of the above John Johnston .....) departed this life .. .. aged (..) years.

JOHNSTON

[Tablet in gothic castellated entablature formerly secured to east wall of upper graveyard, now lost.] The family burying place of Samuel Johnston, Belfast. John Johnston died 1st Dec. 1821 aged 81 years. Martha Johnston died 26th April 1828 aged 76 years. Margaret the beloved wife of Samuel Johnston died 11th December 1835 aged 42 years. Beneath also lies the remains of Margaret wife of James HART, fourth daughter of Samuel and Margaret Johnston, deeply lamented by her husband, and relatives. She died on the 10th of September 1855 aged 32 years. The above named Samuel Johnston died 2nd August 1860 aged 82 years. Elizabeth Johnston, the beloved wife of William Johnston, died 26th October 1859 aged 30 years. William Johnston died 26th January 1866 aged 35 years.

[Samuel Johnston was a tanner, and William was a clerk.]

JOHNSTON

[Smashed and worn tablet formerly secured to east wall of upper graveyard, now lost.] Erected by William Johnston, (No 31 Mill) Street, Belfast, in memory of his daughter Ann Johnston who departed this life the 11th of Septr 1824 aged 19 years. (Also the above named William Johnston (departed this) life on the 13th day of (Sept)ember 1837 aged 68 years. (Also hi)s grandson William Johnston who departed this life on the 14th day of June 1839 aged 8 years. Also his sister Ann Johnston who departed this life on 1(7)th of May 1842 aged 15 years. And their father John, son to the above William Johnston who departed this life on 21st June 183(2) aged 39 years. And his mother Mary, wife to the above named William Johnston who departed this life on the 24th Septr 1842 aged 6(5) years. And her daughter-in-law Ellen wife to John Johnston who departed this life on the 23rd Augt 1843 aged 37 years.

[The family were mostly bakers in Mill Street.]

JOHNSTON

[Horizontal slab.] Erected to the memory of Archibald Johnston of Strabane, who departed this life Decr 3rd 1825 aged 38 years. Also Fanny A. Johnston his daughter died 28th Feby 1828 aged 4 years. Also Archd Kingsmill Johnston his son died 19th March 1828 aged 2 years.

Oh Shade revered this frail memorial take,
T'is all alas thy sorrowing wife can make,
Faithful and just and humble and sincere,
Here lies a valued friend, a husband dear,
Composed in suffering and in joy sedate,
Good without noise, without pretensions great.

JOHNSTON

[Bottom lines buried.] Erected to the memory of Georgeann, the beloved wife of Robert Johnston of Belfast, who departed this life 22nd day of December 1829 in the 26th year of her age and eleventh month of her marriage. Also his father Andrew died 9th Mar. 1830 aged 54 years. And his brother Andrew died 8th Jany 1836 aged 27 years. And his mother Mary died 25th Decr 1841 aged 65 years. Also the above Robert Johnston who died 28th January 1873 in the 75th year of his age. Also Mary Anne, sister of the above Robert Johnston who died 28th Decr 1880 in her 75th year. Also Georgina, daughter of the above Robert Johnston died 23 Feby 1887 in her 57th year.

[In the burial register, Robert Johnston is described as a merchant of 9 College Street.]

JOHNSTON
[Marble tablet in broken surround, now lost.] Here repose the remains of Mary Jane Johnston who died on the 3rd day of February 1834 aged 54 years. Also John Johnston who died on the third day of October 1855 aged 78 years.

JOHNSTON
[Very badly weathered and now lost.] Erected by S(amuel) Johnston, (Prince's Street, Belfast), in memory of (his son James) who (departed this life) 24th January 18(38 aged 34) years. (Also) Mary, the beloved wife of Alexander Johnston who departed this life (Jany 19th 1840 aged 3)3 years. Also the (above Alexander) Johnston who died on the 12th of July 1840 aged (35) years. Also the above Samuel Johnston who departed this life on the 10th Dec 1847 aged (76) years. Also Samuel, son of the (above named) Alexander Johnston, who departed this life on the (4)th of July 1849 aged (4)0 years. Also Isabella, the beloved wife of the above named Samuel Johnston, who departed this life on the 11th of December 1863 aged 89 years. Also Ann B., daughter of the above named Samuel Johnston, who departed this life 8th of January 1864 aged 66 years.

[The will of Anne Bradley Johnston of Wellwood Place, Mountpottinger, in the county of Down, spinster, who died 8 January 1864 at Ballymacarret in the county of Down, was proved at Belfast on the 6 July 1864 by the oath of John McKee of Cregagh (Belfast) in the county of Down, farmer, one of the executors. Effects under £800.

The will of Anne Bradley Johnston of Wellwood Place, Mountpottinger, in the county of Down, spinster, who died 8 January 1864 at Ballymacarrett, county of Down, was proved at Belfast on the 7 October 1864 by the oath of John Wallace of Donegal Street, Belfast, in the county of Antrim, printer, one of the executors. (Double probate, former grant 6 July 1864). Effects unadministered under £600.]

JOHNSTON
[Broken and laid flat.] Erected by Allen Johnston, of Belfast, to the memory of his beloved daughter Elizabeth Johnston who died 3rd March 1840 aged 16 years.

JOHNSTON
[Tablet formerly secured to north wall of lower ground. It has disappeared since being copied in 1907.] Erected by Thomas Johnston in memory of his infant daughter Agnes who died on the 25th January 1861 aged 4 months.

JOHNSTON
See BARNETT, BRYSON, GEMMILL and WHITE

JOHNSTONE
See TEMPLETON

Portrait of Valentine Jones, merchant (1711-1805), (photograph Ulster Museum).

JONES

[Twin marble tablets (now lost) of which right one is blank, in pedimented entablature secured to south wall in high-railed, low-stone enclosure.] Erected in memory of Mr. Valentine Jones, of the town of Belfast, merchant, who lived respected and died lamented by numerous descendants and friends on the 22nd day of March 1805 aged 94 years, and was here buried in the same grave with his son-in-law John Galt SMITH who died on 14th Decr 1802 aged 72 years. And of Margaret Smith, daughter of John Galt Smith, who died on 1st Feby 1844 aged 69 years. Also of Edward Smith, son of Edward Jones Smith who in Montevideo, South America on 4th January 1844, was after a very short illness cut off in the prime of his life aged 33 years. And of his mother Jane Smith, daughter of Hugh CRAWFORD, of Orangefield, banker, who died 9th December 1838 aged 71 years. Also of her husband Edward Jones Smith son of John Galt Smith, grandson of Valentine Jones, died 15th August 1859, being on the anniversary of his birth day aged 79 years.

[Valentine Jones (1711-1805) was one of the early builders of the town of Belfast, both commercially, socially and physically. A West India merchant in his early manhood, he later had an extensive wine trade throughout the North of Ireland, his premises occupying almost one entire side of Winecellar Entry, off High Street. He was involved in practically every public venture of importance in Belfast, particularly the founding and establishing of the Belfast Charitable Society. He contributed substantially to the funds required for the building of the old Poor House in 1774 and the White Linen Hall ten years later. He helped to set up the Belfast Dispensary, and he and his son Valentine contributed to funds for the town's water supply. He belonged to the Irish Volunteer movement in the 1780s and was an early Committee member of the Belfast (now Linenhall) Library. He was responsible for building the range of five houses on the east side of Donegall Place, in one of which he spent his latter years.

He married at the age of sixteen into the Ronchet family of Lisburn and had five children, one of whom, Jane, married John Galt Smith (1730-1802) whose father Samuel was a friend of his.

Like both his father and father-in-law, John Galt Smith was involved in the public life of the town from an early age. He was a founder member of the Belfast Charitable Society and for many years was its Treasurer. A Lieutenant in the Belfast Volunteer Company, he was also a founder member of the Northern Whig Club in 1790. He was for a long time Treasurer of Rosemary Street First Presbyterian Church and personally supervised its rebuilding in 1783. He had many mercantile interests in Belfast, amongst them the manufacture of rope and pottery.

He had a large number of children, many of whom together with their children distinguished themselves both in Ireland and abroad. At least four successive generations were named John Galt Smith.

John Galt Smith's (his mother was Miss Ann Galt of Coleraine) connection with both the Bristow and Thomson families has been alluded to in the biographical note appended to the Bristow monument. A detailed account of

Portrait of Henry Joy, historian of Belfast and owner of Joy's Paper Mill (1754-1835) (Belfast Literary Society, Centenary Volume).

both the Jones and Smith families is given in Benn's *History of Belfast*, Vol. 2 (1880). See also Strain: *Belfast and its Charitable Society* (1961).

John Galt Smith's son Edward married Jane, a daughter of Hugh Crawford who was one of the four founders of the Belfast Bank in 1808. The other three partners were Narcissus Batt, David Gordon and John H. Houston, and from this bank the Belfast Banking Company evolved in 1827.]

JONES

[Tablet formerly secured to south wall beside John Moore's and Roger Moore's obelisk in low-stone enclosure but now lost.] Here lies interred Mrs Katherine Jones, daughter of John and Mabella MOORE of Moorgrove, in the county of Antrim, and wife of Valentine Jones, of Belfast, formerly of Barbados, who in every Christian hope and pious expectation closed a mild and innocent life on the twenty-eighth of October 1806, aged seventy-three years. Here also was interred the above-named Valentine Jones who died on the twenty-sixth of October 1808, at Portpatrick, having recently completed his 79th year. "If a fulfilment of the moral and religious, the relative and social duties of life constitutes a good man, this was one".

[He was the eldest son of Valentine Jones (1711-1805) and is sometimes referred to as Valentine Jones the second. He spent many years as a merchant in Barbadoes and, on his return to this country in 1783, took an active part in the mercantile and institutional life of Belfast, in collaboration with his father. He was an energetic member of the Belfast Charitable Society and was a founder of the Belfast Dispensary in 1792.

His son and grandson were also called Valentine.]

JONES

[Small slate headstone, now missing.] To the memory of George Jones, son to John and Dorothy James, 64th Regt., aged 6 years. 1831.

JONES

[Corroded iron plaque in low-railed enclosure.] The family burying ground of David Jones 1880.

JONES

See ANDERSON

JOY

[Tablet secured to west wall in a high-railed, low-walled enclosure.] To the memory of Henry Joy, son of Robert Joy and Grace RAINEY, and grandson of Francis Joy and Margaret MARTIN, formerly of The Lodge, near Belfast, born 16th Oct. 1754, died 15th April 1835. Also Mary Isabella his wife, eldest daughter of John HOLMES, of Belfast, banker and merchant and Isabella PATTERSON, of Comber, born 14th May 1771, died 7th Oct. 1832. Also Robert, their eldest son, born 12th Feb. 1798, died Feb. 1814. Also Susan BRUCE their youngest daughter, born 7th May 1812, died 5th June 1832. Also Robert Joy, of Belfast, second son of Henry Holmes Joy Q.C. and Catherine Ann LUDLOW and grandson of Henry Joy, born 12th August 1838, died 6th February 1905. Also of William Bruce Rainey Joy, M.C. died

September 1946, aged 69. And his only child Alix Bruce Joy, 3rd Officer, W.R.N.S., lost at sea through enemy action, August 1941, aged 24. And her mother Josephine who died 1st December 1947.

[Administration (with the will) of the estate of Robert Joy of Belvedere, Deramore Park, Belfast, land agent and stockbroker, who died 6 February 1905 granted at Dublin on the 22 May 1905 to Robert C. Joy, solicitor. Effects £1,891 0s.4d.

Henry Joy is best remembered as an historian, and George Benn said of him that he knew more of the history of old Belfast than anyone else. His most important work was *Historical Collections Relative to the Town of Belfast*, published in 1817. He was also a man of considerable literary attainments and published many important articles in the *Belfast News-Letter* of which he was proprietor until 1795. He also compiled *Belfast Politics* in conjunction with Dr Bruce.

Henry Joy owned the Cromac Paper Mill, near the junction of present-day Ormeau Avenue and Ormeau Road, for many years, besides much other property in and around Belfast.

In the late 18th and 19th centuries, the Joy family, more than most others, was identified with building up the commercial life and leading institutions of Belfast. Henry played a considerable part in this development, and for many years was an active committee member of the Belfast Charitable Society. He was one of the founders of the Belfast Library and Society for Promoting Knowledge, and was a most useful member of the Committee from very early in its history.

He was one of the founders of the Northern Whig Club in 1790 and later was both Secretary and President of the Belfast Literary Society. Although an extremely able and efficient man, there is evidence to suggest that his personality was ruthless, cold and lacking in humility.

A member of an old and distinguished family, he was the son of Robert Joy (1722-1785) who with his brother Henry (1720-1789) did so much to found and endow the old Poor House. It is said that Robert was the architect of the Poor House, the plans being approved by Francis Cooley of Dublin. Robert, in conjunction with Nicholas Grimshaw, introduced cotton manufacture to Ireland, the first being woven on looms in the Poor House. They were also proprietors of the *Belfast News-Letter*, founded in 1737 by their father Francis (1697-1790).

Their sister Ann (1730-1814) married Capt. John McCracken and among their children were the famous Henry Joy McCracken, executed in 1798, and Mary Ann McCracken (q.v.). Henry (1720-1789) had a son also called Henry (1766-1838) who subsequently became a noted lawyer and Attorney General, and was created Chief Baron Joy.

Henry (1754-1835) himself had five sons, four of whom survived to manhood and followed distinguished careers. A full account of both the Joy and McCracken families will be found in *The Life and Times of Mary Ann McCracken* by Mary McNeill (1960). See also Ward's memoir in *Belfast Literary Society* (1902), and Benn's *History of Town of Belfast*, Vol. II (1880).

Henry's father-in-law John Holmes was a merchant who, together with

John Brown, John Ewing and John Hamilton, founded Belfast's first Bank in 1787, which for a time during its short life was on the site of the present-day Bank Buildings. Officially called the Belfast Bank, it was popularly known as the "Bank of the Four Johns". His first cousin was Robert Holmes, a brother-in-law of Robert Emmet, the leader of the 1803 Rebellion. See Chambers: *Faces of Change* (1983).]

KEAN
[Marble tablet now lost.] Erected by Major Henry Kean, 97th Regt., in memory of his infant son Daniel, ob.19th Dec. 1833, aged 13 months. And his daughter Emily F. Kean, ob.1st August 1843, aged 7 years. Likewise his beloved wife Martha Caroline, ob.19th October 1857, and his youngest daughter Martha Caroline, ob.3rd November 1857. Here also lie the remains of Major Henry Kean, late H.M. 97th Regt., ob.15th February 1859.

[The will of Henry Kean of Ormeau Road, near Belfast, in the county of Antrim, esquire, a major in the army, who died 15 February 1859 at Queenstown, county Cork, was proved at Belfast on the 13 June 1859 by the oath of Henry Kean of 7 College Square, Belfast, esquire, a captain in the army, one of the executors. Effects under £4,000.]

KEAN
Erected by James Kean to the memory of his beloved and affectionate wife Clarissa who departed this life 30th July 1836, aged 19 years. Also Edward John TUKER who died 2nd March 1841, aged 31. Also his wife Eliza Tuker who died on the 28th January 1858, aged 47 years.

KEARNEY
[Very worn and now lost - supplemented from Society's Inscription book.] This burying (ground, 8 feet by 7 is the property of James Kearney, of Belfast, Ship Master. Here lieth the body of his) daughter, Ann (Kearney) who departed this (life the 25th) of Septr 1801, (aged 5 years and 2) months.

KEITH
[Flaked and lying flat.] Sacred to the memory of Eliza, relict of the late Robert Murray Keith (Esqr), who departed this life, 20th (November), 1853, aged 5(5 years). ("I ha)ve the witn(ess in my breast I know) Christ (died for me").

KELLY
[Cast-iron.] The family burying ground of John Kelly, Belfast, 1873.

KELLY
See AGNEW and WRIGHT

KELSO
[In entablature, formerly with those of John Gray and James Dunlop, and secured to dividing wall, but now lost.] Erected by Charles Kelso, of High Street, Belfast, in memory of his mother who died 28th of August 1830.

KELSO
See GRAY

KENNEDY

[Two tablets in pillared twin entablatures, secured to north wall. The first is badly broken.] (a) Here are deposited the remains of Gilbert Kennedy, D.M., During the period of forty four years by an exemplary decorum of life, purity of precept and (anetity) of manners he taught that virtue to others which he himself eminently possessed. He was ordained at Lisburn, An.1732, translated to Killileagh, An.1733 and removed to Belfast, An.1744, where he died universally esteemed and regretted on the 12th of May 1773, aged 67 years. Beside his are deposited the remains of his wife Elizabeth, daughter to James TRAIL, Esquire, of Marybrook in the County of Down, who died on the 20th April 1786, aged seventy four years, than whom none ever lived more excellent in the various relations of mother, wife and friend. Near this are also deposited the remains of his grandson Gilbert Kennedy who died on the 8th September 1799, aged seven years. Also the remains of his grand-daughter Isabella Kennedy who died the 29th October 1798, aged 9 months.

(b) Here lie the remains of Margaret Kennedy, daughter of the late Rev Gilbert Kennedy, who died the 1st of May 1830, aged 72 years. James Trail Kennedy, of Annadale, Esqr born 8th April 1751, died 28th August 1832. Isabella Kennedy, his wife died 5th April 1833, aged 65 years. Elizabeth Kennedy, daughter of the late Revd Gilbert Kennedy, died 15th April 1833, aged 81 years.

[These three plots were purchased by James T. Kennedy in June 1807.

The Kennedy family was descended from the noble family of Cassilis of Scotland. The first member to appear in this country was the Rev. Gilbert Kennedy (primus) who fled from Girvan, Ayrshire as a result of persecution against the Presbyterians in the reign of Charles II. For a number of years he preached secretly in the district around Comber until the 1690s when, with the introduction of a limited amount of toleration, he became minister of Comber, Dundonald and Holywood.

His son, also the Rev. Gilbert Kennedy (secundus) was minister of Tullylish until his death in 1745.

The son of Rev. Gilbert Kennedy (secundus) was also the Rev. Gilbert Kennedy (tertius) and was minister of the Second Presbyterian Church, Rosemary Street from 1744 to 1773.

Collectively, they were known in the family as the "three Gilberts" and among their many distinguished descendants were the Andrews family of Comber, the Hyndman and McTear families (q.v.) of Belfast and Dr A.G. Malcom (1818-1856), the physician and historian. George Kennedy Smith, a great-grandson of John Galt Smith (1730-1802) was descended from the Rev. Gilbert Kennedy (secundus) through the Barbers of Rathfriland. It would appear that the Kennedy family of Cultra was distantly related to them.

James Trail Kennedy, son of Rev. Gilbert Kennedy (tertius), was a highly prosperous wine merchant with extensive premises in Legg's Lane, which thoroughfare is now occupied by Lombard Street. Regarded as one of the foremost merchants of Belfast, he helped to build up the growing town's prosperity in the late 18th and early 19th centuries.

He was a founder member of the Northern Whig Club in 1790. Greatly respected by all who knew him, he was a highly cultured man, was most charitable, whilst his manner was simple and genuine. In later life he lived at Annadale House where he pursued his literary tastes.

He married Miss Isabella Byron and had several children, all of whom died young except one, Elizabeth, who married, firstly, into the Bomford family, and secondly, Archbishop Beresford of Armagh. She had no children by either marriage.

A fuller account of the Kennedy family will be found in Benn's *History of Belfast Vol.2.* (1880). See also Millin: *History of the Second Congregation of Protestant Dissenters in Belfast* (1900) Chambers: *Faces of Change* (1983).]

KENNEDY

[Wall plot in upper ground. The monument is no longer extant and is copied from Society's Inscription book.]. .... Margaret Kennedy .... of her husband .... Kennedy ...... day of December 180(.)............. March 1811.

[This was a worn flat slab, the plot being purchased by Andrew Kennedy M.D. on 6th December 1804.]

KENNEDY

[Pillar with pedimented capstone topped by an urn, in a high-railed enclosure.] Interred here are the remains of Ann Jane, daughter of John Kennedy, who died 30th April 1812, aged 8 months. Eliza who died 21st Jan. 1818, aged 12 years. Isabella died 3rd Dec. 1829, aged 3 years. William son of John Kennedy, died 27th June 1851, aged 27 years. John Kennedy, of Shrub Hill, Belfast died 24th Nov. 1853, aged 70 years. Sarah Jane, relict of the late John Kennedy, died 28th May 1867, aged 78 years. Sarah Kennedy, born 1st June 1817, died 3rd Jan. 1889. Kate died 19th Dec. 1865.

[Contd. on south side.] Interred here are the remains of John, son of Thomas Kennedy, who died 1st Feb. 1848, aged 8 months. Anna FOWLER, wife of Thomas Kennedy died 6th July 1865, aged 42 years. Thomas Kennedy died 1st June 1868, aged 54 years. Anna Archer Kennedy died 11th May 1926.

[On plinth.] Erected by Thomas Kennedy, A.D. 1848.

[The will of Sarah Kennedy of 15 Victoria Place, Belfast, spinster, who died 3 January 1889 at same place, was proved at Belfast on the 1 May 1889 by John Milliken of Knock, county Down, railway secretary, one of the executors. Effects £659 4s.6d.

The will of Thomas Kennedy of Mountcharles, Belfast, county Antrim, gentleman who died 1 June 1868 at same place, was proved at Belfast on the 3rd July 1868 by the oaths of James Kennedy of Rosetta, Belfast, county Down, esquire, and William McNeill of Upper Cresent, merchant and John Milliken of Queen Street, gentlemen (both in Belfast aforesaid), three of the executors. (Deceased died domiciled in Ireland). Effects in Great Britain and Ireland £9,000.

Kennedy, Anna Archer of Killowan Terrace, Rostrevor, county Down, spinster, died 11 May 1926. Probate Belfast 27 September 1926 to

Thomas Mayne Heron, solicitor. Effects £1,967 4s.7d.]

KENNEDY

[In lower ground and no longer extant.] Erected by Dorothea Kennedy in remembrance of her beloved husband John Kennedy who departed this life 1st March 1854, aged 54 years. Also 3 children who died in infancy. And her grandchild Dorothea Kennedy died 2nd August 1875, aged 6 months. Also Jennie, the dearly beloved wife of Joseph Kennedy, died 23rd Jany 1896, aged 39 years. Also the above Dorothea Kennedy died 21st Dec. 1896. One of the best of mothers.

KENNEDY

[Large headstone in low-walled enclosure, which has been completely demolished and is in fragments. Arms: chevron bearing two hatchets. Three rings and three flowers. Supported by two horses rampant. Crest: Eagle bearing words "The Cooper Arms". Motto: "Prosperity attend the integrity of our cause".] Erected by the Jurneymen [sic] Coopers, of Belfast, May 1812.

[Inscription on worn marble at back.] Names of members interred in Coopers' Burying Ground:

William J. Kennedy died Sept 9th 1838.
Thomas CAMPBELL died June 4th 1847.
James Campbell died Decr 23rd 1849.
George MATTHEWS died June 8th 1855.
Hugh MULLAN died Mar. 9th 1857.
(James) CUMMINGS died Jan. 7th 185(9).
John RODGERS died (May) 12th 1872.
James Rodgers died (Novr) 6th 1872.
William J. DIXON died (Feb) 7th 187(3).
Thomas JACKSON died (Mar) 6th 1874.
James MALLON died (Aug.) 2nd 1875.
John MA(RT)IN died (Sep.) 12th 1877.

[In addition to those commemorated on this monument, one Hugh Crawford, an inmate of the Poor House, who died in 1847 at the age of 102, is buried here. See Strain: *Belfast and its Charitable Society* (1961)].

KENNEDY

See CURLEY, GOURLEY and MILLER

KENNING

[Flaking.] Erected by Thos Kenning to the memory of Jane Kenning his wife who departed this life January 21st 1806, aged 31 years. Also here lieth the remains of the above named Thomas Kenning who departed this life October 11th 1816, aged 48 years.

[Thomas Kenning was a muslin-dealer of Castle Street.]

KENT

[Small plaque now missing from lower ground.] The family burying ground of John Kent, Belfast, 1835.

KERR

See McCUTCHEON and McDOWELL

Memorial to the Journeyman Coopers of Belfast (1812) with its unusually fine coat of arms (photograph R.W.M. Strain).

KING
[Badly weathered sandstone, now lost.] Erected (in) memory of (Jame)s King who departed thi(s life ..) February 1814, age(d .. yea)rs. (Also M)ary his .... who departed (this) life .. (Octo)ber 182(5), aged (.. year)s. ....

KING
[Headstone formerly in upper portion of graveyard, but no longer extant.] Erected to the memory of the late Peter King who died Feby 28th 1837, aged 39 years.

KING
See EWART and MURPHY

KINGAN
[Now lost.] Erected by Mary Kingan in memory of her beloved daughter Letitia RANKIN who departed this life 5th June 1857, aged 29 years. "Watch therefore, for you know not the hour when the Son of Man cometh". Also the above Mary Kingan who departed this life 10th February 1865, aged 57 years.

[The will of Mary Kingan of Smithfield, Belfast, in the county of Antrim, widow, who died 10 February 1865 at same place, was proved at Belfast on the 17 May 1865 by the oaths of David Morton of Berry Street, auctioneer, and Robert Kingan of Townsend Street, boilermaker, both of Belfast aforesaid, the executors. Effects under £200.]

KINGSBERRY
[Slate tablet now loosened from headstone and lost.] Erected by William Kingsberry in memory of his beloved wife Elizabeth who departed this life the 10th of June 1856, aged 30 years.

KINNEAR
[Now missing from lower ground. This plot was purchased by Patrick Kinnear in February 1851.] The family burying place of Patrick Kinnear.

[He was a linen merchant with offices in Waring Street and lived at Harp Hall, Antrim Road.]

KIRKER
[Laid flat.] Erected by Archibald Kirker, Shrubhill, in memory of his much lamented wife Jane who died 17th Novr 1865, aged 52 years. Also the above named Archibald Kirker who died 8th Octr 1886, aged 76 years. Also his wife Mary who died 18th April 1892, aged 67 years.

[The will of Archibald Madowel Kirker, formerly of Belfast and late of The Knock, county Down, gentlemen, who died 8 October 1886 at latter place, was proved at Belfast on the 1 November 1886 by Mary Kirker of The Knock, widow, one of the executors. Effects £829.

The will of Mary Kirker, formerly of The Knock, and late of Strandtown, both in county Down, widow, who died 18 April 1892 at latter place, was proved at Belfast on the 22 June 1892 by Sir James H. Haslett of North Street, Knight, J.P., and James Jenkins of Rosemary Street, rent agent, both of Belfast, the executors. Effects £1,874 18s.4d.]

KIRKPATRICK

[Headstone lying flat and almost completely flaked, but now lost.] Erected by James Ki(rkpatrick), of Belfast in memory (of his mother Rosina who died 6th Decr 1816, aged 35 years. Also his) fat(her James who died 18th Jany 1823, aged 62 years. Also his sister) Mar(garet who died 14th Aug. 1827, aged 35 years [sic]. Also his brother William who died 14th Novr 1827, aged 23. Also his brother Hugh who died 18th May 1832, aged 32. Also 3 of Hugh's children who died young.)

KIRKPATRICK

[Flaking and now lost.] Sacred to the memory of Henry Kirkpatrick, aetatis 1 year 7 months, April 3rd 1848. Also Mrs Margaret Kirkpatrick, who died 10th July 1905, aged 90 years. "Seated with Christ in heavenly places". Also James B. Kirkpatrick who died 17th April 1911, aged 87 years, son of Henry Kirkpatrick, who died in Australia. Also his wife, the above Margaret Kirkpatrick.

[Probate of the will of Margaret Kirkpatrick of 165 York Street, Belfast, widow, who died 10 July 1905, granted at Belfast on the 16 August 1905 to James Benjamin Kirkpatrick, retired grocer. Effects £381.

Probate of the will with one codicil of James Benjamin Kirkpatrick of 165 York Street, Belfast, retired grocer, who died 17 April 1911 at Claremount Street in said city, granted at Belfast on 5 July 1911 to Graham Lemon Owens, bookkeeper, and William Nelson, foreman. Effects £4,035 7s.7d. Re-sworn £3,882 9s.7d.]

KITCHIN

[It was flaking and has now disappeared.] (Erected) to the memory of Elizabeth Kitchin who departed this life 25th March 18(5)5, aged 75 years. John Kitchin, a relative, who died 7th Aug. 1859, aged 23 years. And Sarah Kitchin, daughter of the above, who died 30th April 1860, aged 43 years. Also her son Wm John Kitchin who died 8th April 1870, aged 57 years. Also in memory of John VINT, M.D. who died 30th Oct. 1881, aged 27 years. Her son Thomas Kitchin who died 20th August 1889, aged 73 years. Her daughter Elizabeth Kitchin who died 30th August 1892, aged 73 years.

[The will of Elizabeth Kitchin, otherwise Kitchen, of 95 Madrid Street, Belfast, county Down, spinster, who died 30 August 1892 at same place, was proved at Belfast, on the 30 November 1892 by Robert Howie Saunderson of 7 Broughem Street, Belfast, ironfounder, the sole executor. Effects £1,361 3s.6d.]

KNOWLES

[Laid flat.] Erected by Mr. Jacob Knowles to the memory of his dearly beloved wife Mary Knowles who departed this life 26th September 1822, aged 18 years. Also their infant daughter Margaret who died 19th September 1822.

KNOWLES

See MARSHALL

KNOX

[Flaking stone with cap broken off.] Erected by Margaret Knox in memory of her beloved husband John Knox who departed this life 13th March (1833), aged 73 years.

KNOX

[Badly weathered and now lost.] Sacred to the memory of Robert Knox who departed this life 9th Fe(by) 1837, aged (88) years.

KNOX

[Headstone, formerly in lower ground, now missing.] Erected to the memory of Alexr Knox, late of Dromore, who departed this life 11th Feby 1851 aged 80 years. And his son John Knox, of Belfast who died 1st Feby 1851 aged 45 years. Also his grandchild Margaret MALCOLMSON who died 10th Jany 1850 aged 4 years, and 10 months. Also on the 29th June 1862, Jane Knox aged 82 years. At Calcutta on 7th Feby 1867, Alexr Knox Malcolmson, Lieut. of H.M.S. 46th Regt. aged 25 years. And at Balmoral Terrace on 20th Jany 1868, Sarah, relict of the late John Knox aged 61 years.

KNOX

See GRAHAM

KYD

See HYNDMAN

KYLE

[Flaking extensively.] Erected to the memory of Margaret Kyle, wife of John Kyle of Tullycainet [sic] who departed this life 8th January 1802, aged 35 years. She was an affectionate mother, a loving wife and a steady friend. Also the said John Kyle who departed this life, 23rd day of Decem 1816, aged 57 years. Here also lies the body of their daughter-in-law Sarah Kyle, of Dindonald [sic] who departed this life 11th day of May 1842, aged 43 years. "If virtue, honesty and integrity deserve to live, her memory can never die". Also their son John Kyle who died 30th July 1873, aged 76 years.

LAIRD

[Marble tablet formerly in surround attached to south wall and now lost.] Here rest, awaiting a happy resurrection to Eternal Life, the earthly remains of Margaret Laird, daughter of the Rev. William Laird, formerly of Belfast. She was born 1759, died Octr 16th 1831. "Precious in the sight of the Lord is the death of his saints". Here also of her sister Anne RAMSEY, died 1823. "Distinguished also by her Christian virtues." Of her husband James Ramsey Esq., and others of both families.

[The Rev. William Laird was minister of the Third Presbyterian Church in Rosemary Street from 1747 to 1791, when he died. He was one of the original committee members of the Belfast Charitable Society, when that body was incorporated by Act of Parliament in 1774.

One of his daughters, Jane, was married to the Rev. John Thomson (1741-1828), the minister of Carnmoney and a 1st cousin of the Thomsons of Jennymount. Their sons were well-known merchants, and one of their daughters, Elizabeth, became the mother of Sir Thomas McClure, Bart., the Liberal M.P. for Belfast from 1868-1874, vid. inf.]

LAITHAM
[Flaking and now lost.] Here lieth the body of John Laitham, who departed this life November 8th 1816, aged 48 years.

LAMONT
[Badly flaked sandstone — looks of c.1810-1830.] Sacred (to the) memory of Mrs Ann Lamont who departed this life the (31st) of October 1(8..), aged 74 years. [This plot was bought by Ann Lamont in November 1823.]

LAMONT
[Laid flat.] In memory of John Harrison Lamont who died 2nd (Feby. 1844) aged 56 years. John Lamont who died 11th Sept. 1848 aged 73 years. James William CAUGHEY who died 10th February 1850, aged 22 years. Aeneas Lamont, November 11th 1860 aged 48. Sarah Lamont aged 80. Leah Lamont, November 11th 1866 aged 89.

[Lamont & Co. were opticians, watchmakers, jewellers and marine instrument repairers at 15, Castle Place.]

LANYON
[With cross and circle at the top and inscription in gothic characters.] Owen Mortimer Lanyon, born Augt XXIV, (XLV), died Dec. IV, (XLV). [The plot was bought by Charles Lanyon, in December 1845.

Sir Charles Lanyon (1813-1889) was probably the most important and influential architect to practice in Belfast. His greatest buildings were erected in the 1840s and 1850s and include the School for the Deaf and Dumb, Crumlin Road Gaol and Courthouse, Queen's College (now University), Assembly's College and the Custom House. He was buried at Knockbreda. His father-in-law was Jacob Owen of the Board of Public Works, Dublin. See Clarke *Gravestone Inscriptions, County Down*, Vol. 2 (2nd ed. 1988).

LARMOUR
[Marble in headstone, now removed.] In memory of Catherine SETON, wife of Hugh Larmour, and second daughter of Geo. W. CHISHOLM, Esqr, of Calcutta, died 25th Septr 1849 aged 31 years. William Larmour who died Octr 1(4)th 18(5)9 aged 3(3) years.

LATIMORE
[Undated slate headstone, identical to and beside Thomas Orr's of c.1805.] This stone was erected by Robert Latimore, of Belfast. Here lieth five of his children who died young.

[This plot was bought by Robert Latimore in October 1800.]

LAW
[Worn limestone in surround.] In memory of James Law, of Fairview, who departed this life 1st July 18(3)6. Also Margaret his wife who departed this life 27th August 18(5)9. Also Jessie GARDNER her cousin.

[The will of Margaret Law of Fairview, Belfast, county Antrim, widow, who died 25 August 1859 at Fairview aforesaid, was proved at Belfast on

LAW

[Missing.] Sarah Law died 14th Dec. 1851, aged 21 years.

LE PAN

[Badly flaked.] To the memory of Louis Noailles Le Pan who died June 9th 1837. Also his (aunt) Elizabeth BUCHANAN Also his (two) daughters Margaret (and) Adelaine. Also (his aunt Cath(erine ..M)AIRS who (died) August 1871.

LECKY

See LENNOX

LEECE

[White limestone, now broken and laid flat.] In memory of Jane Leece, relict of the late George Leece, Woodlands Eay...d, who fell asleep in Jesus (26)Nov. 1870. Also of her father Capt (John) REILLY who departed this life (18)th April 18(0)8. Also her sister Eliza Reilly, who departed this life (6)th January 1874. Also Frances Leece died Nov. 28th 1911. "Until the Lord come".

LEMON

[Missing.] The family burying place of Graham Lemon, 1847.

LEMON

See WILSON and WORKMAN

LENNOX

[Broken and very worn horizontal of Castle Espie limestone slab, with Mattear and Drennan stones. Arms: serrated diagonal cross with four stars in chief. Crest: Knight's helmet and plumes. Motto:]. Here lyeth the body of Robert Lennox, of Belfast, merchant, who departed this life the (5) of February 173(3) aged (7)9 years. Here ly(eth the body o)f his first (wife Ann Lennox, alias) LECKY, with three of their (children). And here lyeth (.) of his children by his second wife Ann Lennox, alias (C)NIN.HSE. Here lyeth also his third wife (Marth)a HAMILTON, daughter of (John) Hamilton Esq. who (was Burgess and) Sovereigne of B(elfast by) who he had eleven (children), nine of (wh)ich were (buried here.) She departed this (life the 3) of February 17(.6) aged (6)0 years.

[This plot was purchased by Mrs Drennan in February 1806. It would appear that Robert Lennox's first wife Ann was connected with the Drennan family as well as the Lecky family. This stone probably came from St George's graveyard, High St Robert Lennox was an active member of the First Presbyterian Church in the opening years of the 18th century.

John Hamilton was Sovereign of Belfast in 1683 and 1684.]

LENNOX

See LINDSAY and MATTEAR

LEWIS

[Large tablet with surround, attached to east wall in a high-railed enclosure.] In memory of James Lewis who died the 15th August 1837 aged 70 years. Elizabeth Maria Lewis died 17th Novr 1839 aged 70 years. Elizabeth Ann Lewis died 23rd August 1837 aged 49 years. James Lewis died 25th April 1845 aged 5 years and 9 months. Anne Lewis died 8th April 1848 aged 7 years. Dorcas Tabitha Lewis died 11th September 1857 aged 55 years. Frederick Harry Lewis died at Nettlefield, 15th February 1871 aged 67 years. And of Mary, wife of the above Frederick Harry Lewis who died 8th October 1887 aged 70 years. Also of their son James, Captain 2nd Battn 6th Royal Warwickshire Regt, drowned at Gopulpur 21st December 1881, and buried at Burdwan, India aged 36 years. "Waiting for the coming of Our Lord Jesus Christ" 1.Cor.1, 7.

[The will of Frederick Harry Lewis of Nettlefield, county Down, esquire, who died 15 February 1871 at same place, was proved on the 31 March 1871 at Belfast, by the oaths of Mary Anne Lewis, the widow, and Elizabeth Mona Lewis and Mary Anne Lewis junior, spinsters, all of Nettlefield, Belfast aforesaid, the executrixes. Deceased died domiciled in Ireland. Effects in United Kingdom under £14,000.

Letters of administration of the personal estate of Mary Anne Lewis of Nettlefield, Ballymacaret, county Down, widow, who died 8 October 1887 at same place, were granted at Belfast on the 23 May 1888 to Elizabeth Maria Lewis of Nettlefield, Ballymacarret, spinster, a child. Effects £1,348 3s.7d.

Frederick Harry Lewis and his brother William were prosperous timber merchants in Great George's Street, the firm having originally been known as Thomas Corbett & Co. Frederick Lewis lived in Great George's Street before moving out to Nettlefield in Ballymacarret about the year 1850.]

LEWIS
See BYRTT and McCLELLAND

LIGGET

[Flaking headstone, laid flat.] Erected by Thomas Ligget in memory of his son Captain James Ligget who departed this life 5th of February 1848 aged 35 years. Also his daughter Margaret who departed this life 14th of August 1848 aged 38 years. Also his wife Jane who departed this life 26th of December 1849 aged 66 years. Also his daughter Mary NEIL who departed this life 21st Decr 1850 aged 42 years. His son Capt Thomas Ligget, lost at sea, 1874. His three grand-children who died young. Also his grandson Thomas Ligget who died 20th Jany 1887 aged 30 years. The above Thomas Ligget died Jany 1857 aged 74 years. Catherine Ligget died 29th November 1907 aged 87 years. Elizabeth Ligget, wife of above Thomas Ligget, junior, who died 13th May 1911 aged 52 years. Catherine G. Ligget died 2nd Jany 19(5)2 aged 87.

[The will of Thomas Liggett of Montalto, South Parade, Ballynafeigh, county Down, commercial traveller, who died 20 January 1887 at same place, was proved at Belfast on 1 April 1887 by Catherine Ligget of 19

Brougham Street, Belfast, widow, and Alexander Reid of 5 Hughenden Terrace, Kenbella Avenue, Belfast, draper, the executors. Effects £1,286 13s.4d.

Catherine Garraway Ligget of "Thornlea", Finaghy Road South, Finaghy, county Antrim, spinster, died 2 January 1952. Probate Belfast 1 February 1952 to Ethel Reid spinster, and Thomasina MacIlwaine, married woman. Effects £113 13s.11d.

The Ligget family were largely seafarers and lived in and around Earl Street in the district affectionately known as "Sailorstown".]

LINDEN

Erected by Matthew Linden, of Belfast, in memory of his daughter Jane who departed this life 25th May 1807 aged 20 years.

Here rests a Maid beloved, a daughter,
dear, of manners gentle and of soul sincere,
a tender Mother's hope and pride, who ne'er give
Cause of grief, but when she died.

Also seven of his children who died young. Also his grand-daughter Catharine Linden who died 14th December 1836, aged 13 years. Also the above named Matthew Linden who died 10th May 1837, aged 76 years. Also Ellen'r, wife of Matthew Linden, junr, who died 16th October 1844, aged 24 years.

[Matthew Linden and Sons were confectioners and pastry cooks in Castle Street.]

LINDEN

[Two marble tablets formerly lying loose and probably both part of the same monument. The first is now in a high-railed enclosure.] Erected by Eliza Linden in memory of her husband William Linden who died the (8)th of March 1830 aged 38 years. Also of her son James Linden who died the 21st of April 1830 aged 7 years. And also of her son Matthew Linden who died 5th of August 1848 aged 36 years.

[Now lost] Also the above named Eliza Linden who died the (20)th of August 1850 aged (5)7 years. And her daughter Jane McGUCKIN, who died 28th July 186(3) aged 4(3) years.

LINDEN

[Marble headstone surmounted by casket-shaped block, attached to east wall of upper graveyard in a high-railed enclosure.] Erected to the memory of William Linden who died 12th September 1866 aged 50 years. And his son William J. Linden who died 19th November 1869.

[William Linden was appointed confectioner to the Queen and his shop was in Corn Market. He lived at Martello Terrace, Holywood. His kinsman, Matthew R. Linden (1846-1917) was a Town Commissioner of Holywood, and also prominent as a church warden in Holywood Parish Church.]

LINDSAY

[Horizontal slab on the ground.] Here lieth the remains of Edward Lindsay, merchant of Belfast, who died 31 Augt 1843 aged 84 years. Also his son Lennox Hamilton Lindsay who died 18th Augt 1829 aged 21 years, whose grandfather Lennox YOUNG Esqr was grandson of Robt LENNOX and Martha HAMILTON, as mentioned on a tombstone now lying in Lot 48 of this ground. Here lieth his wife Amelia Lindsay, alias Young, daughter of Lennox Young as above. late of Cotton in the Parish of Bangor, County Down. She died the 8th of October 1845 aged 74 years. Also her dr Martha died 11th of July 1849 aged 51. Also their son Edward died 13th Decr 1852 aged 51 years. Also their dr Amelia M.N. Lindsay died 3rd Augt 1868 aged 64 years.

[The will of Amelia or Amelia Norman Margerette Lindsay formerly of Botanic View, Belfast, county Antrim, and late of Hibernia Place, Holywood, county Down, spinster, who died 3 August 1868 at Holywood aforesaid, was proved at Belfast on the 31 August 1868 by the oaths of Robert Young of Calender Street, Belfast aforesaid, C.E., and the Reverend Joseph William McKay of Stephen's Green, Dublin, Wesleyan minister, the executors. Effect under £3,000.

Edward Lindsay, senr and his son were nursery and seedmen, first in Donegall Street, then later in Waring Street. About the year 1840 they lived at Lennoxvale, Malone Road, which took its name from their family connection with Robert Lennox who died in 1733.]

LINDSAY
See CARSON

(LITTLE)
[Stone in upper ground, no longer extant. It was badly decayed in 1907, and the only clue to its identity is that the plot was bought by Samuel Little in 1815.] Erected to the memory of William ..... of Belfast who departed this life ... April ... aged ...

LLOYD
See MALCOMSON

LOGAN
See CAVART

LOW
[Flaking and now lost.] Erected by John Low, in memory of two of (his children) who died (young). Also his son John Low who died 1st Novr 1837 aged 5 years. His daughter (Ja)ne (died 2)nd August 1838 aged 2 (months). Also his wife Jane Low (died) 3rd November 1848 aged 39 years. Also his son William Neil, who died 11th July 18(48) aged 5 months. And (also to the) memory of his much lamented (wife) Mary Ann who died 19th November 185(4) aged (23) years and 10 months.

LOWRY
[Flaking and laid flat.] This stone was erected by Jacob Lowry of Belfast, in memory of his son Jacob who departed this life the 13th of June 1799 aged 9 mths.

[This appears to be the oldest stone indigenous to the New Burying Ground.]

LOWRY

[Marble tablet now detached from smashed, Gothic-style headstone, laid flat.] Erected in loving memory of John Lowry, born 17th Decr 1805, died 26th April 1881. Grace Lowry died 10th July 1900 aged 96 years. Also three children: Robert, born 16th May 1831, died 1st Sept 1831, Letitia, born 16th April 1834, died 15th Feby. 1836, Anna Maria, born 6th July 1839, died 18th Sept 1840. "Then are they glad because they are at rest, and so he bringeth them unto the haven where they would be."

[The will of John Lowry of Woodlawn, Sydenham, county Down, retired builder and contractor, who died 26 April 1881 at same place, was proved at Belfast on the 13 May 1881 by Grace Lowry of Woodlawn, Sydenham, widow, the sole executrix. Effects under £2,000.

Probate of the will of Grace Lowry of Oakley, Strandtown, county Down, widow, who died 10 July 1900, granted at Belfast on the 17 December 1900 to David Moore, assistant secretary to the Belfast Harbour Commissioners. Effects £2,400 19s.2d.]

LOWRY

[Flaking, and now lost.] Erected by James Lowry, of Belfast, in memory of his beloved wife Elenor H. (Lowry) who departed this life (19th February 1841 aged (40) years. Also the above James Lowry who died 8th November 1853 aged 55 years. Also Catherine Lowry who died 22nd December 1863 aged 60 years.

LOWRY

[White limestone, broken and laid flat.] Erected by Joseph Lowry in loving remembrance of his family. John Harper Lowry died 22nd Jany 1852 aged 8 years. Samuel Lowry died 27th March 1867 aged 20 years. James Alexander Lowry died 14th May 1881 aged 19 years. David Hamilton Lowry died 5th Jany 1882 aged 21 years. Also three other children who died in infancy. Also his wife Ellen Lowry who entered into rest 6th January 1888. The above named Joseph Lowry died 10th April 1890. Their daughter Annie H. Lowry died 21st February 1892.

[The will of Joseph Lowry of 60 Botanic Avenue, Belfast, gentleman, who died 10 April 1890 at same place, was proved at Belfast on the 14 May 1890 by Josephine Mary Lowry of 60 Botanic Avenue, Belfast, spinster, and Thomas Farley of South Parade, Ballynafeigh, county Down, clerk of inland revenue, the executors. Effects £237 5s.]

LUDLOW

See JOY

LUKE

[*M.D.X*,160. Mausoleum surmounted by a thick obelisk which bears the inscription on three sides. [East side.] James Luke of Donegall Place son of James Luke of Island Reagh and Sarah THOMPSON, of Greenmount, his wife died (1st) March 18(09). Catherine Luke, wife of the first named and daughter of Robert and Ann GETTY died 20th April 181(3).

[North face.] John SITLINGTON of Ballygor, died at Ballymacarret in

1803. Ann Getty, of Belfast, daughter of John Sitlington, of Ballyclaverty and sister of the above named died 24th April 181(2) aged 84 years. Her husband Robert Getty with several of their children were interred at the old church, High Street.

[South face.] The following are the sons of James and Catherine Luke: Robert, who died in 1815, John who died in 1814, Samuel who died in 1844, Campbell who died at Phildelphia in 1820, William who died at New York in 1837, Thompson who died in 1834, James who died in Dublin in 1862, by whom this monument was erected to the memory of his parents and brothers.

[Francis Joseph Bigger submitted the following entry to the *Memorials of the Dead in Ireland* for the year 1918: "The Luke Vault in Clifton Street burial ground, has 'W. Graham fecit' cut upon its base. It was probably erected circa 1810 and W. Graham was a well-known Belfast stone-carver in the beginning of the last century. The Lukes come from Islandreagh, near Muckamore, where the Thompsons established themselves, and were allied to the Sitlingtons who had a bleach green in the parish of Ballycor, near Ballyclare. They were intermarried with the Gettys, a well-known family, whose burial-places were in the old churchyard in High Street, and also in Carnmoney. They were also intermarried with the Thompsons of Greenmount on the old Carrickfergus Road, now North Queen Street, and of the Abbey at Muckamore where they were bleachers. In 1783 there was a firm of woollen warehousemen — Luke, Murphy, Hazlett & Co. — whilst Luke, Thompson & Co. were merchants in 14, York Street in 1819. The Lukes were also bankers."

James Luke, a woollen draper of Bridge Street and John Thomson (1798-1874) of Jennymount became partners in 1821 of the Belfast Commercial Bank from which evolved the Belfast Banking Company of which they were to become early directors.

The Gettys were well-known provision merchants in Belfast. Edmund Getty (1799-1857), the antiquarian and Secretary to the Belfast Harbour Board of Commissioners, was of this family and his father Robert was a prominent Volunteer and had a shop at 16, North Street. Robert married a daughter of Nicholas Grimshaw, the pioneer cotton-spinner. See Simpson: *The Belfast Bank 1827-1970* (1975).

The will with one codicil, of James Luke, formerly of Belfast, late of Charles Street, Grosvenor Squire, in the city of London, who died 30 September 1862 at the Gresham Hotel, Dublin, was proved at the Principal Registry on the 21 October 1862 by the oath of Anne Cuningham of Ardverness in the county of Antrim, widow, the sole executrix. Effects under £8,000.]

LUKE

This burying ground belongs to John Luke, of Belfast, mercht. Here lieth the remains of his son Hugh Luke who died the 18th Decr 1804 aged 12 years 7 months. Also the remains of the above named John Luke who died on the 29th of August 1822 aged 89 years.

LUTMAN
See WRIGHT

LYNAS
See BENSON

LYNCH
See EID

LYONS
[Badly worn marble shield in headstone, now lost.] (Erected by Robert Lyons in memory of his daughter Agnes who died 17th January 1851 aged 18 years. Also his daughter Mary Ann who died 18th May 1831 or 1851 aged 8 years.) Also Margaret BAIRD his wife who died 8th (June 1855 aged 51) years. And the above-named Robert Lyons who died on the 9th (March 1860) aged (59) years.

[Letters of administration of the personal estate of Robert Lyons of Bradbury Place, Belfast, in the county of Antrim, grocer and publican, a widower, who died 9 March 1860 at same place, were granted at Belfast on 20 June 1860 to Jane Lyons of Kensington Place, Belfast aforesaid, spinster, the daughter, one of the next of kin of said deceased. Effects under £450.]

LYONS
[Flaking.] The family burial place of Thomas Lyons. His son, William Henry Lyons who departed this life 20th Sept. 1879 aged (31) years.

Though Neptune winds and blustery waves have tossed me me to and fro,
In spite of all, by God's decree, I'm harboured here below,
Here at an Anchor I do lie with many of our fleet,
One day again we shall set sail our Saviour Christ to meet.

LYTLE
[Large black granite monument in the form of a sarcophagus, in railed enclosure and inscribed around three sides.] John Lytle, born on the 12 March 1815, died on the 18 of September 1871, Mary, wife of John Lytle, died April 21, 1857 aged 49. Isabella Jane, daughter died January 11, 1845 aged 6. John Lytle, junr, died March 18 1869 aged 32. Robert Lytle, sen, died March 12 1870 aged 27. "Blessed are the dead which die in the Lord, for they rest from their labours".

[The will of John Lytle junior of Belfast, county Antrim, and Ballynafeigh, county Down, merchant, who died 18 March 1869 at Ballynafeigh aforesaid, was proved at Belfast on the 11 June 1869 by the oaths of Joseph Hugh Lytle and James Haslett, both of Belfast aforesaid, merchants, the executors. Effects under £5,000.

Letters of administration of the personal estate of Robert Lytle of Belfast, county Antrim, merchant, a bachelor, who died 12 March 1870 at same place, were granted at Belfast 1 June 1870 to John Lytle of Belfast aforesaid, merchant, the father and sole next of kin of said deceased. Effects in United Kingdom under £4,000.

John H. Lytle was a linen merchant of A. & S. Henry & Co., Wellington Place.]

McBLAIN

[Smashed and almost completely worn marble tablet in headstone now lost.] ("He loved me and gave Himself for me". In memoriam) John Mc(Blain, who fell asleep in Christ, Jan. 21st 1875) aged (68 years. Also two sons & three daughters).

[The will of John McBlain of Clifton Terrace, Belfast, county Antrim, leather merchant, who died 21 January 1875 at same place, was proved at Belfast 1 March 1875 by the oath of Sarah McBlain of 3 Clifton Terrace, Belfast, spinster, one of the executors. Effects under £7,000.

John McBlain was the founder of the firm of John McBlain & Co. who were well-known leather merchants and tanners, first in North Street, and later in Donegall Street. Their tanyard was situated in Carrick Hill.]

McBRIDE

[In lower ground and now missing. Plot purchased by Miss Margaret McBride in September 1854.] The family burying ground of Joseph McBride.

McCABE

[Large slate cracked down the middle and lying flat.] Here lieth the body of Mary McCabe who departed this life April the 11th 1801 aged 84 years. Also her son Thomas McCabe who departed this life March the 5th 1820 aged 80 years. This tomb is erected to their memory by Isabella McCabe the disconsolate widow of Thomas McCabe.

Thomas McCabe, M.D.,	died 1829.
Isabella McCabe	" 1837.
Jane Maria COLEMAN	" 1861.
James Coleman	" 1866.
Isabella McCabe Coleman	died 1893.
Maria Ann Coleman	" 1905.
Thomas McCabe Coleman	" 8th July 1908.

Elizabeth Hamilton Coleman, died 20th March 1912.

[Letters of administration of the personal estate of Isabella McCabe Coleman of 61 Atlantic Avenue, Belfast, spinster, who died 30 July 1893 at same place, were granted at Belfast 21 August 1893 to Thomas McCabe Coleman of 61 Atlantic Avenue, writing clerk, the brother. Effects £7.

Probate of the will of Maria Ann Coleman of 71 Atlantic Avenue, Belfast, spinster who died 26 May 1905, granted at Belfast 20 July 1906 to Thomas McCabe Coleman, writing clerk, and the Reverend Charles Scott. Effects £2 14s.9d.

Probate of the will with one codicil of Thomas McCabe Coleman of 71 Atlantic Avenue, Belfast, book-keeper, who died 8 July 1908 granted at Belfast 7 August 1908 to the Reverend Charles Scott and Thomas Fisher, house and land agent. Effects £397 0s.8d.

Probate of the will, with two codicils, of Elizabeth Hamilton Coleman of 71 Atlantic Avenue, Belfast, spinster, who died 20 March 1912, granted at Belfast 1 May 1912 to Harriet Elizabeth Scott and Marjorie Scott, spinsters. Effects £341 19s.7d.]

Thomas McCabe (1740-1820) came to Belfast from Lisburn in 1762 and opened at No. 6, North Street his watchmaker's and jeweller's shop which soon became renowned for its excellence of workmanship, McCabe watches being the most fashionable in Belfast. In the late 1780s he, together with Robert Joy, Nicholas Grimshaw and Capt. John McCracken (see inscriptions), was instrumental in starting Ireland's cotton production in the Poor House (now Clifton House). In 1784, the firm of Messrs Joy, McCabe and McCracken built the first mill in Ireland to be driven by water power.

An intensely liberal and humane man, Thomas McCabe successfully opposed the coming of the slave trade to Belfast in 1786. He and his son William Putnam McCabe were both United Irishmen and many of the meetings prior to the '98 Rebellion took place at their home at Vicinage (St. Malachy's College is built on the site). Thomas was an early and active member of the Belfast Charitable Society and the Belfast Philosophical Society. In the mid-nineteenth century the McCabe family moved to London.]

McCALLA
See THOMPSON

McCALLUM
See BROWN

McCAMMON
See ANDREWS

McCANN
[Very badly corroded sandstone headstone, beside James Coleman's, of c.1820, now lost.] Here lieth (the rem)ains of James McC(a)nn who died 5th June aged 50 years. Also Mary Ann died 22nd Feb ..... and their ...

[This plot was bought by James McCann in January 1818.]

McCANN
[Worn marble in Gothic entablature, now lost.] Erected by (Thomas) McCann in memory of his father George McCann died 3rd Jan. 1862 aged 76 years. His mother Letitia McCann died 10th March 1862 aged 67 years. And his brother John died 24th Feb 1855 aged 24 years. And his daughter Sarah Jane died 31st March 185(5) aged 16 months. His son Robert Archer McCann died 27th Feb. 1865 aged 12 years.

[The burial register describes George McCann as a farmer living at 29, Eliza Street.]

McCARTER
[Badly flaked in the centre and now lost.] Erected by Mary MOORE, to the memory of Sarah McCarter who departed this life 15th June 1852 aged (28) years. "Blessed are the (dead) who die in the Lord". (Rev. C)hap. XIV., ver 13. John WILLIAMSON, 23rd (May) 1858 aged 7 yrs. Louisa E. Williamson, 26th May 1858 aged 3 years.

McCARTER
See COEY

McCAVANA
> See GORDON

McCAW
> [Small stone formerly in lower ground and no longer extant. It was copied from the Society's records.] The family burying place of William McCaw, Belfast, 1854.

McCAW
> See McFARLAN

McCLANAHAN
> [Now lost.] Erected by Robt McClanahan in memory of his wife Martha who died 5th Sepr 1847 aged 45 years. Also the above named Robt McClanahan who died 8th May 1854 aged 45 years. And his son Robert who died 23rd July 1854 aged 5 years.
>
> [Robert McClanahan was a captain employed by Belfast Tug Boats.]

McCLEAN
> [Broken tablet with bottom part missing, formerly in surround secured to north wall, now lost.] (Underneath are interr)ed the remains (of) the Revd (Samuel) John McClean, A.M., fellow of Trinity College, Dublin. He departed this life in that University (on the) 7th November 1835 aged 33 years. (Also of his) mother Margaret, (wife of) Adam McClean, of Belfast, Esq., who died 21st Novr 1842 aged 77 years. And of Francis Robert, third son of said Adam McClean Esq., who died 1st May 1846 aged 4(5) years. James his second son died in London 14th Novr 1847 aged 48 years. The remains of said Adam McClean are interred here. He died 14th August 1849 aged 83 years. Also of Sarah Smyth McClean, his fourth daughter who died 12th December 1862 aged 52 years. Also of Andrew Thomas McClean his fifth son who died 14th July 1865 aged 57 years. (Also) Matilda McKEDY, third daughter (wife of the) Revd. J. H. DUCKE, M.A., (who died August) 30th 1874 aged 65 years. Also of Adam McClean his first son, who died 12th January 1878, aged 80 years). "Your Redemption draweth nigh".
>
> [The will of Sarah Smyth McClean of Belfast in the county of Antrim, spinster, who died 12 December 1862 at Finglas in the county of Dublin, was proved at Belfast 29 May 1863 at Belfast by the oaths of John Stevelly of Belfast aforesaid, LL.D., Professor of Natural Philosophy in the Queen's University of Belfast and William Hartley of Belfast aforesaid, public accountant, the executors. Effects in Great Britain and Ireland £6,000.
>
> The will with one codicil of Adam McClean, formerly of Belfast, and late of Tudor Park, Holywood, county Down, esquire who died 12 January 1878 at latter place, was proved at Belfast 29 January 1878 by the oath of the Reverend Macnevin Bradshaw formerly of Gorey, county Wexford, afterwards of Merville near Booterstown, county Dublin, but now of Clontarf, county Dublin, clerk in holy orders, the sole executors. Effects under £14,000.]
>
> Adam McClean (1765/6-1849), had a large cloth shop in High Street. He owned the land nowadays occupied by Linenhall Street (then called

McClean's Fields) and through which the first water pipes were laid in 1814. He was also responsible for building many of the fine terrace houses in Donegall Square South in the 1800s and Wellington Place in 1830. He had 5 sons:

1. Adam McClean (1797/8-1878) is reputed to have owned St. Patrick's Bell which was sold after his death for £150 to Dr Todd and thence to the Royal Irish Academy.
2. James McClean (1798/9-1847) died in London.
3. Francis Robert McClean (1800/1-1846).
4. The Rev. Samuel John McClean (1802-1835) entered Belfast Academical Institution in 1814 (the year it opened), entered Trinity College, Dublin in 1819, graduated B.A. in 1823, Fellow in 1829 and M.A. in 1833.
5. Andrew Thomas McClean (1807/8-1865) also entered the Belfast Academical Institution in 1814.

The Rev. John Hare Duck was born in Cork in 1814/5, son of Thomas Duck, linen draper. He entered Trinity College, Dublin as a sizar in 1838, became a scholar in 1841 and graduated B.A. in 1844, B.D. and D.D. in 1875. He altered his name to Duke in 1875. He was ordained curate of St John's, Dublin 1845-47, of St Michael's, Dublin 1846-47 and 1852-53, of St George's Belfast 1847-50, perpetual curate of Ballymacarret 1853-57, Vicar of Upper Tean, Staffordshire 1857-71 and incumbent of Glencraig, county Down 1872-1905. He married first Matilda McKedy McClean who died at Glencraig Parsonage. He married secondly Jemima. He died on 29 September 1905 aged 90 and his widow died at Eyton House, Leominster, Hertfordshire 11 November 1915.

See Benn: *History of the Town of Belfast*, Vol. II (1880); Fisher and Robb: *The Royal Belfast Academical Institution* (1913); Burtchaell and Sadlar: *Alumni Dublinenses* (1924); Leslie and Swanzy: *Biographical Succession Lists of the Clergy of Diocese of Down* (1936).]

McCLEAN

[Now missing.] The family burying ground of Danl. McClean, Ann St., 1837.

McCLEAVE

[Lying flat, now lost.] The family burying place of James McCleave, Belfast. Sacred to the memory of his son James B. McCleave, died May 11th 1847 aged 29 years. Isabella McCleave died 23rd October 1864 aged 26 years. James McCleave died September 14th 1865 aged 78 years. Sarah McCleave died 24th Decr 1871 aged 82 years. Robert Hyslop McCleave died 2d June 1874 aged 43 years. Stewart Robert McCleave died 3d September 1874 aged (4)6 years.

[The will of James McCleeve of Castle Place Belfast, in the county of Antrim, saddle and harness maker, who died 14 September 1865 at same place, was proved at Belfast 17 March 1866 by the oaths of George McCleeve of Holywood in the county of Down, and Thomas McCleeve of Gloucester Street, Belfast aforesaid, saddlers, the executors. Effects under £1,500.

Letters of administration of the personal estate of Robert Hyslop

McCleeve of 73 Donegall Street, Belfast, watchmaker and jeweller, a bachelor, who died 2 June 1874 at same place, were granted at Belfast 17 June 1874, to George McCleeve of Castle Place, Belfast aforesaid, saddler, the brother of said deceased. Effects under £1,500.

The will of Stewart Robert McCleeve of Donegall Street, Belfast, watchmaker and jeweller, who died 3 September 1874 at Breda Lodge, Newtown Breda, county Down, was proved at Belfast 20 August 1875 by the oath of Edward Gribben of High Street, Belfast, jeweller, one of the excutors. Effects under £1,000.

James B. McCleave (d.1847) was a watch-maker at Millfield. Descendants of George McCleave ran a well-known plumbing firm in Holywood which still operates under that name.]

McCLEERY

[Very badly flaked and now lost.] Erected by Jo(hn) Hay HODGSON in memory (of) Jane (McCleery) daugh(ter of the late John HAY, bookseller who died 5th Feby 1830 aged 79 years. Also of her son John Hay McCleery who died 15th April 1827 aged 34 years.

McCLEERY

[Marble tablet in surround, secured to north wall, in a high-railed enclosure.] Sacred to the memory of James McCleery, surgeon, who died 9th July 1847 aged 53 years. And of Jane his wife who died 19th April 1855 aged 59 years. And of Robert their son who died 2nd May 1860 aged 38 years. And of Henry McGiffert, their son who died 22nd May 1880 aged 46 years.

[Letters of administration of the personal estate of Robert McCleery of York Street, Belfast, in the county of Antrim, gentleman, a bachelor, who died 2 May 1860 at same place, were granted at Belfast 27 June 1860 to James Caughey McCleery of York Street aforesaid, the brother one of the next of kin of said deceased. Effects under £1,500.

Surgeon James McCleery was born in Portaferry and practised in North Street, Belfast. He was surgeon to the Belfast Charitable Institute "who for a period of twelve years had zealously and benevolently fulfilled the laborious duties of surgeon to the male side of this Charity. He died of fever and was suceeded by his son". Robert was a solicitor. See Strain: *Belfast and its Charitable Society* (1961).]

McCLEERY
See CAUGHEY

McCLELLAND

[Flaking slate in broken surround formerly secured to south wall but now lost.] (Sacred) to the memory of Richard McClelland who departed this life on the 17th of September 1807 aged 46. Also his wife Tabitha who departed this life on the 8th of June 1844 aged 76 years. Elizabeth Griffith LEWIS died 29th March 1838 aged 79 years. Sarah BELL, relict of John Bell (M.D.), died 9th October 1854 aged 89 years. Alexander Orr Lewis, died 14th October 1856 aged 86 years. Sarah

Bell, died 15th November 1857 aged 70.

[Alexander Orr Lewis was a retired Army captain and lived at 2, Upper Queen Street.]

McCLELLAND

[Flaking headstone, now lost.] Erected by Sarah McClelland, of Belfast, in memory of her husband Frances [sic] McClelland who departed this life the 16th Novr 1834 aged 55 years.

[He was a grocer in College Square West (now Durham Street).]

McCLELLAND

See CHIRMSIDE and FOSTER

McCLEMENT

[Flaking sandstone, now lost.] Sacred to the memory of David McClement who departed this life 21st May 1815 aged 21 years.

McCLENAHAN

[Missing from lower ground.] The family burying place of William McClenahan, Belfast, 19th July 1848.

[He was a mill-wright at 22, Mustard Street (nowadays Library Street).]

McCLENAHAN

[Now lost.] Sacred to the memory of Catherine, the beloved wife of Thos McClenahan, Qr-Mr, H.P. 2nd Gd Bn., who departed this life, 24th Jany 1859 aged 70 years. Captn Thos McClenahan died 6th August 1867 aged 82 years.

McCLINTON

[Marble tablet in entablature formerly secured to east wall, now lost.] Erected by John McClinton in memory of his son Charles McClinton who died 17th November 1858 aged 9 years.

McCLUNEY

[Worn marble tablet beside George Mitchell's, now lost.] Sacred to the memory of Robert McCluney Surgeon who died on the 21st of January (A.D. 1837) aged ... years (Clara McCluney) who departed this life (....) (A.D. 1842).

[Robert McCluney (1768-1837) was involved in the Belfast Charitable Society as far back as 1792 and was a surgeon to the Belfast Dispensary in 1797. He was on the committee of the newly formed Belfast Medical Society in 1806 and in the period 1827-8 was Chairman of the committee of the Belfast Charitable Society. See Strain: *Belfast and its Charitable Society* (1961).]

McCLURE

[Marble tablet secured to north wall in upper ground, of which the first half has disappeared.] To the memory of William McClure, of Belfast, who died 21st December 1843 aged 86 years. And his daughter Anna who died 11th February 1840 aged 23 years. Also his wife Elizabeth who died 25th January 1848 aged 75 years. Their daughter Eliza who died 27 December

1878 aged 70 years. Sir Thomas McClure, Bart. D.L., J.P., of Belmont, County Down, son of the above William McClure, born 4th March 1806, died 19th Jan. 1893. "Thou wilt keep him in perfect peace whose mind is stayed on thee, because he trusted in thee". Isaiah XXVI.3. The Rev. William McClure, eldest son of the above William McClure, who died 22nd Feb. 1874 aged 73 years. He was interred in Londonderry, having been 49 years Minister of 1st Derry Congregation.

[Letters of administration of the personal estate of Eliza McClure of Belmont, county Down, spinster, who died 27 December 1878 at same place, were granted at Belfast 22 January 1879 to Sir Thomas McClure of Belmont, Belfast, Baronet, the brother of said deceased. Effects under £1,500.

The will with five codicils of Sir Thomas McClure, formerly of Belmont, county Down, but late of Redford House, Colinton, county Midlothian, Baronet, who died 19 January 1893 at latter place, was proved at the Principal Registry 19 April 1893 by Ellison Thornburn, Lady McClure of Redford House, widow, and George Laughy MacLaine of Wandsworth House, Strandtown, county Down, clerk of the crown and peace, two of the executors. Effects £6,037 4s.6d. Re-sworn £8,588 14s.6d.

The will of Reverend William McClure of Rossdowny, county Londonderry, Presbyterian minister, who died 22 February 1874 at same place, was proved at Londonderry 13 April 1874 by the oaths of Thomas McClure of Belmont, Belfast, county Down, Baronet, and Charles Finley of University Square, Belfast, esquire, the executors. Effects under £5,000.

The Rev. William McClure was born on 21 August 1801, eldest son of William McClure, merchant, of Donegall Street, Belfast and Elizabeth Thompson, daughter of the Rev. John Thompson, Presbyterian minister of Carnmoney. He was educated at the Belfast Academical Institution 1818-20, obtaining the General Certificate in 1820, and at Edinburgh University. He was licensed by the Ballymena Presbytery in 1823 and ordained at First Derry on 1 March 1825. He was Moderator of the General Synod 1834-5 and of the General Assembly 1847-8. He married (1) a daughter of Hugh Dickie. He retired in 1868 and died on 22 February 1874, being buried in Londonderry.

Sir Thomas McClure, Bart., D.L., J.P., was born on 4 March 1806 and educated at the Belfast Academical Institution from 1819. He was Liberal M.P. for Belfast 1868-74 and for county Londonderry 1879- . See Fisher and Robb: *The Royal Belfast Academical Institution* (1913) and McConnell: *Fasti of the Irish Presbyterian Church* (1951).]

McCLUSKEY

[With masonic symbols and rose at top, now lost.] Erected by Henry McCluskey, in memory of his daughter Fanny, born 19th Jany 1858, died 28th March 1860.

McCLUSKEY

[Formerly in lower ground and now missing. It appears that William McCluskey acquired the plot in February 1861, and transferred it to the

Dunlavey family in 1876.] The burying place of William McCluskey.

McCOMB
[Pitted.] In memory of Thomas McComb, of Belfast, merchant, (who) died 28th March 1820 aged 58 years. (Also) his wife Elizabeth HUDSON who (died) 26th April 1842 aged 70 years.

McCONKEY
[Stone now missing from upper ground. James McConkey bought one plot in December 1823, and the other in April 1847.] Burial place of James McConkey and his son-in-law James STAKELY.

McCONNELL
[With cross.] I.H.S. Erected by Elanor McConnell to the memory of her husband James McConnell, late of Belfast, who departed this life 8th of June 1830 aged 30 years.

McCONNELL
In memory of William McConnell, who died 1st June 1844 aged 74 years. Also his wife Margaret McConnell who died 17th June 1842 aged 58 years. Also their children: Sarah McConnell, who died 8th Aug. 1880, Mary, wife of James G. ALLEN, died 1st February 1884, William McConnell, died 27th December 1894.

[William McConnell, senior, was a grocer at No. 7, Skipper Street, Belfast.]

McCONNELL
[Capstone and base of large headstone, now missing. Inscription on plinth of draped urn — probably c.1840.] S. McConnell. [Two lots were bought by Samuel McConnell in 1829 and 1839 respectively.]

McCONNELL
See EAGLESON

Mc(CORD)
[Very badly flaked and now lost.] Erected by (Robert) Mc(Cord in memory of .... McCord) who departed this (life) .... (1822) aged (..) years. Also of his (children) ... Isabella aged (10) months. (And) Robert (aged 13) months Likewise Ma(tilda) aged 12 years. Also the above Robert died the 23rd June 1829 aged 55 years.

McCORMICK
[Iron shield, now lost.] John McCormick died 11th August 1884 aged (68).

[The will of John McCormick of 191 York Street Belfast, bookseller and stationer, who died 11 August 1884 at same place, was proved at Belfast 3 October 1884 by Rachel McCormick of 191 York Street, Belfast, widow, the sole executrix. Effects £265 3s.]

McCOY
[Flaking headstone with twin faces, at a slight angle to each other.]
Sacred to the memory of Samuel McCoy, 1815.
Sacred to the memory of Anne HIGGINSON, 1821.

MacCRACKEN/McCRACKEN

[Small stone block in a low marble enclosure.] (a) Mary Ann MacCracken, the beloved sister of Henry Joy MacCracken, born 8 July 1770, wept by her brothers Scaffold, 17 July 1798, died 26 July 1866. "Dileas go h-eag". ["True till death".]

(b) [Inscription on marble enclosure.] In this grave rest remains believed to be those of Henry Joy McCracken, born 31st August 1767, executed 17th July 1798.

[The will of Mary Ann McCracken of Donegall Pass, Belfast, in the county of Antrim, spinster, who died 26 July 1866 at Belfast aforesaid, was proved at Belfast 1 September 1866 by the oaths of Agnes McCormick, widow, and William Erskine, master mariner, both of Adela Street, Belfast aforesaid, the executors. Effects under £100.

Henry Joy McCracken was born on 31 August 1767, the fourth son of Captain John McCracken of High Street, Belfast and Ann Joy (see Joy entry, above). He was associated with Samuel Neilson, Thomas Russell and Theobald Wolfe Tone in the formation of the United Irishmen in 1791. In 1796 he was arrested and sent to Kilmainham Gaol but was released in the following year. When the rising finally began in June 1798 he was the principal leader in county Antrim. Unfortunately their plans were transmitted to General Nugent and, though they had initial success at Antrim, they were eventually routed. Henry hid and travelled for some weeks but was captured in July, tried and hanged in Belfast at the corner of Corn Market and High Street on 17 July 1798. He was buried in the old graveyard of St. George's but in 1909 Francis Joseph Bigger had what were thought to be his bones transferred to his sister's grave plot in Clifton Street.

His brother Francis (1762-1842) and father Captain John (c.1721-1803) were instrumental in establishing the manufacture of cotton in this country.

Mary Ann McCracken was born on 8 July 1770, the younger sister of Henry Joy. She shared many of the views of her brother and as stated on her memorial accompanied him to his execution. After this her energies were channelled first into Irish cultural life and then into a lifelong devotion to the Belfast Charitable Institute. Her life and the whole era is movingly described in Mary McNeill's *The Life and Times of Mary Ann McCracken* (1960). See also Madden: *Antrim and Down in Ninety-eight*; Latimer: *Ulster Biographies Relating Chiefly to the Rebellion of 1798* (1897).

Thomas McCracken who died on 8 January 1914 was buried in this plot. His relationship to the above and that of the McCracken family mentioned below is unknown.]

McCRACKEN

[Small plaque now gone.] The burying place of Robt. McCracken, 1852.

McCRACKEN

[Marble with surround in a low-railed enclosure.] Sacred to the memory of

Photograph of Mary Ann McCracken (1770-1866), (Ulster Museum).

Caroline Leslie McCracken who died on the 4th of January 1864 aged five months. Also Elizabeth Jane McCracken, who died on the 22nd of September 1865 aged eight years and seven months. Also John Francis McCracken, who died on the 12th of December 1867 aged six years and five months.

Not gone from memory, not gone (from love)
But gone to their Father's house above.

[In 1864, the family was living at 4, Brougham Street, Belfast.]

McCRACKEN

[Very corroded iron shield, now lost.] The burying place of (Henry Joy) McCracken, (1892).

[The plot was purchased by Henry McCracken in June 1854.]

McCREA

See SHIELDS

McCREADY

See EWART

McCREEDY

[Lying flat but now lost.] Here lieth the body of John McCreedy, formerly of Downpatrick, who died on the 4th day of February 1806 aged 80 years. Also his grand-daughter Jane, relict of the late Thomas AINSWORTH, of Belfast, died 31st January 1874 aged 83 years. Also her daughter Jane Greer Allen MUSSEN, who died 7th February 1897 aged 87 years.

[The will of Jane Ainsworth of 133 Ormeau Road, Belfast, county Antrim, widow, who died 31 January 1874 at same place, was proved at Belfast 27 March 1874 by the oaths of Jane Mussen, widow, and Catherine Adair, wife of Hugh Adair, printer and stationer, both of 133 Ormeau Road, Belfast aforesaid, the executrixes. Effects under £1,500.

Probate of the will of Jane Mussen of Duncairn Gardens, Belfast, widow, who died 7 February 1897, granted at Belfast 26 February 1897 to William Thomas Adair of Mountcharles, Belfast, merchant. Effects £522 12s.5d.]

McCULLOCH

[Polished granite obelisk, with inscription on the base.]

Erected by Robert J. McCulloch, Glencar, in memory of his father Robert McCulloch who died 25th Nov. 1858 aged 52. Also his mother Sarah Jane McCulloch who died 15th Nov. 1871 aged 60. And his sister and brother who died young. The above named Robert J. McCulloch who died 8th Feb. 1915 aged 74.

[The will of Robert McCulloch of Cumber Place, Belfast, publican, who died 25 November 1858 at Cumber Place aforesaid, was proved at Belfast 2 November 1859 by the oath of Sarah Jane McCulloch of same, widow, the sole executrix. Effect under £300.

The will with one codicil of Sarah Jane McCullough or McCulloch of Hampstead, Belfast, widow, who died 14 November 1871 at same place, was proved at Belfast 15 December 1871 by the oaths of the Reverend William Johnston, Presbyterian minister, and William Walker Pinkerton, gentleman, both of Belfast aforesaid, the executors. Effects £4,000.

Probate of the will of Robert James McCulloch of Heatherview, Ballygomartin, county Antrim, farmer, who died 8 February 1915 granted at Belfast on the 9 June 1915 to Mary McCulloch, the widow, and the Reverend John Gailey, Presbyterian minister. Effects £5,269 18s.3d.]

McCULLOCH
See FERGUSON

McCULLOUGH
[Broken and flaking.] Erected by Agnes McCullough to the memory of her beloved son Edward McCullough who departed this life 5th May 1861 aged 35 years.
[He was a porter and lived at 24, Stephen Street, Belfast.]

McCUNE
[Missing.] The family burying ground of Wm. McCune, Belfast, 1869.

McCUNE
[Iron shield in high-railed enclosure, now lost.] The family burying ground of Samuel McCune, Belfast, 1874.
[Another iron plaque with above and looking of c.1880.] McKEE.

McCUNE
See CAMERON and WARDLOW

McCUTCHEON
Erected by Margaret McCutcheon to the memory of her beloved husband John McCutcheon, of Belfast, architect and builder, who departed this life at Walworth near London, 16th April 1822 aged 47 years. Also here lieth seven of his children who died in infancy.
[He lived at 1, Chichester Street, Belfast. Among the works he supervised, but did not design, were the construction of the Royal Belfast Academical Institution in 1810-14 and the Commercial Buildings in 1822. See Brett: *Buildings of Belfast*, (1967 and 1985).]

McCUTCHEON
[Very badly pitted, now lost.] Erected by Captn McCutcheon in memory of his mother Elizabeth McC(utcheon) who departed this life the 10th Nov(ember 184)0 aged 64 years. Also his au(nt) ..... KERR, who departed this (life) .... December (182)4 aged (.. years).

McDONAGH
See DEMPSY

McDONALD
See DUNLAP

McDONNELL
Erected by Jane McDonnell, in memory of her father Alexander McDonnell who departed this life January the 8th 1831 aged 55 years. Also his beloved wife Elizabeth Mary who departed this life April the 5th 1849 aged 75 years.
[He was a bricklayer and lived in Lagan Street, Belfast.]

McDORNAN

[In upper ground and now missing.] The family burying place of John McDornan, Belfast, 1856.

McDOWELL

[Painted headstone in low-granite enclosure.] Raised to the memory of Henry McDowell, eldest son of Henry McDowell, Belfast, who died the 15th day of April 1826 in the 7th year of his age. For ea...

This engaging boy (was intelligent) and pleasingly inquisitive,
Evincing (an eager desire for) information,
And blending (with sweetness) of temper,
A disposition (the most) affectionate,

By (his endearing) manners
Exciting early and warm attachments,
By his death,
Leaving behind him deep and sincere regret.

Here also is interred Ann, wife of said Henry McDowell, who died 3rd August 1831 aged 36 years. [Continued on plinth.] Also of the above named Henry McDowell who died Sept. 30, 1836 aged 59 years. His daughter Rose McDowell.

[Continued on granite enclosure.] Also of James CHARNOCK, son-in-law of the above Henry McDowell who died June 30, 1855. Anna Maria Charnock, daughter of the above Henry McDowell, who died April 30, 1906 aged 86 years.

[Probate of the will and codicil of Ann Maria Charnock of 6 Lower Cresent, Belfast, widow, who died 30 April 1906 granted at Belfast 11 June 1906 to Maurice Frederick Fitzgerald, Professor of Engineering. Effects £20,855 9s.

James Charnock of Charnock Brothers, general merchants at 65 Corporation Square, Belfast, died at his residence at Brooklyn, Victoria Road, Holywood, aged 46.]

McDOWELL

[Twin slate tablets in pedimented entablature of the Regency style, secured to north wall, in enclosure that was formerly high-railed.] Erected in memory of Rose, wife of Robert McDowell, of Belfast, merchant, who died 2d January 1839 aged 45 years. Agnes MOORE, niece of Robt McDowell, died 16th July 84 aged 72 years.

Robert McDowell, of Belfast, merchant, died 31st August 1850 aged 75 years.

[Robert McDowell lived at 35, Arthur Street, Belfast.]

McDOWELL

[Headstone, cracked across the middle in a low-stone enclosure.] Erected by Sarah McDowell, in memory of her beloved husband John McDowell, of Saintfield, in the County of Down, who departed this life on the 6th day of December 1850 aged 78 years. Here also are interred the remains of the above named Sarah McDowell, who died at Glasgow, 13th March 1874 aged

84 years. And Margaret KERR, their faithful servant for 40 years, who died at Ballyholme, 18th July 1878 aged 80 years.

[The will of Sarah McDowell of Ballydavey, county Down, and late of Kilcreggan in Scotland, widow, who died 12 March 1874 at Eton Terrace, Glasgow, was proved at the Principal Registry 15 June 1874 by the oaths of William Anderson Donaldson of 103 St Vincent Street, Glasgow, merchant, and Robert Meharey of Belfast, grocer, two of the executors. Effects under £1,500.]

McFADDEN

[Large headstone with broken twin tablets, in a low-stone enclosure.] To the memory of Archibald McFadden who departed this life April 6th 1811 aged 45 years. Also his beloved wife Ann McFadden who departed this life May 24th 1816 aged 45 years. Also one of their children Ann McFadden who died in infancy. Isabella HALLIDAY, eldest daughter of the above, who died 14th June 1862 aged 65 years.

Erected to the memory of James IRELAND, of Belfast, who departed this life April 26th 1837 aged 35 years. Also his son David who departed this life Novemr 22nd 1831 aged 3 years. James Ireland, junr died 13th May 1845. Wm Thos Ireland died 16th June 1847. Anne Ireland died 20th Sep. 1881 aged 48 years.

[James Ireland, senior, was a baker in Prince's Street, Belfast.]

McFARLAN

[Small cast-iron memorial later replaced by a granite headstone.] The family burying place of A. McFarlan & W. COATES, Belfast, 1866.

McFARLAN

[Polished granite in low-railed enclosure.] In memory of Adam McFarlan, died 29th March 1868. Elizabeth his wife died 25th Decr 1905. William McFarlan, son, died 16th July 1868. Isabella McFarlan, daughter, died 4th Sept 1874. Andrew Spence, son, died 3rd March 1877. George Coates, son, died June 1892. Thomas McCAW, son-in-law, died 31st July 1923. Margaret McCaw, his wife, died 1st Oct. 1923. Jane McFarlan, daughter, died 20th February 1930. "I am the resurrection and the life; he that believeth in me shall never die".

[The will of Adam McFarlan of Great Patrick Street, Belfast, county Antrim, cooper and publican, who died 29 March 1868 at Belfast, was proved at Belfast 23 September 1868 by the oaths of Elizabeth McFarlan of Great Patrick Street, Belfast aforesaid, the widow and executrix. Effects under £1,000.

Letters of administration of the personal estate of William McFarlan of Great Patrick Street, Belfast, county Antrim, muslin manufacturer, a bachelor, who died 16 July 1868 at Belfast aforesaid, were granted at Belfast 23 September 1868 to Elizabeth McFarlan of Great Patrick Street, Belfast aforesaid, widow, the mother and next of kin of said deceased. Effects under £450.

Thomas McCaw of Kingswear, Knockburn Park, Belfast, gentleman, died 21 July 1923. Administration Belfast 26 November 1923 to George

McCaw, clerk. Effects £928 14s.3d.

Jane McFarlan of Kingswear, Knockburn Park, Belfast, spinster, died 20 February 1930. Probate Belfast 15 May 1930 to Stanley St George Harvey C.E. Effects £3,002 4s.6d.]

McFERRAN
[Slate with willow tree carved at top.] Sacred to the memory of Jane, daughter of Capt. James McFerran, of this town, who departed this life on the 11th January 1852 aged 15 months. Also two of his children who died in their infancy.

[The family lived at 39, James Street, Belfast (nowadays Corporation Street), many sea-farers inhabiting the district at that time.]

McGAHAN
[Very badly flaked and weathered headstone, now lost and mostly copied from Inscription Book.] (Erected to the memory of Christopher McGahan who departed this life the 17th of March (....) aged 14 years ..... of Ellen BRA)DDELL (who departed this life the 18th of December 1807 AE 3 years. Henry Braddell, departed this life the 8th of February) 1829 aged (19 year)s.

McGEAH/McGEAGH
Erected to the memory of John McGeah, of Cookstown. Superior talents and acquirements distinguished his academical course; and faith in the Son of God supported him under his last illness: he died in hope of Eternal life, 18th March 1817 aged 17 years. Also of Wm Wilberforce McGeagh, son of Robert McGeagh Senr, of Belfast, who died September 9th 1862 aged 19 years.

[Robert McGeagh, senior, was a partner in McGeagh, Wilson & Co., wool and cloth merchants, at 39 Castle Place, Belfast. He lived at 4 Franklin Place, Belfast.]

McGEE
[Altar-tomb with well-cut lettering.] Here lyeth the body of James McGee, former in Belly Robert & parish of Holliwood, who departed this life the 6 day of Febr 1714 & of aged 80 years. Here lyeth the body of James McGee, merchant in Belfast, son to James McGee, in the parish of Holliwood & town land of Ballyrobart who departed this life the 22 of January 1703 and of age 25 years [sic].

[This stone was brought from its original site at the old church at Craigavad about the year 1890 and placed in the present plot which was purchased by Carlile McGee. See O'Laverty: *An Historical Account of the Diocese of Down and Connor*, Vol. II, (1880).]

McGEE
See EID and SLOAN

McGLADERY
[In upper ground and now missing.] Sacred to the memory of William McGladery of (Belfast) who departed this life 9th (December 1860) aged 73 years. Also his beloved wife (Ruth) who departed this life 20th March 1865 aged 75 years.

[The will of William McGladery of Antrim Road, Belfast, in the county of Antrim, carpenter, who died 9 December 1860 at same place, was proved at Belfast 8 March 1861 by the oath of Samuel McGladdery of Antrim Road, Belfast, carpenter, and Samuel McAdam of Old Park, Belfast, farmer, the executors. Effects under £20.]

McGOWAN

[Missing from lower ground.] The family burying ground of William McGowan, Belfast, 1847.

McGUCKIN
See LINDEN

McHENRY
See GARDNER

McILWAINE/McILWAIN

[Painted sandstone headstone with winged angel at top. Clearly, this headstone came from another graveyard, probably what is now St. George's.] Here lieth the body of the Revd Mr Andrew McIlwaine, A.M., who departed this life August ye 5th 1764 aged 33 years. Died 9th Janr 1777, Thos McIlwain, of Belfast, mercht aged 69 years.

[The Rev. Andrew McIlwaine was born in 1731, son of Andrew McIlwaine, farmer, of county Donegal. He was educated by Mr Babington, entered Trinity College, Dublin as a Sizar in 1749 and graduated B.A. in 1753. He was ordained on 21 October 1854 as curate of Drumholm and of Lettermacaward, both in the Diocese of Raphoe. He appears to have been replaced in these parishes in 1755 and 1760 respectively but nothing further is known of him. See Leslie: *Raphoe Clergy and Parishes* (1940).

The will of Thomas McIlwain, merchant, of Belfast, was proved in the Prerogative Court in 1777.]

McINTYRE

[Worn marble in large headstone now lost.] In memory of George Joy McIntyre died Oct (5th) 1834 aged (4)9 years. Also three of his children who died young. Also his daughter Eliza McIntyre, died Oct (21st 1851) aged 27 years. And also his wife (Jane) McIntyre died (Sept ....) 18(54) aged 6(7) years. Also his son George McIntyre died (Sept 30th) 1865 aged (51) years. Also his son James McIntyre died (March 15th) 1880 aged (68) years. ("He giveth) his beloved (sleep".)

[The will with one codicil of James McIntyre of 16 Kensington Gate, London, esquire, who died 15 March 1880 at same place, was proved at the Principal Registry 25 June 1880 by the oath of James Alexander Johnson of same place, gentleman, one of the executors. Effects under £6,000.]

George McIntyre, senior, was a stationer in Arthur Street, Belfast. His son George was a partner in McIntyre and Patterson, linen yarn and flax merchants; he lived in Martello Terrace, Holywood].

McKEAN
See McMULLIN

McKEDY

[Sandstone tablet with broken surround formerly secured to west wall, now lost.] Died on the 18th of May 1802, Mary McKedy, widow of the late Henry McKedy, of Belfast, merchant aged 68 years. Elenor their daughter departed this life on the seventh of January 1828 aged 52 years. Elizabeth McKedy died 2nd Feb. 1837 aged 71 years. Ann McKedy died 11th July 1840 aged 72 years. Jane McKedy died 25th July 1854, aged 84 years. Catherine McKedy died 15th January 1860 aged 80 years. Mary McKedy died 25th Septr 1861 aged 89 years, being the last survivor of the family.

[The will with one codicil of Catherine McKedy of York Street, Belfast, in the county of Antrim, who died 15 January 1860 at Belfast aforesaid, was proved at Belfast 14 February 1860 by the oaths of James Walker of the Knockagh, near Carrickfergus, gentleman and William Hartley of Belfast aforesaid, agent, the executors. Effects under £7,000.

The will with one codicil of Mary McKedy of York Street in the town of Belfast and county of Antrim, who died 25 September 1861 at same place, was proved at Belfast 1 November 1861 by the oaths of James Walker of the Knockagh, near Carrickfergus, in the county of the town of Carrickfergus, gentlemen, and William Hartley of The Castle in the town of Belfast aforesaid, public accountant, the executors. Effects under £7,000.]

McKEDY
See McCLEAN

McKEE
See McCUNE

McKELVEY
See HOWARD

McKENDRY

[Badly flaking and ivy-covered, now lost.] Sacred to the memory of James McKendry who departed this life, 18th February 1821 aged 43 years. Also four of his children.

McKENNA
See WILSON

McKENZIE
See BROWN

McKEY

[Slate tablet in headstone of neo-Egyptian style, now lost.] Erected by William McKey in memory of his wife Mary McKey who died 6th May 1837 aged 50 years. His son, Capn James McKey's two children, Mary Ann, died 18th Novr 1842 aged 13 months, Rosanna died 23rd April 1845 aged 3 years & 6 months.

[The family lived at Fortwilliam, Belfast.]

McKIBBIN

[Twin marble tablets in entablature, now lost.] (The family burial place of

Robert) McKibbin. The family burying place of Robert McKibben. In memory of: Esther McKibbin, junr who died 18th August 1814 aged 7 years, Robert McKibbin, jun., who died 12th July 1831 aged 2 years and 5 months, John Robinson McKibbin who died 8th August 1836 aged 27 years. Esther McKibbin, sen, who died 26th Feb. 1841 aged 100 years. Robert McKibbin, sen, who died (31)st March 1843 in the 62nd year (of his age). James McKibbin (who died at 66 Rathmines) Road, Dublin, 20th (December 1849 aged 36 yrs. Mary McKibbin, relict of Robt McKibbin, senr, who died 13th October (1852 in the 69th year of her age.) Adam (Wilson McKibbin died 22nd Septr 1871 aged 46 years.)

(The family burying place of Ann Wilson.) Interred here (Adam WILSON, born 25th) February 1815, (died 10th November 1832.) Also Ann (Wilson, mother of Adam Wilson), died 7th July (1864 aged 78 years). James McKibbin (son of the late J. McKib)bin, Dublin, born 18th (Oct. 1845, died at Banbridge, 25th) April 1891.

[The will of Adam Wilson McKibbin of No. 5 Adelaide Place, Belfast, gentleman, who died 22 September 1871 at Belfast aforesaid, was proved at Belfast 13 October 1871 by the oath of Charlotte McKibbin of No. 5 Adelaide Place, Belfast aforesaid, widow, the sole executrix. Effects under £600.

The will of Anne Wilson of Ballyoran, in the county of Down, widow, who died 7 July 1864 at same place, was proved at Belast 10 August 1864 by the oath of John Robinson of Ballyoran, Dundonald aforesaid, gentleman, one of the executors. Effects under £4,000.

The womenfolk of the McKibbin family were milliners, first in Donegall Street, Belfast, then later in Adelaide Place. The womenfolk of the Wilson family were milliners in Donegall Street.]

McKIBBIN

To the memory of Hugh McKibbin, of Belfast, who departed this life on the 3rd of Decr 1817 aged 45 years. Also on the 15th March 1824, his daughter Mary Eliza aged 11 years. On the 23rd September 1842, his son Stevenson aged 26 years. On 20th September 1845, his grand-daughter Matilda DICKSON died aged 12 years. On 27th December 1859, his wife Sarah died aged 77 years. On 13th May 1863, his daughter Sarah died aged 52 years. On 20th July 1869, his son Robert Dickson died aged 54 years. On 6th May 1871, his daughter Anna GAMBLE died aged 53 years.

[The will of Sarah McKibbin, formerly of Belfast, and late of Farmhill, near Dunmurry, both in the county of Antrim, spinster, who died 13 May 1863 at Farmhill aforesaid, was proved at Belfast 14 September 1863 by the oath of Anne Gamble McKibbin of Farmhill aforesaid, spinster, the sole executrix. Effects under £300.

[Hugh McKibbin was a tanner and glue manufacturer at 22 Mill Street (nowadays the upper part of Castle Street) and Robert Dickson McKibbin appears to have been a felt manufacturer in Waring Street in the 1840s.]

McKIBBIN

[Badly flaking and now lost.] Erected by Margaret McKibbin, in memory of her husband John McKibbin who departed this life May 15th 1833 aged 58 years. Margaret WARNOCK, died 16th (Februa)ry 1844 aged (48) years.

McKIBBIN

[Stone formerly in upper ground, but it has disappeared since 1907.] Erected in memory of George McKibben who died 21st June 1850. Also Jane his wife who died 24th Jany 1871.

[George McKibbin (1782/83-1850) was Dock-Pilot and Harbour Master for the port of Belfast (1832-50) as well as being surveyor for Lloyds. He lived at 1, Corporation Street, at that time at the corner with Great George's Street, Belfast. He was related to the Hyndman family (q.v.). See Owen: *A Short History of the Port of Belfast* (1917).

McKIM

[Now lost.] Erected by Catherine McKim in memory of her beloved mother Margaret who departed this life April 5th 1848. Also in memory of her beloved husband William SANDYS, who died 22nd April 185(3) aged 5(0) years.

[Catherine McKim (1790/91-1848) was employed as a lady's maid in Donegall Place, Belfast.]

McKISACK

[Small headstone with family name, looking of c.1880-1910, and in low railing.] McKisack.

[The plot was bought by James McKisack of Donegall Square on 3rd August 1847.]

McKNIGHT

See GLENDINNING

McLAINE

See RITCHIE

McLAUGHLIN

[Laid flat.] Erected by Henry McLaughlin in memory of his mother Catherine who died 4th Septr 1849 aged 55 years. Also his daughter Catherine who died 17th Decr 1856 aged 7 years. Here also lieth the remains of the above named Henry McLaughlin who died 11th Augt 1871 aged 53 years. And of his wife Mary who died 10th March 1901 aged 83 years. "He giveth his beloved sleep".

[The will of Henry McLaughlin of Osborne House, Malone, county Antrim, builder, who died 11 August 1871 at same place, was proved at Belfast 6 December 1871 by the oaths of William Harvey of Wellington Park, Belfast, builder, and Martin Shaw of Belfast, accountant, both in said county, the executors. Effects under £7,000.

Probate of the will of Mary McLaughlin, of Osborne House, Osborne Park, Belfast, widow, who died 10 March 1901, granted at Belfast 10 May 1901 at Belfast to William H. McLaughlin builder and contractor. Effects £195 2s.3d.]

The now very extensive building and civil engineering firm of McLaughlin and Harvey came into being in the late 1850s at 146, York Street, Belfast, when William Harvey, previously working alone at 22

Little May Street, entered into partnership with Henry McLaughlin. At that time McLaughlin lived at 10, Bentinck Street, not far from their builder's yard.

The firm moved to their present premises at 26 (contemporary numbering) York Road (Castleton Building Works) in the 1890s.]

McLEARN
See SMYTH

McMANN
[Polished granite headstone broken and laid flat in a low-granite enclosure with cap-stone of an older memorial bearing carving of a sailing clipper. The latter is now lost.] In loving memory of Captain George McMann, master of the "Thomas Hughes", who died at sea, February 1840 aged 34 years. Also his wife Ellen who died 13th January 1839 aged 26. Their daughter Elizabeth died April 1839 aged 8. Their daughter Jane died 20th June 1857 aged 24. Their only son John died 24th November 1864 aged 28. Erected 1910 by their last surviving daughter Georgina McMann who died 3rd March 1913 aged 78.

[Probate of the will with one codicil of Georgina McMann of The Retreat, Richhill, county Armagh, spinster, who died 3 March 1913, granted at Dublin 18 April 1913 to the Right Reverend Charles F. D'arcy, Bishop, and William B. Galway, solicitor. Effects £4,266 5s.9d.]

McMASTER
[Badly flaking headstone.] Erected by William McMaster, senior, in memory of Elizabeth McMaster, his daughter-in-law who departed this life 11th September 183(3 aged) 22 years. Also his son (William) who dep(arted this life) on the 3rd day of September 18(41) aged 3(3) years. Also of (his daughter, I.......] who departed this life) on the 10th of Sept(ember 184.) aged (11) years. Also of his beloved wife Margaret, who departed this life on the 9th day of February 1849 aged 64 years..

[William McMaster, senior, was a tavern-keeper at 11, Frederick Street, Belfast.]

McMEEKIN
[Badly flaking at the top, now lost.] Erected by Mary McMeekin, in memory of her husband Thomas McMeekin, of Belfast, who departed this life 10th Feby 1815 aged 46 years.

McMILLAN
[Missing.] In memory of Sarah McMillan, died July 20, 1861 aged 63 years.

[Her husband Robert was a clerk living at 70 Johnston's Buildings, Shankill Road, Belfast.]

McMILLAN
See MARTIN

MacMULLIN
[In a low-railed enclosure.] In loving memory of Agnes, daughter of James & Susan MacMullin, died Oct. 21st 1885 aged 25 years. And Alexander

their son died May 6th 1889 aged 30 years. And Susan their daughter died March 21st 1894 aged 32 years. And Susan, daughter of John McKEAN, of Belfast, and widow of James MacMullin, of Glenarm, died March 19th 1906 aged 75 years. And Martha their daughter died November 3rd 1915 aged 53 years. And Maria their daughter died October 5th 1924 aged 66 years. "In thy presence is fulness of joy".

[Alexander McMullin and his sister Agnes were both teachers at Miss A. Martin's Boys' Preparatory School at 11 Fitzwilliam Street, Belfast.]

McMURRAY
See FERGUSON

McNABB
[Flaking near the top.] Erected by Sarah HODGKINSON, in memory of her sister Maria Jane McNabb, daughter of the late Geo. Hodgkinson, of Lisburn, who departed this life 16th Sept. 1828 aged 44 years.

McNAIR
[Laid flat.] Erected to the memory of John McNair who died the 13th February 1830 aged 53 years. Also Elizabeth McNair his wife, who died the 23rd September 1851 aged 56 years.

McNEIGHT
[Pitted in centre, now lost.] The family burying place of Robert (Mc) Neight whose father (and) mother are in(terred) here. Also Mary .... his beloved wife who departed this life on the 1(5th) February 1845 aged 39 years. Likewise four of his children who died young.

[Robert McNeight was a merchant tailor at 6 Pottinger's Entry, Belfast.]

McNEILL
Erected by Elizabeth McNeill, in memory of her daughter Elizabeth McNeill who departed this life on the 1st of June 1828 aged 22 years. Also her son Robert McNeill who departed this life on the 6th of July 1828 aged 16 years. Likewise her son James McNeill, who departed this life on the 6th of October 1829 aged 28 years. Also her son William McNeill who departed this life on the 15th of August 1830 aged 19 years.

McNEILL
[Now removed.] (Erected by Daniel McNeill .... in memory of his mother Mary died 13th Septr 1844 aged 61 years. Also his sister) Elizabeth (died 14th Novr 1849) aged 2(3) years.

McSORLEY
See HARPER

McTEAR
[Polished granite against south wall, now lost.] In memory of David McTear, Hazelbank, died 1840 aged 84 years. His wife Elizabeth died 1836 aged 71 years. His son George died 1871 aged 74 years. Margaret, wife of George died 1861 aged 54 years. Also their children: Elizabeth Anne, died 1852 aged 13 years, David, died 1895 aged 58 years, Mary, wife of David, died

1898 aged 50 years. George died 1909 aged 69 years. Sarah May Nelson McTear, born 15th December 1871, died 6th April 1937.

[The will with one codicil of George McTear of Belfast, county Antrim, merchant, who died 8 August 1871 at Moygara, Whitehouse, county Antrim, was proved at Belfast 28 June 1872 by the oaths of John Galt Smith, esquire, and George Kennedy Smith, solicitor, both of Meadow Bank, Whitehouse, in said county, the executors. Effects under £8,000.

Letters of administration with the will annexed, of the personal estate of David McTear of 5 Mount Charles, Belfast, merchant, who died 10 April 1895 at same place, were granted at Belfast 10 June 1895 to Margaret Smith McTear of 5 Mount Charles, Belfast, spinster, one of the residuary legatees in remainder. Effects £1,157 10s.9d.

David McTear (1755/56-1840), merchant, bought Hazelbank, Whitehouse, Co. Antrim in 1796, and it was there that his three surviving sons, George (1796/97-1871), Thomas (1800-84) and James, were born. Thomas and James were among the foundation pupils at Royal Belfast Academical Institution in 1814 and all three sons trained as merchants, becoming agents in some of the private shipping companies of Belfast. In the mid-1820s a Joint Stock Company was formed for the Belfast and Glasgow trade under the title of the Belfast and Glasgow Steamboat Company with George and Thomas McTear as Belfast managers and agents. Thomas left for Liverpool in 1828, his brother James taking over his interest. The Company prospered and following, some opposition from rival companies, the Glasgow agents, James and George Burns established their own line of steamers, eventually buying up the Cunard Line. J. & G. Burns continued to employ George McTear as their Belfast agent until his death. Thomas recounted the changing fortunes of the shipping companies in a series of articles, published in the *Ulster Journal of Archaeology* (2nd series), Vol. 5 in 1898-99.

Their mother's sister was married to James Hyndman (q.v.).

McTEAR
    See SMITH

McTIER
    [White limestone, now broken.] In memory of James McTier, of Vernant Lodge, who departed this life 7th April 186(4) aged 93 years. And Margaret his wife who departed this life 10th November 1875 aged 72 years. "Because I give ye shall live also". Also in memory of their only son James McTier, born 1844, died 1880, buried at Castlebar, Co Mayo. And his wife Mabella Frances Miller, dau. of Rev. Henry CARTER D.D., Rector of Ballintoy, Co. Antrim, born 1846, died 1898, buried at Dean's Grange, Dublin.

[The will of James McTier of Vernant Lodge Belfast in the county of Antrim, gentleman, who died 7 April 1864 at same place, was proved at Belfast 12 August 1864 by the oaths of Margaret McTier of Vernant Lodge, Belfast, widow, James Kennedy and Robert Wakeman, both of Bedford Street, Belfast, merchants, all in the county of Antrim, the executors. Effects under £450. Re-sworn at Belfast, 3 March 1866, under £600.

The will of James McTier of Belfast, gentleman, who died 7 November 1880 at Castlebar, county Mayo, was proved at Belfast 13 December 1880 by the oath of Mable Frances Miller McTier, Hopefield Terrace, Antrim Road, Belfast, widow, the sole executrix. Effects under £500.

McWILLIAM

[Worn tablet formerly secured to north wall and now lost.] (The burying) ground of John McWilliam, merch: Belfast. Here lieth the remains of his wife Mary McWilliam who departed this life on the 8th of April 1808 aged 41 years. And also of their daughters, Margaret who died 23rd June 1816. Elizth NEILSON, ob.22nd October 1859.

[John McWilliam owned a cotton-yarn warehouse at 68 Donegall Street, Belfast.]

McWILLIAM

See ANDREWS

MACARTNEY

[Badly flaking stone, now lost.] (Erected by A(rthur Macartn)ey in memory of his wife Ann who died 14th Feby 1823 aged 19 years.

MACARTNEY

[Small memorial now lost. The plot was bought by John Neill Macartney in April 1849.] The family burying place of J.N. Macartney, Belfast, 1850.

MACAULEY

[Worn marble in broken headstone now lost.] Sacred to the memory of Mary, wife of Thomas Macauley, Belfast, and daughter of Adam DICKEY, Hollybrook, Randalstown who (departed this life .. November) 1866 aged (73) years. And their three children Fred(erick Wil)liam who died (5th March 1836) aged 17 years, Alexander who died (11th December 1838) aged (9) years, Jane who died (13th November 1840) aged (24) years. Also Jane, wife of James Macauley J.P. Ben Neagh of Crumlin, who died (5th November 1842) aged (82) years. Thomas Macauley who died 14 August 1848) aged (63) years.

[The will of Mary Macaulay of Chichester Street, Belfast, widow, who died 16 November 1866 at Belfast aforesaid, was proved at Belfast 11 January 1867 by the oaths of Adam Thomas Macaulay and Francis Montgomery Macauley, both of Chichester Street, Belfast aforesaid, gentlemen, the executors. Deceased died domiciled in Ireland. Effects in Great Britain and Ireland under £450.]

MACK

[Very worn.] (Erected by Robt Mack in memory of Robert Black) his son, died (11th January) 1827 aged (10) years. Eliza (Hall) Mack his daughter died 11th) June (1830) aged (9) years. (Four) of (his children: Robert), Charlotte, (Caroline) and Matilda, died in infancy. Jane his beloved wife died June 22nd 1838 aged (44) years. And the above named Robert Mack who died 29th (April 1840) aged (56) years. His daughter Margaretta Mercer Mack died 19th November 1861 aged 46 years. His youngest daughter Elizabeth Hall REED died 20th Nover 1864 aged 32 years. Also James Reed her infant son.

[The will of Margaretta Mercer Mack of Belfast, in the county of Antrim, spinster, who died 19 November 1861 at same place, was proved at Belfast 5 December 1861 at Belfast by the oath of Catherine Stannus of Belfast aforesaid, widow, the executrix. Effects under £4,000.]

MACK
See GILBERT

MACKAY

[Twin tablets in entablature secured to south wall, in high-railed enclosure.] Dedicated to the memory of Agnes Mackay, wife of Alexander Mackay, many year a proprietor and publisher of "The Belfast News-Letter". She died 10th September 1826 aged 61 years. Three sons, James, John and Alexander repose beside their mother. On the 7th of November 1844, the above-mentioned Alexander Mackay departed this life aged 81 years. Respected and venerated by all who knew him. Robert Allan Mackay, born 29th June 1795, died 29th June 1872.

Dedicated by Jane Mackay to the memory of her beloved husband Alexander Mackay, jun., a proprietor and also publisher of The Belfast News-Letter, who departed this life 2d March 1829, aged 35 years. Jane Mackay, his wife died 9th July 1857. "Looking unto Jesus". Also Katharine Mackay, their daughter, born 18th August 1820, died 2nd January 1903, and Elizabeth Murray Mackay their daughter, born 16th August 1823, died 11th June 1905.

[Probate of the will of Catherine Mackay of Fortwilliam Park, Belfast, spinster, who died 2 January 1903, granted at Belfast 11 February 1903 to James Boyle, J.P. and Robert M. Young, civil engineer, J.P. Effects £6,625 14s.6d.

Probate of the will of Elizabeth Murray Mackay of Fortwilliam Villas, Antrim Road, Belfast, spinster, who died 11 June 1905, granted at Belfast 26 July 1905 to James Boyle, J.P. and Robert Magill Young, civil engineer. Effects £6,480 18s.7d.

In 1795 Henry Joy, junr. sold the *Belfast News-Letter* to a consortium of five Edinburgh men consisting of Robert Allan, George Gordon, Ebenezer Black, James Blair and Alexander Mackay, senr. Ebenezer Black died in 1801, and in 1804, Mackay bought up the interests of the three surviving partners, so making himself the sole proprietor of the paper. In the ensuing years his many improvements included moving the offices from Joy's Entry to Bridge Street where the *Belfast News-Letter* had started in 1737, and also enlarging the scope and format of the paper.

He was one of the founders of Fisherwick Place Presbyterian Church in 1827 and he lived in Mount Collyer Park.

His son Alexander became a partner and publisher in 1820 — one of the books he published was George Benn's *History of Belfast* in 1823 — and died in 1829 aged only 35. He was married to a daughter of David Murray of Edinburgh and had three daughters of whom the second,

Agnes, married James Alexander Henderson (1823-1883) whose father James was a close friend and adviser of the Mackay family.

James Alexander Henderson made the *Belfast News-Letter* a daily paper and was one of the founders of the Press Association. He was Mayor of Belfast in 1873 and 1874 and was a member of the Harbour Board. His son was Sir James Henderson who was Lord Mayor in 1898, and he was also the great-grandfather of the present proprietor.

Alexander Mackay junr.'s other two daughters, Katherine and Elizabeth, never married and resided at Fortwilliam Park.

See Benn: *A History of the Town of Belfast* (1877); Campbell: *Belfast Newspapers, Past and Present* (1921).]

MACKAY
See MULHOLLAND

MACKENZIE
See GIBBS

MACKEY

[Twin marble tablets, of which one is blank, in entablature secured to dividing wall.] In memory of Thomas Mackey, of Glenbank, who died 9th January 1841 aged 57 years. His wife Agnes Mackey died 11th November 1873 aged 73 years. Their children: Mary died 8th February 1829 aged four years and seven months, Anna died 15th February 1840 aged six years and two months, Eliza died 18th February 1840 aged two years and one month. Their grandchild Martha Eliza REID, died 10th May 1856 aged 9 months. His sister Mary Mackey died February 1843 aged 53 years. Their son William Alexander Mackey died 9th February 1884 aged 50 years. Their daughter Charlotte Mackey died 1st April 1894 aged 58 years.

[The will (with one codicil) of Agnes Mackey of Glenview, Strandtown, county Down, widow, who died 11 November 1873 at same place, was proved at Belfast 19 January 1874 by the oaths of William Alexander Mackey of Glenview, Strandtown and George Washington Charters of Craigavad, Holywood, both in said county, esquires, and Forrest Reid of Londonderry, county Londonderry, solicitor, the executors. Effects under £2,000.

The will of William Alexander Mackey of Belfast, engineer, who died 9 February 1884 at Clifton Lodge, Belfast, was proved at Belfast 1 October 1884 by the Reverend George Brydges Sayers of Ballinderry Glebe, clerk, and Hugh Hyndman of Belfast, solicitor, both in county Antrim, the executors. Effects £4,471.

The will of Charlotte Mackey of 5 Wilmount Terrace, Belfast, county Antrim, spinster, who died 1 April 1894 at same place, was proved at the Principal Registry 4 May 1894 by John Kelso Reid of The Elms, county Londonderry, solicitor, the sole executor. Effects £2,137 10s.9d.

Thomas Mackey of Glenbank was a linen merchant who purchased the plot in May 1829. Glenbank at Ballysillan was subsequently occupied by the Ewart family.

MACLURCAN

[Marble tablet in surround surmounted by a draped urn in a high-railed enclosure.] Erected by S. J. Maclurcan, late Captain 19th Regt, in memory of his father Thomas Maclurcan, of Belfast, born 1800, died December 18th 1846. To Jane, his wife who died May 1826, aged (20). (To Wm.) Maclurcan who died March 1856 aged (54) and James Maclurcan, brothers of the above named Thomas Maclurcan, who died August 12th 1857 aged 50. "Requiescant in pace".

MACLURCAN

[Inclining forwards.] Erected in memory of William Maclurcan who died 19th June 1847 aged 73 years. Margery Maclurcan his wife who died 3rd August 1825 aged 48 years. Margery Maclurcan their daughter who died 16th Jany 1837 aged 26 years. Joseph WHITE their son-in-law who died 30th March 1848 aged 59 years. Mary, wife of (James) REYNOLDS, their daughter who died 28th August 1852 aged 39 years, Also William Maclurcan junr who died 17th Decr 1879 aged 64 years. And his three sisters: Agnes BLAIN, Margaret White, and Ann Maclurcan. Also Peter RAMSEY, son-in-law of Margaret White.

[The will of William Maclurcan of Warrenview, Dunmurry, county Antrim, mercantile clerk, who died 17 December 1879 at same place, was proved at Belfast 12 January 1880 by the oaths of James Reynolds of Albert Terrace, Belfast, iron founder, and Joseph Orr of Ann Street, Belfast, seed merchant, two of the executors. Effects under £1,500.]

MACLURCAN

[Large headstone, now smashed, and of which the inscription on the marble tablet is completely worn away, copied from the Society's books.] Erected by John Maclurcan, to the memory of his daughter Sarah, who died 13th April (1845) aged 13 years. And three children who died in infancy. (Eliza Maclurcan died 31st March 1848 aged 43 years. John Maclurcan died 18th March 1858 aged 55.)

[Letters of administration of the personal estate of John Maclurcan of Belfast in the county of Antrim, merchant, who died 15 March 1858 at Victoria Place, Belfast, were granted at Belfast 19 April 1858 to John Herdman of Belfast aforesaid, merchant, the maternal uncle, and guardian of the minor children of said deceased. Effects under £10,000.

John Maclurcan was a silk mercer, first in High Street, then in Donegall Place on the site later occupied by Anderson and McAuley's shop. He lived in Donegall Street before moving to Victoria Place.]

MACLURCAN
See BLACK

MACOUN
See MONTGOMERY

MADILL

[Iron plaque in low-railed enclosure.] The family burying place of James Madill, Belfast, 1886.

MAGAIN
   See NIBLOCK

MAGEE
   [Now missing.] Here lieth the remains of Sarah DONNELLY, wife of Henry Magee, mariner, died 28th Feby. 1848.

MAGEE
   [Marble in carved entablature, secured to south wall.] Sacred to the memory of Matthew Jordan Magee who departed this life 23rd Oct. 1857 aged 34 years. Also his daughter Eliza Jane who died in infancy. Also his daughter Margaretta Magee who departed this life 26th March 1862 aged 8 years.

MAGUIRE
   See EWART and WEIR

MAHON
   See GILLIS

MAIRS
   See LE PAN

MAJOR
   [Worn tablet in pedimented entablature attached to south wall together with small plaque on each side, in high railed enclosure. Arms: Ship's anchor in chief, with three roses. Crest: Horse's head on wreath. Motto: "Fidus ad extremum".] To the memory of Ann Major who was interred here the 6th of March 1805 aged 11 years. Also Thomas Major, of Brickfield, her grandfather who departed this life on the 4th of June 1815 aged 76 years. And Jane his wife who died on the 3rd December 1816 aged 74 years. Also Jane Major, mother to the above named Anne Major who died the 1st of May 1857 aged 87 years. Isabella Major, daughter of Thomas Major, Sydenham, died 27th June 1862 aged 21 years. Also William Henry Major his son, Lieutenant, 5th Fusiliers, died 16th September 1868 aged 2(5) years. Agnes, wife of Thomas Major, of Sydenham, died 27th December 1875, Thomas Major died 29th September 1881.
   [Small plaque badly flaked in the middle.] Sacred to the mem(ory) of Andrew M(ajor), son of McKe(ady) Major and nephew of (above me)ntioned Thomas (Major), died 21(st .... 18.)9. "No mo(....n..."). Jane McKeady Major, sister of Andrew Major, died and was buried at Bournmont, 1898.
   [Plaque on other side.] Sacred to the memory of McKeady Major who died 26th Dec. 1889 and was buried at Hamilton, Bermuda aged 84 years, grandson of the first named Thomas Major. Mary Graham Major died 26th January 1922.
   [Letters of administration, with the will and one codicil annexed, of the personal estate of Thomas Major of Cambridge Villa, Sydenham, Belfast, esquire, who died 29 September 1881 at same place, were granted at the Principal Registry 8 July 1882 to Edward Ernest Knox of Saint Alban's, Bray, county Wicklow, esquire, the person appointed to be administrator of said deceased. Effects £8,398 19s.7d.]

Portrait of Dr Andrew Marshall (Photograph   )

MALCOLMSON
See KNOX

MALCOMSON
[Flaking near the bottom.] Erected to the memory of John Malcomson who departed this life 22nd November 1835 aged 73 years. Also his wife Janet, 23rd February 1840 aged 73 years. Their daughter Elizabeth, 8th February 1843 aged 50 years. Their son, Thomas, 6th January 1846 aged 44 years. Their daughter Margaret TAYLOR, 18th June 1846 aged 33 years. Charles FRAZER, 29th July 1855 aged 44 years, and an infant son. William John Malcomson, 12th March 1860 aged 44 years. Thomas LLOYD 22nd November 1862 aged 64 years.

MALLON
See KENNEDY

MANSFIELD
[Slightly flaking and capstone fallen.] Erected by James Enery Mansfield, in memory of his wife Jane who departed this life the 30th day of March 1848 aged 37 years. Also rest here the remains of the above named James Enery Mansfield who died 17th March 1854 aged 67 years. And of his daughter Martha HIG(G)... who died November (..)th .... aged 95 years.

MARKS
See CAMERON

MARSDEN
See HIND

MARSHAL
[Small headstone.] Isabella Marshal, died 14th August 1857.

MARSHALL
[Flaking slightly.] This stone was erected by Hugh Marshall, of Belfast, to the memory of his daughter Margaret who departed this life Feby 6th 1816 aged 12 years. And his son James who died 8th Feby 1816 aged 19. Also his wife Margaret Marshall who died Nov. 1st 1816 aged 44 years. Here lieth the remains of the above named Hugh Marshall who died July 3rd 1832 aged 59 years. Also his son John who died Septr 21st 1832 aged 38 years.

MARSHALL
[Worn marble tablet in sandstone surround formerly secured to north wall but now lost.] In memory of Andrew Marshall, M.D., of Belfast, born 24th Dec. 1779, died 5th March 1868. And of his wife, Isabella, daughter of William DRUMMOND surgeon (N.V.) born 15th Sept 1776, died (16)th Jan. 1845. "The memory of the just is blessed".

[The will, with one codicil, of Andrew Marshall of Gortalie, Carrickfergus, doctor of medicine, who died 5 March 1868 at same place, was proved at Belfast 3 April 1868 by the oaths of the Reverend John Scott Porter of Belfast, county Antrim, Presbyterian clergyman, and William John Campbell Allen of Fawnoran, Greenisland, Carrickfergus aforesaid, banker, the executors. Effects under £2,000.

Dr Marshall began his medical career as a naval surgeon during which he witnessed the action in which Heligoland, off the Danish coast, became a British possession. He obtained the L.R.C.P. (Ed.) in 1804 but did not take an M.D. until 50 years later, in Glasgow. In 1805, during an interval in his naval career he came back to Belfast and entered into partnership with James Drummond, his future brother-in-law, as an apothecary in High Street. He was the first Secretary and Treasurer of the Belfast Medical Society, founded in 1806. He finally left the Royal Navy in 1808. He was a surgeon to the Fever Hospital, then in West Street, and to the Belfast Charitable Society, practising first at 3 Wellington Place and later living at Greenisland, county Antrim. Dr Marshall took an active part in the founding of the General Hospital in Frederick Street in 1815, and was its first consulting surgeon when it opened two years later.

In 1810 he became a committee member of the Belfast Library and Society for Promoting Knowledge, now the Linenhall Library.

Three of his daughters married well-known Belfast men — Margaret married the Rev. John Scott Porter, a well-known author, Isabella married William John Campbell Allen, banker, and Rosa married Richard Rothwell, painter.

Another brother-in-law of Dr Marshall's was the Rev. William Hamilton Drummond D.D., a noteworthy literary figure in Belfast in the early years of the 19th century and proprietor of a well-known boys' school at Mount Collyer from 1805-1815.

See Drummond: *Belfast Literary Society* (1902); Strain: *Belfast and its Charitable Society* (1961); Allison: *The Seeds of Time* (1972).]

MARSHALL

[Very worn marble shield in sandstone headstone.] (Sacred to the memory of James Marshall, late of Donegall Street, Belfast, who departed this life, 20 Sept. 1853) aged (39) Also Jane (his beloved wife who died on the 23rd May 1869) aged 47 years. Also Margaret Marshall his (sister) who died 11th June 1880 aged (60 years.)

[Letters of administration of the personal estate of Margaret Marshall of Rathmore Cottage, Dunadry, county Antrim, spinster, who died 11 June 1880 at same place, were granted at Belfast to John Marshall Weir of Cookstown, county Tyrone, merchant, a nephew of said deceased. Effects under £200.]

MARSHALL

[Marble tablet in base of cross, around arms of which is entwined a collarette bearing inscription "Thy will be done".] Sacred to the memory of Jane wife of J.D. Marshall, Esqr, M.D., of Holywood, and daughter of the late Sheridan KNOWLES, Esqr, died on the 4th of April 185(4) aged 41 years.

[James Drummond Marshall was a son of Dr Andrew Marshall and a well-known apothecary at 8, High Street, Belfast and held the appointment of chemist in ordinary to Her Majesty the Queen.

Sheridan Knowles ran a boys' school in Crown Entry in the early years of the 19th century, though one account has it that it was off North Street. He had previously been assistant to his father James who was the first Head Master of the English School at the Royal Belfast Academical Institution, and whose stormy expulsion in 1817 is described in Fisher and Robb: *Royal Belfast Academical Institution* (1913) and Jamieson: *History of the R.B.A.I.* (1959). Sheridan was also an accomplished actor and playwright. His great-grandfather was the Rev. Dr Sheridan who was a 1st cousin of Richard Brinsley Sheridan and a friend of Dean Swift.]

MARSHALL

[In upper ground and now missing, but recorded in the 1907 transcript.] Sacred to the memory of James Drummond Marshall who died at Holywood on the 27th March 1868 aged 59 years.

[For biographical note, see above.]

MARSHALL

See GLENDINNING

MARSHAW

See SIMMS

MARTIN

[Inscription gleaned from fragments of flaked headstone (now lost) - remainder copied from Society gravestone book.] Erected (to the) memory of (Jane) Martin (who departed this life in) Belfast (on the 4th July 1816 aged 50 years. And also Ellen Martin who died 16th Feb. 1835 aged 75 years. Also Mr. Robert Martin who departed this life the 30th June 1841, aged 72 years. Also William MURDOCK, nephew of above Robert Martin, who departed this life on the 18th March 184 . aged 12 years.

MARTIN

[Very worn marble in headstone, now lost. It has been mostly copied from Society's records.] Erected by Margaret Martin to the memory of her husband Samuel Martin, of Donegall Street, who departed this life 28th of December 1834 aged 38 years. Also their only child Margaret who departed this life on the 4th of January 1835 aged five years and .. months. "Reader prepare to meet thy God". Also Margaret, relict of the above Samuel Martin who departed this life on the 28th July 1857 aged (63) years.

MARTIN

[Slate, now laid flat.] Erected to the memory of Hamilton Martin who died 23rd Jany 1845 aged 70 years.

MARTIN

[Now lost.] Erected by Robert McMILLAN, in memory of his neice Mary Martin, obit, 18th Octr 1847 aged 34 years. Also Agnes McMillan died 4th Decr 1860 AE 71. Also Isabella McMillan died 3rd March 1877 in her 83rd year. The above Robert McMillan who died 7th September 1878 in the 83rd year of his age.

MARTIN

[Slightly flaking.] Sacred to the memory of Sarah Martin who died 29th

Memorial to Dr John Mattear (1727-1806), (photograph R.W.M. Strain).

October 1849 aged 56 years.
>   Heard ye the sob of parting breath,
>   Mark'd ye the eyes last ray,
>   No! life so sweetly ceased to be,
>   It lapsed in immortality.

Isabella Martin who died 16th October 1880 aged 84 years.

MARTIN
See JOY and KENNEDY

MASSEY
[Broken and very badly weathered, largely copied from Inscription Book.] Erected (by) William Massey (of Saltwater Bridge to the memory of his wife Elizabeth) Ma(ssey who) departed this life (on the 5th day of January 1825 aged 38 years. Also four of his children who died young. Also the above-named William Massey) who departed this life (on the) 2nd (day of) May 184(6) aged (65) years. (Also Samuel, son of the) above died 29th June 1866 (aged 38) years. Also Sarah, second wife of the above William Massey died 8th January 1896 aged 89 years.

[The Saltwater Bridge was a small structure which spanned the river Blackstaff where the Boyne Bridge is now.]

MASSEY
[Memorial now missing from lower ground. The plot was bought by George Massey in November 1842.] The burying place of George Massey, Belfast.

MASSEY
[Surface badly broken away and now lost.] (Erected by (William Masse)y, jun., (of Belfast in memory of) his beloved wife Catherine Ann Mass(ey who depa)rted this life 24th Septr. (185)1 aged 26 years. Also his son William who died young.

MASTERSON
See MUNCE

MATEER
[Small plaque in the ground. The ground was purchased by Samuel Mateer in May 1830.] Erected by Samuel Mateer of Belfast.

MATEER
See GILBERT and SINCLAIR

MATHERS
[Slate tablet in entablature, formerly pedimented, secured to south wall.] Erected by (John M. ATKINSON) to the memory of his uncles, John Mathers Esqr, departed this life the 18th April 1803 aged 78 years, Samuel WOOLSEY Esqr, the 9th December 1817 aged 67 years, Thomas Woolsey Esqr the 6th March 1819 aged 45 years.

MATHERS
[Now lost.] Erected by Margaret Mathers in memory of her beloved husband Thomas Mathers who died June 27, 1847 aged 56 years. Also of their three

daughters who died in infancy. Their son Henry who died at Singapore, January 22nd 1845. Their son William who died at Charleston, W.S. Also the above named Margaret Mathers who departed this life the 8th August 1862 in her seventy-second year. "She is not dead but sleepeth".

The sweet remembrance of the Just,
Shall flourish when they sleep in dust.

Also Francis their fourth son, drowned at Bangor, May 27th 1865 aged 15 years [sic].

MATHEWS
See MORRISON

MATTEAR
[Sandstone tablet secured to west wall in enclosure with Lennox and Drennan Stones.] In memory of John Mattear M.D., who departed this life the 15th day of February in the year of our Lord 1806 aged 79 years. Also his niece Margaret Mattear, daughter of the late Samuel Mattear, born 1762, died April 1845.

[Dr John Mattear was a noted early physician to the Belfast Charitable Society and was also an active committee member. He was also one of the founders of the Public Dispensary in 1792.

His brother Samuel (who often spelt his surname McTier), died 1795 was also a prominent Committee member of the Belfast Charitable Society and was for a time its Chairman. He was married to Dr William Drennan's sister Martha, and for a time was President of the Belfast Directory of the Society of United Irishmen. See Strain: *Belfast and its Charitable Society* (1961). Chart: *The Drennan Letters* (1931).]

MATTHEWS
See KENNEDY and REID

MAWHINNEY
[Flaking and now lost.] Erected by James Mawhinney, teacher of English in the Belfast Academy, to the memory of an affectionate wife, and other dear relatives, Nov. 1825.

[At this time the Belfast Academy was situated in Academy Street, and did not move to the Cliftonville Road until 1880. James Mawhinney was appointed English teacher at the Academy by Dr Bruce in 1814 but was involved in a bitter dispute when Bruce retired in 1822. This continued when the Rev. Reuben John Bryce became Principal and finally in 1827 Mawhinney was induced to resign over a question of charges to pupils for coal to heat the classrooms. He set up his own academy in York Street but it does not appear to have flourished. See Stewart: *Belfast Royal Academy, the First Century* (1985).

MAWHINNY
See BOYD

MAXWELL
[Raised horizontal slab.] Erected by Jane Maxwell in memory of her husband William Maxwell, late of Belfast, merchant, who departed this life

22nd of December 1806 aged 42 years. Also their son James died 23rd of March 1810 aged 8 years. Likewise their son Thomas died 13th of August 1812 aged 8 years.

MAXWELL
See ROGERS

MAY
See GILBERT and SINCLAIRE/SINCLAIR

MEEK
See ANDREWS

MEGAW
See BARNETT

MEHARY
[Formerly in upper ground, but no longer there.] Erected by Robert Mehary, Belfast, to the memory of five of his children, who died in infancy. Also his eldest son Robert Mehary who died 13th July 1872 aged (24) years. And his dearly beloved wife Eliza Mehary who died 17th October 1874 aged 54 years.

MENESY
[Polished granite in low-railed enclosure, now lost.] The burying place of Edward Menesy, Belfast, 1851.

MENOWNE
See GRAHAM

MILBURN
See CAMPBELL

MILFORD
[In low-railed enclosure.] The burying ground of the late John Milford, Belfast, A.D. 1802. Jane Milford, his daughter, born 3rd April 1798, fell asleep in Jesus, 8th July 1890.

[The will of Jane Milford of Belfast, spinster, who died 8 July 1890 at same place was proved at Belfast 1 August 1890 by Richard Barnett of 14 Dublin Road, Belfast, M.D., and John Milford Barnett of 54 Elmwood Avenue, Belfast, M.D., the executors. Effects £6,398 5s.5d.]

MILLAR
[Worn raised horizontal slab, now lost.] Sacred to the memory of Samuel Millar, (merchant) of Belfast, who departed this life the (30)th [sic] day of (February) 1830 aged 6(4) years. Also his wife Anne Millar who departed this life (the 7th) day of November 1830 aged 6(3) years. Also William (Bell) Millar, eldest son of the above Samuel Millar, who departed this life the (6th) day of November 18(1)7 aged 23 years. Likewise David Millar who departed this life the (11)th day of September 18(5)2 aged (66) years. And Thomas Millar, merchant of Belfast, who departed this life the (15th) day of November 18(55) aged (.9) years. Also his daughter Annabell Millar who departed this life the (28th) day of Sept. 18(35) aged (2) years and (6

months). And his daughter (Helen) Millar who departed this life the (7)th day of May 18(77) aged (4) years and (8) months.

MILLAR
[Cracked across the middle and now lost.] In memory of Lenora Millar, born at Gracehill, 3rd July 1861, died 3rd April 1895. [Inscription on the back is mostly hidden by Thomas White's stone which is cemented to it, but looks older.] Erected by James .... in in(fancy) .... who departed (this life) ....his.........who departed (this life).........

MILLAR
See SINCLAIRE

MILLER
Erected by Ann Miller to the memory of her mother Jane, wife to John Miller, baker, who departed this life 16th May 1811 aged 28 years. Also two of her children, John and Robert, who died young.

MILLER
[Two worn marble tablets in entablature secured to east wall of upper graveyard, but now smashed and only a few fragments remain.] (a) Erected by William Miller of Belfast in memory of his mother-in-law Jane KENNEDY who departed this life 27th June 18(23) aged 76 years. Also his son John Cunningham Miller, who departed this life (29th Nov 1824) aged 24 years. Also his (daughter) Jane Kennedy Miller who departed this life 13th (Aug. 1831) aged 2(1) years. Also his wife Eliza Miller who departed this life (6th) Octr 1840 aged 73 years. (The above named) William Miller who departed this life (16th Apr 1844) aged (8)2 years, (Margaret) Cunningham BLOW, wife of Edwin Blow, (and daughter of the above William) Miller departed this life 16th (July 1849) aged 42 years. Edwin Blow (who departed this life 17th July 1849 aged 49 years.) William Blow his brother who departed this life 17th July 1849 (aged 46 years).

[The burial book states that William Blow who died 17th July 1849 was Edwin Blow's son and not brother and was 16 years old — see CUNNINGHAM.

The Miller family was connected to the Cunninghams of Macedon by marriage. John Cunningham bought Macedon in 1813, and was a widely respected linen merchant. His son, also John, was a co-founder of the Belfast Commercial Bank.

William Miller's daughter Margaret married Edwin Blow who, together with his brother William, owned the Cromac Paper Mill for some years prior to disposing of it in 1842. They were grandsons of Daniel Blow (1718-1810), the well-known printer.]

MILLER
[Formerly with the above.] Erected by John BREAKEY, M.D., R.N., in memory of his father-in-law Arthur Kennedy Miller who departed this life 17th July 1849 aged 50 years. Also his (mother-in-law) Margaret Miller who depar(ted this life 16th) Oct 1861 aged (62) years. Also (his brother Kennedy) Breakey who departed this life 20th Feb 1868) aged 40 years.

[Letters of administration of the personal estate of Margaret Miller of Prospect Place in the town of Deal in the county of Kent, widow, who died 16 October 1861 at same place, were granted at the Principal Registry 11 March 1862 to Jane Kennedy Breakey otherwise Miller, wife of John Breakey of Prospect Place aforesaid, the daughter and only next of kin to said deceased. Deceased died domiciled in Ireland. Effects within Great Britain and Ireland under £3,600.

Arthur Kennedy Miller was a son of William Miller (d.1844).]

MILLIKEN
[In high-railed enclosure.] Interred here are the remains of Hugh Milliken, White Park, Co. Down, who died 7th October 1856 aged 48 years. Hugh, son of the late Hugh Milliken, who died 16th February 1868 aged 15 years. Annie, wife of the late Hugh Milliken, who died 31st Decr 1897 aged 82 years. Elizabeth "Bessie", daughter of the late Hugh Milliken, who died 18th Decr 1904 aged 61 years. Sarah J.K. "Jeannie", last surviving daughter of the late Hugh Milliken, who died 10th March 1937 aged 95 years. [On base.] Erected by Hugh Milliken, A.D.1848.

[Probate of the will of Elizabeth Milliken of Beechville, Knock, county Down, who died 18 December 1904, was granted at Belfast 22 May 1905 to Sarah Jane Kennedy Milliken, spinster. Effects £376 1s.3d.

Sarah Jane Kennedy Milliken of Ros-na-Ree, Rostrevor, county Down, spinster, died 10 March 1937. Probate Belfast 16 June 1937 to Johnena Kathleen Martin, married woman, and John Alexander Standfield, agent. Effects £962 14s.7d.

Hugh Milliken was a linen manufacturer, whose premises at White Park, near Ballynahinch were among the most imposing in all county Down. Little is known of him except that he is thought to have been a close associate of John Cromie of Draper Hill, near Castlewellan, who was the leading linen manufacturer in county Down in the 1820s and 1830s.]

MILLIKEN
[Formerly in upper ground and now missing.] Erected by Robert Milliken in memory of his children, James ..... who died 20th Aug. ... aged 3 years, and (.. months). Also his wife Isabella Milliken who died 4th January 1874 aged (55) years.

MILLIKEN
[In a high-railed enclosure near the above.] Wilhelmina Seeds, beloved wife of John Milliken, Knock, Co. Down, and daughter of the late Francis GLENFIELD, who died 2nd December 1904 aged (4)9 years. John Milliken who died 16th November 1910 aged 71 years. Also his wife Gertrude ANDREWS, who died 4th March 1926, interred in Cheltenham. [On base] John Milliken, Knock, Co. Down.

[Probate of the will and one codicil of John Milliken of East Hillbrook, county Down, secretary (retired), who died 16 November 1910 at Erere Cresent Gardens, Belfast, granted at Belfast 24 December 1910 to Sara Gertrude Milliken, the widow. Effects £2,033 7s.8d.

Sara Gertrude Milliken otherwise Gertrude Andrews of 26 Stranmillis

Road, Belfast, widow, died 4 March 1926 at Cheltenham in England. Probate Belfast 27 July 1926 to Thomas Brown. Effects £1,494 12s.5d.]

MILLIN

Erected to the memory of the late John Millin of Princess Street, who departed this life 24th December 1844 aged 69 years. Also his daughter Isabella AE 16 months, Also Ann, his beloved wife, 18th July 1854 AE 69. And John, eldest son to Adam Millin, of Princess Street, died 26th July 1854 AE 17. And two of his daughters, Martha and Sarah Jane who died in infancy. Also Agnes the beloved wife of Adam Millin, died 14th April 1861 AE 49. And his son Adam who died in America, aged 20. Adam Millin died 8th Augt 1889 aged 79 years. Agnes Millin, daughter of Adam Millin, died 28th June 1903.

MINE

[Very worn.] Erected by Samuel Mine, of Belfast, in memory of his wife Mary Mine who departed this life the 2nd of June 181(.) aged (53) years. Also his daughter Susa(nnah) who died the 11th of April (1808) aged 22 years.

MINNIS

See SMITH

MINNISS

Charles Minniss, jnr., who departed this life March 25th 1806 aged 24 years.

How loved how valued once avails thee not,
To whom related or by whom begot,
A heap of dust alone remains of thee,
T'is all thou art and all the proud shall be.

[His father Charles was a peruke maker at 37, Ann Street, Belfast.]

MITCHELL

[Two worn marble tablets in identical carved entablatures secured to east wall of upper graveyard, in a low-stone enclosure but now lost.] Erected by George Thomas Mitchell in memory of his sister (F)ann(y) Mitchell who died on the 16th of February A.D. 18(23). And of his mother Clara Mitchell who died on the (19)th of Oct. A.D. 18(42) aged (80 years. Also of his wife Catherine Mitchell who died on the 7th of Aug 1845 aged 43 years). Also of George Thomas Mitchell who died (13)th November (1856) aged (7)0 years. Also of his (daughter) Clara Mitchell who died 8th September 1857 aged (22) years.

[George Thomas Mitchell was an original member of the Northern Banking Company's Shareholders' Committee, and in May 1831 became a Director of the Belfast Banking Company in succession to Thomas Batt, and remained in that position until his death. He was also Treasurer of the Harbour Board. He lived at no. 6, Wellington Place, and also built "Olinda" at Craigavad, Co. Down where he died. He was a cousin of Alexander Mitchell (q.v.) the blind engineer. See Simpson: *The Belfast Bank 1827-1970* (1975).]

MITCHELL

[Horizontal slab.] Erected by John Mitchell, of Gosford, Markethill, to the memory of his father William Mitchell, of Belfast, merchant, who departed this life on the 25th of October 1826 aged 76 years. Also his son William Mitchell who departed this life on the 2nd of December 1841 aged 41 years. Also two of his children, Amelia Matilda and James who died in infancy. Also the above John Mitchell who departed this life 4th April 1849 aged 72 years. Mary Ann Mitchell who died 20th December 1869 aged 38 years, wife of William John Mitchell. Mary Ann Mitchell, wife of the above William Mitchell, who died 23rd April 1873 aged 64 years. William John Mitchell, son of the above William Mitchell who died 1st August 1886 aged 57 years. Eleanor Amelia Mitchell, eldest daughter of the above William John Mitchell, who died 24th August 1924 aged 68 years. Louis Benjamin Mitchell, second son of the above William John Mitchell, who died 23rd October 1924 aged 57 years, buried at sea.

MITCHELL

[Badly flaking sandstone.] Erected to the memory of the late David Mitchell, hardware merchant, 35 Castle Street, Belfast, who departed this (life) on the 11th April, 1846 aged (59) years.

MITCHELL

[It is not known if a monument was ever erected but Alexander Mitchell, the famous blind engineer and inventor of the screw pile, is buried in the graveyard. Born in Dublin on 13th April 1780, his family came to Belfast when he was still a boy and very early he showed an unusual aptitude for mechanics. Although he went totally blind by the time he was twenty he continued his work and patented his invention in 1833. Among the pile light-houses constructed under his supervision was that in Belfast Lough in 1844. He died on 25th June 1868. For a fuller account, see *Belfast Naral History and Philosophical Society Centenary Volume* (1921).

MOFFAT

[Very large and ornate Gothic monument in a railed enclosure, now removed.] Erected by a few of his numerous friends in memory of William Moffat, Doctor of Medicine, died 27th April 1852 aged 38 years. Here also lie the remains of his wife Mary Moffat who died at Cookstown, on 31st May 1889 aged 68 years.

[The will of Mary Moffat of Cookstown, county Tyrone, widow, who died 31 May 1889 at same place was proved at Armagh 26 July 1889 by the Reverend Hamilton Brown Wilson of Cookstown, D.D., and Thomas Greer Carson of Coleraine, county Londonderry, solicitor, the executors. Effects £4,261 4s.1d.

He was a M.D. of Edinburgh University and a physician to the General Hospital in Frederick Street from 1841 until his death. See Allison: *The Seeds of Time* (1972).]

MOLYNEUX

[Twin tablets and two modern marble tablets in sandstone monument against dividing wall.] Erected by Joseph Molyneux, of Belfast, in memory of his daughter Fanny Margaret who departed this life 13th June 1831 aged 21 years. Also his wife Ann who departed this life 10th day of February 1837 aged 74 years. Also his grandson John HUNTER who departed this life on the 13th of May 1840 aged 9 years. Also his son Joseph Molyneux who departed this life on the 31st of July 1841 aged 39 years. Also Ellen wife of Joseph Molyneux junr who departed this life on the 19th of June 1849 aged 37 years. And of his grandson William Hunter who departed this life on the 16th Nov. 1848 aged 13 years.

Also the above named Joseph Molyneux who departed this life on the 25th of May 1843 aged 85 years. John Hunter died 23rd February 1855 aged 51 years. His son John Hunter died 13th March 1863 aged 17 years. His daughter Anna Hunter died the 23rd March 1863 aged 23 years. Mary Ann Hunter died the 7th July 1866 aged 70 years. Agnes, wife of the above John Hunter, died 16th Aug. 1877 aged 74 years. Eliza WILSON, daughter of the above Joseph Molyneux senr died 16th Dec. 1873 aged 74 years. Also her daughter Eliza Jane CONNOR died 27th June 1866 aged 41 years. And her grandchildren, John Cromie FULTON, died 8th June 1845 aged 1 year. Sarah Fulton died 13th May 1862 aged 9 years.

[Right-hand marble tablet.] In memory of our father and mother, Joseph Hunter died 9th May 1913 aged 76, Ann Jane Hunter died 3rd Feb. 1914 aged 70. 55 Cavehill Rd.

[Left-hand marble tablet.] In memory of Catherine beloved wife of Alexander Hunter, died 11th Aug. 1939 aged 52 years.

[The will of Mary Ann Hunter of Henry Street, Belfast, county Antrim, widow who died 7 July 1866 at Belfast aforesaid, was proved at Belfast 23 November 1866 by the oaths of Joseph Hunter of Wellington Street, linen lapper, and John Anderson of Henry Street, builder, both of Belfast aforesaid, the executors. Effects under £20.

The will of Eliza Wilson, formerly of Belfast, and late of Rialto Place, South Circular Road, county Dublin, widow, who died 16 December 1873 at Rialto Place, was proved at the Principal Registry 27 March 1874 by the oath of John Fulton of Rialto Place aforesaid, provision merchant, one of the executors. Effects under £100.

Letters of administration of the personal estate of Eliza Jane Connor of Earl Street, Belfast, in the county of Antrim, who died 27 June 1866 at Newtownbreda in the county of Down, were granted at Belfast on the 20 August 1866 to Eliza Wilson of Lower Earl Street, Belfast aforesaid, widow, the guardian during the minority only of Edward Connor the son, only next of kin of said deceased, by order of court. Effects under £100.

Probate of the will of Joseph Hunter of 55 Cavehill Road, Belfast, linen-lapper, who died 9 May 1913, granted at Belfast 5 September 1913 to Ann Jane Hunter, the widow, and Robert Johnston, posting master. Effects £1 2 8s.9d.

Joseph Molyneux came from the parish of Killead, Co. Antrim and the family were artisans in the John Street and York Street districts of the town.]

MONTGOMERIE
See ANDERSON

MONTGOMERY
[Worn marble tablet in entablature surmounted by urn, secured to south wall.] In memory of Robert Montgomery died 2nd Oct. 1806 AE 66. Anne BLACKLEY, his wife died 9th March 1845 AE 85. Also of Robert their only child died 9th Septr 1851 AE 68. Jane JACKSON, his wife died 1st Septr 18(1)5 AE 29. And of their children: Robert died in Antwerp 27th Jany 184(4) AE 33, John died young, Anne died 1(4)th May 1835 AE 24, Hugh died 4th August 1838 AE 25, and Jane, widow of T.R. Blackley, died 10th May 1885.

[The will of Jane Blackley of Sandymount, Strandmillis Road, Belfast, widow, who died 10 May 1885 at same place, was proved at Belfast 10 June 1885 by Robert Edward Merie Montgomery of 22 Rue Mozart, Antwerp, Belgium, esquire, one of the executors. Effects £6,087 8s.3d.

In the burial register, Robert Montgomery (d.1851) is described merely as a gentleman and lived at Sandymount.]

MONTGOMERY
[Limestone tablet in pedimented entablature secured to south wall in lowstone enclosure.] Erected to the memory of James Montgomery, surgeon, died 4th Decr 1846 aged 89. Mary Ann Montgomery died 1stDecr 1824 aged 42. Elizabeth MACOUN died 25th Decr 182(3) aged 72. Hugh Montgomery died 11th June 1826 aged (19). John Montgomery died 30th March 1816 aged 11. Elizabeth Montgomery died 27 May 1830 aged 17. Maria Montgomery died 31st August 1833 aged 32. William Montgomery died at New Orleans 17th Sept. 1837 aged 27. James Montgomery died at Calcutta 12th May 1850 aged 47. And his daughters: Mary Anne & Maria died 1831 aged 3 and 1. And his brothers: Robert and Robert Graham Montgomery, who died in infancy in 1811 and 1816.

[Dr James Montgomery was an apothecary in High Street.]

MONTGOMERY
[Large and twin panelled headstone, now laid flat.] In memory of Sarah Montgomery who departed this life on the 27th of October 1838 aged 75 years. And of Catharine Montgomery her sister who departed this life on the 14th of February 1832 aged 74 years.

In memory of the Rev. James RADCLIFFE, Minister of the Gospel in Londonderry, Manchester, and Wigan who was suddenly removed from this life by his Heavenly Master whilst walking in the street in Belfast on the 17th November 1848 aged 56 years. And of his widow Anne Jane Radcliffe who died at Sale, Cheshire, 21st September 1874 aged 73 years. "When Christ our Life shall appear, then shall we also appear with him in Glory".

[Ann Jane Radcliff, formerly of Belfast, Ireland, and late of 18 South Grove, Sale, county Chester, widow, died 21 September 1874. Probate granted herein from District Registry, Chester, 30 October 1874. Re-sealed at Principal Registry, Dublin. Effects in Ireland £284.

Sarah was the widow of H. Montgomery and lived in Upper Arthur

Street. This family which was largely made up of lawyers and gentry, gave its name to nearby Montgomery Street.]

MONTGOMERY

[Formerly in upper ground, but now missing.] Anne, wife of Alexander Montgomery, Belfast, and daughter of the late Rev. John FISHER .... died 17th Nov. 1864 aged (2)4 years.

MONTGOMERY

See BARNETT, CAVART, DUFFIELD, SINCLAIR and SINCLAIRE (X2)

MONTEITH

[Raised and worn horizontal slab.] Erected by Maria Monteith in memory of her husband, John Monteith, surgeon, R.N., who departed this life (28th) April 1837 aged 49 years. Maria Monteith his wife who died on the 17th Nov. 1856 aged 63 years. Also (Matilda) (sic) Monteith (his wife) (who died at Brooklands, Carrickfergus, (12th) April 1880 aged (5)8 years.

[Letters of administration of the personal estate of Mary Monteith formerly of Belfast and late of Rocklands, Carrickfergus, spinster, who died 12 April 1880 at latter place, were granted at Belfast 14 May 1880 to Henry Owens Johnson of 2 Riversdale Road, Liverpool, merchant, a cousin of said deceased. Effects under £4,000.]

MOON

[At the time of E.W. Pim's survey, a tablet with the date 1844 was on a plot bought by Alexander Moon in 1843. He was a merchant and worked for William Todd & Co., linen drapers and silk mercers of 13 Donegall Place.]

MOORE

[Badly flaking.] Here lyeth the remains of (Mary) Moore of Belfast, who d(ied) 2nd June 1815 aged 54 years.

MOORE

[Worn sandstone tablet secured to south wall beside Katherine Jones's.] In memory of John Moore (son of) William and (Saraha)nn Moore, of Ardmoore, (in the County of Antrim who)departed (this life) on the 27th day of February) 1817 (aged 17 years. Also in memory of Margaret, sister to the above named John Moore who departed this life on the 12th day of January 1821 aged 18 years.

MOORE

[Flaking and now lost.] Erected in memory of Henry Moore, Mooremount, Malone, who died 21st July 1823 aged 40 years. Also his son David who died 16th April 1838 aged 22 years. Also his daughter Hannah who died 23rd August 1845 aged 26 years. Also his daughter Rebecca, wife of Peter HANLON, R.E., died 2nd March 1852 aged (3)5. Also his youngest daughter Margaret Jane, wife of Revd J. DAVIS, Ballynahinch, died 18th Sept 1854 aged 31. Also his wife Anna Maria who died on the 10th June 18(6)9 aged 75 years.

[Henry Moore was a prosperous linen merchant.]

MOORE
[Small oval-ended marble tablet bearing the one word and set into the dividing wall.] Moore.

[Plot bought by James Moore in February 1832. He was proprietor of the Donegall Arms Hotel in Castle Place and died in 1857, at which date the building ceased to function as a hotel. The building, which was latterly Robb's department store, was pulled down in 1988 to make way for Donegall Arcade].

MOORE
[Weathered sandstone, now lost.] 1843. Erected by Alex Moore (in) memory of Isabella, his beloved w(ife, w)ho departed this life July 16th 184(3) aged 32 years. Also three of their children, viz: Margt Eliza who died Novr 8th 1836 aged 13 months, Thos George who (died) Jany 3rd 1837 aged (3) years & (3) months, and Isabella who died in infancy. Also his belov(ed son) John Allen who died 26th Decr 1846 aged 8 months and (7) days.

[This stone is next to that of Henry Moore of Mooremount, Malone.]

MOORE
[Twin stones from which the capstone has been toppled.] Erected by Hugh Moore and James G. WALLACE, in memory of their wives, sisters, viz: Mary Moore died 20th June 1837 aged 32 years. Also her infant child. Also his father Gideon Moore, died 8th Jan. 1847 aged 74. His daughter, Mary A. Moore died 14th Nov. 1852 aged 11. His son Stewart M. Moore, died 23rd Dec. 1852 aged 9. His mother Mary Moore died 13th Dec. 1863 aged 85. The above Hugh Moore died 2nd Nov. 1866 aged 66.

Eliza Wallace died 11th June 1837 aged 23 years. The above James G. Wallace died 23rd June 1845 aged 33. Also his nephew Andrew Wallace, died 20th Jan. 1860 aged 11. And William Wallace died 2nd June 1868 aged 15.

[Gideon Moore was a cooper in Nile Street, Belfast.]

MOORE
[Obelisk bearing badly worn marble plaques (now lost) in enclosure with Katherine Jones' and John Moore's tablets. Arms: Lion rampant in dexter, sinister indistinguishable. Crest: Knight's helmet on boar's head. Motto: illegible.] (Sh...n Moore ...

[Broken plaque formerly on pedestal.] (In hope of a blessed Resurrection. Here lieth the body of Catherine Moore, relict of) Roger (Mo)ore Esqr, who departed this life 27th November 18(4)1 aged 73 years.

In life, they were most united,
and in death are not divided.

[She was the second daughter of Valentine Jones (secundus), 1729-1808. (q.v.)]

MOORE
[Sandstone headstone, now lost. The first portion has been copied from the Society's records.] (Sacred to the memory of William John Moore who departed this life 27th November 18.. aged .. years. His wife Grace Moore who

departed this life 10th March 1861 aged 51 years. Of his daughter Matilda Moore who departed this life) 9th March 1850 aged 23 years. Of his daughter Grace Moore who departed this life 4th March 1861 aged 31 years.

MOORE

[Smashed marble now flat.] Family burying ground of D.W. Moore. In memory of his daughter Agnes Moore who died 22nd Mar. 1856 aged 4 years. And of his daughter Agnes Moore who died 9th Jany 1861 aged 1 year and 7 months. Also his daughter Catherine Moore who died 9th Decr 1864 aged 8 mos. And his brother John Moore who died 26th Septr 1855 aged 30 years. His eldest son Edward Coey Moore who died 29th November 1867 aged 18 years. His youngest son Edward Coey Moore who died 13th Augt 1876 aged 6 years.

MOORE

[Slate headstone with sandstone surround, inscribed on both sides. It is now lying loose.] Burying place of Saml Moore, who died 14th Feby 1867 aged 60 years. Also his wife's nieces Allie HAMILTON who died 4th Decr 1881 aged 17 years. Also Maggie Hamilton who died 19th May 1882 aged 21 years. Also Sarah Jane Hamilton who died 3rd Jany 1883 aged 27 years. "As in Adam all die, even so in Christ shall all be made alive".

[Inscription on the back which is flaking.] Also Samuel Hamilton who died (16)th December 1885 aged 28 years. (Also Ellen) dearly loved (wife) of James Hamilton (who died) 24th December (18.)8 (aged 83) years. Also (James), dearly loved husband of (Ell)en Hamil(ton who) died 24th Decemb(er ...) aged 88 years.

[Samuel Moore was a pawnbroker at 39, Cromac Street, Belfast.]

MOORE

[Rough granite base with polished face bearing inscription, surmounted by cross.] In loving memory of Hugh Moore, died 9th Jan. 1891 aged 63 years. His wife Elizabeth died 27th Oct. 1909 aged 70 years. Their son Hugh died 16th May 1873 aged 3 months.

[On cross.] Erected by their children Isa, William and Jackson.

[At foot.] In affectionate rembrance of my dear wife Isa WALSH who died 20th January 1915.

[Hugh Moore was a retired tailor living at 13, Eglinton Place, Belfast.]

MOORE

See EAGLESON, JONES, McCARTER and McDOWELL

MOORHEAD

[Now lost.] Erected by James Moorhead, to the memory of his mother Ann Moorhead who departed this life 25th of Augt 183(4) aged 50 years. Also his father Archibald Moorhead who departed this life 26th of May 1836 aged 50 years. Also to the memory of his wife Mary Moorhead who departed this life 22nd Augt 1843 aged 28 years.

MORELAND

[Split slate headstone with elegant geometric motifs at the top.] This stone was erected by Arthur Moreland, victualler, of Belfast. His son

Robert who died 17th Jany 1801 aged 3 years. Also Robert who died 27th Jany 1808 aged 7 years.

[Arthur Moreland was a victualler at 14, Cornmarket, Belfast.]

MORELAND

Erected by Thomas Moreland, of Belfast, in memory of his son Robert who died 21st May 1828 aged 2 years & 1 months.

Ere sin could blight, or sorrow fade,
Death timely came with friendly care,
The opening bud to heaven conveyed,
And bid it bloom for ever there.

MORELAND

[Worn marble in carved sandstone entablature, now lost.] Erected by William Moreland in memory of his beloved (wife) Sarah who died (8)th October 1862. Also his son Alexander who died in infancy. The above William Moreland who died 2nd October 1877 aged (44) years.

[Letters of administration of the personal estate of William Moreland of Belfast, county Antrim, and of Croft Hall, Holywood, county Down, merchant, who died 2 October 1877 at latter place, were granted at Belfast 19 October 1877 to Sophie Moreland of Croft Hall, Holywood, the widow of said deceased. Effects under £4,000.

William Moreland was the proprietor of William Moreland & Co., drysalters and merchants at 11, Waring Street, Belfast].

MORGAN

[White limestone, broken and laid flat.] In memory of Charles Morgan who died 17th Nov. 1845 aged 60 years. And his wife Mary Morgan who died at Holywood, 2nd Jan. 1886 aged 83 years. "Patient in suffering". Also their two sons, James, Philip who died at Ballarat in 1866, and Charles who died at Jarrow-on-Tyne in 1868. Also Mary who died at Newcastle-on-Tyne, 24th Feb. 1927 in her 85th year, and was interred in St. Peter's churchyard, Stocksfield, Northumberland, "The Lord is good: a stronghold in the day of trouble".

[The will of Mary Morgan of Auburn Place, Holywood, county Down, widow, who died 2 January 1886 at same place, was proved at Belfast 20 January 1886 by Mary Morgan of Auburn Place, Holywood, spinster, the sole executrix. Effects £2,733 5s.7d.]

MORRISON

[Very badly flaked headstone of which only part has survived.] (Erected by the shipwrights of ...... in memory of Robert Morrison, shipwright, who was assasinated by a Portuguise sailor), 22nd of April 1810 aged 23 years.

Array'd in hope that fatal morn arose
He knew no guilt and therefore felt no dread
He little dream't that ere the evening's close
He should be numbered with the silent dead.

Ye mourning friends suppress your cries
Who like the early blessed flower he fell,

If Truth and Virtue shall to Heav'n arise
There with his God, the youth is going to dwell.

[The sailor, Antonio de Silva by name, belonged to the crew of an American ship, then in port, and stabbed Morrison to death near Prince's Street. He was tried and convicted at the Summer Assizes, and was executed at a gallows called the "Three Sisters" on the sea-shore, about one mile from Carrickfergus. The event was witnessed by a very large crowd. See Benn: *History of the Town of Belfast,* Vol. II 1880.]

MORRISON

[Twin slate tablets of which one was broken and lying down, in a broken entablature secured to the dividing wall, now both removed.] Sacred to the memory of Alexander Morrison of Belfast, who departed this life 3rd March 1832 aged 53 years. Also his third daughter Margaret who departed this life 8th January 1836 aged 22 years. Also his daughter Sarah who departed this life 19th day of November 1838 aged 20 years. Also Margaret, relict of Alexander Morrison, who departed this life 18th day of May 1839 aged 57 years. Also his eldest daughter Mary MATHEWS, who departed this life 20th day of September 1840 aged 35 years.

Sacred to the memory of Mary Morrison, mother of Alexander Morrison, who departed this life 24th January 1833 aged 83 years.

[Alexander Morrison was a muslin manufacturer, first in Gordon Street, and subsequently in Donegall Street.]

MORRISON

[Slightly flaking.] Erected by Joseph Morrison in memory of his beloved wife Mary Morrison who departed this life 25th May 1842 aged 27 years. Also his son Hugh who died on the 1st of February 1854 aged 13 years. Also his daughter Elizabeth died on the 2nd of April 1855 aged 19 years. Also Elizabeth Lamb GRACEY who departed this life 12th Jany 1861 aged 69 years "When Christ, who is our Life, shall appear then shall ye also appear with him in (glory)".

MORROW

[Slate in large headstone, of which capstone is fallen, in low railing.] Erected by Patrick Morrow in memory of his beloved wife Eliza NELSON who departed this life 29th May 1852 aged 42 years. Also the above Patrick Morrow who died suddenly while bathing in Carnlough Bay on the 16th August 1875 aged 68 years.

MOYLE

[Now lost.] In memory of Captain T.J. Moyle, late of the 66th Regt, who died on the 20th October 1843 aged 45 years. This tablet is erected by his brother officers, as a mark of their esteem.

MUIR

[Missing from lower ground.] Sacred to the memory of Thomas Muir Matthew, son of Thomas Matthew & Catherine Muir, Kincardine, Perthshire, Scotland. He was born at Edinburgh 1814, died in Belfast, (May 1833). [His father was from Muir Park near Glasgow.]

MULHOLLAND

[Polished black granite tablet secured to east wall of upper graveyard, in low-stone enclosure.] Sacred to the memory of Thomas Mulholland of Belfast who departed this life December 4, 1820 aged 64 years. Also to the memory of his son Thomas who departed this life May 5, 1830 aged 44 years. Also to the memory of his son William who departed this life May 11, 1847 aged 51 years. Also to the memory of his wife Anne, who departed this life January 13, 1858 aged 92 years. "In Christ shall all be made alive" 1 Cor. XV, 22.

[The will of Anne Mulholland of Mount Ogle, near Belfast in the county of Antrim, widow, who died 13 January 1858 at Mount Coyller, was proved at Belfast 2 March 1858 by the oaths of Andrew Mulholland of Spring Vale and Saint Clare Kelburne Mulholland of Eglantine, both in the county of Down, esquires, the executors. Effects under £10,000.

Thomas Mulholland senr and his son Andrew (1790-1866) started busisness as manufacturers of calico and muslin in the very early years of the nineteenth century. They purchased McCammon, Milford & Bailey's cotton mill in Winetavern Street, said to be the very first of its kind in Belfast, and later they acquired McCracken's old mill in Francis Street, there installing the first power-driven looms in the town. By the early 1820s Andrew had built cotton mills in York Street which, on being burnt down in 1828, were rebuilt as a linen factory. From this evolved the world-famous York Street Flax Spinning Company, Ltd. This firm was largely responsible for making Belfast the chief linen centre of the world.

Andrew Mulholland also took an active part in the life of the community, being a co-founder of Fisherwick Place Presbyterian Church, and one of the first councillors of the new Town Council of 1842, representing Dock Ward.

He married a sister of T. McDonnell, the noted Q.C. and purchased, amongst other property, Ballywalter Park, county Down, building the present very fine mansion. His son John was M.P. for Downpatrick, and was ennobled as Lord Dunleath twenty-five years after succeeding to Ballywalter Park where his descendants still live. The family had previously lived in York Street, then later at Mount Collyer.

Andrew's brother Sinclair Kelburn added a wing to the General Hospital in Frederick Street.]

MULHOLLAND

[Badly flaking.] Erected by Margaret Mulholland in memory of her husband John M(ulholand, late of Belf(ast who) departed this life Jan ...h 1822 aged 3(4 years). Also 3 of their (children) who died in (infancy). Margaret REI(D) alias (the) above Margt Mulh(llan)d who died (Jun)e the 7th 18(.3) aged (..) years, leaving on .... William Mackay Mulholland, (died 23rd July 1867).

MULLAN

[In lower ground and no longer extant.] Erected by James Mullan, 41 Hopeton St., Belfast, in memory of his beloved wife Isabella who died 14th February 1875 aged 53 years.

MULLAN
See KENNEDY

MULLIGAN
[With lead letters and in a high-railed enclosure.] Interred here are the remains of John Mulligan, of Belfast, who died 27th November 1847 aged 40. Thomas Mulligan, son of the above, who died in New York, 1877. Eliza Ker BROWN, widow, daughter of above John Mulligan, who died August 1893. John M. Brown, son of above. Eliza, wife of the late John Mulligan, who died 23rd Novr 1897. Sara J. Kennedy, daughter of above John Mulligan, who died 5th January 1907. Erected by Eliza, widow of John Mulligan, A.D. 1848.

[Probate of the will of Sarah Jane Kennedy Mulligan of 74 University Street, Belfast, spinster, who died 5 January 1907 granted at Belfast 18 February 1907 to John Simpson, M.D., and Thomas Chisholm Houston, solicitor. Effects £5,367 3s.9d.

John Mulligan who lived in Donegall Pass was a partner in J. & T. Mulligan whose wholesale calico warehouse was at 6 Donegall Street.]

MULLIN
[Horizontal slab, now lost.] I.H.S. Erected by Dennis Mullin, (mariner) to the memory (of) his (Uncle) Captain John Mullin, of Belfast who departed this life on the (7)th of May 1837 aged (73) years. [Two indecipherable lines of verse follow.]

MUNCE
[Large headstone, badly flaked, leaning forward, now removed.] Erected (by William Munce in memory of his beloved wife Ann Munce who departed this life 15th August 1852 aged 42 years.) Ann MASTERSON, wife of Samuel STEPHENS, died 29th September (1866 aged 67 years). William Munce died 25th August 18(76).

[The will of William Munce of 8 Wellington Park, Belfast, builder, who died 25 August 1876 at same place, was proved at Belfast 1 November 1876 by the oaths of Elizabeth Harriet Munce of 8 Wellington Park, Belfast, widow, and James Milling of Malone Park, Belfast, builder, the executors. Effects under £4,000.

MUNFOAD
[Badly flaking and ivy-covered, now lost.] Sacred to the memory of James Munfoad who departed this life 22nd November 1832 aged 76 years. Jane Munfoad his wife died (..)th February 1814 aged (6)2 years. Margaret (his) daughter died (12)th July 1820 aged 3(8) years. Mary his (daughter), wife of Joy D(.Y.), died (..)th November 18(.. aged 51) years. Elizabeth (his dau)ghter died (17th Fe)bruary 1841 (aged) 53 years.

[James Munfoad was an active committee member of the Belfast Charitable Society whose records tell of his frequent and interesting spells of duty as orderly. From 1797 until his death he was secretary and treasurer of the Linenhall Library and, for 2 months in 1829, he was Librarian until forced by ill-health to resign. He was organised and diplomatic, to judge by his B.N.L. obituary. See Killen: *A History of the Linen Hall Library* (1990).]

MUNFOAD
See REID

MUNN
See COLEMAN

MUNSTER
[Flaking and broken horizontal slab.] This (stone) is erected to the memory of Marianne Munster by a fond mother and an affectionate husband. She surrendered up into the Creator's hand that life which she had held in trust for 32 years on the 25th day of January 1818.

Invidious grave! how dost thou rend in sunder,
Whom love has knit, and sympathy made one.

MUNSTER
[No longer extant. Captain Paul Munster bought the ground in January 1831.] Erected by Paul L. Munster of Belfast, 1832.

[He was a broker and shipping agent in Prince's Street.]

MURDOCK
See MARTIN and SPRING

MURPHY
[Now lost and copied from the Society's gravestone record book.] Sacred to the memory of Robert, father of John Murphy who died 12th March 1832 aged 40 years. Also his beloved mother Eliza who died 30th July 1854 aged 62 years. Also the above named John Murphy, of Catherine St., North, who died on the 9th January 1863 aged 45 years. And his sister Sarah Murphy, died 28th October 1873 aged 41 years.

[The will with one codicil of John Murphy of Belfast in the county of Antrim, grain merchant, who died 9 January 1863 at same place, was proved at Belfast 30 January 1863 by the oaths of Catherine Murphy and Sarah Murphy, both of Belfast aforesaid, spinsters, the executrixes. Effects under £100.

The will of Sarah Murphy of Little May Street, Belfast, spinster, who died 28 October 1873 at same place, was proved at Belfast 3 December 1873 by the oath of Catherine Berryman, wife of Thomas Berryman of Mill Street, Belfast aforesaid cabinet manufacturer, the sole executrix. Effects under £100.]

MURPHY
[Large and thick pillar, inscribed on two sides and surmounted by a wreath, in a low-walled enclosure.] The family burial place of John Murphy, whose mother Sarah was interred here A.D. 1834. Also John his father, A.D. 1836. The above named John Murphy formerly of York Street, Belfast, and late of Scrabo Cottage, was interred here 11th Nov. 1870. "I know that my Redeemer liveth". There is also interred in this vault his beloved wife. Jane Murphy who died 27th August 1874. Their

daughter Ursula died 28th January 1906 in her 83rd year.

[East side.] Their daughter Jane, widow of Robert KING, died 22nd April 1920. "I have fought a good fight, I have kept the Faith". Her beloved and devoted youngest daughter Margaret Josephine died 25th May 1920. "She hath finished the work thou gavest her to do". "There is a green hill far away". Also Robert King, her only and beloved son, died 21st January 1942. "A valiant soul, fearless in the defence of right". "His memory to those who cherish it most". Edith King, 1877-1958. Caroline Ursula King, 1875-1960.

[Robert King of 43 Fitzroy Avenue, Belfast, engineer and draughtsman, died 21 January 1942. Administration Belfast 9 March 1942 to Caroline U. King, spinster. Effects £395 6s.10d.]

MURPHY

[Laid flat.] Erected to the memory of Alexander Murphy, of Belfast, who departed this life 1st July 1847 aged 56 years. Also his grand-daughter M.. Jane THOMAS died February 1854 aged 3 months. Also his best beloved daughter Anna PORTER who departed this life 19th August 1872.

The beautiful and pure is gone,

But yet the sun is shining on.

Also his youngest daughter Mima who died 14th October 1895, the dearly beloved wife of John HERRON. Also the above named John Herron who died 18th March 1901.

[Probate of the will of John Heron of 74 Mountpottinger Road, Belfast, writing clerk, who died 18 March 1901 granted at Belfast 24 April 1901 to Elizabeth Murphy, spinster, and Hugh L. Orr, mill furnisher. Effects £384 7s.8d.

Alexander Murphy was proprietor of the Union Iron Foundry at 12 Weigh-house Lane, off High Street. After Weigh-house Lane was cleared away in the late 1840s to make way for Victoria Street, the firm was continued by John F. Murphy.]

MURPHY

See ATKINS and RUTHERFORD

MURRAY

[Now lost.] Here lieth the body of Archibald Murray who departed this life the 4th Septr 1807 aged 20 years.

MURRAY

[Badly eroded headstone.] Ere(cted) to the memory of Archd Murray, bricklayer, of Belfast, who departed this life Septr (10)th 1810 aged (43) years. Also one of his daughters, Sarah Jane who died a child.

MURRAY

[Undated flaking stone, now lost, of c.1820.] Erected by James Murray in memory of his two sons who died young. [The plot was purchased by Dr. Murray in December 1813.]

[This was the famous Sir James Murray (1788-1871), inventor of Milk of Magnesia. He began his career by becoming apothecary to the Belfast

Dispensary in 1807 at the early age of 19. Only a year later he set up his own surgeon's and apothecary practice in High Street, though there is a tradition that he started in Winetavern Street. The turning point in his career came about 1829 when he invented a special medicine to cure a sudden ailment that the Marquis of Anglesea, Lord Lieutenant of Ireland, was seized with on a visit to the Marquis of Donegall. The treatment was so successful that he was appointed resident physician, to the Lord Lieutenant, and he moved to Dublin where he had a brilliant career. He obtained the M.D. of Edinburgh in 1829 and of Trinity College, Dublin in 1832.

He was also responsible for building a very fine set of gentlemen's houses known as Murray's Terrace, where Murray Street is now, in 1828.

His son was John Fisher Murray (1811-1865), the distinguished satirist and poet.

See *Dictionary of National Biography* (1913); Gaffikin: *Belfast Fifty Years Ago* (1894); Burtchaell and Sadleir: *Alumni Dublinenses* (1924).

MURRAY

[Large granite triangular-topped altar-tomb, probably c.1840-1870.] The burial place of John Murray, Arthur Street, Belfast.

[The plot was bought by John Murray in November 1814. His family founded the tobacco firm of Murray, Sons and Company.]

MURRAY

[Smashed marble in headstone now lost.] The family burying place of George Murray. Underneath are interred the remains of his daughter Euphemia Murray who died on the 28th day of (Decr) 1828 aged (7) years. And of his sister (Mary) Murray who died on the 17th day of Decr 18(4)6 aged 48 years. And of his sister Eliza Murray who died on the 17th day of April 1847 aged 63 years. Also the above named George Murray who died on the 5th day of Febry 1855 aged 70 years. "There remaineth therefore a rest for the people of God". Hebrews IV.6. Esther ORR, his sister widow of the Rev. Robert Gamble Orr, who died on the 14th of March 1864 aged 73 years. Also George, son of the late John Murray, of Arthur Street, who died September 28th 1868 aged 32 years. Also Sarah Ann, widow of the first named George Murray, of Strandtown, who died November 22nd 1896. "For of such is the Kingdom of Heaven".

[Probate of the will of Sarah Anne Murray of Strandtown House, Strandtown, county Down, widow, who died 22 November 1896, granted at Belfast 15 January 1897 to George Murray Rogers of Hazelbank, Laurencetown, said county, esquire, J.P., Robert Wallace Murray of Fortwilliam, Belfast, esquire, J.P., and Edgar Rogers of Creevy, Strandtown, esquire. Effects £6,057 2s.5d.

The Murray family were wholesale grocers and tobacconists in High Street and Queen's Square and later in Arthur Street. The tobacco firm of Murray Sons & Co. evolved from their concern. George Murray, senior, came from Banbridge.

The Rev. Robert Gamble Orr was born in 1787 at Brigh, county Tyrone, the third son of James Orr, farmer. He entered Glasgow University in 1804 and (like so many at that time) does not appear to have taken a degree. He went on to the Reformed Presbyterian Divinity Hall in Stirling and was licenced by the Southern Presbytery. He was ordained Minister of Limavady in 1815 but resigned in 1827 to emigrate to the U.S.A. He died at Paterson, New Jersey in 1837 and presumably his widow then returned home. See Addison: *Matriculation Albums of the Univeristy of Glasgow* (1913); Loughridge: *Fasti of the Reformed Presbyterian Church of Ireland* (1970).]

MURRAY

[Now lost — copied from inscription book.] To the memory of John Murray, born 11th January 1813, died 9th January 1850. "He might have said as (said Obidiah) — I fear the Lord from my youth". 1st Kings XVIII,12. Also his wife Jane Murray who died 23rd Feby 1854 aged 42 years.

[Jane Murray was born at Rostrevor, Co. Down.]

MURRAY

[Broken headstone near "cholera ground", but now missing.] .... Margaret Murray in memory of her beloved daughter Mary Sarah Murray who died 6th April .... aged 4 years and 6 months.

MUSSEN

See McCREEDY and WELDON

M.......

[Stone with portion missing from centre. It was near the cholera or Strangers' ground, but has disappeared since 1907.] Erected by James M..... in memory of his son ...... who died March 7th 1827 ...... years.

NAPIER

[Limestone tablet in large entablature of the doric order, secured to west wall, in a low stone enclosure.] Here are interred the remains of William Napier who died 25th May 1830 aged 75 years. Also the remains of Samuel his second son who died 31st March 1835 aged 33 years. Also the remains of Rosetta, widow of William Napier, who died 30th June 1836 aged 67 years.

[William Napier ran a brewery in Bank Lane (now Street) and went into partnership with John Dunville (q.v.) in 1808, the latter buying him out entirely in 1825. Mrs Napier spent her remaining years at Wellington Place, Belfast. Their son, Sir Joseph Napier, was subsequently Lord Chancellor of Ireland.]

NEIL

See LIGGET

NEILL

[Flaking in centre.] Erected to the memory of Samuel Neill who departed this life Jany 4th 1832 aged 60 ys. Also his wife Rachael who departed this life Decr the 7th (183)2 aged 59 years. Also Mary Ann ANDERSON, who departed this life June 23rd 1841 aged 31 years. And of Mary Neill who departed this life 31st Decr 1845 aged 3(1) years.

[Samuel Neill was a dealer in old clothes in Smithfield.]

NEILL
[Polished granite tablet attached to east wall in a high-railed enclosure.] Sacred to the memory of Robert Neill, merchant, Belfast, born 2nd April 1804, died 26th Feb. 1854, buried at Longford. And of his wife Margaret, daughter of Henry RIDDEL, Comber, who died 30th November 1892 aged 82 years, and is buried here. Victoria, born 15th March 1840, died 26th Dec. 1843, Victoria, born 2nd Jan. 1844, died 15th Nov. 1846. John, born 21st Nov. 1829, died 10th Nov. 1881.

[The will of John Neill of 47 Balmoral Terrace, Belfast esquire, who died 10 November 1881 was proved at Belfast 8 December 1882 by James William Thomas Smith of 3 Glengall Place, M.D., one of the executors. Effects £217 10s.7d.

Robert Neill was a grocer and tobacconist at 21, Church Lane, Belfast. His son John was a co-proprietor of the Belfast Foundry at 118 & 120 Donegall Street. He lived at 47 Great Victoria Street.]

NEILL
[Broken marble in headstone, now flat.] Sacred to the memory of Robert Neill of Belfast, died 27th Jany 1857 aged 82. And of his wife Letitia Neill died 15th July 1845 aged 57. And of their son Robert Neill, died at Naples 2nd July 1849 aged (32). Also their grandchild Letitia Neill, daughter of John Neill, who died in infancy. Robert Neill, born 20th Ja(nuary) ...., died 17th Novr 18(5)0.

[Robert Neill, senior, founded in c.1800 the well-known firm of watchmakers and jewellers, initially located at No. 1, and later at 23, High Street, Belfast before moving to Donegall Place. The firm is best remembered from the 1930s as Sharman D. Neill. Robert and his two sons James and John lived at Holywood.]

NEILL
See HYNDMAN and RUSSELL

NEILSON
[Tablet now loose from headstone.] John Neilson, M.D., F.R.C.S., who died on the 17th July 1839 aged 23 years. Also his sister Sarah Jane Neilson who died on the 22nd July 1838 aged 19 years.

[The burial register records that Dr Neilson died at the Old Lodge, Cliftonville, Belfast, having been taken ill whilst visiting S. McDowell Elliott.]

NEILSON
See GARRETT and McWILLIAM

NELSON
See MORROW

NEWSAM
[Twin marblet tablets, now lost, formerly in entablature secured to south wall.] Erected by ..... Newsam, of Belfast.

Sacred to the memory of William Newsam who departed this life 28th March 1830 aged 68 years. Also of four of his children who died in infancy. Also of Mary, relict of the above named William Newsam who departed this life the 10th day of May 1847 aged 70 years. Also Eliza, daughter of the above William Newsam who died at Walsall, 21st Decr 1881 in the 63rd year of her age and was buried at Great Barr, Staffordshire.

Sacred to the memory of Jane, wife of James Ramsey Newsam, who departed this life 10th October 1842 aged 25 years. Also her son William who departed this life 9th Jany 1854 aged 11 years. Also James Ramsey Newsam who died at Walsall 13th Septr 1856 in the 46th year of his age, and was buried at Gr(eat) Ba(rr, Staffo)rdshire.

[Eliza Newsam of Walsall, county Stafford, spinster, died 22 December 1881. Probate granted at London 3 June 1882. Re-sealed at Principal Registry, Dublin. Effects in Ireland £1,000.

James Ramsey Newsam was a merchant at 72, Waring Street, Belfast.]

NIBLOCK
[Now lost.] Erected by David Niblock in memory of his wife Mary Ann who died September 10th 1837 aged 37 years. Also his mother-in-law Margaret MAGAIN who died January 1841 aged (6)8 years.

NICHOLS
See CRABB

NICHOLSON
See CONNELL

NORWOOD
[Very badly worn headstone, now lost.] Erected by David Norwood, of Belfast 1805, who departed this life (12th) March (1816) in the (63) year of his age, and was interred here.

NOTT
See FORRESTER

NOWLAN
[Laid flat and flaking with geometric design at the top.] To the memory of Arthur Nowlan, son to Lieutenant William Nowlan of the 50th Regiment of Foot, who departed this life at Belfast the 24th of May 1815 aged 7 years, 7 months and eighteen (days).

NUGENT
[Weathered.] Here lieth the (body of) Elizabeth Nugent (who departed) this life November (the) 20th 1804 aged 64 years."... is no ... where the Wicked cease from troubling and the w(ea)ry be ever at rest".

NUGENT
See BARTON

OFFICER
[Flaking.] Erected to the memory of Robert Officer of Belfast, who died 10th January 1825 aged 66 years. Also his wife Sarah Officer, who

died 28th August 1828 aged 58 years. Also their daughter Margaret Officer who died 18th September 1824 aged 18 years. Likewise their son Doctor Alexander Officer who died on the 8th of June 18(5)7 aged 51 years.

[Dr Alexander Officer was a licentiate apothecary and surgeon at the York Street Medical Hall at 43, York Street, Belfast. He lived at Mountainview Terrace, Crumlin Road.]

OGILVIE
See GRAHAM

OGSTON
[Worn tablet, now lost.] Erected in memory of William Ogston who died 6th Dec. 18(31) aged (42) years. Also two of his children who (died in infancy). William Ogston aged 21, (184.) Mary Rochead Ogston, died 26th November 1860 aged 68.

[William Ogston, senior, a native of Greenock, Scotland was a confectioner at 39, High Street, Belfast and the shop was continued by his widow Mary until her death in 1860].

OLLIVER
[Badly worn small sandstone, now lost.] This stone is erected to the memory of Robert Oliv(er) who departed this life January the (..) 1826 aged (2)2 years. Also (of) his sister ...an.. died January the (..), 182(.) aged (7) years. Likewise Jane died February the (..) 18(2.) aged (..) years. Also .... child .... Also (Susana Oliver) who departed (this life) December the 10th (18.)9 aged (1)0 years.

   Their lamps were
   The
   The
   .....g the

ORMISTON
See ANDREWS

ORR
[Slightly pitted.] Sacred to the memory of Robert Orr, Barrister at Law, who departed this life Sept 7th 1817 aged 47 years. Also of Elizabeth Mary his wife who died Decm 1st 1823 aged 41 years. And also of Ann their youngest daughter who died May 25th 1836 aged 18 years.

[Robert Orr practised as a barrister both in Belfast and had an office at 76, Marlborough Street, Dublin.]

ORR
[Undated slate headstone identical to and beside Robert Latimore's looks of c.1805-1825.] This stone was erected by Thomas Orr, of Belfast.

   The blustrous winds & Neptune's waves
   Hath toss me too & fro,
   In spite of all, by God's decree I am harboured here below,
   Where at an anchor I do lie with many of our fleet,
   One day we shall set sail again,

Our Saviour Christ to meet.
Here lieth five of his children who died young.
[This plot was purchased by Thomas Orr in September 1800.]

ORR

[Iron plaque now missing from lower ground. The plot was bought by Robert Orr in January 1846.] The family burying ground of Edward Orr.

[Robert Orr was a spirit dealer at 202, North Street, Belfast.]

ORR

See BLAIN, HUNTER and MURRAY

OWEN

[Headstone with marble tablet and capstone now flat.] Erected by Wm H. Owen, to the memory of his brother Edward who departed this life 11th October 1840 aged 30 years. Also his father Hugh who died 27th November 1843 aged 69 years. Also W. H. Owen, infant son of J. B. Owen. Also Margaret, wife of the above named W. H. Owen, who departed this life 5th April 1846 aged 37 years. Also the above Wm H. Owen died on 14th Aug. 1860 aged 48 years. Also Hugh, son of the above named W. H. Owen who died 21st Febr. 1865 aged 28 years. And Anna, wife of the above W. H. Owen, died 7th March 1889 aged 64 years. "Through the Valley of Death, my feet have trod, and I reign in glory now". "Blessed are the dead which die in the Lord".

[The will of William Hayes Owen of Henry Street, Belfast, county Antrim, gentleman, who died 14 August 1860 was proved at Belfast 7 September 1860 by the oath of Anna Owen, widow, one of the executors. Effects under £4,000.

The Owen family hailed from County Limerick. Edward of Stanhope Street was a writing clerk. His father Hugh, of Henry Street was an Excise Officer. William Hayes Owen was a rent agent.]

OWEN

[Missing from lower ground.] Erected by J. B. Owen in memory of his dear children, Margaret, died 29 Oct. 1849 AE 3 years. And (Hugh) on 5 Nov. 1849 AE 19 months. Also his beloved wife Ruth died 17 August 1855 AE 31 yrs.

[James B. Owen was a pawnbroker at 29, Townsend Street, Belfast.]

OWEN

See CARSON

OWENS

[Undated iron shield now lost, probably of c.1860.] The family burying ground of Thomas Owens.

[The plot was purchased by Thomas Owens in November 1843, for his five month old son Robert. He was a grocer and provision dealer at 48, Gordon Street, Belfast.]

O'DONNELL

See FERGUSON

O'FARRELL
[Formerly in upper ground and no longer to be seen.] Erected by Fergus O'Farrell of Belfast, 1839.

O'HAGAN
[Cracked.] I.H.S. Sacred to the memory of Edward O'Hagan who departed this life 11th Novr 1836 aged 57 years. Also in memory of his beloved wife Mary the eldest daughter of Captain Thomas BELL, who died near Rosstrevor 27th October 1836 aged 50 years.

[Edward O'Hagan, originally from Dungiven, county Londonderry, was a merchant in Gordon Street, Belfast.]

O'HARA
[In upper ground and now missing.] This stone is erected to the memory of Robert O'Hara who departed this life January the .. 1820 aged 15 years. Also of his sister Rosina died January the 12th 1828 aged 7 years. Likewise Jane died February the 20th 1828 aged 2 years. Also Susan O'Hara who departed this life December the 10th .... aged 10 years.

O'NEILL
See GIFFORD

PALMER
[Very badly flaking and now lost.] This stone was erected by John Palmer of Belfast, in memory of his wife Ann who departed this life 9th Jan(uary) 1809 (aged 3)4 years.

PALMER
[Smashed marble in large headstone, now removed.] Erected to the memory of (William Palmer who died on the 19th September 1856 aged 51 years. Also four children who died in infancy. Here also is interred Agnes, relict of the above William Palmer, [by whom this tablet was erected] who died on the 23rd of January 186)7 (aged 59 years. Also William their eldest) son who died on the (13th of Janu)ary 1877 aged 38 years.

[The will of Agnes Palmer of Queen Street, Belfast, widow, who died at Belfast 23 January 1867, was proved at Belfast 6 April 1867 by the oaths of John Miller Pirrie of Belfast, M.D., and William Pirrie Sinclair of North John's Street, Liverpool, merchant, the executors. Effects under £2,000.

Letters of administration of the personal estate of William Palmer of Belfast, county Antrim, merchant, who died 15 January 1877 at Glasgow, a bachelor, were granted at Belfast 9 April 1877 to Thomas Palmer of Holywood, county Down, merchant, a brother of said deceased. Effects under £300.

[William Palmer, senior, was a boot and shoemaker at 3, Church Lane, Belfast, and 88, High Street.]

PARK
[Wall plot in upper ground. It is no longer extant, but was recorded by E. W. Pim in 1907.] Here lieth the bod(y of) Mary Park, widow of .... died 19th October .... James Park, their elde...... and Mary Ann Park the

youngest .... Sarah .... their eldest daughter died ..... April 1823.
[This lot was purchased by James Park on 19th October 1805.]

PARKE
See PIRRIE

PATISON
[Pitted.] In memory of Major Andrew Patison late of his Majesty's 29th Regt, born at Leith, Anno 1778, died here Anno 1821.

PATRICK
See JAMESON

PATTERSON
[Laid flat. The plot was bought by John Patterson in May 1812.] Cleland Patterson and Wm Rt Patterson, the infant children of John Patterson.
[See next stone].

PATTERSON
[Broken and badly weathered sandstone headstone. The top is separate, laid flat in the ground.] John Patterson, born 14th May 1784, died 27th March 1843; is buried at Ballyachron, near Coleraine. Here are interred his infant sons, (Cleland), died 1813 & Wm. Robert (died 1816). His wife Ann CLE(LAND) died 17th Ma(rch) 182(9) aged (43) years. Their (daughter Sarah) died 29th (May 1836 aged 19 years.) John (Cumming, first born of their son James died 12th March 1852 aged 12 days. Mary Anderson Cumming), wife of the (same James Patte)rson, born 16th Jan (1822, died 19th Sept) 1858. Christopher, third son of) James Patterson, (born 27th) October 1855, died (26th) August 1861.

[Sarah Patterson was a governess living at Castle Place, Belfast. Her brother James was an Inspector of National Schools and lived in Downpatrick, County Down.]

PATTERSON
[Slate tablet with painted sandstone surround secured to west wall.] Here rests the remains of Robert Patterson who died 1st June 1831 aged 81 years. Also of his children who died young. Also of two infant grandchildren, and of William his son who died 12th June 1837 aged 32 years. Also of Catherine, wife of the above named Robert Patterson who died 14th Jany 1842. Also of David Jonathan his son who died 1st May 1847 aged 37 years. Also his only daughter Catherine who died 16th May 1857 aged 51 years. Also his grandson John son of the above named David Jonathan who died 24th March 1864 aged 23 years. Also of Elizabeth wife of the above named David Jonathan who died 13th August 1902 aged 83 years.

[Probate of the will with one codicil of Elizabeth Patterson of Dunallen, Windsor Avenue, Belfast, widow, who died 13 Aug. 1902 granted at Belfast, 29 August 1902 to John Fleming Patterson, merchant and Elizabeth Jones, married woman. Effects £2,327 13s.5d.]

Robert Patterson and his brother John, originally from near Ballymoney, county Antrim, started their ironmongery and hardware shop at 24 High Street, Belfast in 1786. On the entry of David Jonathan, the firm was known as R. & D. J. Patterson and in about 1860 took on its present title of Robert Patterson & Son Ltd. In the late nineteenth century they moved to Bridge Street and subsequently to Ann Street. Richard, a grandson of the founder, bought Musgrave Brothers hardware firm in 1865 and ran it as Richard Patterson & Co. It was sold in 1920. Richard was a chairman of Holywood Urban District Council.]

PATTERSON
[Laid flat.] Erected by James Patterson, of Belfast, in memory of his wife Margaret who departed this life 18th Septr 1836 aged 52 years. Here also lieth the above named James Patterson who departed this life the 5th July 1846 aged 77 years.

PATTERSON
[Marble headstone broken in two, and lying flat.] Erected in loving memory of Francis Patterson, died 6th June 1888 aged 64 years. Also his children Helena died 8th April 1859 aged 2 years, Sarah, 26th June 1860 aged 8 years, Thomas died 18th April 1867 aged 4 years, Harriett, died 17th Decr 1872 aged 16 years, Charlotte Elizabeth died 25th Novr 1898 aged 30 years. And his wife Margaret, died 22nd Octr 1911 aged 82 years. "Asleep in Jesus".

[Francis Patterson was an inspector of gas meters and at the time of his death he lived at 22 Newington Avenue, Belfast. Previously, he had lived at 3, Sandy Row.]

PATTERSON
See CAUGHEY and JOY

PATTON
[Tablet with surround secured to west wall in a low-railed and low-stone enclosure.] Sacred to the memory of David Patton, of Belfast, who departed this life on the 19th of July 1814 aged 64 years. Also Barbara Patton his sister who was interred here on the 28th of January 1809 aged 52 years.

[Barbara Patton was a haberdasher at 121, High Street, Belfast.]

PATTON
[Horizontal slab in above enclosure.] Here lie the remains of Anne Patton, wife of Isaac Patton, of Belfast, merchant, who dep this life 21st February 1802 aged 40 years. Also Isaac Patton who departed this life on the 23rd day of July 1827 aged 63 years. Also his second wife Sarah daughter of John SHAW, of Maze, who departed this life September 15th 1846 aged 72 years. John Patton died 10 May 1853 aged 63 years. Anna Patton died 8 Feby 1898 aged 77 years. Elizabeth Patton died 3 August 1899 aged 70 years. Jane Patton died 4 December 1899 aged 73 years.

[Probate of the will of Anne Patton of 4 Wellwood Street, Belfast, spinster, who died 4 February 1898 was granted at Belfast 11 March 1898 to David McKelvey of 85 Royal Avenue, Belfast, rent agent. Effects £1,373 18s.1d.

Probate of the will of Elizabeth Patton of 4 Wellwood Street, Belfast, spinster, who died 3 August 1899 was granted at Belfast 23 October 1899 to David McKelvey of 85 Royal Avenue, rent agent. Effects £1,234 6s.3d.

Probate of the will of Jane Patton of 4 Wellwood Street, Belfast, spinster who died 2 December 1899 was granted at Belfast 19 December 1899 to John Magee of Woodland Avenue, stationer, and Charles K. Moore of 4 Duncairn Terrace, corporation official, both Belfast. Effects £1,305 4s.8d.

The plot was purchased by Isaac Patton on 23rd February 1802.

Isaac Patton was a haberdasher at 124, High Street, Belfast at the beginning of the nineteenth century. By 1820 his concern was known as Isaac Patton, wholesale printed calico warehouse at 20, High Street. He lived in Hammond's Court, off Corn Market. After his death his widow continued the concern.]

PAUL

[Headstone in upper ground, now missing, but recorded in burial book.] Sacred to the memory of Mary Frances who died on the 2nd August 1864 aged 10 days. Also of Chester Bateman who departed this life on the 11th November 1864 aged 4 years. And Reginald Bertram on the 24th of the same month aged 2 years and 8 months, the much loved children of Captain W. H. Paul.

PEARCE

[Missing from lower ground.] The burying ground of Samuel Pearce, 1839.

[He was a partner of Holden & Pearce (see under James Holden), proprietors of the Phoenix Foundry, 16 Great George Street, Belfast. Samuel Pearce lived at 10, Trafalgar Street.]

PEEL

[Headstone now missing from lower ground. Even in 1907 it had deteriorated very badly. Robert Peel acquired the plot in April 1856.] Erected by Robert Peel .... Belfast, to the memory of his .... 13th.

[Robert Peel was a publican, and ran a bakery and flour stores on the Shankill Road, Belfast.]

PELLING

[Small stone in lower ground, now missing.] The family burying place of Charles Pelling, 1844.

[He was a sewed muslin manufacturer at 79, Academy Street, Belfast and later at 30, Donegall Street. He bought the grave plot for his son Richard in April 1844.]

PENNEY

[Worn, raised horizontal slab, now removed.] Erected in memory of William Penney of (Whitehouse) [sic] who died at Belfast (23rd) Feby 18(3)7 aged (3)0 years.

[A native of Whitehaven, he was a builder and died at William Hall's guest house at 57, Waring Street, Belfast.]

PENTLAND

[Mounted on north wall in a high-railed enclosure.] Sacred to the memory of John Pentland who died 5th October 1843. And of his wife Mary Pentland died 16th March 1878. Also of their children, John Allen Pentland died 14th February 1869, Charlotte Pentland died 9th March 1891. Also

Thomas Pentland who died 16th December 1903.

[Letters of administration of the personal estate of John Allen Pentland of Belfast, county Antrim, merchant, a bachelor who died 14 February 1869 at London, were granted at Belfast, 11 June 1869 to Thomas Pentland of Belfast, bank clerk, a brother and one of the next of kin. Effects under £3,000.

Letters of administration of the personal estate of Charlotte Pentland of 25 Victoria Place, Belfast, spinster, who died 9 March 1891 at same place, were granted at the Principal Registry, 16 June 1891 to Hugh M. Pentland of Dungannon, county Tyrone, bank manager, the brother. Effects £7,158 10s.

Probate of the will of Thomas Pentland, late of 25 Great Victoria Street, Belfast, retired bank manager, who died 16 December 1903, were granted 5 February 1904 at Belfast to Ernest D. Pentland, bank manager. Effects £29,074 5s.2d.

John Pentland, senior, was a merchant's clerk and lived at 48 Mill Street, Belfast, aged 42. John Allen Pentland, aged 37, was a linen merchant at 57, Great Victoria Street. Thomas Pentland, aged 76 worked for the Belfast Bank.]

PHILLIPS

[Flaking badly.] In this spot repose the earthly remains of Jane, wife of George Phillips, of Belfast, who departed this life the 23d of June 1840 aged (34) years. "And all wept and bewailed her but (Jesu)s (said, weep) not; she is not dead, but sleepeth". Also of her children, James Russell aged 9 months, and (Eliza) Maria aged 20 months. Also her sister Mary RUSSELL, who departed this life 5th May 1876 aged 7(.) years. Also the above George Phillips, who departed this life 24th May 1877 aged 73 years.

[The will of Mary Russell of Sydenham, county Down, spinster, who died 5 May 1876, was proved at Belfast 14 July 1876 by the oaths of Dorothea Phillips and Mary Phillips, both of Sydenham, spinsters, the executrixes. Effects under £800.

The will of George Phillips, formerly of Sydenham, county Down, and late of University Square, Belfast, county Antrim, gentleman, who died 24 May 1877, was proved at Belfast 20 June 1877 by the oaths of Dorothea Phillips and Mary Phillips both of 7 University Square, Belfast, spinsters, the executrixes. Effects within UK under £14,000.

George Phillips was a bookseller, stationer and publisher with a shop at 27 (later 26) Bridge Street, Belfast. In the 1860s the firm was George Phillips & Sons. He lived in Linenhall Street.]

PINKERTON

[Twin marble tablets in large entablature in low-stone enclosure. Only the plinth and enclosure remains.] Pinkerton, Belfast.

(a) Here lie the remains of James Pinkerton, of Belfast, merchant, born 1751, died 1803. His son James Pinkerton, of Belfast, born 1799, died 1866. Jemima Pinkerton, wife of last named James Pinkerton died 1847 aged 38 years.

Joseph Culloden Pinkerton, of Belfast son of James and Jemima Pinkerton, born 1832, died 1886. Sarah Rodgers Pinkerton, wife of J. C. Pinkerton, junr, born 1861, died 1895. Joseph Culloden Pinkerton, of Belfast, son of J. C. Pinkerton, born 1861, died 1895. Eliza Pinkerton, daughter of James and Jemima Pinkerton, born 1827, died 1912. [Continued on plinth.] In memory of James Pinkerton junr, son of last named James Pinkerton, born 1829, died 1854, at Halifax, Nova Scotia.

(b) Here lie the remains of John DAVIDSON, merchant, Belfast. His wife died 1805. Patrick CULLODEN, of Stranmillis, died 1843. His son Michael died 1837. His wife Eliza, died 1841. The children of J. C. Pinkerton and infant daughter of J. C. Pinkerton, junr. Elizabeth Hull Pinkerton, wife of James Pinkerton, of Belfast, merchant, and daughter of Anthony HULL, Esq., of Lisburn, born 1781, died 1808. [Continued on the plinth.] In memory of Anthony Hull Pinkerton, son of James Pinkerton, born 1801, died 1845, at Quebec. "Forgive us our trespasses".

[Letters of administration of the personal estate of Joseph Culloden Pinkerton of Ballyhackamore, county Down, merchant, who died 6 December 1886, were granted at Belfast 17 January 1887 to Joseph Culloden Pinkerton of Victoria Street, Belfast, shipping agent, a child. Effects £17,018 11s.11d.

Administration of the unadministered estate of Joseph Culloden Pinkerton of Ballyhackamore, county Down, merchant, who died 6 December 1886, granted at Belfast, 15 June 1887 to Robert McMurtry of Helens View, Antrim Road, Belfast, accountant, and Pakenham Erskine of Jordanstown, county Antrim, mercantile clerk, executors of the son. (Former grant 17 January 1887). Effects £200.

The will of Joseph Culloden Pinkerton of Victoria Street, Belfast, and Ballyhackamore House, Strandtown, county Down, shipping agent, who died 29 December 1895, was proved at Belfast, 19 February 1896 by Robert McMurtry of Helen's View, Antrim Road, Belfast, accountant and Pakenham Erskine of Jordanstown, county Antrim, mercantile clerk, the executors. Effects £7,462 12s. Re-sworn £8,462 12s.

Probate of the will of Eliza Pinkerton of Montalto, South Parade, Belfast, spinster, who died 11 September 1912, granted at Belfast, 9 October 1912 to John Weir, stockbroker, and Arthur James Weir, bankruptcy court deputy registrar. Effects £2,910 5s.9d.]

James Pinkerton, senior, was an established wine and general merchant in North Street, Belfast. He was a member of the Belfast Volunteer Company and the Linen Hall Library, as well as being a promoter of the Belfast Charitable Society early in its history. His wife Elizabeth was a daughter of Anthony Hull of Lisburn and niece of Major Trevor Hull who had been agent to the Hillsborough Probate and Sovereign of Hillsborough Corporation from 1736 to 1748. See *Catalogue of Museum Exhibition*, 1927.

Joseph Culloden, senior, was a partner of George Clotworthy in the firm of Clotworthy & Pinkerton, ship-brokers and general merchants in Tomb Street, Belfast in the 1860s. In the following decade the partnership appears to have broken up, George Clotworthy forming his own company, Clotworthy & Co., dealers in dry fish, whilst Pinkerton remained in the ship-broking and insurance business, moving to 10, Victoria Street. From the early 1860s until his death Pinkerton was the local Italian and Hanoverian Consul. In the 1860s he lived in High Street, Holywood, later moving to Ballyhackamore House.

PIRRIE

[Twin slate tablets formerly in pedimented entablature of Regency Style, against north wall, now smashed and scattered.] In memory of Eliza, wife of William Pirrie who died 4th Decbr 1855 aged 74 years. William Pirrie, died 8th June 1858 aged 78 years. "Believe in the Lord Jesus Christ and thou shalt be saved and thy house".

Also the undernamed grandchildren of William and Eliza Pirrie: John Sinclair HEYN, died July 1837 aged 14 months. Agnes Pirrie Heyn, died January 1842 aged 2 years. Emma Heyn died March 1842 aged 9 months, Eliza Morison Heyn, died 20th July 1844 aged 11 years. Caroline Frederica Heyn died 15th Septr 1855 aged 21 years. George Holmes PARKE died 6th Decbr 1854 aged 8 years.

[The will of William Pirrie, late of Belfast in the county of Antrim, esquire, who died 8 June 1858 was proved at Belfast 30 June 1858 by the oaths of William Pirrie of Liverpool in England, merchant, and John Miller Pirrie of Belfast aforesaid, Doctor of Medicine, the executors. Effects under £4,000.]

William Pirrie was born on 24 January 1780 at Wigton, Scotland. He travelled much in his early years, becoming a ships' captain, merchant and shipowner and later became a naturalised citizen of the U.S.A. He settled in Belfast with addresses at Donegall Street and Conlig House, and when the new Harbour Board was created in 1847 he was appointed one of the first Harbour Commissioners. As the senior member of these he opened the new Victoria Channel on 10 July 1849.

He married on 3 December 1810 Elizabeth Morrison and had 4 sons and 4 daughters. The most notable of these was James Alexander Pirrie who was born at Belfast on 26 November 1822 at Belfast and died on 20 August 1849 of cholera at Quebec. He married on 28 June 1844 Elizabeth, daughter of Alexander Montgomery and niece of the Rev. Henry Montgomery of Dunmurry. They had 1 son and 1 daughter, the son being William James Pirrie who entered the firm of Harland and Wolff, worked his way up to become a partner and was eventually ennobled as Viscount Pirrie. The daughter Eliza Pirrie married the Right Hon. Thomas Andrews of Ardara, Comber (1843-1916).

Chevalier Gustavus Heyn was the father of the five children commemmorated, and was therefore married to the future Lord Pirrie's aunt. In the 1840s the family was in Henry Street and in the following decade they moved out to Bunker's Hill, Sydenham. He was one of the leading shipping agents in Belfast in the late nineteenth century and as G. Heyn & Sons the firm was manager of the Ulster Steamship Company. The concern was continued after the death of Gustavus by his son Frederick Ludwig (born 1850). Both father and son were Consuls. George Parke was the son of Andrew Parke who lived at the Grove and was born in 1846 in Quebec.

See Jefferson: *Viscount Pirrie of Belfast* (undated); *Burke's Irish Family Records* (1976).]

PITTENDRICH
[Worn marble headstone, now lost.] (Sacred to the memory of Mary) Josephine (Louisa), daughter of (J.G.) Pittendrich (Esq) 3d "The Buffs" Regt) died 1(8)th July 1867 aged (4) months.

POLLOCK
Erected by Ellen Pollock, Belfast, in memory of her husband George Pollock, who died 19th Nov. 1846 aged 30 years. Also two of their children who died young. Also their daughter Anna Pollock who died 1st April 1858 aged 15 years.

[George Pollock was a printer at 40, Academy Street, Belfast and had been born at Bunker's Hill.]

POLLOCK
[Iron plaque no longer extant, but formerly beside that of William Sherry.] The family burying ground of James Pollock, Belfast, 1847.

POLLOCK
See DUGAN and SINCLAIRE/SINCLAIR

PORTEOUS
[In lower ground and missing, but recorded by the Society.] Sacred to the memory of John Carmichael (Porteous), died on 15th July 185(1) aged 9 years and 11 months.

[His father James was a native of Glasgow and ran a sewed muslin factory at 15, Church Street, Belfast.]

PORTER
See HENDERSON and MURPHY

PRENTER
[Small undated granite headstone looking of c.1900.] The burying ground of William Emerson Prenter.

PRETTY
[Now lost.] "I am the Resurrection and the Life". Sacred to the memory of Elizabeth HARDY, the beloved wife of Edward James Pretty, of Her Majesty's Civil Service, who departed this life 2d April 1854 aged 42 years.

[Edward James Pretty was a landing waiter, employed by the Inland Revenue and lived at 2, College Place North, Belfast before moving to Mount Prospect. He later married a daughter of James Ritchie (q.v.).]

PRETTY
See RITCHIE

PRICE
[Large monument with twin slate tablets, topped with draped urn, now broken up and scattered.] Erected by Thomas Price, Belfast, A.D. 1843.

(a) In memory of Anne HARPER, his wife who died 5th February 1815 aged 38 years. Also eight of their children who died in infancy. And of

Mary his daughter.

(b) In memory of Thomas Price who died 10th December 1843 aged 70 years. Here also lie the remains of his daughter Elizabeth Price who died 11th September 1849 aged 50 years. And of Thomas Price his son who died 23d April 1871 aged 56 years.

[The will with 2 codicils of Thomas Price of No. 149, North Queen Street, Belfast, N.P. who died 23 April 1871 at Belfast, was proved at Belfast 10 May 1871 by the oaths of the Reverend Josias Leslie Porter of College Park, Belfast, professor of the Presbyterian College, and James Hamilton of Corporation Street, Belfast, merchant, the executors. Effects under £600.

Thomas Price, senior, a native of Templepatrick, was an architect and lived at 1, North Queen Street, Belfast. His son Thomas was a junior ballast master in the 1840s and later was a commission agent.]

PRICE

[Slate headstone, formerly with weeping willow at top but now broken.] Erected by Wm. Price, master mariner, August 1st 1857, in memory of three children who died young.

[He lived at 13, Shipboy Street, Belfast.]

PRING

See GRATTAN

PRITCHARD

See THOMSON

PURDY

[Now lost.] Erected to the memory of George Purdy who died the 9th of January 183(1) aged 20 years. Also William Purdy who died 9th May 1847 aged 69 years. And Mary Purdy who died 18th February 1853 aged 72 years. And Mary, wife of James Purdy, died 9th June 1858 aged 33 years.

[The family were boot- and shoe-makers and lived at 2, William's Lane, off Green Street (now Exchange Street), Belfast.]

PURKIS

[This has disappeared since E. W. Pim's survey.] The burying ground of Richard Purkis, heckle [sic] maker, Belfast, Augt. 2nd 1842.

[Richard Purkis bought the plot for his wife Ann, and lived at 4, Seymour Lane, off Seymour Street near May Street, Belfast.]

QUIGLEY

[Very corroded iron plaque, now removed.] The burying (place) of Samuel Q(uig)ley, Belfast, 1844.

[He was a grain merchant and baker at 18, Cromac Street, Belfast.]

QUIN

[Now lost and recorded in the Society's Gravestone book] In memory of John Quin, surgeon, who departed this life 9th March 1853 aged 60 years.

[John Quin, a native of Armagh, was a Member of the Royal College of Surgeons of England and was in private medical practice at 3 Bank Lane,

Belfast, until he was appointed Certifying Factory Surgeon in 1849. He replaced in this post his brother William who died in that year. The competition with Dr Andrew Malcolm and all its intrigue is described in detail by Calwell: *Andrew Malcolm of Belfast* (1977).]

RADCLIFF

[Formerly against east wall but now only fragments remain.] Sacred to the memory of Mr William Radcliff, of Belfast, merchant, who departed this life the 11th day of December 1817 aged 47 years. Also Jane Radcliff his daughter who departed this life the 6th day of June 1810 aged 7 months. Also Margaret Ann Radcliff his daughter who departed this life the 6th day of September 1811 aged 7 years.

RADCLIFFE

See MONTGOMERY

RAINEY

See JOY

RAMSEY

[Iron shield, now lost.] The family burying ground of Sinclare Ramsey, Belfast, 1874.

[Sinclaire Ramsey ran a haberdashery and trimming warehouse at 12, Hill Street, Belfast and lived in Great Patrick Street. Margaret Ramsey died in February 1874. The plot had been bought by Robert Donaldson in March 1830.]

RAMSEY

See LAIRD and MacLURCAN

RANKIN

[Small and badly flaked headstone, laid flat.] Erected by Ha(riet Ra)nkin in me(mory of he)r father A(ndrew Ran)kin, who d(eparted this life) 6th Mar. 1821 aged 6(8) years. Also his wife Margaret who departed this life 8th Jan. 1826 aged (7)2 years.

RANKIN

See KINGAN

RAPHAEL

[Horizontal slab.] Underneath are interred the remains of David Raphael, of Belfast, merchant, who departed this life, 7th December 1826 in the 45th year of his age. Also two of his children, David & Ann who died young.

REA

[Badly weathered in the middle.] Erected by Samuel Rea, of (Bel)fast, in memory of his wife Jan(e who) departed this life on the 2. (Nov)r 1822 aged 42 years. Also James Rea his son who died on the 4th June 1824 aged 15 years.

REA

[Broken marble slab with top portion missing and now lying loose.

First half is copied from Society's transcript.] ("Precious in the sight of the Lord is the death of his saints" Psalm CXVI-XV. Sacred to the memory of John Rea who died 23rd Augt 1841 aged 73 years. Also his wife Agnes Rea who died 12th March 1861) aged 90 years. Also their son James Rea who died 1st Decr. 1834 aged 21 years. Also their son Hugh Rea who died 25th Augt 1836 aged 28 years. "And if I go and prepare a place for you, I will come again and receive you unto myself: that where I am there ye may be also". John XIV,14.

[The Rea family lived at 92, Millfield, Belfast where John was a grocer. His son James is described in the burial register as a tutor, and Hugh was the keeper of the Ulster Religious Tract and Book Repositary at 17 Waring Street. After his death it was continued by Miss Agnes Rea, presumably his sister.]

REANEY
See STEVENSON

REED
See ANDERSON and MACK

REFORD
See HERDMAN

REID
[Badly flaking and now lost.] Erected to the memory of Sarah Reid, relict of the late Captain James Reid, who departed this life 9th Feby 18(31) aged 41 years. Also the above named Captn James Reid who perished in a gale with 19 of his crew, 1847 [sic] aged 33 years.

[Sarah Reid lived in Trafalgar Street, Belfast.]

REID
[Very badly worn marble in a low-railed enclosure, and of which most of the inscription was copied from the Society's Gravestone Book.] (In memory of Mary MATTHEWS, wife of James Reid, who died in 1832 aged 40 years. The above James Reid who died 10th July 1853 aged 67 years. Their daughter Margaret Reid who died 19th Dec. 1895 aged 76 years.) And their son Stafford Matthews Reid who died young.

[James Reid was a cooper at 60, Ann Street, Belfast.]

REID
[Flaked and now lost.] In memory of James Reid who died 11th April 18(53) aged 84 years. Also his son Robert Reid who died 2(7)th August (1861) aged 35 years. Also his wife Jane Reid who died 9th Dec. 1867 aged 8(5) years.

[The family originated at Templepatrick, county Antrim. James lived in Ship Street Place, Belfast and Robert was a provision merchant at Broughshane.]

REID
[Tablet in carved and pedimented entablature, surmounted by draped urn, formerly attached to north wall in a high-railed enclosure, with

the next but now destroyed.] The family burying place of James Reid departed this life 2nd of August 1857 aged 88 years. Jane, wife of James Reid, and daughter of James MUNFOAD, died 24th May 1867 aged 86 years. Eliza, daughter of the above, died 1st January 1861 aged 50 years.

[Letters of administration, with the will annexed, of the personal estate of Eliza Reid, formerly of Clarendon Place, late of Glenfield Place, both in Belfast in the county of Antrim, spinster, who died 1 January 1861 at Belfast, were granted at Belfast 7 June 1861 to the Reverend Robert Knox of Linenhall Street, Presbyterian minister, and Henry Kingsmill of Hamilton Street, mercantile clerk, both of Belfast aforesaid, the trustees. Effects under £1,500.]

REID

[Small tablet in carved surround attached to north wall in enclosure with the above.] In memory of Henry Reid who died 27th March 1888 aged 85 years. And of Catherine Barnett his wife who died 31st October 1894 aged 87 years. And of their daughter Jane Reid died 11th May 1887 aged 50 years.

[The will of Henry Reid, late of College Gardens, Belfast, gentleman, who died 27 March 1888 at same place, was proved at Belfast 7 May 1888 by James Reid of Greenock, county Renfrew in Scotland, merchant, and John Barnett Reid of 24 Crutched Friars, London, E.C., merchant, the executors. Effects £6,064 19s.3d.

Letters of administration of the personal estate of Jane Reid of College Gardens, Belfast, spinster, who died 11 May 1887 at same place, were granted at Belfast 10 June 1887 to Henry Reid of College Gardens, Belfast, gentleman, the father. Effects £153 7s.10d.]

Henry Reid was a retired insurance agent and stockbroker who had practised at 8, Donegall Street Place, Belfast. In the 1860's he had lived at Glenfield Place.]

REID

[Undated low-stone enclosure, bearing family name — looks of c.1900] Reid.

REID

See CRAWFORD, FOLINGSBY, GARLAND, MACKEY and MULHOLLAND

REILLY

See LEECE

REYNOLDS

[Missing.] In memory of John H. Reynolds, late of London, died Dec. 12th 1844, aged 67 years.

[John H. Reynolds was an excise officer and lived at 22, North Queen Street, Belfast.]

REYNOLDS

See MACLURCAN

RICE

[Iron shield now missing from lower ground.] Family burying place of James Rice, Belfast, 1851.

RICE

[Headstone now missing from lower ground.] Erected by Thomas Rice, Belfast, in memory of his beloved daughter Susanna Rice who departed this life on the 27th of September 18(5)1 aged 4 years.

Snapped like a rose, in early bloom,
An early tenant for the tomb,
Here mouldering lie her frail remains
Her ransomed soul with Jesus reigns.

Also the above named Thomas Rice who departed this life on the 28th of April 18.. aged (5)2 years. Also his wife Susanna who died Feby 1st 1889 aged 72 years.

[The will of Susanna Rice of Roseville, Windsor, Belfast, widow, who died 1 February 1889 at same place, was proved at Belfast 18 February 1889 by Maria Rice of Roseville, Windsor, Belfast, spinster, the sole executrix. Effects £1,780 7s.6d.]

[Thomas Rice was a dealer in meal at 7 Castle Market, and he lived at 3, New Bond Street, Belfast.]

RICHARDSON

[Worn horizontal slab.] In memory of Martha Richardson, who was the wife of Thomas Richardson Esqr. of the county of Tyrone. She departed this life on the 4th day of January 1810 aged 62 years. This stone is erected by one of her daughters who owes to her instruction and example under favour of Almighty God whatever she enjoys of earthly blessings and who lives in hope by an humble imitation of her virtues through the mediation of Our Blessed Redeemer to rejoin her in a better world. Also of Thomas Richardson, abovenamed, who died the 9th August 1836 aged 7(5) years. Also their daughter Eliza, wife of John BROWN, of Belfast, who died 29th June 1862 aged 77 years. Her husband John Brown who died 31st August 1865 aged 79 years. Dunbar JAMISON their son-in-law who died 1838 aged 27 years. And of Thomas Henry Browne J.P. youngest son of John and Elizabeth Browne, who died 21st April 1908 aged 84 years.

Dear heart, asleep beneath this sod,
Thy guileless soul at peace with God,
In echo sweet thy gentle voice,
Bids my lone heart in God rejoice.

Thy kindred, too, from far and near,
Sleep in this ground, are buried here,
On earth they loved God's Holy Name,
In Realms afar with Saints now reign.

Thy way was peace, God's Law was thine,
In all thy walks his light did shine,

Portrait of Hugh Ritchie, shipbuilder (1766-1808), (Ulster Museum).

In Bible class, in Sabbath school,
The youth you taught God's Holy Rule.

Shall I too sleep beneath this sod,
My weary soul at peace with God,
In Realms afar with those I've loved,
In perfect peace with thee beloved.

[Probate of the will and codicil of Thomas Henry Browne J.P., late of Rathcoole, Sydenham Park, Belfast J.P., who died 21 April 1908 at The Groves, Witton, Droitwich, Worcestershire, granted at Belfast 22 June 1908 to Jane Florence Brown, the widow, Alexander Crawford Browne, timber merchant, and Frederick W. Johnston, insurance agent. Effect £9,174 4s.2d.

In the early part of the nineteenth century the Richardson family were prominent in the Dungannon area of county Tyrone.

John Brown and his son John were builders in Gloucester Street, Belfast from the 1830s to the 1870s. Thomas Henry, son of John Brown, senior, was for long a partner with Lawson A. Browne in the firm of L. A. & T. H. Browne, timber and slate merchants at 45 & 47, Chichester Street.]

RIDDEL
See NEILL

RITCHIE
(a) [Tablet with urn and round-headed entablature secured to west wall.] Interred here is Hugh Ritchie, ship-builder who died 1st January 1808 aged 41 years. William Ritchie, shipbuilder, brother to the former who died 18th January 1834 aged 79 years. And his wife Agnes Ritchie who died 15th January 1812. John WATT, shipmaster, who died about 1802. And his wife Jane Watt who died 17th January 1807.

(b) [Very worn marble tablet (now lost) in pedestal of broken pillar, within low-stone enclosure of above.] In memory of ...... (Patt)erson Ritchie who died 21st Novr 18(37) aged 5(0) years. Also of his wife Anna who died 2nd July 1840 aged 4(3) years.

[William Richie was born in 1755 and came to Belfast from Ayrshire in 1791. He founded his shipyard on a site now covered by Corporation Square and also built a graving dock just north of the Harbour Commissioners' Office, which he completed in 1800. He was a member of the Academical Institution and the committee of the General Hospital and Chairman of the management committee of the Charitable Society. When he came to Belfast, he found only 6 jobbing ship-carpenters in the town, but by 1811 he employed 44 journeymen carpenters, 56 apprentices, 7 pairs of sawyers, 12 blacksmiths and several joiners. William's brothers John and Hugh were also shipbuilders, Hugh arriving with him. They remained partners until 1798 after which date Hugh built ships on his own until he died. John did not arrive until 1807.

William is credited with building in partnership with Alexander MacLaine, another Scot, the very first steamship constructed in Ireland. This was the *Chieftain*, launched in 1826.

See Owen: *History of Belfast* (1921); Owen: *A Short History of the Port*

Portrait of William Ritchie, shipbuilder (1755-1834) by Thomas Robinson (Ulster Museum)

of Belfast (1917); Strain: *Belfast and its Charitable Society* (1961).]

RITCHIE
[Oval tablet in large surround secured to east wall of upper graveyard.] Interred here, John Ritchie, shipbuilder, who died 4th April 1828 aged 77 years. Also his wife Jane Ritchie who died 26th January 1837 aged 81 years. Likewise four of the children of Alexander and Martha McLAINE, namely: Helen, Lachlan, Robert and Lachlan, who died in infancy. And Major Lachlan McLaine, first or Royal Reg., who departed this life 30th November 1845 aged 66 years. The above Alexander McLaine departed this life 22nd August 1856 aged 73 years. Agnes Ritchie who died 2d May 1857 aged 73 years. Susanna McLaine who died 17th September 1857 aged 25 years. Robert McLaine who died 4th January 1864 aged 29 years. The above Martha McLaine who died 8th August 1864 aged 69 years. And Susanna Ritchie who died 14th October 1867 aged 78 years.

[Small elliptical tablet beneath above.] Also in loving memory of Jane CHAMBERS, daughter of above John Ritchie, who died 16th Feb. 1840.

[Letters of administration of the personal estate of Martha McLaine of Corporation Street, Belfast, widow, who died 8 August 1864 at same place, were granted at Belfast 1 September 1864 to John McLaine of Corporation Street, Belfast aforesaid, esquire, the son, one of the next of kin of said deceased. Effects under £450.

The will with three codicils, of Susanna Ritchie, late of Belfast, spinster, who died 21 October 1867 at same place was proved at Belfast 27 November 1867 by the oaths of Alexander McLaine, shipbuilder, and George Langtry MacLaine, solicitor, both of Belfast aforesaid, the executors. Effects under £3,000.

John Ritchie arrived in Belfast from Ayrshire in January 1807, and commenced shipbuilding near the future site of Pilot Street as John Ritchie & Co. (later Ritchie & McLaine).]

RITCHIE
[In carved entablature, secured to east wall, in low-stone enclosure.] Erected by James Ritchie, of Belfast, in memory of his beloved wife Anna who died 10th February 1837 aged 26 years. Also their son James Hutton Ritchie died 5th October 1854 aged 22 years. Also sacred to the memory of above named James Ritchie who died 2nd Oct. 1867 aged 73 years. And Margaret Ritchie who died 24th June 1873 aged 83 years. Florence Carson Ritchie beloved daughter of Thos Ritchie, died 5th Nov. 1874 aged 3 years & 8 months. Sarah PRETTY, daughter of James Ritchie, died 13th Feby 1900 aged 67 years. Also Thomas Ritchie who died 19th September 1907 aged 71 years.

[The will with one codicil of James Ritchie of Seaview House, Antrim Road, Belfast, merchant, who died 2 October 1867 at same place, was proved at Belfast 5 December 1867 by the oath of Sarah Pretty, wife of Edward James Pretty of Seaview House aforesaid, esquire, daughter of deceased and one of the executors. Effects under £450.

James Ritchie, senior, was born in Downpatrick. A successful grain merchant in the Docks area, he lived at Seaview, Antrim Road, Belfast where his son Thomas, for long the New Zealand agent in Belfast, also lived. There is nothing to connect this family to the ship-builders.]

ROARK
[Flaking stone, now lost.] Erected by Robert Roark, in memory of his son Thomas who died in infancy. Also his affectionate son Robert who died the 26th Jany 1837 aged 8 years. Also the said Robert Roark who died 23rd March 1849 aged 45 years.

[Robert Roark was a carpenter in Little George's Street, Belfast.]

ROBERTSON
[No longer extant. The ground was bought by Major-General Bainbrigge in November 1847.] In memory of Ensign George Robertson of the ...... who died at Belfast on the 2nd of .... in the 21st year of his age. This stone is erected by his surviving ....

ROBINSON
[Headstone broken off base and now lost.] Allgood Robinson, son of Thos Robinson, departed this life June 3d 1806 aged 11 years.

ROBINSON
[Slate with three flowers at the top.] Erected by John Robinson of Belfast Anno Domini 1812. And here lieth the body of his son John who departed this life 2d October 1806 aged 1 month.

ROBINSON
[Large flat slab.] Erected to the memory of Templeton Robinson, of Belfast, who departed this life 14th January 1826 aged 36 years. Also of his brother John Robinson who departed this life 4th November 1813 aged 15 years. Also of his daughter Ellen who departed this life 18th August 1845 aged 21 years. Also of his widow Margaret Robinson who departed this life 28th September 1846 aged 54 years.

[Templeton Robinson was the son of James Robinson. The family lived at 4, Chichester Street, Belfast in the 1840's.]

ROBINSON
[Weathered.] Erected in memory of James Robinson, of Belfast, who departed this life on the (2)nd of May 1826 aged (5)2 years. Also ( ) of his children who died in infancy. Also Isabella Robinson, relict of the above named James Robinson, who departed this life on the 4th of April 1842 aged 60 years.

ROBINSON
[Flaking with bottom lines buried.] The burying place of William I. Robinson and family. Here rest the remains of his wife Ellen Robinson who departed this life on the 27th August 1830 aged 30 years. Also four of his children who died young, viz: Sarah Robinson who died 5th August 1828 aged 3 years, William Robinson who died 17th January 1832 aged 4 years, Harriet Robinson who died 22nd February 1837 aged 2 years, John Robinson who died 18th September 1839 aged 11

days. Also the above named William I. Robinson who departed this life on the 13th July 1841 aged 45 years.

[In the 1830s William Irvine Robinson, a linen merchant, was living at 11, Queen Street, Belfast, and moved to Botanic Road a few years before he died.]

ROBINSON

[Now missing from lower ground.] The burying place of Richd. Robinson, Belfast, 1853.

[Richard Robinson was an agricultural implement and bobbin manufacturer at 13, Eliza Street, Belfast and lived at no. 29. His wife Jane died in May 1853 aged 44.]

ROBSON

[Marble in large entablature, formerly topped by a draped urn, now lost.] (Erected by John Robson of Belfast) in memory of his father Richard Robson who departed this life 27th Novr 1858 in the 64th year of his age. Also his son Richard who died 10th July 1867 aged 7 years. Also his mother Margaret Robson died 22nd March 1870 aged 84 years.

[Richard Robson, senior, a native of Whitehaven, England, is first listed in the 1835 Belfast Directory as the agent for the Whitehaven Pottery Warehouse at 130, High Street. By the 1850s he was a partner in John Robson's funeral and posting establishment at 31 Chichester Street, Belfast (founded 1842). When he died, he held the position of Posting Master. The firm later evolved as the Royal Victoria Horse Bazaar. See Anon: *Industries of Ireland, Part 1* (1891 and 1986).]

ROCHE

[Modern Celtic Cross with inscription on the base in low-railed enclosure.] In loving memory of Sarah Gelston Roche, beloved wife of William John Roche, who died 4th December 1906 in her 80th year. Also of their children: Alice Maria aged 7 years, Samuel Gelston, aged 6 weeks, William Howard aged 17 years, Julia Florence aged 20 years. And the above William John Roche who died 20th April 1920 in his 94th year.

From love's shining circle the gems drop away,
When true hearts lie withered and fond ones are flown,
Oh, who would inhabit this bleak world alone.

[William John Roche was a manufacturer of linen and cambric handkerchiefs with offices at 5, Donegall Square South, Belfast. He lived in Fortwilliam Terrace, Antrim Road, before moving to Sans Souci Park.]

RODGERS

[Flaking very badly and now lost.] Erected by David Rodgers, (in memory) of his father Edward (Rodgers who died Augt) 9th 18(17 aged 59 years). Also his sister Eliz(abeth Rodgers (died May 25th 1818 aged 22 years. Also his son Henry Rodgers March 15th) 1838 (aged 15 months Likewise) his bro(ther Will)iam Rodgers, (Augt 29th) 1839 (aged 50 years. And his mother Agnes) Rodgers, (March 28th 1848 aged 81 years.) David Rodgers died Oct. 28th, 1866 aged 37 years. Edward Rodgers, (died Oct 31st) 1866 aged (33)

FUNERAL UNDERTAKING

AND

POSTING ESTABLISHMENT,

31 CHICHESTER STREET,

BELFAST.

JOHN ROBSON,

PROPRIETOR of the above Establishment, takes the present opportunity of returning his sincere thanks to the Nobility, Gentry, and the Public generally, for the liberal support and encouragement he has received these last 10 years, and more especially since his removal to the above Premises, and now wishes to inform them that he has considerably improved and enlarged his establishment, and has made every arrangement necessary for the extension of his business, and for the execution of all orders (especially funeral ones), in the shortest possible time; and he trusts, from strict attention to business, and MODERATE CHARGES, to always merit a continuance of their support.

HEARSES, MOURNING COACHES,

OPEN AND CLOSE CARRIAGES,

COVERED, SOCIABLE, AND OUTSIDE CARS,

ALL OF THE BEST DESCRIPTION.

COFFINS OF ALL DESCRIPTIONS ON HAND OR MADE TO ORDER

SHOULDER SCARFS, HAT BANDS, GLOVES, &c.,

ALWAYS READY FOR USE.

Full-page advertisement for the posting establishment of John Robson, to become one of the leading horse bazaars in Belfast (from Belfast and Ulster Directory for 1854).

years. (Also) David Rodgers their father died Febry 9th 1867 aged 72 years. Annie, wife of David Rodgers, died 20th June 1869 aged 72.

[The Rodgers family were saddle and harness manufacturers at 51, North Street, Belfast until the 1850s when they took up residence at 201, York Street. David, junior, was a sea-captain.]

RODGERS

[Mostly flaked away and therefore largely copied from Society's records, now lost.] Erected by Edward Rodgers of Belfast (in memory of his father Richard Rodgers who departed this life 29th Jany 1855 aged 72 years. Also his mother Catherine Rodgers) who departed this life 30th Novr. 1856 aged 6(6) years.

[Richard Rodgers kept a carman's inn at 11, Upper Church Lane, Belfast.]

RODGERS

See KENNEDY

ROGERS

[Very badly flaked.] In memory of Joseph Rog(ers) who departed this life 7th of (May 1811) aged 21 years. Also his (sister Jane who dep)arted this life ... Novr. (1816) aged (.4 years). Likewise their mother Sarah departed th(is life) 6th of (Mar)ch 1820 aged 7(0) years. Mary Rogers, who departed this life 6th of Sep. 1843 aged 66 years. Her sister Rachel CORRY, who departed this life 12th of Nov. 1843 aged 60 years.

[The Rogers family originally hailed from Banbridge, county Down.]

ROGERS

[Very badly flaked and now lost.] Erected in mem(ory of La)scellas Rogers, (formerly of Clo....) who departed (this life) on th(e) 5th day of April 1829 aged 85 years. His wife Matilda Rogers died 13th February 1842 aged 82 years. Lascellas Rogers MAXWELL, infant son of William & Rachel Maxwell, died 1st June 1814.

ROGERS

[Flaking on right side and now lost.] Sacred to the memory of John R(ogers), of Belfast, who departed this (life) on the 10th January 1832 aged (60) years. Also his daughter Mary who died 18th April 18(5)2 aged 30 years. His daughters: Sarah Rogers who died 17th July 1861 aged 53 years, and Rachel Rogers who died 2nd June 1904 aged 74 years.

[Probate of the will of Rachel Rogers, late of 4 Chadwick Terrace, Lisburn Road, Belfast, spinster, who died 2 June 1904, granted at Belfast 1 July 1904 to John Rogers, gentlemen. Effects £787 2s.6d.

John Rogers was a grocer and breeches maker at 14, Castle Place, Belfast. He was born in Banbridge (see Joseph Rogers) and lived for some time in Dundalk.]

ROGERS

See WARDLOW

ROSE

[Marble tablet in ornate headstone.] In memory of Robert Rose, died July 18, 1849 AE 37. Also his wife Jane died Nov. 21, 1855 AE 44. Helen, their second daughter died AE 53, interred at Magilligan.

[Robert Rose, a native of Saltcoats, Ayrshire, was a sewed muslin manufacturer, with a small warehouse in Nelson Street, Belfast. He lived in Great Patrick Street.]

ROSS

[Badly flaking small headstone, now lost.] (Erect)ed (to the me)mory of Archibald Ross, Belfast, who departed this life the 3d of September 1805 aged 46 years.

ROSS

[Badly weathered.] Erected by Henry Ross, of Belfast, late of Dublin. Sacred to the memory of his beloved daughter, Letitia Isabella who departed this life 8th June 1829 aged 14 years & 10 months. Also the above named Henry Ross who died 6th May 1863 aged 77 years. Also Mary Ross daughter of the above-named who died 10th June 1881 aged 68 years. Also Charlotte HODGES, sister-in-law of the above named H. Ross, and wife of Thomas Hodges, late of Dublin, died 12th April 1888 aged 75 years. Also the above named Thomas Hodges died 27th Oct. 1891 aged 80.

[Letters of administration of the personal estate of Mary Ross, late of 12 Ontario Terrace, Rathmines, county Dublin, spinster, who died 10 June 1881 at same place, were granted 3 August 1881 at the Principal Registry, to William Adolphus Ross of Craigavad, county Down, merchant, the brother. Effects £60.

Henry Ross, who died at his residence in Holywood, was the father of William Adolphus Ross who in 1879 founded the firm of W. A. Ross & Co. and who ran the Royal Belfast Ginger Ale and Aerated Water Works at William Street South. Thomas Hodges died at Whiteabbey. See Anon: *Industries of Ireland, Part I* (1891 and 1986).]

ROWAN

[Now lost. Plot purchased by Captain Rowan in March 1850.] Sacred to the memory of Sidney Rowan aged 3 years. Emily H. Rowan aged 14 years.

[In the burial register Captain Rowan is described as the Barrack Master.]

RUSSELL

[Very badly flaked.] Here lieth (the bo)dy of Margret (Russell, wife) of James Russell, baker, of B(elfast wh)o departed this li(fe the 17th) of January 180(9) aged 67 years.

RUSSELL

[Very badly worn marble tablet with surround secured to the east wall of upper graveyard and in a low-stone enclosure.] The burying place of Mary Russell, daughter and only child of Captain John Russell, formerly of Belfast (by) Mary (NEILL) his first wife. (She departed this life of ....) the 25th of August 182(1) aged (..) years. (and desired that in the inscription on her tombstone she should simply be designated as "An Honest Woman".)

RUSSELL
[Large stone, now lost and recorded in Society's gravestone book.] Erected by Thomas Hart Russell in memory of Caroline Elizabeth, his beloved wife who departed this life 6th of January 1841 aged 40 years. And on the 3rd March 1869, Mary Elizabeth their beloved daughter aged 40 years. Also the above named Thomas Hart Russell died on the 20th April 187(.) aged 91 years.

RUSSELL
See PHILLIPS

RUTHERFORD
[Laid flat.] Erected to the memory of Jordan Rutherford, of Belfast, who departed this life the 22nd September 1813 aged 44 years. Here also rest the remains of his mother Ann Rutherford and of his daughter Margaret, wife of Alexr MURPHY, of Belfast, who died 3rd July 1840 aged 36 years. With those of her son Jordan who died 13th May 1837 aged 7 years and 8 months, and of an infant son. Also the remains of Margaret his wife who died 11th February 1842 aged 72 years. Also the remains of his son Archibald who died 9th October 1857 aged 51 years.

[Jordan Rutherford & Co. were muslin manufacturers at 197, North Street, Belfast. His son Archibald kept muslin warerooms at 37 John Street (now Royal Avenue) and a sizing establishment at 27, Little Donegall Street.]

RYANS
[Flaking and now lost.] Erected by (Lew)is Ryans to the memory of his son James who departed this life 5th day of January 1829 in the 7th year of his age. Also the above named Lewis Ryans who died 30th October 1836 aged 40 years. And Mary his wife who died 16th January 1859 aged 59 years. Sarah Ryans who died Oct 25th 1880 aged 53 years. Lewis Ryans who died Nov. 15th 1890 aged 63 years. Also six of their children who died young. William John Ryans died Oct. 9th 1891 aged 71 years.

[The will of William John Ryans, late of 58 Great Victoria Street, Belfast, retired bookkeeper, who died 9 October 1891 at same place, was proved at Belfast 16 November 1891 by James McLean of 23 Chichester Street Belfast, solicitor, one of the executors. Effects £333 10s.6d.

Lewis Ryans, senior, was a ladies' boot- and shoemaker at 2, Ann Street, Belfast, and Lewis junior was a carver and owner of a toy shop at 38, Mill Street (now upper part of Castle Street).]

RYANS
[Very worn, now removed.] (In memory of) Sarah (Jane Ryans) who departed this (life 27th August 1853 aged 18 years. Also William (Ryans) who departed this life (5th) March 18(62) aged (63) years.

SALMON
[Tablet with broken sandstone surround formerly secured to west wall but now lost.] Here lieth the remains of Christopher Salmon, of Belfast, Esquire who died November 28th 1824 aged 75 years. Also the remains

of Elizabeth, relict of the above mentioned Christopher Salmon, who died 13th June 1844 aged 75 years.

[Christopher Salmon lived at 18, Prince's Street, Belfast.]

SALTERS

[Very badly flaking sandstone headstone now lost.] Sacred to the memory (of) John Henry Salters, (who departed this life 11)th June 1853 (aged 9 yrs & 11 mo)nths. ("And they brought unto him al)so infants that (he would touch them: but wh)en his disciples (saw it) the(y rebuked them. But Jesus call)ed them and said suffer little children to come unto me and forbid them not for of such is the Kingdom of God". (Also his father) Captain Robert Salters departed this life on the 26th November 1855 aged 47 years. And his daughter Mary Jane Salters who died 4th July 1873 aged 32 years.

[Captain Robert Salters, a master mariner, lived at 6, Ship Street and finally moved to Spencer Street.]

SANDERS

[Large monument with marble tablet in arched recess, with two small tablets on either side and surmounted by a casket and a draped urn, in a railed enclosure with the next.] To the memory of James Maxwell Sanders M.D., born at Greenhead, Glasgow, the 24th of April 1814, died at Shrubhill, Belfast, the 26th of July 1846. Erected by a number of friends, many of them his professional brethren to whom he was greatly endeared by the amiability and benevolence of his disposition; the integrity and purity of his life, the accomplishments of a liberal education, and the highest professional attainments. "The righteous shall be in everlasting remembrance". Here also is interred the remains of Marianne Sanders, wife of the above, who died 26th March 1896.

[Left hand tablet.] Here rests the body of Sutherland Sanders, eldest son of the late James Maxwell Sanders M.D., born in Belfast 24th Sept. 1844, died at Shamrock Vale, conuty Down, 15th Jan. 1887. "Dearly loved and sorely missed".

[Right hand tablet which is worn.] Also their son Richard Barnsley Sanders, C.E. and County Surveyor, King's Co., who died 13th February 1900. "The grass withereth, the flower fadeth, but the Word of Our God shall stand forever". Isaiah XL, 8.

[The will of Marianne Sanders of Shamrock Vale, Lisburn, county Down, widow, who died 26 March 1896 was proved at Belfast 1 June 1896 by Richard B. Sanders of Parsonstown, county surveyor, of King's County, executor. Effects £12,538 18s.2d.

Letters of administration of the personal estate of Sutherland Sanders of Shamrock Vale, Lisburn, county Down, gentleman who died 13 January 1887 at same place were granted at Belfast 18 May 1887 to Richard B. Sanders of Parsonstown, King's County, surveyor, the brother. Effects £2,393 19s.7d.

Probate of the will of Richard Barnsley Sanders of Shamrock Vale, Lisburn, county Down, and Parsonstown, King's County, civil engineer, who died 13 February 1900 at latter place, granted at Dublin 1 September 1900 to Hendrew Crawford and Alexander A. Lockhart, solicitors. Effects £43,512 16s.6d.

James Maxwell Sanders was born at Greenhead, Glasgow on 24 April 1814. His parents died when he was 3 and he was brought up by an uncle and aunt. After they moved to Belfast in1826 he went to the Academical Institution until 1830 and then trained as a doctor in Belfast, Dublin, Glasgow and Edinburgh, graduating M.D. at the last in 1835. Apart from a year in charge of the Ardglass Dispensary in 1837, he practised in Belfast from 1835 until his death. From 1838 he was on the surgical staff of the General Hospital and for most of this period he was secretary of the Belfast Medical Society and also gave two papers at the Belfast Natural History and Philosophical Society. He married on 12 December 1843, at Donaghadee, Marianne Barnsley, eldest daughter of Richard Barnsley of Lisburn. He appears to have died of tuberculosis and Andrew Malcolm states that "None, probably, at his early age, ever before enjoyed so high a place in the public mind". See Malcolm: *The History of the General Hospital, Belfast* (1851); Deane: *The Belfast Natural History and Philosophical Society, Centenary Volume* (1924); *Belfast Commercial Chronicle*, 13 December 1843; Logan: "Doctor Sanders' silver lancet case" (1991).]

SANDERS

[Very badly flaked and now lost.] Sacred (to) the m(emory of Agnes Sanders) who (departed this life) April 15th 18(20) aged (.8) years.

SANDERS

[Tablet formerly with the above.] Sacred to the memory of Mr Maxwell Sanders, born at Wood Side, near Glasgow, in the year 1777, died in Belfast 12th January 1853 aged 76 years, for 26 years a merchant in Belfast, and an Elder in the Presbyterian Church. He was distinguished by kindness, virtue and christian worth in all the duties and relations of life. This monument was erected by his only surviving sister as a token of affection and respect to the memory of a beloved brother. This sister Agnes Sanders is also interred here, died April 1866.

[Maxwell Sanders appears to be the uncle who brought up Dr J. M. Sanders (see above). See Malcolm: *History of the General Hospital, Belfast* (1851). He was a manufacturer at 13, Commercial Court, Belfast.]

SANDYS

See McKIM

SANSON

[In lower ground and no longer extant.] Sacred to the memory of George Sanson, deceased 11th January 1843.

[The burial register describes him as a native of Edinburgh and as a 67 year old printer resident in Donegall Street, Belfast.]

SAUNDERSON

[Flaking.] Erected to the memory of Captain Robert Saunderson who departed this life on the 27th day of April 1826 aged 23 years. Also his daughter Mary who departed this life in infancy.

SCHENCK
[No longer extant and copied from Society Inscription Book.] In memory of Robert Brett Schenck, born in New York, U.S.A., 4th June 1808, died in Belfast 10th December 1849 aged 41 years.

[Robert Brett Schenck was a flax merchant and lived at Ballynafeigh Cottage on what is now the Ormeau Road (on the country side of the bridge). A later resident of this house was Francis D. Finlay (q.v.).]

SCOTT
[Now lost.] Here lyeth the body of Hester Scott who departed this life on the 2d of September 1831 aged 32 years.

[Her father was James Scott of Smithfield, Belfast.]

SCOTT
[Badly worn in the middle and now lost.] In memory of William Scott, son of David ..... Scott, of Belfast, ... who died ...... (April 28th 1833) aged (35 yrs).

[William Scott was a commission agent, resident in Gloucester Street, Belfast.]

SCOTT
[Large headstone, formerly in lower ground, but no longer extant.] Erected by her sorrowing family to the memory of Elizabeth Scott, relict of John Scott of Anerum, Roxburghshire, Scotland, who died at Ballyhackamore House, Co. Down, March 20th 1842 aged 70 years.

They mourn a widowed mother mouldering here,
Dear to themselves and to their offspring dear.

Also to the memory of John Scott, son of the above John and Elizabeth Scott, who died at Brighton, Sussex, 21st Jan. 1855 aged 53 years, and whose remains are interred here. And of Peter Scott, son of the above named John and Elizabeth Scott, who died at Newcastle, Co. Down, 11th Feb. 1862 aged 63 years, and of Jessie TROWSDALE, only daughter of the above-named John and Elizabeth Scott and wife of Wm. Trowsdale who died at Newcastle, Co. Down, 17th March 1868 aged 62 years.

[John Scott, junior, ran a nursery and was a seedsman. He lived at Ballyhackamore. The whole family came from Roxburgh.]

SCOTT
[Very worn and now lost.] In memory of John Sc(ott), aged (1)2 years, Oct 25th 18(4)8. Likewise (Ann) Scott aged 7 years, Octr 25th 18(55).

[There were children of James Scott, butcher and provision merchant with business premises, first in Grattan Street and then in Queen's Square. He lived in Great George's Street, Belfast.]

SCOTT
[Polished granite in low-railed enclosure, broken up.] The family burying place of Joseph Scott. Sacred to the memory of Ruth his wife who died 6th January 1852 aged 48. Also two of his daughters who died in infancy. Also Joseph Scott who died 5th March 1867 aged 62.

[Joseph Scott was a farmer from Killead, county Antrim.]

SCOTT
[Marble tablet in headstone, in a high-railed enclosure.] Sacred to the memory of John Scott who departed this life on the fourth of July eighteen hundred and sixty two aged fifty eight years. Also Eliza Murphy, of Craigavad, widow of the above John Scott, died 17th December 1907.

SCOTT
See TROWSDALE and WILLIAMSON

SEED
[Iron shield laid flat.] The family burying place of John Seed, December, 1854.

[John Seed was Secretary to the Corn Exchange at 109, Victoria Street, Belfast. The plot was bought for his daughter Margaret.]

SELBY
See FALOON

SEMPLE
[Worn and flaking stone, now lost.] Dedicated to Elizabeth the only and affectionate child of John & Sarah Semple, Ardoyne, who departed this life 22nd March 1857 aged 16 years. "Weep not; she is not dead, but sleepeth". Luke VIII,52. Also her mother (Sarah) Semple, who departed (this) life 27th Feb. 1876 aged (73) years. John Rea Semple, died Feby 5, 1892 aged 89 years.

[The will of John Rea Semple, formerly of 133 Shankill Road, late of 56 Glenfarne Street, both in Belfast, toll collector, who died 4 February 1892 at latter place, was proved at Belfast 25 November 1892 by Joseph McKibbin of 136 Shankill Road, merchant, one of the executors. Effects £157 10s.5d.]

SHANKS
See WARD

SHAW
[Now missing from upper ground. In 1907, this flat stone was almost obliterated. The plot was bought by John Shaw in September 1800.] This stone was erected by Alexander (Shaw) in memory of his .... who departed.................

SHAW
[Laid flat and upper part very worn.] Erected by the Rev. Thomas TOYE in memory of his mother-in-law Charlotte Shaw who died June 1st 1851 (aged 81 years). "Thanks be to God who giveth us the victory through our Lord Jesus Christ". Also to (the memory) of his beloved (wife) Harriet who died (July 24th) 1852. 1. John,IV.14. Also in memory of the Rev. Thomas Toye who was born at Clonakilty on the 6th October 1801, and died at Belfast on the 15th May 1870, after a faithful ministry of 34 years in which much people was added unto the ...... He left for his own epitaph, "A sinner saved by grace". Jane GALWAY, relict of the late Rev. Thomas Toye, died 2nd Jan. 18(86).

[The will of the Reverend Thomas Toye of Great George's Street, Belfast, county Antrim, Presbyterian minister, who died 15 May 1870 at Belfast aforesaid, was proved at Belfast 8 June 1870 by the oath of Jane Toye of same place, the widow and sole executrix. Effects under £100.

The Rev. Thomas Toye was born at Clonakilty, county Cork on 6 October 1801. He was a Congregational minister 1836-41 and changed to be Presbyterian minister of the Macrory Memorial Church, Belfast, first in James's Street and then in Great Georges's Street. He married (1) 1825 a daughter of J. F. Hogg; (2) a daughter of William Shaw of Cork; (3) Jane, daughter of William Galway of Dundonald. See Barkley: *Fasti of the General Assembly*, 1840-70 (1986).

James Shubridge purchased the plot in November 1833.]

SHAW
See CORDUKES and PATTON

SHEKLETON
See GIFFORD

SHELSWELL
[Small and flaking headstone, partly buried.] In memory of Elizth Shelswell, wife of Qr. Mr. Sergt. Shelswell, 43 Regt., Lt. Infy., who died in child bed, 1st of April 1820 aged 28 years. Had isue [sic] two sons and two daughters, three of which survives [sic] her to deplore the loss of an affectionate mother. Also Elizth who died at Naas aged 3 years.

SHERIDAN
[Formerly in lower ground, but now gone.] In memory of Mark Sheridan Esqr., late of 13th P.A.L.I., who died on the 2nd March 1849 aged 69. Also of Bt. Major James Henry FENWICK 13th P.A.L.I. who died on the 14th July 1849, aged 39.

[Both were attached to the 13th Light Infantry and lived in Antrim Place.]

SHERRY
[Small plaque now missing.] The family burying ground of William Sherry, Belfast, 1847.

SHIELDS
[No longer extant, but recorded by Society.] Erected by Margaret Shields to the memory of her ..... (William) Shields who departed this life (Novr. 22) 1843 aged (41) years. Likewise .... Shields who .... June .... years.

[William Shields was a tailor at 15, Skipper Street, Belfast.]

SHIELDS
Erected by James Shields, Belfast, 1846, who died on the 16th of February 1851 aged 64 years. Also his son William Booth Blair who died 17th of June 1851 aged 23 years. Also his wife Charlotte who died 16th of March 1852 aged 54 years. Cunningham McCREA died 11th Novr 1851 aged 57 years.

[James Shields was a grocer at 20, Albert Square, Belfast, and Cunningham McCrea was a writing clerk living in Grattan Court.]

SHUBRIDGE

[Slate tablet in broken pedimented entablature, formerly secured to dividing wall but now broken.] Erected by Jane Shubridge, of Belfast, in memory of her beloved husband James Shubridge who died 26th July 1847 aged 54 years. Also their son George McCaughey Shubridge who died 13th December 1869 aged 26 years. And two of their children who died in infancy. Also his wife Susanna who died 12 May 1838 aged 33 years. And his father David Shubridge who died 20th November 1830 aged 64 years. And his mother Hannah who died 23rd February 1833 aged 65 years.

[James Shubridge was a butcher at 5, Arthur Square, Belfast. See also SHAW.]

SIBBIN

[Very worn marble in large headstone, now lost.] Erected by George Sibbin, of Belfast, in memory of his beloved (parents) Mary Sibbin (who departed this life) Jan. 20th, 1841 (aged 49 years) and William Sibbin (who died March 17th 1843 aged 49 years.)

[The Sibbin family were pawnbrokers in the Smithfield and Chapel Lane districts of Belfast.]

SILLY

[Polished red granite, topped by a draped urn in low-stone enclosure.] In loving memory of Thomas Silly, master mariner, who departed this life 3rd Sep. 1867 aged 48 years, and was interred here with four children who died in infancy. Also his son Sweetland Silly aged 24 years, who was lost at sea in 1869. "For ever with the Lord". 1.Thess.IV.17.

[Thomas Silly who was born at Morecambe, Lancashire, was a sea-captain, resident at 84, Great George's Street, Belfast.]

SIMMONS

[Stone in upper ground and now no longer extant. The plot was purchased by Hugh Simmons in October 1826.] Erected by Hugh Simmons of Belfast.

[Hugh Simmons was a hat-maker at 24 Bridge Street, Belfast.]

SIMMS

[Worn horizontal slab in the ground. David Simms bought the plot in 1817.] Sacred to the memory of David Simms, of Belfast, who died 30th December 1841 aged 70 years. Also of Robert Simms who died 1(4)th January 18(1)6 aged 1(3) months. And of Anne MARSHAW, died (..) May 18(22).

[David Simms started printing in 1797 when he formed a partnership with one J. Doherty, after the wrecking of the *Northern Star* printing works. This partnership lasted till 1803, and four years later Simms entered into partnership with one Mr McIntyre. The firm of Simms & McIntyre, based at 22, Donegall Street, Belfast, became well-known as pioneers of cheap fiction. The partnership between his son John and McIntyre broke up in the 1850s. See Adams: *The Printed Word and The Common Man* (1987).]

SIMMS

[Slate tablet in entablature secured to east wall of upper graveyard in low-stone enclosure.] Sacred to the memory of Sarah Simms daughter of Robert Simms of Belfast, who died on the 13th of February 1824 aged 19 years.

> The hour of my departure's come,
> I hear the voice that calls me home,
> I leave this World without a tear
> Save for the Friends I hold so dear.

Sacred also to the memory of her sister Marianne Simms, who died on the 25th of October 1830 aged 36 years. And to the memory of their mother Mary Simms who died on the 18th of September 1832 aged 73 years. And to the memory of their sister Eliza Simms who died on the 11th of June 1843 aged 52 years. Also to the memory of their father Robert Simms who died on the 23rd of June 1843 aged 82 years. And to the memory of their sister Jane Simms who died on the 31st of October 1892 in her 94th year.

[Robert Simms was a prominent Committee member of the Linenhall Library in its early days, and in the 1820s and 1830s held the position of Chamberlain to the White Linenhall. By calling he was a merchant and insurance agent. See Killen: *History of the Linen Hall Library* (1990).]

SIMMS

[Very worn marble, in large headstone now lost.] In memory of Arthur Simms, (who died 1825 aged 48 years). His wife Mary) Simms died (1865 aged 70 years. Their daughter Susanna Simms died 1840 aged 20 years. Mary (Simms died 23rd November) 1891. Sarah Simms died 27th January (1898).

[Letters of administration of the personal estate of Mary Simms of 75 Ormeau Road, Belfast, spinster, who died 25 November 1891 at Richmond Asylum, Dublin, were granted at Belfast 30 March 1892 to Sarah Simms of 75 Ormeau Road, Belfast, spinster, the sister. Effects £4,090 18s.2d.

Probate of the will of Sarah Simms of 95 Ormeau Road, Belfast, spinster, who died 27 January 1898 granted at Belfast 23 March 1898 to Hugh Simms and William Simms, both of Newtownards, county Down, manufacturers, and Felix Simms of North Queen Street, Belfast, notary public. Effects £13,763 19s.11d.

[Arthur Simms was a merchant at 25, Donegall Street, Belfast.]

SINCLAIR

[Twin marble tablets in carved surround topped with urn, now lost.] In memory of.

(a) William Sinclair of Brookvale, who died 10th August 1842 aged 84 years. Elizabeth his wife who died 18th March 1834 aged 65 years. Ann MONTGOMERY, his sister-in-law, formerly of Killead, and late of Brookvale, who died 28th August 1819 aged 44 years.

(b) William Sinclair, junr, of Broo(kva)le, who died 8th August 1841 aged 37 years. Also his wife Mary GIBSON, who died 11th December 1887 aged 81 years. Also his children: James Gibson, who died 24th March 1840 aged 3 years, Jane and James, who died in infancy, Elizabeth Sinclair, daughter of the late Wm Sinclair, died 24th July 1900 aged 68 years.

[The will of Mary Sinclair of 14 Kenilworth Square, Rathgar, county Dublin, widow, who died 11 December 1887 at same place, was proved at the Principal Registry 6 April 1888 by Samuel Dobbin of Ellerslie, Glenageary, county Dublin, Vicar Choral of Christ Church and Saint Patrick's Cathedral, one of the executors. Effects £2,059 13s.5d.

Probate of the will of Elizabeth Sinclair formerly of 14 Kenilworth Squire, Rathgar, county Dublin, and late of Patrick's Hospital, Dublin, spinster, who died 24 July 1900 at latter place, granted at Dublin 26 September 1900 to Samuel Dobbin and Hanbury C. Geoghegan, esquires. Effects £4,347 15s.5d].

SINCLAIR

[Two slate tablets with lettering formerly picked out in gold paint, in very ornate entablatures in the classical style, and both are surmounted by draped urns, attached to north wall and in a low-walled enclosure.]

Sacred to the memory of John Sinclair, of the Grove, who died 17th January 1856 aged 47 years. William Pirrie Sinclair, his son who died 30th October 1836 aged 6 months.

Sacred to the memory of Thomas Sinclair, J.P., of Hopefield, who died 2nd January 1867 aged 56 years. Sarah ARCHER his wife died 27th June 1849 aged 49 years. Mary their daughter died 30th November 1853 aged 10 years. William their son died 25th May 1854 aged 18 years.

[The will, with one codicil, of Thomas Sinclair of Hopefield, Belfast, county Antrim, merchant, who died 2 January 1867 at London was proved at Belfast 1 March by the oath of William Symms of Mountjoy Square, Dublin, gentleman, one of the executors. Effects under £35,000.

John Sinclair and his brother Thomas were provision and general merchants and ship-owners at 5-11, Tomb Street, Belfast.

Thomas Sinclair of Hopefield House, Belfast, J.P. married Sarah, daughter of William Archer of Rockshill, Hillsborough. Their son the Rt. Hon. Thomas Sinclair, P.C., J.P., D.L. for counties Antrim and Down, was born on 23 September 1838. He was Chairman of Convocation of Queen's University, M.A. and Hon. D. Lit. See Burke's *Landed Gentry of Ireland* 1912 edition; also Young and Pike: *Belfast and the Province of Ulster in the 20th century* (1909).]

SINCLAIR

[Bottom lines buried.] Erected by John Sinclair. Andrew Sinclair died 20th October 1855 aged 8 years. Edward Sinclair died 14th September 1860 aged 19 years. Robert Sinclair died 2nd October 1861 aged 22 years. The above John Sinclair died 1st May 1862 aged 59 years. Mary Sinclair, wife of George MATEER died 19th June 1863 aged 26 years. Jane ARMOUR, the beloved wife of the above John Sinclair, died 29th September 1872 aged 67 years. Thomas Sinclair, son of Henry Sinclair died 17th June 1892 aged 14 years.

[The will, with one codicil, of John Sinclair of King Street in the town of

Belfast, house carpenter, who died 1 May 1862 at same place, was proved at Belfast 3 June 1862 by the oath of Henry Greer of King Street, Belfast aforesaid, salesman, one of the executors. Effects under £200.

John Sinclair was a house carpenter at 6, King Street, Belfast and Henry Sinclair was a house painter at 40, King Street.]

SINCLAIRE/SINCLAIR

[Very large monument of three tablets in entablature of Doric columns surmounted by two eliptical and two round urns and secured to west wall.] (a) [Central tablet.] William Sinclaire of Belfast, ob.11th February 1807 aged 47. Also Charlotte Sinclaire his widow who died on the 9th day of January 1850 in the 87th year of her age.

(b) [Right-hand tablet.] James POLLOCK of Newry, died the 4th of February 1816 aged 68 years. Also his daughter Hester Pollock died the 15th of June 1800 aged 20. Agnes Sinclaire died the 16th of January 1825 aged 74.

(c) [Left-hand tablet, now lost.] Cecil Charles MAY, died 10th of January 1857 aged 13 months. Elizabeth May, widow of the Rev. E. May, born 16th June 1785, died 24th April 1857. Also of Edward Stephen May, eldest son of the Revd Edward May and Elizabeth Sinclair his wife who died on the 13th day of August 1864 in the 52nd year of his age.

[The Sinclaire family, originally from Scotland, first settled in the Newtownards area.

Thomas Sinclaire, grocer and linen merchant, was born in 1719, married in 1749 Hester Eccles Pottinger and lived first in High Street and later in Mill Street. He had bleach greens at Mountain Green, Lodge Green and Falls Green. He died in 1798 and was buried in the graveyard in High Street. He had 4 sons:

1. Thomas Sinclaire.

2. William Sinclaire (1760-1807) lived at Donegall Place and Fortwilliam, Belfast, and enlarged and mechanised his father's bleach mills. He married Charlotte Pollock (1763-1850) and had 3 daughters:

(a) Elizabeth Sinclaire married on 13 June 1809 the Rev. Edward May, Rector of Belfast and brother of Sir Stephen May, Kt, and brother-in-law of the second Marquis of Donegall. She died at Rockport, near Holywood. Her son Edward (1813-64) was a retired army officer.

(b) Charlotte Maria Sinclaire married on 26 August 1826 Conway Richard Dobbs of Castle Dobbs.

(c) - Sinclaire married the Rev James Strange Butson, M.A., Archdeacon of Clonfert.

Many of this branch are buried in this grave.

3. John Sinclaire (1763-1857) of Donegall Place, Belfast, married Margaret Clarke (1768/9-1839) and had 4 sons and 2 daughters:

(a) Thomas Sinclaire (1796/7-1860) married Augusta Montgomery (1801/2-1870) and had issue:

(b) (Son)

(c) William Sinclaire was alive c.1880.

(d) Richard Ker Sinclaire (1810/1-1905) of Avoca Park, Falls Road mar-

ried Isabella McKee (1830/1-1881) and had issue. This branch is buried in Balmoral Cemetery.
   (e) Jane Sinclaire (1804/5-1819)
   (f) Margaret Sinclaire (1807/8-1900)
Most of this branch are buried in another plot, see below.
   4. George Sinclaire had 3 sons and is presumably the George listed below.

William Sinclaire (1760-1807) was, like the rest of his family, a successful linen merchant and bleacher, and as such was an active member of the Belfast Chamber of Commerce from its inception in 1783. Actively involved in the politics of the day, he was a member of the Belfast Volunteer Company, and joined the United Irishmen on their formation in 1791, being the first chairman of the Northern Directory. He was also an early and keen member of the Linenhall Library. He lived in Donegall Place, not far from the corner with Castle Lane, and there kept an assortment of animals and hawks. His brother John (1763-1857) was also a Volunteer and a United Irishman and had the distinction of being the last surviving Volunteer at the time of his death. He lived on the west side of Donegall Place, opposite his brother William, and there he kept a pack of hunting hounds and a monkey. Dressed in a green frock coat with brass buttons and a top hat, he cut a very colourful figure in his later years.

See Benn: *A History of the Town of Belfast*, Vol II (1880); Leslie: *Ferns Clergy and Parishes* (1936); *Burke's Irish Family Records* (1976); Clarke: *Gravestone Inscriptions, Belfast*, Vol. 3 (1986); also Chambers: *Faces of Change* (1983).]

SINCLAIRE
[In upper ground and no longer extant. This plot was bought by Capt. George Sinclaire in February 1818.] The graves of Capt. G. Sinclaire and his wife Mary Sinclaire, Belfast.

SINCLAIRE
[Slate headstone with surround, formerly against south wall in low-stone enclosure with next but now lost.] Erected to the memory of John CLARKE died April 1810, Jane Sinclaire died 4th Septeber 1819 aged 14 years. Margaret Sinclaire died 9th January 1839 aged 70 years. Mary MONTGOMERY died 21st January 1844 aged 82 years. Augusta Sinclaire died 11th March 1845 aged 13 years. John Sinclaire died 29th June 1857 aged 94 years. Thomas Sinclaire died 8th October 1860 aged 63 years. Augusta Sinclaire died 23rd March 1870 aged 68 years. Mary Caroline Sinclaire died 11th October 1870 aged 34 years. Thomas Sinclaire died 25th September 1884 aged 50 years. Margaret Sinclaire died 1st July 1900 aged 92 years.

[The will of Thomas Sinclaire of Annavale, Windsor, Belfast, esquire, who died 25 September 1884 at same place, was proved at Belfast 14 November 1884 by Emily Sinclaire of same place, spinster, one of the executors. Effects £1,129 8s.3d.

Mary Montgomery (d.1844) was the widow of Conway Heatly Montgomery.]

SINCLAIRE

[Polished granite in enclosure with the above.] Sacred to the memory of John Sinclaire died 29th June 1857 aged 94 years. And Margaret his wife, only child of John CLARKE, died 9th Jany. 1839 aged 70 years. Also their daughters, Jane died 14th Sept. 1819 aged 14 years, and Margaret died 1st July 1900 aged 92 years. Their eldest son Thomas Sinclaire died 8th Octr. 1860 aged 63 years. And his wife Augusta, daughter of Conway Heatly MONTGOMERY, died 23rd March 1870 aged 68 years. Also their daughters, Augusta, died 11th March 1845 aged 13 years, Mary Caroline died 11th Octr. 1870 aged 34 years. And their eldest son Thomas Sinclaire, died 25th Sept. 1884 aged 50 years. This stone is erected by Emily Sinclaire MILLAR, 1901.

[John Sinclaire (1763-1857) is commemorated above and an outline of his career is given under Sinclaire/Sinclair.]

SITLINGTON

See LUKE

SKELTON

[Headstone formerly in upper ground, and no longer extant.] Erected by William Skelton, of Belfast, to the memory of his son David who died 26th of September 1841 aged 14 years. Likewise the above named William Skelton who departed this life on the 25th March 1845 aged 55 years. Also his son-in-law Henry CONNOR who departed this life on the 24th January 1851 aged 24 years. His eldest daughter Jane, relict of Henry Connor, who died 9th November 1855. His third son Hugh James who died 23rd January 1870. His son William who died 28th February 1878. His widow Anne who died 14th September 1880.

[Letters of administration of the personal estate of William Skelton of Cliftonville, Belfast, manager of the Belfast Steam Ship Company Limited, a bachelor, who died 28 February 1878 at same place, were granted at Belfast 18 March 1878 to Ann Skelton of Cliftonville, Belfast, widow, the mother of said deceased. Effects in United Kingdom under £600.

The will, with one codicil, of Ann Skelton of 20 Cliftonville, Belfast, widow, who died 14 September 1880 at same place, was proved at Belfast 8 October 1880 by the oaths of Francis Brown of 34 Mill Street, rent agent, Elizabeth Skelton of 20 Cliftonville, spinster, and Joseph Skelton of 7 Duncairn Terrace, linen manager, all in Belfast, the executors. Effects under £200.

[William Skelton, senior, was a cabinet maker and mahogany merchant at 57, Donegall Street, Belfast.]

SKILLEN

[Polished granite.] Erected by Agnes GRANT in memory of her father William Skillen, died Sept. 17, 1845 aged 59 years. Her mother Agnes Skillen died April 30, 1857 aged 62 years. Her brother William died

Aug. 24, 1865 aged 40 years. Her husband William Grant who was accidentally drowned in Belfast Lough, July 15, 1868 aged 37 years. Her daughters: Elizabeth died Aug. 3, 1864 aged 2 years. Mary died Aug 11, 1864 in infancy, Wilhelmina Skillen, Nov. 6, 1868 aged 7 months, and Agnes, June 6, 1886 aged 26 years. The above named Agnes Grant died Feb. 1, 1903 aged 73 years.

[Letters of administration of the personal estate of William Grant of York Street, Belfast, county Antrim, baker, who died 15 July 1868 at Holywood, county Down, were granted at Belfast on the 4 September 1868 to Agnes Grant of York Street, Belfast aforesaid, the widow of said deceased. Effects under £1,000.

Administration of the estate of Agnes Grant of 1 Gosford Terrace, Dufferin Avenue, Bangor, county Down, widow, who died 31 January 1903, granted at Belfast 13 March 1903 to Margaret Grant, spinster. Effects £1,748 12s.8d.]

[William Skillen was a mechanic and lived at 10, Thomas Street, Belfast. William Grant was a baker and biscuit manufacturer at 221, York Street.]

SLOAN

[Two identical tablets formerly secured to north wall, but only the first remains.] Erected by George Sloan, in memory of his beloved daughter Jane who died 30th May 182(5) aged 23 years. And also of his daughters, Susanna Jane who died young, Eliza, wife of Wm McGEE, M.D. who died 27th Jany 1832 in her 36th year.

[Now lost.] Sacred to the memory of John Sloan, of Belfast, who departed this life on the 16th day of June 1831 aged 63 years.

[John Sloan, a native of Church Hill, near Moneymore, lived in Donegall Square, Belfast, and was one of the original four partners of the first Northern Bank when it was formed in 1809. The Sloan family were linked to that of John Galt Smith (q.v.). Dr William McGee who lived in Arthur Street was the first lecturer in midwifery when the Belfast School of Medicine opened at R.B.A.I. in 1830.]

SLOAN

[Very badly weathered sandstone monument formerly secured to the dividing wall and now removed.] .... of (March) ...... years. .....Spia (on the 11th) day of ...... 1875 (aged 77) years.......... their daughter Janet on the 23rd day of Jan. 1837 aged (45) years. (John their son on the 10th) day of (February 1837 aged 43) years. (And to James) their son who died on the 11th day of (July 1856 aged 57) years. (Also) Margaret (their daughter) who died on the (1st) day of February 1862 aged 72 years.

[The will, with two codicils, of Margaret Sloan of Donaghadee, county Down, spinster, who died 1 February 1862 at same place, was proved at Belfast 20 February 1862 by the oaths of Alexander John Bruce of Ayrshire in Scotland, banker and the Reverend John McAuley of Donaghadee aforesaid, Presbyterian minister, the executors. Effects under £7,000.

This plot was purchased by James Sloan in May 1829.

John Sloan (d.1837) was the owner of the Donegall Arms Hotel, Castle Place, Belfast. His brother James was an inn-keeper and died at Donaghadee. Their father was called James.]

SLOAN

[Damaged.] Erected in memory of David Sloan who departed this life 11th Sept. 1845 aged 80 years. Also his beloved wife Agnes who fell asleep in Jesus, 14th March 1858 aged 81 years. And their daughters, Margaret, who, died 25th Dec. 1859 aged 51 years, Mary, who died 13th Jany 1861 aged 51 years. Also his son-in-law James BYERS, who died 1st April 1877 aged 68 years. And Elizabeth, relict of James Byers, who died 7th Dec. 1885 aged 73 years. Also Elizbeth [sic] THOMSON, who died 23rd June 1921 aged 67 years.

[The will of Agnes Sloan of Belfast in the county of Antrim, widow, who died 14 March 1858 at same place, was proved at Belfast 19 April 1858 by the oaths of Samuel Edgar of Arthur Square, draper, and Elizabeth Byers otherwise Sloan, wife of James Byers of Prince's Street, both in the town of Belfast aforesaid, the executors. Effects under £450.

The will of Mary Sloan, formerly of Belfast, in the county of Antrim and late of Ballymacarret in the county of Down, spinster, who died 13 January 1861 at Ballymacarret aforesaid, were proved at Belfast 8 March 1861 by the oath of Samuel Edgar of Belfast in the county of Antrim and Elizabeth Byers, wife of James Byers of Ballymacarret. Effects under £300.

The will of Elizabeth Byers of 12 Joy Street Belfast, widow, who died 9 December 1885 at same place, was proved at Belfast 19 April 1886 by William Harper of Victoria Street, Belfast, merchant, and David Sloan Thomson of Whiteabbey, county Antrim, mill manager, the executors. Effects £845 4s.2d.

David Sloan ran a boarding-house at 47, Prince's Street, Belfast. James Byers was a sea-captain.]

SLOAN

See EWART

SMALL

[Headstone at head of the next stone.] Here lyeth the body of Mary Small, wife to Hugh Small of Belfast, who departed this life the 12th of April 1820 aged 57 years. Also the body of the above named Hugh Small who departed this life the 3rd of September 1838 aged 70 years.

[Hugh Small was a leather-cutter at 77, North Street, Belfast.]

SMALL

[Horizontal slab at the foot of the above stone.] Sacred to the memory of John Small who died 21st March 1852 aged 42 years. And of Sarah his wife who died 16th May 1852 aged 40 years. And of Mary their child who died 20th October 1848 aged 4 years. And of their son Hugh Alexander who died at Chicago, U.S., 7th August 1873 aged 33 years. And also their son William who died at Chicago, U.S., 9th October 1882 aged 35 years.

[Letters of administration of the personal estate of William Small of Chicago in the U.S. of America, merchant, who died 9 October 1882 at same place, were granted at the Principal Registry on the 14 November 1882 to Elizabeth Ferris, wife of James Caldwell Ferris of Newry, county Down, Presbyterian Minister, the sister. Effects £3,450.

John Small was a merchant at 129, York Street, Belfast.]

SMITH
[Very large memorial with twin tablets in pillared granite entablature with unicorn's head at the top with motto "Mea gloria fides", against east wall, in high-railed enclosure.] John Galt Smith born March 23rd 1770, died February 9th 1832. His wife Margaret born August 12th 1782, died May 21st 1875. Her sister Frances BARBER, born March 29th 1780, died October 5th 1866. Infant daughter, born March 17th 1810, died March 25th 1810. Mary Jane, born March 17th 1806, died January 5th 1812. Fanny, born April 30th 1814, died July 9th 1815. Elizabeth, born October 14th 1804, died July 2nd 1817. Agnew, born July 19th 1817, died January 11th 1818. Jones Agnew, born July 2nd 1819, died September 10th 1819, Edward born August 15th 1825, died August 23rd 1831. John Smith McTEAR, born 1842, died 1913. Margaret McTear, born 1837, died 1916. Frances Mary McTear, born 1845, died 4th February 1934, grandchildren of the above John Galt Smith.

Thomson born September 25th 1820, died February 17th 1844. Francis, born August 22nd 1822, died January 16th 1857. John Galt, born March 5th 1809, died September 8th 1872. Charlotte, born March 27th 1816, died June 26th 1876. George Kennedy, born July 19th 1812, died July 25th 1886. Samuel Smith, born February 19th 1811, died August 2nd 1849. His wife Mary-Anne born October 5th 1819, died January 3rd 1878. Their children, Maggie "Primus", died in infancy 1842, Mary-Anne born November 15th 1840, died April 12th 1848, Willie, born March 6th 1847, died April 19th 1850. Samuel Thomson Smith, son of Sam. Smith and grandson of John Galt Smith, born 1849, died 1891. [On plinth.] Erected by George Kennedy Smith.

[The will, with one codicil, of Margaret Smith of Meadowbank, county Antrim, widow, who died 23 May 1875 at same place, was proved at Belfast 17 September 1875 by the oath of George Kennedy Smith of Meadowbank, Whitehouse, solicitor, the surviving executor. Effects under £4,000.

The will of Frances Barber, formerly of Glengall Place, Belfast, and late of Meadow Bank both in the county of Antrim, spinster, who died 5 October 1866 at Meadow Bank aforesaid, was proved at Belfast 18 October 1866 by the oaths of George McTear of Belfast aforesaid, merchant, and George Kennedy Smith of Meadow Bank, Belfast aforesaid, solicitor, the executors. Effects under £3,000.

Frances Mary McTear of Creevelea, Kings Road, Knock, Belfast, spinster, died 4 February 1934. Probate Belfast 18 June 1934 to Robert Watts, solicitor, and the Reverend Herbert John Rossington, unitarian clergyman. Effects £2,268 0s.1d.

The will of George Kennedy Smith of Meadowbank, Whitehouse, county

Antrim, solicitor, who died 25 July 1886 at same place, was proved at Belfast 4 October 1886 by John Galt Smith of Meadowbank, Whitehouse, merchant, and John Smith McTear of The Castle, Belfast, solicitor, the executor. Effects £19,161 12s.7d.

Letters of administration, with the will annexed, of the personal estate of Mary Anne Smith, formerly of Croom and of Moygaret and late of Meadowbank, Whitehouse, all in county Antrim, widow, who died 3 January 1878 at Meadowbank, were granted at Belfast 18 July 1879 at Belfast to Samuel Thomson Smith of Whitehouse, one of the residuary legatees. Effects under £2,000.

John Galt Smith I (1731-1802), West India and general merchant, was son of Samuel Smith (1693-1760) and Ann Galt. He married Jane Jones, daughter of Valentine Jones, both being buried in the Jones grave (q.v.). They had at least 5 sons and 3 daughters.

1. Samuel Smith (1766-1829), linen bleacher, married in 1794 Letitia Bradish of Kilkenny and had 11 children, including John Galt Smith III, who died in Australia, and the Rev. William Smith F.L.S., Professor of Natural History in Queen's College, Cork. He had a daughter Jane who married James Bristow (q.v.).

2. Valentine Smith died young.

3. John Galt Smith II (1770-1832) married Margaret Barber and had 14 children including John Galt Smith IV.

4. William Smith, West India Merchant married – Wentworth.

5. Edward Jones Smith (1780-1859) married Jane Crawford of Orangefield and had several children including John Galt Smith V and Edward Smith.

6. Mary Ann Smith married Josiah Bryan.

7. Margaret Smith (1774/5-1844) died unmarried.

8. Charlotte Smith died unmarried.

See Benn: *A History of the Town of Belfast* (1877-80); also Chambers: *Faces of Change* (1983) for an extensive description of this family. See also entries under BRISTOW, JONES, KENNEDY, McTEAR and Samuel THOMSON.]

SMITH

[Twin slate tablets in carved and pedimented entablature secured to south wall in low-stone enclosure.] (a) Erected A.D. 1845, in memory of Samuel Smith, formerly of Woodville, near Belfast, who died at Balnamore, near Ballymoney 21st day of Decr 1830, and Letitia his wife who died at same place 9th day of Feby 1835. "Mark the perfect man and behold the upright, for the end of that man is peace". Psalms XXXVI, 37V. "Whom the Lord loveth he chasteneth". Heb.XII, 6V. Also of Samuel their son, who died at Woodville, 19th day of Novr 1804, and Abby their daughter who died at Belfast after a few hours illness, 13th day of Decr 1814. And of Charlotte sister of the above named Samuel Smith, who died at Belfast, 9th day of Novr 1822.

(b) Also of Mary Anne, daughter of the aforesaid Samuel and Letitia Smith and beloved wife of James Thomson BRYAN Esq. who died in child bed at Rose Lodge, near Magherafelt, 26th day of Decr 1844, and whose remains with those of her infant son are interred here.

Awake my Soul with anxious care,
For the great day thyself prepare,
With steadfast faith that path betrod;
Which thro' the grave conducts to God.

[See Benn: *A History of the Town of Belfast*, Vol. II (1880); also entries under BRISTOW and JONES.]

SMITH
Sacred to the memory of Elizabeth Smith, wife of Sergeant Thomas Smith of the 45th Regiment of Foot, who died on the 11th of February 1816 aged 38 years.

SMITH
[Stone formerly in upper ground, but no longer extant. Plot purchased by George Smith in April 1817.] Sacred to the memory of Margaret WORKMAN, wife of George Smith, manufacturer, died (.... 1817) aged (..) years. James Smith, Master Mariner died 1828 aged (..) years. Jane Workman, wife of William ...., merchant, Glasgow, died .... Oct. ...... aged ......

SMITH
[Worn marble tablet, of which the upper half is obliterated, in broken entablature.] Sacred (to the memory of James Smith, of Belfast, who died on the 8th Novr 1826 aged 43 years. Of Eleanor his wife who died on the 12th Novr 1841 aged 37 years. And of their son Isaac George who died on the 20th May 1802 (sic) aged 2 years. Also their daughter Anna Rosetta, wife of Thomas Henry AICKIN, of Belfast who died on the 17th March) 1847 aged (23) years. Also of her three children who died in infancy. Also Jane Maria Elizabeth, wife of Thomas Waring (COULTER), of Belfast, who died on the 2(3d) of December 18(5)0 aged (2)8 years.

SMITH
[Missing.] The burying ground of William Smith, upholsterer, Belfast, 1837.
[He lived (and presumably worked) at 2, Skipper Street, Belfast.]

SMITH
Erected to the memory of Jane Smith, relict of the late James Smith, of Garvagh, who departed this life June 21st 1839 aged 80 years.

SMITH
[Formerly in lower ground and now gone.] The family burying ground of Alexander Smith, Belfast, 1840.

SMITH
[No longer extant.] Family burying ground of John Smith, Belfast, 1840.

SMITH
[Slate formerly in large neo-Egyptian style headstone, now laid flat.] Erected by James Smith in memory of his beloved wife Isabella Smith, who departed this life 27th June 1845 aged 61 years. Also his beloved daughter Jane MINNIS who departed this life 16th February 1849 aged

27 years. Also his beloved son Thomas who departed this life 23rd February 1862 aged 47 years. Also the above named James Smith who departed this life 15th April 1867 aged 86 years.

[The will of Thomas Smith of Henry Street in the town of Belfast, merchant, who died 23 February 1862 at Belfast aforesaid, was proved at Belfast 14 April 1862 by the oaths of Matilda Richardson alias Smith, widow and Isabella Smith, spinster, both of Henry Street, Belfast, aforesaid, the executrixes. Effects under £2,000.]

SMITH

[Weathered in the centre, now lost.] Erected by John Smith, in memory of his mother Sarah Smith who departed this life on the 18th day of April 1847 in the 60th year of her age. Also of his father (Th)omas Smith who departed this life on the 4th day of June 185(2 aged 64) years.

SMITH

[No longer extant. Date of purchase not given in Society's records.] Erected by Samuel Smith, Belfast, to the memory of ...... Smith who departed this life .. April .....

SMITH

See BRISTOW, JONES and STEEN

SMYTH

[Very worn and broken horizontal slab, now lost, largely copied from Inscription Book.] (Erected by Mr. Samuel Smyth to the memory of his brother) John Smy(th ..... Constable of Belfast, who departed this life the 8th of) April 181(0 aged .. years. Here) also (are interred the mortal remains of his sister Miss) Mary Smyth (who departed this life on the 21st day) of March 1838 aged (75).

[In the opening decade of the nineteenth century, the policing of the streets of Belfast was a voluntary and loosely organised affair. Generally speaking, groups of four constables took it in turns to escort night patrols of soldiers looking for vagrants and drunkards. There was a small and rather crude prison in Ferguson's Entry, off Smithfield. In 1808, one J. Smyth was on the police committee.]

SMYTH

Erected by Jos Smyth, Belfast, to the memory of his mother Eliz. Smyth died 1820 AE 84. Also to his wife Rebecca Smyth died 1824 AE 27 [sic]. And two of their children. Also Ann McLEARN died 1829 AE 32. The above named Joseph Smyth died 27th June 1858 AE 84. Also daughters, Ann Jane died 30th Novr 1888, Margaret died 19th Octr 1893, Elizabeth died 7th March 1896.

[The will of Joseph Smyth of Belfast in the county of Antrim, gentleman, who died 27 June 1858 at Belfast aforesaid was proved at Belfast 24 July 1858 by the oaths of Elizabeth Smyth and Anne Jane Smyth, spinsters, the executrixes and Henry Greer, bookseller, the surviving executor, all of same place. Effects under £4,000.

Letters of administration of the personal estate of Anne Jane Smyth of

Belfast, spinster, who died 30 November 1888 at same place, were granted at Belfast 25 July 1889 to Eliza Smyth of Belfast, spinster, a sister. Effects £2,460 1s.9d.

Letters of administration of the personal estate of Margaret Smyth of 22 University Street, Belfast, spinster, who died 19 October 1893, were granted at Belfast 25 September 1896 to James Agnew of 9 Chichester Street, Belfast, law clerk, executor of her sister. Effects £744 8s.10d.

The will of Elizabeth Smyth of 21 Ulsterville Avenue, Belfast, spinster, who died 7 March 1896 was proved at Belfast 20 April 1896 by James Agnew of 9 Chichester Street, Belfast, law clerk, one of the executors. Effects £7,387 0s.6d. Re-sworn £7,399 0s.6d.

Joseph Smyth, printer, publisher & stationer formed a partnership with David Lynas at 115, High Street, Belfast in about 1800. By the time the Smyth & Lynas partnership dissolved in about 1818, they had published some of the earliest Belfast directories and almanacs. Smyth then continued alone at new premises at 34 High Street (near corner with Bridge Street) until he retired in about 1851. During this time he continued to publish his almanacs which were popular all over the north of Ireland and in Scotland. After 1851, they were printed by Alexander Mayne. Smyth died at 2, William's Place, off Wellwood Place, off Great Victoria Street. See Notes by J. J. Marshall, *Belfast Telegraph* 24th Oct. 1934.]

SMYTH

[Very worn raised horizontal slab, broken down the centre and now lost.] Erected (to the memory of) Samuel Smyth (who departed this life the .. March 1827 aged 65 years.)

SMYTH

To the memory of James Smyth who died 18th October 1845 aged 64 years. Also his daughter Fanny who died 14th May 1856 aged 26 years. And Dorothea his wife who died 31st Decr 1861 aged 77 years. And James Smyth, son of above died 22nd October 1883 aged 69 years. And Eliza Smyth, daughter of above, died 1st January 1885 aged 66 years. And Thomas Smyth, son of above, died 30th March 1907 aged 87 years.

[James Smyth, senior, was a coach-maker, employed by Hasting Duprey at 11, Fountain Street, Belfast. His sons James and Thomas were engravers and printers at 31, Castle Street. In the burial register James, Junior, is described as a coach-painter.]

SMYTH

[Broken and fallen.] Sacred to the memory of Edward Smyth who died 3rd Sept 1852 aged 55 years. And of his beloved wife Anna Maria Smyth who died 19th Decr 1860 aged 76 years.

SMYTH

[Flaking.] Erected to the memory of Matilda Smyth, relict of Capt Wm Smyth, died 18th Nov. 1871 aged 56 years. Also Ann HUNTER, sister to the above died Feb 16th 1872 aged 72 years. Also to the memory of William, youngest son of the above Matilda Smyth, who died at

Beleize, British Honduras, 15th Dec. 1891. Also Jane Smyth eldest daughter of the above died 4th February 1907.

Time is winging us away,
To our immortal doom,
Life is but a Winter's day,
A journey to the tomb.

[Letters of administration of the personal estate of William Smyth of 68 Clifton Park Avenue, Belfast, master mariner, who died 15 December 1891 at Belize, British Honduras, were granted at Belfast 16 March 1892 to John Smyth of 68 Clifton Park Avenue, master mariner, brother. Effects £639 13s.4d.

Letters of administration of the personal estate of Jane Smyth of 14 Sunbury Avenue, Belfast, spinster, who died 4 February 1907, were granted at Belfast 22 March 1907 to Matilda Smyth, spinster. Effects £213 10s.7d.]

SMYTH

[Worn marble in a low railed enclosure.] Erected by Wilson Smyth in memory of his father John Smyth who died 8th Decr. 1876 AE (62) years. Also his mother Ann Jane Smyth (died 31)st Jany 1874 AE 61 years. And his niece Annie Wilson HILL, (died ..)th Decr. 1874 AE (10) years. The above named Wilson Smyth who died 28th March 1916 AE 66 years.

[The will, with one codicil, of John Smyth of York Street, Belfast, county Antrim, pawn broker, who died 8 December 1876 at same place, was proved at Belfast 23 July 1877 by the oaths of William Smyth of Virginia Street, Belfast, pawnbroker, and Robert Cleland of York Street, Belfast, baker, the executors. Effects under £600.

Letters of administration of the personal estate of Ann Jane Smyth of Great Patrick Street, Belfast, who died 30 January 1874 at same place, were granted at Belfast 15 April 1874 to John Smyth of Great Patrick Street, Belfast aforesaid, pawnbroker, the husband of said deceased. Effects under £50.]

SMYTH

See GETTY

SNODDY

[Small iron plaque, now lost.] The burying ground of Arthur McCune Snoddy, 1(9)06.

[The ground had been bought by Andrew Snoddy in May 1818.]

SPENCE

[Badly flaking sandstone.] Erected by Andrew Spence in memory of two children who died young. Also his daughter Isabella who died 25th of February 1839 aged 17 years. Also the above-named Andrew Spence who died 24th August 1848 aged 74 years. Also his grandson John Spence who died young. Also Jane, relict of the above named Andrew Spence, who died 8th Nov. 1856 aged 74 years.

[Andrew Spence was a provision merchant and publican at 33, Tomb Street, Belfast.]

SPILLER

[Squat pillar with marble tablets on three sides, formerly topped by a casket and draped urn.] In memory of William M. H. Spiller, late Captain 94th Regt died 11th May 1841 aged 51 years. Also Mary Anne his wife died 30th October 1871 aged 67 years.

[East tablet.] Charles Spiller, third son of William M. H. Spiller, died 25th August 1862 aged (3)4 years. Also James Spiller his eldest son, died 16th November 18(90) aged (66) years.

[West side.] William Spiller, second son of William M.H. Spiller, died 19th Novr 1906 aged 81 years. Catherine his eldest daughter died 3rd March 1908 aged 86 years. Susan, his younger daughter died 8th Jany 1914 aged 83 years.

[Letters of administration of the personal estate of Mary Ann Spiller of No. 5 Henry Street, Belfast, widow, who died 30 October 1871 at Belfast aforesaid, were granted at Belfast 17 November 1871 to William Spiller of Belfast aforesaid, bank manager, the son and one of the next of kin of said deceased. Effects under £1,000.

The will of James Spiller of Eirene, Fortwilliam Park, Belfast, gentleman, who died 16 November 1890 at same place, was proved at Belfast 3 December 1890 by William Spiller of Eirene, Fortwilliam Park, Belfast, bank cashier, the sole executor. Effects £1,554 6s.

Probate of the will of William Spiller of Eirene, Fortwilliam Park, Belfast, esquire, who died 19 November 1906 granted at Belfast 4 January 1907 to Edward Ashley Spiller, bank cashier, and Susan Spiller, spinster. Effects £225.

Probate of the will, with one codicil, of Susan Spiller of Eirene, Fortwilliam Park, Belfast, spinster, who died 8 January 1914, granted at Belfast 20 March 1914 to Reverend Henry Robert Brett, clerk, and Samuel Arthur Robinson, bank cashier. Effects £6,949 12s.7d.]

[William Spiller, junior, was a bank manager in the employ of the Belfast Bank.]

SPRATT

See DAVIS

SPRING

[Broken headstone laid flat beside the dividing wall in a low-stone enclosure.] Erected by Joseph MURDOCK, of Belfast, in memory of his father-in-law Edward Spring, who departed this life the 1st day of September 1830 aged (69) years. Mary Spring his wife, who departed this life on the 8th day of September 1831 aged 61 years. Also their daughter Isabella, wife of Joseph Murdock, who died A.D. 1833. The remains of the above named Joseph Murdock lie here, who died 14th Decr 1840 aged 46 years.

[Edward Spring was a cork-cutter at 39, Hercules Street, Belfast. The burial register describes Joseph Murdock as a linen merchant, living at Pakenham Place.]

STANDFIELD

[Laid flat and damaged. It is obviously the same person who is commemorated on the horizontal slab.] Erected to the memory of Charles Standfield, who died 27th November 1808 aged 19 years.

STANDFIELD
[Badly flaking slate horizontal slab, now lost.] (Charles Standfield born) in Coleraine, (..) January 1789, and died in Belfast, 27th of November 1808.

STANDFIELD
[Slab now lying flat and badly broken.] The remains of Margaret Standfi(eld) who died the 23rd July 1810 aged 36 years, are deposited beneath this stone.

STANDFIELD
[Broken horizontal slab, formerly beside the above, now lost.] Erected to the (memory of) Margaret Stan(dfield) who died 23rd July (1810) aged 36 ye(ars.)

STANDFIELD
[Very badly flaking sandstone, now lost.] Erected by (Jame)s Standfield of Belfast in memory (of) his beloved daughter Margaret who departed this life (on) the 25th day of Novr 1826 in the 12th year (of) her age.

STANDFIELD
[Worn and flaking stone, now lost.] Sacred to the memory of Eliza, the beloved wife (of) Charles Standfield, Belfast, who departed this life 2nd Novem(ber), 1833 aged 62 years. Charles Standfield, husband of the above named Eliza, died 19th May 1843 aged 78 years. Robert Standfield, eldest son of Charles & Eliza Standfield departed this life the 29th December 1858 in the 61st year of his age.

[The will with one codicil of Robert Standfield of Eglinton Street, Belfast, in the county of Antrim, gentleman, who died 29 December 1858 at Belfast aforesaid, was proved at Belfast 19 January 1859 by the oath of Samuel Vance of Chichester Street, Belfast aforesaid, gentleman, the sole executor. Effects under £2,000.

Charles Standfield, a native of Greencastle, county Donegal, arrived in Belfast sometime prior to 1807. He was a grocer and spirit dealer at 85 (old numbering) High Street, and retired to Murphy Street a few years before he died.]

STANDFIELD
[Large headstone with lead letters, in low railing.] The family burying ground of James Standfield, who was born 30th March 1781, and who died 3rd January 1867. Thomas Standfield died 9 September 1903 aged 74. Jane Younghusband Standfield died 31st January 1907.

[The will, with one codicil, of James Standfield of Belfast esquire, who died 3 January 1867 at same place, was proved at Belfast 7 May 1867 by the oath of Thomas Standfield, gentleman, and Jane Younghusband Standfield, spinster, both of Belfast aforesaid, executors. Effects under £450.

Probate of the will of Thomas Standfield of 2 Fortwilliam Terrace, Antrim Road, Belfast, gentleman, who died 9 September 1903 at 13

Lower Crescent, Belfast, granted at Belfast 20 November 1903 to Matthew Pollard, gentlemen, and John A. Murphy, stationer. Effects £12,299 14s.11d. Re-sworn £12,407 12s.11d.

Probate of the will and codicil of Jane Younghusband Standfield of 2 Newington Terrace, Belfast, spinster, who died 31 January 1907, granted at Belfast 8 March 1907 to John A. Murphy, wholesale stationer. Effects £4,545 17s.1d.

James Standfield, who hailed from the Inishowen peninsula of county Donegal, appears to have settled in Belfast sometime before 1807 and opened a grocer's shop at 95 (old numbering), High Street. He later added the wine and pickle trades to his activities, and seems to have retired before he was fifty. He was also an active member of the Committee of the Belfast Charitable Society. See Strain: *Belfast and its Charitable Society* (1961)].

STARK

[Oval tablet in headstone, formerly topped by a draped urn.] In memory of Peter Stark, Lieut. R.N., died 11th May 1852 aged 59 years. Marion his daughter died 1st August 1844 aged 17 years. Sarah his daughter died 18th Oct. 1849 aged 19 years. Margaret Stein his wife died 26th May 1867 aged 73 years.

[Lt Peter Stark was born in Scotland and was the local Emigration Agent appointed by the Government. He lived in Holywood.]

STAVELY

See McCONKEY

STEED

[Headstone formerly in upper ground, now missing and recorded in the Society's transcripts.] Erected by Daniel Steed in memory of his ... sons Daniel & ..... who died in infancy, 1812.

[Daniel Steed was a publican at 20, Lime-Kiln Dock (nowadays Albert Square), Belfast.]

STEELE

Erected to the memory of Mary Steele, wife of William Henry Steele, of Belfast, who departed this life the 5th day of March 1814 aged 30 years.

STEELE

See HUMPHRYS.

STEEN

[Now missing from lower ground.] Erected by (Revd. Isaiah Steen) in memory of (his wife) Isabella who died (16th August, 1841) aged 39 years. Also his infant son William who died 28th September 1841 aged 7 weeks. Also his son James who died 30th March 1868 aged 33 years. Here also lie the remains of the above Rev. Isaiah Steen who died 3rd August 1871 aged 73 years. Also of his wife Dorothy SMITH who died 30th March 1889 aged 74 years.

[The will of Reverend Isaiah Steen of No. 46 Pakenham Place, Belfast, Presbyterian Minister, who died 3 August 1871 at Belfast aforesaid, was proved at Belfast 6 September 1871 by the oaths of Robert Steen of the Royal Academical Institution, Belfast, classical teacher, and Hunter Steen of No. 1 Willmont Terrace, Belfast, fancy box manufacturer, two of the executors. Effects under £3,000.

Letters of administration of the personal estate of Dorothy Smith Steen, formerly of 46 Pakenham Place, Dublin Road, Belfast, and late of North Circular Road, Lisburn, both in county Antrim, widow, who died 30 March 1889 at latter place, were granted at Belfast 24 April 1889 to William Peile Steen of Lisburn, schoolmaster, the child. Effects £479 18s.

The Rev. Isaiah Steen was born in 1798, the 6th son of John Steen of Dunbo, county Londonderry. He was educated at the Academical Institution, receiving the General Certificate in 1818, though his name is in the list of pupils entering in 1820. He was ordained Minister of Ballycopeland in 1823 and resigned in 1832 having also been Moderator of the Secession Synod in 1831-32. He became headmaster of the Mathematical School, R.B.A.I., in 1833. He was a good teacher but was subsequently involved in disputes with other teachers until he retired in 1869. He married (1) in 1824 Isabella, only daughter of John Carmichael and their son Robert, a distinguished scholar, was for 35 years headmaster of the Classical Department of the R.B.A.I. They had 5 other sons and 2 daughters. He married (2) in 1855 Dorothy Smith, daughter of William Peile of Harrington, Cumberland. They had 1 further son William Peile Steen who was headmaster of Sullivan Upper School, Holywood 1880-86 and of Lisburn Intermediate School 1886-90, before moving to Cambridge.

See Jamieson: *History of the Royal Belfast Academical Institution* (1959); Stewart: *The Seceders in Ireland* (1950); Fisher and Robb: *Royal Belfast Academical Institution, Centenary Volume* (1913); Kilpatrick: *Millisle and Ballycopeland Presbyterian Church* (1934).

STEPHEN

[Polished granite laid flat.] Erected by Alexr Stephen in memory of his father John Stephen who died 26th Oct. 1857 aged 82 years. Also of his mother Catherine Stephen who died 18th Jan. 1861 aged 81 years. Also of his brother-in-law Richard FAINT, who died 28th Sep. 1867 aged 38 years. Also of his wife Ann Stephen who died 19th June 1876 aged 66 years. The above named Alexander Stephen who died 12th March 1884 aged 73 years. Olivia Stephen, wife of the above Richard Faint, who died 7th September 1896.

[The will of Richard Faint of Sydenham, county Down, and of Belfast, draper, who died 28 September 1867 at Sydenham aforesaid, was proved at Belfast 2 December 1867 by the oath of Olivia Faint of Sydenham, Belfast aforesaid, widow of deceased, the sole executrix. Effects under £100.

The will of Alexander Stephen of Mountpottinger, county Down, gentleman, who died 12 March 1884 at same place, was proved at Belfast 16 May 1884 by Olivia Faint of Mountpottinger, widow, one of the executors. Effects £429 10s.

Probate of the will of Olivia Kinnaird Faint of 221 Lorne Terrace,

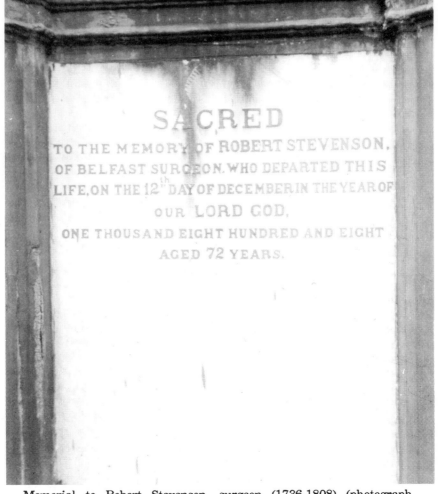

Memorial to Robert Stevenson, surgeon (1736-1808) (photograph R.W.M. Strain).

Mount Belfast, widow, who died 7 September 1896 granted at Belfast 14 October 1896 to Sir James H. Hazlett of North Street, William J. Turtle of 219 Lorne Terrace, Mountpottinger, bookkeeper, and Charles W. Black of 19 Arthur Square, solicitor, all in Belfast. Effects £3,431 5s.4d.]

Alexander Stephen was a wine and spirit dealer at 37, Rosemary Street, Belfast. The burial register describes him as a retired architect living at 217, Albertbridge Road.]

STEPHENS

[Large and well cut horizontal slab, now broken in two.] In memory of Isabella Stephens, wife to Joseph Stephens, of Belfast, who departed this life 20th day of August 1810 aged 70 years. She was universally beloved and deeply regretted by all that knew her. Here lieth the body of Joseph Stephens who departed this life 21st day of Decr 1834 aged 90 years. Also the infant child of John and Mary CHAMBERS. Here also are interred the remains of Thomas Gihon FERGUSON who departed this life 11th May 1852 aged 70 years. And of Isabella his wife who died 22nd June 1870 aged 82 years. "Then shall the dust return to the earth as it was: and the spirit shall return unto God who gave it". Eccles. XII,7.

[Joseph Stephens returned to Ireland as a linen merchant from Liverpool having been born near Dromore, county Down and lived at The Lodge, Old Lodge Road and later at Rose-vale. He married firstly Isabella Mitchell of Monaghan, sister of John Mitchell of Banbridge (father of Isabella Ferguson above). She died on 20 August 1810 and he married secondly Margaret McDowell. He died on 21 December 1834 at Joy Street leaving a will dated 13 June 1833 and his widow died between 10 March 1841 and 7 September 1843 being also buried here. Her niece's husband, John McDowell (not related) died between 1834 and 1843 and is also buried here.

Joseph and Isabella Stephens had a daughter Mary who married John Chambers, merchant, of Dublin, as his second wife and had the child who died in infancy also buried here.

Thomas Gihon Ferguson was a merchant of 36, Queen Street Belfast and married Isabella Mitchell, daughter of John Mitchell above.

See *Memorials of the Dead*, 1909, VII, 511-513.]

STEPHENS

See MUNCE

STERNE

See GARLAND

STEVEN

[Oval slate tablet with lettering formerly picked out in gold paint on monument surmounted by draped urn, against south wall, in railed enclosure.] Erected by Robert BOAG, Crescent, in memory of his mother-in-law Margaret Steven who died 27th March 1849 AE 58. Also his son James who died 12th Oct. 1864 AE 17. Also Mennie HILL who died 5th Jany 1877 aged 87 years. Also his grandchildren, Mina Hill STUART, who died 17th May 1872 aged eleven months. And Sara Edith Stuart who died 6th March 1877 aged 8 years, daughters of D. B. Stuart, banker, Ballyshannon.

[Margaret Steven was born in Glasgow and was the widow of John. Robert Boag ran the Albion Cloth Company, merchant tailors, at 22 High Street, Belfast. He lived at 6, Upper Crescent.]

STEVENSON

[Marble tablet, in entablature bearing urn, secured to south wall, in high-railed enclosure.] Sacred to the memory of Robert Stevenson, of Belfast, surgeon, who departed this life on the 12th day of December in the year of our Lord God, one thousand eight hundred and eight aged 72 years.

[Malcolm records that he was "for 26 years a most active and zealous member of the Committee of the Charitable Society, to whom he bequested the munificent sum of £1,000." See Strain: *Belfast and its Charitable Society* (1961).]

STEVENSON

[Very large tablet with wide sandstone entablature, secured to west wall — looks of c.1810-1840.] The family burying place of William Stevenson, Belfast.

STEVENSON

[Flaking badly and laid flat.] Erected by Maria Jane Stevenson in memory of her beloved & affectionate husband Thomas Stevenson who departed this life on the 20th of November 1850 aged 39 years. Also her father James REANEY, who departed this life on the 4th of January 1852 aged 65 years. Also her mother Mary Reaney who departed this life 22nd September 18(5)7 aged 71 years.

Remember man as you pass by
As you are now so once was I
As I am now so shall you be
Remember man that you must die.

[Thomas Stevenson was a master mariner and lived at Trafalgar Street, Belfast. James Reaney was a grocer in Green Street (nowadays Exchange Street.]

STEVENSON
See CARSON

STEWART

[Large slate monument with sandstone surround in a low-stone enclosure.] The burying ground of William Stewart, Belfast.

William, son of William Stewart died 1810 aged 11 years, William Stewart, senr died February 1811 aged 61 years, Jane his wife died 5th February 1832 aged 74 years, Mary, wife of George HOUGHTON, of Dublin, died 18th Decr 1840 aged 66 years. Ann wife of James Stewart, of Cherryvale, died 4th May 1850 aged 45 years, James Stewart died 18th November 1858 aged 79 years, William his son died 11th November 1862 aged 33 years. Also James his eldest son died 16th September 1883. "And they shall be mine saith the Lord of Hosts, in that day when I make up my jewels".

[The will of William Stewart of Greencastle in the county of Antrim, secretary to the Belfast Water Commissioners, who died 11 November 1862 at same place, was proved at Belfast 12 December 1862 by the oath of Anne Stewart of Greencastle aforesaid, spinster, the sole executrix. Effects under £300. See Loudan: *In Search of Water* (1940).

Letters of administration of the personal estate of James Stewart of Rosetta, Ballynafeigh, county Down, gentlemen, who died 16 September 1883 at same place, were granted at Belfast 26 November 1883 to Anne Kennedy of Rosetta, widow, the sister. Effects £1,294 18s.11d.

James Stewart, senior, was a wine and spirit merchant in Legg's Lane, Belfast (near the present-day Lombard Street) for many years. He lived at both 18, Arthur Street and Cherryvale, Ballynafeigh before finally retiring to Greencastle.]

STEWART

[Raised limestone slab with lead letters in a railed enclosure. Arms: Twin crescents, with chequee rectangle, and extended right arm, in chief.] Erected by James Forsythe WILSON, in memory of his grandfather John Stewart, who died 26th Jan. 1814 AE 40 years. Also his uncle John Stewart who died 14th Jan. 1824 AE 19 years. And his mother Mary WILSON who died 3rd March 1853 AE 47 years. Also his grandmother Nancy Stewart who died 9th Dec. 1854 AE 75 years. And his aunts: Nancy Stewart who died 20th Nov. 1870 AE 64 years, and Margaret Stewart who died 9th Oct. 1879 AE 81 years.

[Letters of administration of the personal estate of Nancy Stewart of 4 Ventry Street, Belfast, spinster, who died 20 November 1870 at same place were granted at Belfast 7 December 1870 to Margaret Stewart of 4 Ventry Street, Belfast aforesaid, the sister and one of the next of kin of said deceased. Effects under £200.

Nancy Stewart (d.1854) was a resident of Union Street, Belfast.]

STEWART

[With foliage and scroll at top, now broken.] Sacred in memory of Horatio Agnew Stewart M.D., born 12th August 1820, died 15th May 1857. His sons: Horatio Robert Stewart, born 8th April 1845, died 29th Decr 1850, James Brenan Stewart, born 10th June 1846, died 4th July 1846, Alexander Brenan Stewart, born 31st July 1847, died in Florida in 1893, Horatio Robert Stewart, born 7th Sept 1854, died 9th Feby 1863. His daughter Elizabeth Stewart, born 14th March 1850, died 20th Feby 1899. And his widow Elizabeth Stewart, born 10th Novr 1810, died 30th April 1902.

[Probate of the will of Elizabeth Stewart of The Crescent, Ardglass, county Down, spinster, who died 20 February 1899, granted at Belfast 21 April 1899 to Edward O' R. Dickey of 29 Donegall Street, Belfast, solicitor, and Mary H. Armstrong of 22 Wellington Park, Belfast, widow. Effects £1,678 19s.3d. Re-sworn £1,779 3s.7d.

Probate of the will of Eliza Stewart of The Crescent, Ardglass, county

Down, who died 30 July 1902 granted at Belfast 8 October 1902 to Edward O'Rorke Dickey, solicitor. Effects £334 16s.1d.

Horatio Agnew Stewart was born on 12 August 1820, the son of the Rev. Robert Stewart, Presbyterian Minister of First Broughshane. He was educated at the Royal Belfast Academical Institution 1835-6 and at Glasgow University from 1836, graduating M.D. in 1841, also at Paris, Edinburgh and Dublin, taking the Diploma of the R.C.S.I. in 1840. He was attending surgeon at the Belfast General Hospital 1847-57 and professor of Materia Medica at Queen's College, Belfast 1849-57. He died at Rose Lodge.

See Addison: *Matriculation Albums of the University of Glasgow* (1913); Moody and Beckett: *Queens, Belfast* (1959); Allison: *The Seeds of Time* (1972).]

STEWART

[Two wide tablets in headstone, in enclosure that was formerly high-railed.] Sacred to the memory of William Stewart, died 15th July 1859 aged 67 years. Also his wife Sarah died 3rd Nov. 1864 aged 69 years. And of their children:

Anne, died 1st Decr 1828 aged 3 years.
James, died 17th Sept. 1839 aged 21 years.
George, died 5th June 1840 aged 18 years.
William, died 29th May 1847 aged 24 years.
Charles, died 21st April 1857 aged 21 years.
Samuel, died 6th April 1869 aged 35 years.
Ellen, died 11th July 1884 aged 52 years.
[Contd. on next tablet.]
George died 19th Augt 1890 aged 50 years.
John died 2nd Jany 1894 aged 66 years.
Anna died 10th Marh 1895 aged 66 years.

"Him that cometh to Me, I will in no wise cast out". John VI.37.

[Letters of administration of the personal estate of William Stewart of Belfast in the county of Antrim, merchant, who died 15 July 1859 at Silverstream in said county, were granted at Belfast 1 August 1859 to Sarah Stewart of Silverstream. Effects under £450.

Letters of administration of the personal estate of Sarah Stewart of Donegall Street, Belfast, widow, who died 3 November 1864 at Belfast aforesaid, were granted at Belfast 24 November 1864 to Ellen Stewart of Donegall Street aforesaid, spinster, the daughter, one of the next of kin of said deceased. Effects under £100.

William Stewart, senior, was a muslin manufacturer with premises in Church Street, Belfast and towards the end of his life he opened additional accommodation at 4, Lower Kent Street.]

STEWART

[Laid flat.] Erected by James Stewart, plumber, of Belfast, in memory of his beloved child Margaret Stewart who died 17th December 1835 aged 2 years and 4 months. Also his beloved wife Isabella Stewart who departed this life 21st January 1837 aged 25 years. "Blessed are the dead who die in the Lord". Died on the 5th of January 1843, Jane Stewart his second wife aged 28 years. Much respected. Also the above named James Stewart who died 30th December 1845 aged 41 years. Also his nice [sic], Mary BORLASE who departed this life 8th Decr 1852 aged 27 years. And her daughter Caroline Elizabeth aged 1 year.

[James Stewart was a plumber and a manufacturer of hydraulic engines and water closets of his own design. He had premises at 101, High Street, Belfast and he lived nearby at 5, Hanover Quay.]

STEWART

[Laid flat.] Erected by Margaret Stewart, to the memory of her beloved husband Hugh Stewart, of Belfast, who departed this life on the 25th of June 1836 aged 57 years. "Reader! prepare to meet thy God". Also his grandchild Stewart INNIS, who departed this life on the 19th of June 1837 aged 5 months. Also the above named Margaret Stewart who departed this life 13th February 1856 aged 77 years. Also her grand-daughter Mary Innis who departed this life 28th February 1856 aged 12 years. Also her son-in-law John Innis who departed this life 1st July 1856 aged 51 years. Maggie Innis died Feby 1858 aged 19 years. John Innis died 13th Augt 1881 aged 40 years. Margaret Innis died 13th April 1897 aged 89.

[Hugh Stewart was an inn-keeper at 95, High Street, Belfast.]

STEWART

[No longer extant. It has been copied from the Society's inscription book.] Erected by William Stewart to the memory of his beloved wife Priscilla who departed this life on the 12th July 18(37) aged (20) years. Also of his daughter Margaret Frances who departed this life 9th October 18(5)7 aged 2 years and 5 months. And his son William James who died in infancy. Also his daughter Rachael Stewart died (23rd Decr. 1853) aged 10 months. And William Stewart died 2nd November (1854) aged 53 years.

[William Stewart was a cashier in the Provincial Bank and lived at 16, North Queen Street, Belfast.]

STEWART

Sacred to the memory of Fanny the beloved wife of James Stewart, Librarian to the Belfast Library and Society for promoting Knowledge. She was a person of refined taste, high literary attainments and ardent piety. She departed this life on the 28th November 1840 aged 34 years. Henry James Stewart, born 9th of Nov. 1835, ob.14th Oct. 1859. "Jesus saith unto her, thy brother shall rise again". John XI.23. James Stewart, ob.9th of July 1868 AE 69. "There remaineth therefore a rest to the people of God." Heb.IV.9. Also in loving memory of David IRVING who departed this life Aug. 4th 1877 AE 55. "Why seek ye the living among the dead?"

[Letters of administration of the personal estate of James Stewart of Hibernia Place, Holywood, county Down, librarian, a widower, who died 9 July 1868 at Holywood aforesaid, were granted at Belfast 25 September 1868 to Elizabeth Ann Stewart of Camberwell Terrace, Belfast, county Antrim, spinster, the daughter and only next of kin of said deceased. Effects under £200.

The will of David Irving of 5 Richmond Crescent, Belfast, county Antrim, dealer in music, who died 4 August 1877 at same place, was proved at Belfast 10 October 1877 by the oath of Bessie Irving of 5 Richmond Crescent, Belfast, widow, one of the executors. Effects within the United Kingdom under £12,000.

James Stewart was born in Belfast in 1798/99 and was elected librarian of the Linen Hall Library on 6 October 1836. He was an energetic librarian for 31 years preparing some seven catalogues and acquiring some of its most valued possessions, the run of the *Belfast Newsletter* and the first 6-inch Ordnance Survey maps. He died at his home, 1 Hibernia Place, Holywood. See Killen: *History of the Linen Hall Library* (1990).]

STEWART
[Polished granite headstone in low-railed, low-stone enclosure against north wall.] Erected in memory of Alexander Stewart, of Ligoneil, who died 17th June 1848. Also his wife Anna Gage Stewart who died 1st October 1852. "And so shall we ever be with the Lord". 1.Thess.IV.17.

[Alexander Stewart (b.1775) seems to have started his career as a linen merchant at 12, Chichester Street in the 1810s. By the mid-1830s the firm by this time known as Alexander Stewart & Co. had offices in the White Linen Hall, and flax-spinning was added to its activities at Ligoniel.]

STEWART
[Polished granite in a low-railed enclosure.] The family burying ground of James Stewart, Upper Arthur Street. In memory of his wife Mary Stewart who died 13th July 1850 aged 46 years. And his mother Mary THOMPSON who died 20th May 1862 aged 82 years. Also his children, Isabella who died January 1863 aged 5 weeks, Eleanor who died 25th April 1863 aged 7 years, Mary who died 23rd January 1875 aged 14 years, Susan who died 20th May 1878 aged 23 years, James who died 10th October 1878 aged 21 years. Also the above James Stewart who died 13th October 1882 aged 73 years. Also his second wife Eleanor Stewart who died 12th November 1909 aged 84 years. Also his youngest son Frederick Charles Courtney Stewart who died 9th November 1918 aged 46 years.

[The will of James Stewart of Belfast, gentleman, who died 13 October 1882 at same place, was proved at Belfast 19 February 1883 by the Reverend Hugh Hanna of Belfast, Presbyterian clergyman, and Hugh Anderson and John Stewart, both of Coleraine, county Londonderry, merchants, the executors. Effects £19,557 1s.7d.]

[James Stewart, senior, ran the Theatre Tavern at 17, Castle Lane, Belfast, from the early 1830s until his second marriage in about 1854. Following his departure it became known as the Shakespeare Hotel and Tavern. Stewart then moved in to the house of his second wife Eleanor (nee Courtney), a milliner at 67, Upper Arthur Street.]

STEWART
[Small and very badly flaked slate, now lost.] Erected by Isabella Stewart, in (memory of) her husband James Stewart died (1)st June 1859.

[James Stewart (b.1812/13) was a night constable, employed by the Police Office which in the 1840s was located in Poultry Square (nowadays Victoria Square). Apart from keeping watch, one of their duties was to call out the hour, banging their staves on the ground as they did so. Stewart lived in Greenland Street, Belfast.]

STEWART

[Worn marble tablet in obelisk lying on the ground, now lost.] (Erected by) Chas Stewart (as a tribute of affection to the memory of his dear sister) Mary Ann who died (19) of Sept 18(59) aged (31) years. And (beloved daughter) Annie who died (1st) June 18(59) aged (3) years.

[According to the burial register Mary Ann was the wife and not the sister of Charles Stewart. Her address is given as Richmond Terrace, Great Victoria Street, Belfast.]

STEWART
See IRELAND

STEWART-WALLACE
See HODGENS

STILWELL
See CLOSE

STIRLING

[Headstone now missing from upper ground.] The grave of Isabella Stirling who died 8th July 1834, and of James Stirling her father who departed this life the 13th February 1856 aged 76 years. And also his wife Agnes Stirling who died 5th July 1862 aged 86 years.

[James Stirling, a native of Scotland, was a muslin manufacturer, with premises at 4, Commercial Court in the early 1830s; he lived nearby at 80, Donegall Street. Soon afterwards he went to live in Glengall Place, and he also moved his office to 6, York Street.]

STIRLING

[Oval tablet of c.1820-1840, on iron backing, now lying beside William Cochran's altar-tomb.] The burying place of James Stirling, merchant, Belfast.

[This stone is beside that of Isabella Stirling, above.]

STIRLING
See TOBIAS

STOCKMAN

[Broken slab in the ground.] Erected by Ralph Stockman jnr in memory of his beloved children: Mary Ann Hunter Stockman died 25th Feby 1835 aged 16 months, Hugh, died 24th July 1839 aged 8 years, Eloner [sic] died 4th Feby 1840 aged 4 years, Robert died 12th Feby 1843 aged 15 years. Sarah, the beloved wife of Ralph Stockman, departed this life 21st Dec 1852 aged 4(9) years. Eliza WIGHTMAN died 8th May 186(1) aged (5)1 years. James Wightman died (Jan)uary 1862 aged 36 years. The above Ralph Stockman died 22nd Nov. 1868 aged 70 years. Hugh Stockman who died at Holywood

2nd Sept 1872 aged (3)3 years, and is interred here.

[Letters of administration of the personal estate of Ralph Stockman of Nelson Street, Belfast, county Antrim, nail manufacturer, a widower, who died 22 November 1868 at Belfast aforesaid, were granted at Belfast 14 December 1868 to William John Stockman of Great Wellington Street, Bonnington, Edinburgh, Scotland, merchant, the son and one of the next of kin of said deceased. Effects under £450.

James Wightman was also a nail manufacturer at 7, Nelson Street.]

STRACHAN

[White limestone, laid flat.] Sacred to the memory of Charlotte Augusta, the beloved wife of James Strachan, Provincial Bank, Belfast, who departed this life 1st Octr 1858 aged 41 years. And their children: Helen Elizabeth, died 5th March 1850 aged 9 years, Ada Mary, 13th Feby 1850 aged 5 years, Henry Bremner, 17th Feby 1850 aged 3 years, and Louisa Nora, 12th May 1857 aged 3 years.

[James Strachan was the manager of the Belfast branch of the Provincial Bank of Ireland, and the family resided over the bank which was then at 36, Donegall Street.]

STUART

[Now lost.] Mary, relict of the late James Stuart Esq. LL.D., died on the 15th November 1853 aged 73. The remains of the late Dr. Stuart, the historian of Armagh, are deposited in this burial ground. A memorial to his memory has been erected in Christ Church, Belfast.

[James Stuart was born in Armagh in 1764, the son of James Stuart who was originally from county Antrim. He was educated at Armagh Royal School and entered Trinity College, Dublin in 1784, graduating B.A. in 1789. He was called to the Irish Bar but did not practice. He published a book of Poems on Various Subjects in 1811 and became first editor of the *Newry Telegraph* in 1812, also editing the *Newry Magazine* 1815-19. His great work, *Historical Memoirs of the City of Armagh* was published in 1819. He then moved to Belfast in 1821 and became editor of the *Belfast Newsletter*. He was subsequently editor of the *Belfast Guardian*. He also published in 1825 some theological letters entitled the *Protestant Layman* and for a short time in 1827 edited the *Guardian* and *Constitutional Advocate*. He died on 28 September 1840 and was buried here, but he is also commemorated by a memorial in Christ Church, Belfast.

See Coleman's edition of the *Historical Memoirs* (1900); Burtchaell and Sadleir: *Alumni Dublinenses* (1924); Ferrar: *Register of The Royal School, Armagh* (1933); Clarke: *Gravestone Inscriptions, Belfast*, Vol. 1, (1982); also Campbell: *Belfast Newspapers, Past and Present* (1921).]

STUART
See STEVEN

(SUFF)ERN

[Very badly weathered, now lost.] Erected by Catherine (Suf)fern in mem(ory of her mother) Mary (Ann Suff)ern who departed (this life 12) August (1844 aged 71). Also her (sister Mary Ann) who died 5th April 1847 aged 49 yrs. Her fa(ther Andrew Suffer)n (who died 1st July) 1849 (aged 80 years). Also (Catherine Suff)ern who died Novr 23d 1861 aged (49) years.

[Andrew Suffern was a carpenter and builder, living at 99, Sandy Row, Belfast.]

SUFFERN

[Polished granite obelisk with urn, now toppled, in low enclosure.] In memory of Mary Suffern died 26th June 1871 aged 41 years. Also her husband Robert Suffern died 12th Novr 1883 aged 54 years. Captn Edmund Suffern, born 1st January 1859 died 25th September 1938. Also his wife Martha died 16th November 1940.

[West face.] W.H. Suffern who was lost at sea, 1869 aged 19 years. Also Fred. Suffern who was lost at sea, 1884 aged 19 years. W.H. Suffern, died 1908 age 78. J.T. Suffern, died 1911 age 59.

[Martha Pauline Suffern of 9 Castleview Road, Belfast, widow, died 16 November 1940. Probate Belfast 16 December 1940 to Frank McKee, solicitor. Effects £73 19s.9d.

Robert Suffern was an accountant living at 46 Norwood Street, Belfast. Captain Edmund Suffern was in the merchant navy.]

SUFFERN
See HANNA

SWAN
See ASH

TAIT
See WILSON

TAYLOR
[Badly flaking slate headstone, formerly secured to south wall.] Jane Taylor, wife of William Taylor, cabinet-maker, was laid here 9th May 1811 aged 36.

TAYLOR
[Iron plaque laid flat.] The family burying ground of William Taylor, 1887.

TAYLOR
See MALCOMSON

TELFORD
[Missing.] The family burial ground of Thos. Telford, June 19, 1839.

[The family came from Edenderry, county Offaly. Thomas Telford lived at Merview, Belfast, and bought the ground for his son James.]

TEMPLETON
[Flaking near the top and in low-stone enclosure.] Sacred to the memory of John Templeton Esq., of Orange Grove, Malone, who died on the 15th Dec., 1825 aged 60 years. Also of Katharine his wife, daughter of the late Robert JOHNSTONE Esq., of Seymourhill, who died on the 28th Dec.

1868 aged 95 years, 9 mo.

[John Templeton was born at Bridge Street, Belfast in 1766, the son of James Templeton, merchant of Belfast and Mary Eleanor Legg of Malone. He was educated by David Manson and lived at the family home of Orange Grove, later known as Cranmore, Malone. The lovely old house was noted for its former owner John Eccles having entertained William III on his way from Carrickfergus to the Boyne in 1690. John Templeton established there a notable collection of trees and plants and devoted his life to the study generally. He was also prominent in the Belfast Society for Promoting Knowledge (Linen Hall Library), the Belfast Literary Society, the Belfast Natural History and Philosophical Society and the Belfast Academical Institution. He published little and appears to have given few talks to these societies but his manuscript material which is still extant was influential throughout the world. He married Katherine Johnston and had a son Robert, who was also a naturalist, and Deputy Inspector-General of Hospitals in Ceylon (died 1894).

See the *Dictionary of National Biography*; Benn: *History of the Town of Belfast*, Vol. 2 (1880); *Belfast Literary Society, Centenary Volume* (1902); Deane: *Belfast Natural History and Philosophical Society, Centenary Volume* (1924); Praeger: *Some Irish Naturalists* (1949); Killen: *A History of the Linen Hall Library* (1990); Wilson: *Fragments that Remain* (c.1950); McNeill: *The Life and Times of Mary Ann McCracken* (1960); also Chart (ed.): *The Drennan Letters* (1931).

TEMPLETON

[Tablet formerly in enclosure with stone to John Templeton but now lost.] In memory of Catharine Templeton who died 29th January 1875 aged 62. And of Matilda Templeton who died 8th June 1893 aged 81, daughters of John Templeton, of Cranmore, formerly called Orange Grove.

TENNENT

[Wall plot in upper ground, but no longer extant.] Sacred to the memory of Eliza Tennent. [This lot was purchased by William Tennent on 23rd February 1802.]

[William Tennent (1759-1832) was one of many children of the Rev. John Tennent of First Kilraughts Presbyterian Church near Dervock, county Antrim. That he was destined to become one of the most brilliant businessmen of Belfast of his time was evident from a very early age. He was a founder member of the Belfast Chamber of Commerce in 1783, spent many years on its Council, rising to be Vice-President. He was a partner of Tennent, Knox & Co., noted sugar-refiners, at the corner of Sugar-house Entry and Waring Street. He was one of the four founders in 1809 of the Belfast Commercial Bank and remained the senior partner until it merged with the Belfast Bank in 1827. In politics he was equally active, first as a Volunteer, then as a committee member of the Society of United Kingdom, as well as being a principal founder of the *Northern Star* newspaaper in 1791. Arrested shortly after the '98 Rebellion, he was imprisoned for the next four years at Fort George, Scotland. He was also a life-long supporter of both the Linenhall Library and the First Presbyterian Congregation in Rosemary Street. He died of cholera during the 1832 outbreak. His daughter Letitia married James Emerson Tennant the noted lawyer and politician. See Chambers: *Faces of Change* (1983); also Simpson: *The Belfast Bank 1827-1970* (1975).]

THIEL

[In surround and in low-stone enclosure.] Erected by Alicia Thiel in memory of her beloved husband John Ferdinand Thiel, of Brannsberg, Prussia, who died at Belfast, 2nd Oct. 1837. Also three of their children who died in infancy. Here also are interred the remains of the above Alicia Thiel who died at Stranraer, 18th Sept. 1862.

[John Thiel (b.1802/03) was a partner of J. F. Thiel & Heyn, flax and linen merchants at 19, Gordon Street, Belfast. He died at his house at 45, York Street.]

(THO)BURN

[Badly flaked and undated, but now lost. The plot was purchased by Joseph Thoburn in September 1803.] (In memory of) Joseph (Tho)burn.

THOMAS

[Badly weathered and flaking, now lost.] Erected by Henry Thomas, in memory of his wife Isabella who departed (this life) the (9)th of November 18(2)8 aged (..) years. (Also) two of his children who died in (infancy).

THOMAS

See MURPHY

THOMPSON

[Flaking.] Erected to the memory of Thomas Thompson who died 31st January 1816 aged 50 years. Also his daughter Sarah who died 29th June 1817 aged 15 years. Also his wife Margaret who died 28th April 1819 aged 58 years. Also his daughter Margaret who died 18th June 1820 aged 23 years. Also four children who died young. Also Joseph HINDS who departed this life the 11th March 1844 aged 50 years. Likewise Hannah Hind, relict of the late Joseph Hind, who departed this life the 9th December 1848 aged 57 years. And Peter CLARK, son-in-law to the above Joseph and Hannah Hind who departed this life July 18th 1852 aged 42 years. Also John Hind who died 21st Augst 1856 aged 24 years.

[Joseph Hinds was a commission agent and shipping agent with an office at 1, Chichester Quay. He lived at 24, Great George's Street, Belfast. Peter Clark was a master mariner at 31, Corporation Street.]

THOMPSON

[Fragments of tablet formerly secured to north wall in carved entablature and within the same low-stone enclosure as Thompson tablets, now lost.] Erected (in memo)ry (of) (William Thompson, of Donegall Square who died 15th June 1819 aged 55 years. Elizabeth his daughter who died 26th May (1835) aged 31 years. William his son, (who die)d in London 17th February 1852 aged 4 years. (Also Eli)zab(eth his re)lict, (who died in) Dublin (26th Sept)ember (1853 aged 84 years. Nathaniel, his so)n (who died) at Holywood (15th) February 1873 aged 61 (years).

[William Thompson was a linen merchant living at Donegall Square West, Belfast. William, junior, his eldest son was one of the most distinguished naturalists of Ireland. See Deane (ed.): *Belfast Natural History and Philosophical Society Centenary Volume, 1821-1921* (1924).

THOMPSON

[Broken and laid flat.] Erected by Eliza Thompson, of Belfast, to the memory of her beloved husband Robert Thompson who departed this life the 27th of December 1839 aged 58 years. And also two of their children who died young. Also the above named Eliza Thompson who died 14th February 1879 aged 81 years. And Eliza Thompson HAMILTON, her grand-daughter who died 8th May 1864 aged 3 years.

[Robert Thompson was a publican at 16, John Street, Belfast. John Street is nowadays represented by that section of Royal Avenue between North Street and Donegall Street.]

THOMPSON

[Slate laid flat.] Sacred to the memory of Jane, the beloved wife of Samuel Thompson, who departed this life January 24th 1840 aged 66 years. Also the above Samuel Thompson who departed this life 23rd August 1854 aged 88 years. Also Mary, the beloved daughter of the above Samuel Thompson, who departed this life on the 17th December 1857 aged 48 years.

THOMPSON

[Horizontal slab in the ground.] In memory of Henry Thompson Esq., late Captain, in the 66th Regiment. He died at Belfast, where he held the office of Barrack-Master, on the 9th day of Novr 1842 aged 59 years. This stone is erected by his attached and sorrowing family.

THOMPSON

[No longer extant.] Erected in memory of Elizabeth, daughter of Joseph and Mary Thompson, died 12th April 1843 aged 16 months.

THOMPSON

[White limestone broken up and lying loose, but recorded in Society's gravestone book.] Erected by Thomas Thompson M.D., Belfast, in memory of his beloved wife Anne WILLIAMS who died on the 29th of November 1862 aged 61 years. His son James McCalla, Barrister-at-Law, who died Aspringe, Kent, by Railway Accident, 2nd June 1862 aged 34. And William who died at Malta, 19th May 1862 aged 27. Also his daughter Annie Mulholland who died 12th January 1859 aged 16, and Emily Barton who died 25th January 1858 aged 18. And four children who died in infancy. Also in memory of his wife's mother Esther McCALLA who died 17th March 1848 aged 84.

[Dr Thomas Thompson was a naval doctor, in memory of whom the Thompson Memorial Fountain in Ormeau Avenue, Belfast was erected in 1885 by his sole surviving child, Eliza. He died at Harrogate on 27 May 1867 and was buried at Clifton Street, although the name is not on the stone. See Garner: *Robert Workman of Newtownbreda* (1969); also Brett: *Buildings of Belfast* (1967 and 1985).]

THOMPSON

[Tablet secured to east wall of upper graveyard in same low-stone enclosure as Jane Thompson's below.] In memory of Robert Thompson, Ardtulagh, Co. Down, died 19th April 1862 aged 53 years. His son Robert, died 9th Nov. 1861 aged 13 years. Emily, wife of the above named Robert Thompson, died 12th August 1888 aged 79 years. Also his son William, died 27th Nov. 1891 aged 52 years.

[The will of Emily Thompson otherwise Sinclair, late of Riverside, Holywood, county Down, widow, who died 12 August 1888 at same place, was proved at Belfast 12 November 1888 by Emily Thompson and Louisa Thompson both of Riverside, Holywood, spinsters, the executrixes. Effects £1,161 0s.6d.

Letters of administration of the personal estate of William Thompson, late of Riverside, Holywood, county Down, gentleman who died 27 November 1891, were granted at Belfast, 1 April 1892 to Emily Thompson of Riverside, spinster, a sister. Effects £261 2s.10d.]

Robert Thompson was a partner of Robert Thompson & Co., flax-spinners and linen manufacturers with offices at 1, Donegall Square West, Belfast. Originally a bleacher, he built the Wolfhill Mill in the late 1830s. He lived at Holywood most of his adult life. See also his father William Thompson, senior, above. See Beckett: *Belfast, The Making of the City* (1983)].

THOMPSON

[Undated polished red granite, looking of c.1880, in low-railed enclosure.] The family burying place of Fulton Thompson, R.H.A. Also his wife Maria Ravinscroft, who rest here with two of their family, Edward and Anne Jane. Erected in loving remembrance by their son Joseph Thompson. [The ground was bought by Fulton Thompson in July 1844.]

THOMPSON

[Tablet secured to east wall of upper graveyard in same low-stone enclosure as Robert Thompson.] In memory of Jane Thompson, daughter of William Thompson, who died in Dublin 29th June 1894 aged 83 years.

[The will, with one codicil, of Jane Thompson late of 16 Fitzwilliam Place, Dublin, spinster, who died 29 June 1894 was proved 20 August 1894 at the Principal Registry by James Thompson J.P. of Macedon, Whitehouse, near Belfast, and Francis Dwyer of Belvidere near Belfast, J.P., the executors. Effects £8,083 8s.6d.

Jane Thompson was a sister of William Thompson, the noted naturalist, and Robert, the builder of Wolfhill Mill (both q.v.).].

THOMPSON

See CORBITT, DYER, GRAHAM, LUKE and STEWART

THOMSON

[In broken entablature secured to dividing wall, now lost.] Erected by James Thomson LL.D., Professor of Mathematics, Belfast College, in memory of Margaret his wife who died May 1830 aged 4(0) years. And their daughter Margaret who died May 12th 1831 aged (4) years.

[James Thomson was born on 13 November 1786, the son of James Thomson, farmer of Annaghmore, near Ballynahinch, county Down. He was educated by his father and at an academy conducted by the Rev. Samuel Edgar. He entered Glasgow University in 1810 and graduated M.A. in 1812. He had intended to enter the Presbyterian ministry but in 1814 was appointed teacher of mathematics in the Belfast Academical Institution and in the following year was appointed Professor. In 1829 the University of Glasgow conferred on him the degree of LL.D. and in 1832 he was appointed Professor of Mathematics in that university. Over his life he published many works on mathematics as well as an *Atlas of Modern Geography*. He married in 1817 Margaret, daughter of William Gardner, and had 4 sons and 4 daughters. She died before he moved to Glasgow. His son James was Professor of Engineering at Queen's College, Belfast, 1857-73 and at Glasgow, 1873 until his death in 1892. Another son William later became Professor of Natural Philosophy at Glasgow and was ennobled as Lord Kelvin. His statue is in the Botanic Gardens, Belfast. See *Dictionary of National Biography*; Fisher and Robb: *Royal Belfast Academical Institution, Centenary Volume* (1913); also Deane (ed.): *Belfast Natural History and Philosophical Society Centenary Volume, 1821-1921* (1924)].

THOMSON

[Broken and laid flat.] Erected by James Thomson to the memory of his daughter Mary Ann Thomson who departed this life 17th January 1844 aged 6 years.

In the soft season of her youth
In natur's smiling bloom,
Ere age arived with trembling steps,
She was hurryed to the tomb. [sic]

Also Mary Ann died August 14th 1848 aged 2 years, 6 months. Sarah died August 17th 1848 aged 9 months. James died June 16th 1851 aged 1 year 11 months. Also his daughter Elizabeth, wife of Thomas COPLAND, who departed this life 8th July 1863 aged 21 years. And two of their children who died in infancy. Also his son-in-law Aniel PRITCHARD, who departed this life on the 8th October 1867 aged 24 years.

[James Thomson lived at 42, Hill Street, Belfast and was a spirit grocer. The Copeland family lived at Ballynafeigh.]

THOMSON

[In surround against north wall, badly broken.] Erected by Thomas Thomson in memory of his infant daughter Agnes who died on the 25th January 1861 aged 4 months.

[He was a partner of McClinton & Thompson, chandlers at 53, Academy Street, Belfast, and lived at 4, Lonsdale Street, off Crumlin Road.]

THOMSON

[Beside William Byrtt's grave and no longer extant — copied from Society's burial book.]

The burying place of Samuel Thomson, merchant, Belfast. Sacred to the memory of Sophia BELLANY, his beloved wife departed this life 4th June

1866 aged 70 years. Also Elizabeth Agnes, their eldest daughter, wife of William H. ALLEY, died 28th Feby 1869 aged 41 years. Also above-named Samuel Thomson who died 7th November 1873 aged 76 years.

[The will, with two codicils, of Samuel Thomson of No. 14 University Square, Belfast, gentleman, who died 7 November 1873 was proved at Belfast 3 December 1873 by the oath of Richard Lewis Thomson of No. 14 University Square, Belfast, merchant, one of the executors. Effects under £10,000.

[Samuel Thomson was a merchant, and one of the directors of the Belfast branch of the Provincial Bank, then located at 1, Corporation Street, Belfast.]

THOMSON
[Undated block in low-stone enclosure, looks of c.1900, now lost.] Thomson.

THOMSON
See BRISTOW, BYRTT and SLOAN

TILLEY
[Broken tablet with carved surround in a high-railed enclosure with a large tree growing in front of it.] (Erected by) James Tilley to the memory of his mother Margaret Anne Tilley who departed this life 13th July 1827 aged 3(0) years. Here also rest the remains of Sarah EWART his grandmother who died 12th May 1835 aged 72 years. William Wallen & James, two of his sons who died in infancy. And of William Ewart his grandfather who died 22nd Nov. 1851 aged 93 years. Sacred also to the memory of his father Hugh Tilley who died at Philadelphia, U.S. 1st March 1860 aged 71 years.

[William Ewart was born in Hillsborough, County Down and his family's biography has been covered under EWART].

TISDALL
[Small and badly flaked headstone — looks of c.1800, now lost.] Hunter Tisdal(l) .... (died) 11th March (1806 aged .. years.)

[John Tisdall bought the ground in November 1800.]

TITTLE
[Worn marble formerly in enclosure with William Blackwell's stone.] Erected by his loving mother & sister (..)th June 187(6) to the memory of John Moore Tittle, eldest son of James H. V. Tittle, solicitor, born 31st December 18(58), died 10th December 18(62). "Suffer little children to come unto me and forbid them not, for of such is the Kingdom of Heaven." Matt XIX.11.

[James Tittle was a solicitor at 19, Arthur Street, Belfast (later he moved to 53, Upper Arthur Street) and a branch at 107, Capel Street, Dublin.]

TOBIAS
[Twin slate tablets of which one is uninscribed, in neo-Egyptian entablature, from which capstone has fallen, in high-railed enclosure.] The Revd Matthew Tobias, Wesleyan Minister, who departed this life, 13th June 1845 aged 75 years. Also his daughter Jane who died in infancy.

Here also lie the remains of his wife Jane STIRLING who survived him nearly seven years and died on Wednesday the 28th April 1852 aged 82 years.

[The Rev. Matthew Tobias was born in Charlemont, county Armagh in 1770 and was admitted for trial as a Methodist minister in 1791 at Charlemont. He was a minister all over Ireland: in Waterford in 1800, in Dublin in 1810 in Bandon in 1823 and in Belfast from 1829. His son the Rev. James Tobias was admitted as a minister in 1829 and married a Miss Rowe, daughter of Moses Rowe of Wexford. When he was in Belfast he lived in College Street South; his widow subsequently moved to Waring Street. See Gallagher: *Pioneer Preachers of Irish Methodism* (1965); Crookshank: *History of Methodism in Ireland* (1858-8).]

TOLEN
See CRAWFORD

TOMKINS
[In upper ground and no longer extant.] Erected by Mary Tomkins in memory of her husband George Tomkins who departed this life the 23rd November 1808 aged 37 years.

TORBETT
See DAVISON

TORNEY
[Very corroded and undated iron shield looking of c.1850, now lost.] The burying place of James Torney, mariner, Belfast.

[The plot was bought by James Torney in August 1849.]

TOYE
See SHAW

TRAIL
See KENNEDY

TRIPP
[Rough granite cross broken off plinth.] I.H.S. In memory of our loving and beloved mother Kate S. Tripp, 25th April 1926. Dorcas D. Tripp, 30th December 1937. Anna C. Tripp, 2nd December 1945. Florence S. Tripp died 21st Feb. 1952 aged 84.

[Plate in ground, now separated from the above.] The family burying place of Thomas Tripp, 1844.

[Thomas Tripp was a distiller, whose stores were at 4, Chapel Lane, Belfast in the 1830s. He built the Brookfield Distillery, the firm being known as Thomas Tripp & Co. For many years he lived at Brookfield, Shankill Road.]

TROTTER
[Marble tablet in surround, formerly secured to north wall now removed.] In memory of John William son of Robt Trotter, banker, Belfast, and his wife Catherine Gordon FOWLER. He died 7th Jany 1858 aged 19 years.

Take Comfort, Christians, when your friends
in Jesus fall asleep,
Their better being never ends,
Why then dejected weep?

Why inconsolable as those
in whom no hope is given?
Death is the messenger of peace,
And calls the soul to heav'n,

As Jesus died and rose again,
Victorious from the dead,
So his disciples rise and reign,
With their triumphant Head.

[In the early 1850s Robert Trotter was the manager of the Belfast branch of the Provincial Bank of Ireland, then at 36 Donegall Street. He was succeeded by James Strachan (q.v.). His son John William was born at Worcester, England.]

TROWSDALE

[Large horizontal marble slab in Yeates family enclosure, of which the tablets have now crumbled and only the inscription on the capstone remains.]

Erected by their sorrowing children in affectionate remembrance of their beloved mother Jessie Trowsdale who died at Newcastle, Co. Down, 17th March 1868 aged 60 years. Also their beloved father William Trowsdale who died at Newcastle, Co. Down, 13th May 1876 aged 66 years. Also their uncle Thomas SCOTT who died 14th June 1869 aged 60 years.

[William Trowsdale is described in the burial register as a retired Custom House Officer.]

TROWSDALE
See SCOTT

TUKER
See KEAN

TURNER

[In the "Cholera Ground".] Sacred to the memory of John Turner, son of Ben Turner, late Superviser of Excise, Belfast, who departed this life 10th Octr 1831 aged 12 years. Also his son William Turner who died 22nd Augt 1832 aged 11 years.

[In 1831, the Turner family lived in Gloucester Street, Belfast.]

TURNLY

[Small tablet in the manner of a Roman tomb, and with a weeping robed figure carved in relief, secured to east wall, in high-railed enclosure with Rev. William Batt's.] "Blessed are the dead which die in the Lord". Sacred to the memory of Alexander Turnly Esq., who died on the 22nd Sept. 1850 aged 75. This tablet is erected by his affectionate children.

[Alexander Turnly (b.1774/75), was the youngest son of Francis Turnly (d.1802) (see BATT), noted brewer and property owner. He was born at Newtownards and died at his home at 1, Chichester Street, Belfast in 1850. His sister was married to the Rev. William Batt (q.v.). See Benn: *History of Town of Belfast*, Vol. II, (1880); also Clarke: *Gravestone Inscriptions, Belfast*, Vol. III (1986).]

TURNLY
See BATT

VANCE
[Top broken off.] Erected by William Vance, to the memory of his son George who perished on the evening of the 26th January 1828 aged 13 years.

> Oh! hapless youth! how sudden was thy doom!
> That dawning morn, how lightly didst thou tread
> And little thought that in a watery tomb
> At day's decline thou shouldst repost thy head.

> But now thy happy spirit dwells on high,
> And guardian Angel pointed out the way,
> Thu'll rise at last when Time itself shall die,
> And live with God thro' never ending day.

VANCE
[Worn marble in large headstone, now lost.] Erected by (Gilb)ert Vance in memory of his beloved wife Margaret who died 10th April 1854 aged (40) years. Also their daughter Maria Jane who died 1(9)th Jany 1841 aged 3 years.

[Gilbert Vance lived at 40, Rosemary Street, Belfast, which was the premises of John R. Vance & Son, muslin manufacturers and merchants. Their weaving factory was next door at No. 38.]

VANCE
[Formerly large pedimented monument with centre tablet in arched recess and two slate tablets on each side. Now all laid flat in the ground.] Erected by William Vance in memory of his four children who died in infancy.

[Left-hand tablet.] William Vance died 8th October 1855 aged 56 years. Jane Martin, his wife died 9th March 1860 aged 57 years.

[Right-hand tablet.] Also their daughter Jane Martin Vance died 5th January 1911. Also Annie Vance, born May 1836, died Jan. 1925.

[The will of Jane Vance of Upper Crescent, Malone Road, Belfast, county Antrim, widow, who died 9 March 1860 was proved at Belfast 18 June 1860 by the oaths of Samuel Martin of Shrigley near Killyleagh, county Down, and William Gamble of Corporation Street, Belfast, merchants, the executors. Effects under £600.

William Vance of 63, Great George Street, Belfast, was a starch manufacturer and his will was proved in 1856. See P.R.O.N.I. *Connor Will Index*.]

VEACOCK
See WARD

VINT

[Worn marble tablet formerly in entablature bearing carving of urn, now lost.] Erected by James A. Vint in memory of his father William Vint who died 3d May 1848 aged 51 years. And his mother Elizabeth Vint who died 4th November 1845 aged 50 years. Also his brother William who died 9th April 1854 aged 33 years. And his sisters: Ann who died 14th April 184(3) aged 1(3) years, Elizabeth who died (.1)st July 184(7) aged 24 years, (Sarah Jane who) died 2(7)th March 1848 aged (17) years. The above James A. Vint died on the 8th July 186(3) aged 3(5) years.

[The will of James Atkinson Vint of Armagh, county Armagh, esquire, who died 8 July 1863 was proved at Armagh 5 August 1863 by the oath of John Vint and George Vint, gentlemen, and Sarah Atkinson, spinster, all of Belfast, county Antrim, the executors. Effects under £1,500.]

William Vint, senior, owned the Cross Keys Inn at 104, North Street, Belfast which was a depot for the carriers and conveyance of parcels and letters to and from much of the north of the country including counties Antrim, Louth, Monaghan, Cavan, Londonderry and Tyrone. The premises were located at the corner with 88 Hercules Street which was the stabling accommodation.]

VINT
See KITCHIN

VIRGIN

[Large stone, now lost — copied from Society's gravestone book.] Sacred to the memory of Nicholas Virgin, Belfast, who departed this life 7th September 1874 aged (5)4 years.

[The will of Nicholas Virgin late of 2 and 4 Great Edward Street, Belfast, publican, who died 7 September 1874, was proved at Belfast 6 November 1874 by the oaths of James Frazer of Great Edward Street, provision merchant, and James Wilson jnr of Skipper Street, wine merchant, both in Belfast, executors. Effects under £1,500.

Nicholas Virgin owned the "Ulster Tavern" at Nos. 2 and 4, Great Edward Street, Belfast, which thoroughfare is nowadays that portion of Victoria Street which runs from Chichester Street to Cromac Street.]

WALKER
[Iron shield.] The family burying ground of David Walker, Belfast, 18(3)4.

WALKER
[Small undated tablet of c.1910, now lost.] The burying ground of W. Walker.

WALKER
See DICKSON

WALKINGSHAW
See CAMERON

WALLACE
[Large pedimented monument, against north wall and in enclosure, for-

merly high-railed, now removed.] Erected by (Mary Wallace) as a tribute of affectionate regard to the memory, of her departed father Robert Wallace who died on the 8th of May 1831 aged 90 years. Also of her brothers, Thomas Wallace who died on the 9th of July 1833 aged 45 years, and James Wallace, who died on the 18th of October 1834 aged 55 years.

[Robert Wallace was born in Stranraer, Scotland and, at the time of his death, was domiciled in Rosemary Street, Belfast. He was a retired merchant.]

WALLACE
See HODGENS and MOORE

WALSH
[Cast-iron tablet in a low-railed enclosure.] The family burying ground of Thomas Walsh, Belfast, 1817.

WALSH
See MOORE

WARD
[Twin slate tablets in entablature secured to north wall in low-railed enclosure. The first is now broken and loose.] Sacred to the memory of Marcus Ward who died in 1801, and Mary SHANKS, his wife who died Nov. 1809. Here also rest the remains of their eldest son John Ward, of Jackson Hall, Co. Down, who died Dec. 6, 1830 aged 60. And Margaret Fowler DAVIS his wife who died Aug. 14, 1832 aged 50. Here also lie four children of the said John Ward, namely: James Barrington who died in 1823 aged 11, Francis Davis who died April 14 1841 aged 36, Marcus who died June 22, 1847, as the adjoining stone shows, and Elizabeth who died June 21, 1851 aged 47. Sacred also to the memory of Ellen VEACOCK, widow of Marcus Ward, who surviving him nearly 48 years, died April 23, 1895 aged 84. "Till the day dawn".

Sacred to the memory of Marcus Ward who died suddenly on 22nd June 1847 aged 40. Here also lie the earthly remains of his first wife Catherine HYNDMAN, who died July 30, 1830 aged 22. And five of his children who died in infancy. Also his youngest beloved child, Ellen Veacock Ward who was early taken to her Saviour on 21st July 1849 aged 2 years and 2 months. Also his beloved child Robert Fowler Ward who died May 8, 1858 aged 12 years and 9 months. Erected by the sorrowing widow of the above named Marcus Ward. Here also are interred three grandchildren of Marcus and Ellen Ward: William Augustus Ward CARROLL, died Nov. 25, 1870 aged 2, Ellen Veacock Ward Carroll, died Nov. 29, 1870 aged 11 and Letitia Bowman Carroll, died Dec. 1, 1870 aged 9. The darling of Benjamin and Letitia Carroll. "He shall gather the lambs with His arm".

[John Ward (1769/70-1830) of Jackson Hall, county Down, was son of Marcus Ward and Mary Shanks. He was one of the early papermakers of Belfast, a partner in the firm of Blow, Ward, Greenfield & Co., who started on his own account in Ann Street in 1824. He married Margaret Fowler

Davis and his son Marcus Ward (1807-47) added a printing business in 1833 and moved to 6 Corn Market in 1841. It was managed after his death by his three sons, Francis Davis Ward, John Ward (1832-1912), artist and Egyptologist and William Ward. After moving to Donegall Place and finally to large purpose-built works on the Dublin Road, it expanded with some fine chromolithography to be one of the largest publishing firms in the United Kingdom, handling all Vere Foster's educational material in the 1860s. However it broke up in the last quarter of the century as a result of a bitter lawsuit and was finally dissolved in 1901. See Deane (ed.): *Belfast Natural History and Philosophical Society, Centenary Volume* (1924); Gracey: The decline and fall of Marcus Ward. *Irish Booklore*, 1971, 1, 186-202; McNeill: *Vere Foster* (1971).]

WARD

[Large slate now lying flat.] Capt Ward of the Waterford Regt, three beloved children died of the hooping cough in Belfast Jany 1804, Henrietta, 6 years old, Edward 3, Mary Ann 2.

Each opening sweet of early bloom,
Shall blush upon this infant tomb
Where in three lovely babbies lye [sic]
Who can refuse a tear and sigh.

The redbreast oft at evening hours
Shall scatter moss & sweetest flowers
And kindly lend his little aid
To deck the ground where they are layd.

The parents feel afflictions deepest load
The Christians yield their children up to God,
Secure to meet again in bliss above,
And join their Angles [sic] in the realms of love.

WARD

See CAMPBELL

WARDLOW

[Polished red granite headstone, topped by a draped urn, in a low-railed enclosure.] Erected by Sara ROGERS in loving remembrance of her uncle Hugh Wardlow who died 3rd June 1880 aged 61 years. Helena McCUNE, his sister died 7th June 1837 aged 33 years. James Wardlow, their brother died 18th May 1844 aged 28 years. Sara Wardlow their mother died 25th May 1867 aged 86 years.

A few short years of evil past,
We reach that happy shore,
Where death-divided friends at last,
Shall meet to part no more.

[In the 1840s James and Hugh Wardlow & Co. were timber merchants at 5, Great George's Street, Belfast. After his death Hugh continued as a merchant at 11, Henry Street, becoming a ship-owner as well. James was born at Bangor, county Down.]

WARE
[Corroded iron shield laid flat.] The family burying ground of William Ware, New York, 1856.

WARNICK
See CAUGHEY

WARNOCK
See McKIBBIN

WATERMAN
[Stone in lower ground, now missing. It seems to have been in poor condition even in 1907. The plot was bought by William Waterman in October 1852.] Sacred to the memory of Margaret Waterman wife of William .... Waterman (who departed this life) 8th October (1852) aged 32 years.

[William Waterman was a soldier of the 46th Regiment.]

WATERSON
[Very worn white limestone headstone with indecipherable arms, crest and motto at top.] In memory of William Thomas Waterson, of Belfast, solicitor, who departed this (life 4th Se)pt 186(4) aged (54) years. ("Blessed are the pure in heart) for they) shall see God".

[The will of William Thomas Waterson, late of Saville Lodge, Sydenham, Belfast, county Antrim, who died 4 September 1864 was proved at the Principal Registry 10 January 1865 by the oath of Arabella Greer of Seville Lodge, spinster, the sole executrix. (By decree). Effects under £2,615.

This firm of family solicitors appears to have been started by Henry Waterson in about 1815 at 128 (renumbered 132), Ann Street, Belfast where it was to remain until it went out of existence half a century later. By 1831 his son William Thomas had joined and two or three years later a branch was opened in Marlborough Street, Dublin (later moved to Gt. Brunswick Street). By about 1840 Henry had become Master Extraordinary in Chancery and a Commissioner for Oaths. Following his death in about 1850 William Thomas continued the firm until his own death in 1864.]

WATT
See RITCHIE

W(AUGH)
[Carved sandstone, completely eroded down the middle.] In (memory of) John W(augh) who died (12th January) 1850, Mary Ann (Jenkins his) wife died (8th Sepr 1862). Char(lott)e his mother) died (.. March 1825) Robert (his eldest son) junior di..... of the general as...... (Decr) 18(52), and four of (his children) who died (in infancy.

[John Waugh was a baker at 11, North Queen Street, Belfast, having moved from North Street in about 1830.]

W(EBSTER)
[Badly flaked headstone, now lost.] H(ere) lieth the (body of) JNo Henery W(ebster) who departed this (life) 3d April 1819 aged 2(. years).

WEIR

[Headstone belonging to upper ground, but has largely disappeared since it was copied by E. W. Pim in 1907.] Erected to the memory of Matthew Weir who departed this life 19th of June 1820 aged 41 years. And Eleanor Weir his wife who departed this life 17th Aug. .... aged 33 years. Also John Weir, son to Matthew Weir of Belfast who departed this life 11... 1812 aged 2 years. And Eleanor Weir who died 9th of February 1816 aged 2 years and 4 months. And also M. Ann Weir who died 14th of June 1816 aged 6 months.

WEIR

[Headstone smashed into seven fragments.] Erected by George Weir, of Belfast, in memory of his son George Weir who departed this life the (1)3th day of June 1824 aged 15 years. Also his wife Margaret Weir who departed this life the 3rd day of December 1833 aged 65 years. Also the above named George Weir who departed this life 27th of May 1837 aged 66 years. Also William Weir who departed this life 1st September 1863 aged 64 years. Also Margaret MAGUIRE, daughter of the above named George Weir, who departed this life 18th Dec. 1880 aged 76 years. Also her brother Daniel Weir who departed this life 10th Jan. 1881 aged 78 years. Also Harriet, beloved wife of Daniel Weir, who departed this life 27th Oct. 1890 aged 79 years.

[The will of Harriette Isabella Weir of Warrenpoint, county Down, spinster, who died 20 October 1890 was proved at Belfast 21 November 1890 by John Marshall, sub-land commissioner, the sole executor. Effects £314.

[George Weir was a dealer in flour and oatmeal at 154, North Street, Belfast. William Weir was a weaver at Lisburn, Co. Antrim and his brother Daniel was a tailor at 7, Frazer Street, Newtownards Road, Belfast.]

WEIR

[Marble tablet in surround that is believed to have formerly been a fireplace in an old house where Queen's University now stands. It was secured to east wall and in high-railed enclosure, all now removed.] Sacred to the memory of Thomas Weir, born 28th Dec. 1813, died 30th Aug. 1867. Also Bessy Weir, his daughter, born 17th July 1842, died 22nd May 1852. Harriet, his wife born 11th Feb. 1814, died at Brussels, 19th Feb. 1891. "The mercy of the Lord is from everlasting to everlasting, on them that fear him, and his righteousness unto children's children". Psalm 103 c.,17v.

[Letters of administration of the personal estate of Thomas Weir of Lisnabreeny, Castlereagh, county Down, merchant, who died 30 August 1867 at Troon in Ayrshire, Scotland, were granted at Belfast 10 March 1868 to Harriett Weir of Lisnabreeny, Belfast, the widow of said deceased. Effects under £600.]

Thomas Weir went into partnership with Henry Smith in about 1850, as Smith, Weir & Co., linen manufacturers, bleachers and merchants, with offices at 11, Donegall Place, Belfast. Within ten years the partnership seems to have broken up and the offices were occupied by William

Memorial to Thomas Weir, linen manufacturer (1813-1867). The surround is believed to have been a fireplace in the old house where Queen's University now stands (photograph R.W.M. Strain).

WELDON

[Polished granite, broken in two.] In affectionate memory of Francis Weldon who died 21st Feb. 1851 AE 43. And of his wife Charlotte MUSSEN who died 16th June 1860 AE 51.

[Francis Weldon was a writing clerk and lived in Mill Street, Belfast.]

(W)ELLS

[Badly flaked stone, now lost.] To (the mem)ory of Edw(ard) (W)ells, late (Cap)tain (in the 54)th Regiment who dep(arted this life) on (the 27th July 1853) aged (69 years). Also El(eanor) his wife who (died on the 30th) of August (1857 aged 76 years.)

[Capt. Wells lived at 3, Ingram Place, Donegall Pass, Belfast.]

WELSH

[Iron shield, now lost.] The family burying ground of Thomas Welsh, Belfast, 1817.

WETHERED

See DOBBIN

WHINNERY

[Marble tablet formerly secured to the north wall and now lost.] Sacred to the (memory) of Thomas Whinnery Esq. Postmaster of this town for 36 years died 28th February 1830 aged 70. He was the steady friend of every religious and Charitable Institution. He was Elder of the Secession Church for forty years the duties of which he discharged with ....

[He sat on the General Board of the Belfast Charitable Society and was its Secretary in 1800. See Strain: *Belfast and its Charitable Society* (1961).

Thomas Whinnery is credited with being the first Postmaster of Belfast. He ran the town's only Post Office in his house at 6, Church Street from 1794 in which year that thoroughfare was created, connecting that part of Donegall Street with North Street. As well as receiving the mails from all over the north of Ireland, Dublin, Scotland and the North of England, he was the agent for the London newspapers. After his death, the Post Office continued at the same address for a few years until his successor James Dickey (q.v.) moved the concern to 65 Donegall Street.]

WHITAKER

[Polished granite.] The family burying ground of Joseph Whitaker, 1845.

WHITE

[Stone in upper portion of graveyard, now missing, and therefore copied from Society's records.] Erected by John White in memory of his wife Margaret who departed this life the 2nd July ..... aged 23 years. Also his son John who died the 9th May 1809 aged 3 weeks. And also Mary JOHNSTON, mother of the above Margaret, who departed this life 19th August 1813 aged 73 years.

WHITE

[Very worn and mostly copied from Society's records.] Erected (by) Thomas B. White, (of Belfast) in memory of his mother Hannah White (who died June 10th 1814 aged 48 years. Also Sarah, daughter of the above named Thomas B. White who met with her death by poison through the mistake of a servant, on 3rd May 1830 aged 2 years & 3 months.

[There are six lines of poetry below, but they are impossible to read.]

WHITE

[Small memorial, now missing.] Family burying ground of Thomas White, Belfast, 18(34).

WHITE

Erected in memory of William White, late of Belfast, ironmonger, who died 17th November 1835 aged 46 years.

[William White was an ironmonger and hardware merchant at 6, Bridge Street, Belfast.]

WHITE

[Completely smashed marble in large headstone, of which only two pieces remain — largely copied from gravestone record book.] (In memory of Isabella, the beloved wife of Hugh White who died 17th Octr 1868 aged 28 years. Also his father Nathaniel White) aged 78 years. His sister Mary (aged 25 years). His sister Matilda, (aged 17 years. And) his brother James Snod(dy White) aged 10 years.

[Hugh White was a partner of Neill & White, wholesale wine and spirit merchants at 7 & 9, Winecellar Entry, Belfast. He lived at Mountview, 53, Crumlin Road. This is a typical example of the by now growing trend to live in salubrious districts some distance from one's place of work.]

WHITE

[Very badly flaked stone, now lost.] In memory of Edwin A(lexander) White (son) of Alexa(nder and Justina) Wh(ite), Bandmaster (Royal Antrim Rifles) who died at Belf(ast), 28th Oct 1868 aged 5(yrs & 7 months). "Suffer little (children to) come unto me".

O Father, I have (prayed for strength)
For summer (tide of joy) That longest H(ours and sunny days) I might for (thee employ.
An) lo! t'was (but so weak and faint
And early (winter came)
It) is Thy will, (Thy will) be done
And blessed be thy name.

[The family lived at 17, Comber Place, Belfast.]

WHITE

See MACLURCAN

WHITMORE

See JAMES

WHITTLE
[Very badly flaked headstone, now lost — mostly copied from Society's record book.] (In memory of James Whittle who) departed (this life the 5th of) Feby 1820 (aged 40 yea)rs. (This stone is erec)ted by (Quarter Master WIL)LIAMS, (43 Regt., Lt., Infy., as) a mark of (esteem for his) faithful (services).

WIGHTMAN
See STOCKMAN

WILKINS
See GRATTAN

WILKINSON
[Iron plaque laid flat.] The family burying ground of John Wilkinson, Belfast, 1841.

[John Wilkinson bought this plot in May 1841 for his daughter Margaret.]

WILLIAMS
[Loose slate with top corner missing.] Sacred to the memory of Samuel Williams of Belfast, who departed this life on (the) 31st day of October 18(37) aged 38 years. And Sarah Williams his wife who departed this life on the 28th day of February 1858 aged 60 years. Also five of their children who died in infancy. This monument is erected by the surviving children to commemorate the virtues of their parents, who in the fear of God, and realizing the importance of the trust committed to them, endeavoured to bring up their family in the nurture and admonition of the Lord.

WILLIAMS
See THOMPSON and WHITTLE

WILLIAMSON
[Large flaking headstone, broken in two and lying flat.] Sa(cred) to the (memory of) James W(illiam)son, Jam(es P)lace, Belfast, who died May 11th (1832 aged 76 years.) Also to his sister-in-law Mary SCOTT aged 7(3) years. Also Barbara Williamson, relict of (the) above James Williamson, died 13th March 1840 aged 74 years. Lendrick Williamson (died) August 22nd 1840 aged (38 years).

[James Williamson was a land surveyor and lived at 5, James Place, Belfast.]

WILLIAMSON
See McCARTER

WILLIS
[Large monument, now lost, but recorded in Society's gravestone book.] In memory of John Hind Willis, aged (1)7 years, died .... 18(3)7. Also his (father) John Willis .... aged 61 years. And of Jane, wife of the above John Willis who departed this life 6th Jan. 1870 in the 70th year of her age.

[John Willis, senior, was a professor of Music and in the 1830s and 1840s was organist of St. Anne's Parish Church. He lived at 32, King Street, Belfast and later moved to 4, College Street South.]

WILSON

[South slate tablet on pedestal bearing urn-topped pillar (now broken) in a high-railed enclosure.] Sacred to the memory of Hugh Wilson, jun., who died 9 March 1801 aged 11 years, being the son of the late Hugh Wilson of Belfast, merchant.

[West tablet.] Sacred to the memory of Hugh Wilson, of Belfast, merchant, who died 27 Dec. 1822 aged 75 years. And also to the memory of Jane his wife who died 12 Aug. 1823 aged 72 years.

[North tablet.] Sacred to the memory of Jane Wilson who died 19 Dec. 1823 aged 27 years, being the daughter of the late Hugh Wilson, of Belfast, merchant.

[East tablet.] This monument was erected by the surviving family as a memorial to the revered memories of their departed parents & brother & sister, A.D. 1823.

[Hugh Wilson & Sons were merchants at 2, Corporation Street, Belfast. Hugh Wilson was a member of the committee of the Belfast Charitable Society in the first two decades of the nineteenth century.]

WILSON

[Undated polished granite triangular-topped block, looking of c.1850-1890, over a low vault, against the dividing wall.] The family vault of William Wilson, of Belfast.

[This plot was bought by William Wilson in April 1830. William Wilson was a merchant at 2 Corporation Street, Belfast. He lived at 11, Wellington Place.]

WILSON

[Flaking.] Erected by Thomas Wilson, surgeon, of Belfast, in memory of his dearly beloved child Margaret Eliza who departed this life 2nd July 18(3)4 aged 13 months.

[Surgeon Thomas Wilson lived at 13, Arthur Street, Belfast.]

WILSON

[Weathered headstone, now lying flat.] Erected by Arthur Wilson in memory of his beloved mother Eleanor Wilson who departed (this life 9th) Sept. 1851 aged (5)8 years. Also (his grandson) Joseph LEMON, who died in infancy.

"The L(ord gave and) the Lord hath (taken away). Blessed be the name of the Lord". Also (Eleanor Lemon) who died 7th (Oct. 1834) aged 24 years. Also (Joseph Wilson) who died 4th March .... aged 62 years.

[The Wilson family lived at 4 Henry Place, Belfast, very near the New Burying Ground.]

WILSON

[Flaking and hard to identify.] Erected by Robert Wilson, shipmaster, Belfast, in memory of his daughter Sarah who departed this life 21st Nov. 1835 aged 5 years & 2 months. Also the above named Robert Wilson who departed this life 28th Jany 1856 aged 57 years.

WILSON

[Large and broken headstone, now lost, copied from the Society's records.]

(Erected by Elizabeth Wilson in memory of her beloved son, James Wilson, surgeon, of Belfast, who departed this life January 27th 1847) aged (28) years. Also the above Elizabeth Wilson who departed this life January 18(61) aged (70) years.

[Surgeon James Wilson lived in Great Patrick Street, Belfast.]

WILSON

[Large headstone, with top broken off.] (Erected by Margaret Wilson) to the memory of her beloved husband James Arbuckle Wilson who departed this life 8th April 1847 aged 63 years. Also her beloved mother Jane TAIT who departed this life 29th October 1845 aged 78 years.

[James A. Wilson was born in Greenock, Scotland. He appears to have arrived in Belfast during the 1810s and opened his first cabinet-making and upholstery works at 1, York Street. At the time of his death he was at 7, Ann Street.]

WILSON

[Broken headstone, now lost.] Erected by R. Wilson in memory of her beloved husband James Wilson who died 26th March 1852 aged 26 years. Also the above Rebecca Wilson who died 24th April 1903 aged 78 years. "Asleep in Jesus".

[James Wilson was a writing clerk at 59, Little York Street, Belfast.]

WILSON

[Badly weathered stone, now lost.] Erected by John (W)ilson to the memory (of his four beloved) children, (Ellen Jane), Wm John, (James and John). Also the above named John (Wilson) who died 6th March 1856 aged (58) years. And his daughter Mary who died 17th April 1856 aged 15 years.

[John Wilson was appointed Steward of the Belfast Charitable Society in about 1815, and held that post until he retired on a pension in 1845. He then went to live at 19, Gloucester Street, Belfast. The burial register gives his age as 65.]

WILSON

[Very worn tablet in headstone, now removed.] (In memory of) Robert (Wilson, D.D., Professor) of (Biblical Criticism in) Assembly's (College, Belfast, and for) eleven (years previously Minister) of the (Congregation of Linen Hall Street, who died October 11th 1859 aged 52 years. Also of his son Frederick Hill who died November 26th, 1858 aged 13 months. And of his sister-in-law Jane Alderdice McKENNA who died December 21st 1859 aged 20 years. Also of Annabella, widow of the Rev. Professor Wilson D.D., who died on the 23rd February 1879 aged 51 years.

[Letters of administration of the personal estate of the Rev. Robert Wilson of Upper Crescent, University Road, Belfast, county Antrim, D.D., who died 11 October 1859 were granted at Belfast 11 January 1860 to Annabella Wilson of Upper Crescent, the widow. Effects under £2,000. Re-sworn at Belfast Jan. 1861 under £1,400.

Letters of administration of the personal estate of Annabella Wilson of Maitland, Glenart Avenue, Blackrock, county Dublin, widow, who died 23

February 1879, were granted at the Principal Registry 13 March 1879 to William Wilson of Sparrow Hill House, Loughborough, Leicestershire, M.D., and Robert C. Wilson of Maitland, Glenart Avenue, esquire, the sons of the deceased. Effects under £3,000.

The Rev. Robert Wilson was born in 1808, eldest son of the Rev. William Wilson, Secession minister of Crossgar, near Coleraine. He was educated at the R.B.A.I., taking the General Certificate in 1828. He was minister of Berry Street Presbyterian Church 1831-39 and of the newly erected Linenhall Street Church 1839-42, Professor of Biblical Criticism, R.B.A.I. and Presbyterian College 1834-40, of Christian Ethics 1840-42 and of Biblical Criticism 1842-59. He obtained the D.D. of Glasgow in 1849 and was Moderator of the General Assembly 1856-57. He married (1) 1836 Mary, daughter of John Barnett of Belfast; see above under CAVART. (2) 1841 a Miss Thompson; (3) Annabella, daughter of William McKenna, M.R.C.V.S., of Belfast. See Fisher and Robb: *Royal Belfast Academical Institution* (1913); Allen: *The Presbyterian College, Belfast,* (1954).]

WILSON

[Now missing from lower ground. Copied from Society's Inscription book.] Sacred to the memory of Hans Wilson who died 1st of April 1870 aged 73 years. Also his wife Jane died 8th of May 1873 aged 90 years [sic].

[Hans Wilson was a grocer at 103, New Lodge Road, Belfast. The burial register gives his wife's age as 80, not 90.]

WILSON

[In upper ground, but no longer extant. The plot was bought by William Park of Crumlin, Co. Antrim in March 1828, and subsequently transferred to Samuel Wilson.] The family burying ground of Samuel Wilson, Belfast.

[Samuel Wilson was a grocer and spirit dealer at 2, Great Edward Street, Belfast.]

WILSON

See BLACKWOOD, CAVART, GORDON, MOLYNEUX, McKIBBIN and STEWART

WINNING

See JACKSON

WIRLING

[Flaking slightly but now lost.] I.H.S. Erected by Edward D. GRIBBIN in memory of his grandmother and uncle Ann and Robert Wirling, the former who died the 9th of May 1810 aged 80 years, the latter the 6th of March 1823 aged 65 years. Also Edward D. Gribbin M.D. who died 24th May 1888 aged 70 years. And his son Edward who died 11th June 1873 aged 4 years.

[The will of Edward Dominick Gribbin of 25 Great Edward Street, Belfast, M.D., who died 24 May 1888, was proved at Belfast 20 June 1888 by the Rev. Alexander Quinn of St. Malachy's presbytery, Belfast, and the Rev. James McArdle of St. Paul's presbytery, Belfast, R.C. priests, the executors. Effects £1,054 16s.3d.

Robert Wirling spent his latter years at 6, Church Street, Belfast where his nephew Edward Gribben also lived from childhood until he was about 30 by which time he had qualified as a surgeon, and gone to live at 23, Great Edward Street where he remained until he died.]

WOOD
See HENDERSON

WOODBURN
[Small headstone, now lost.] Here lie the remains of Wm Woodburn, who departed this life 16th June 1808 aged 78 years.

WOODS
[Headstone in upper ground and now missing.] Erected in memory of David Woods, merchant, died 14th Octr. 1807 aged 40. Also his sister Mary who died 21st Novr 1802 aged 46, both of Belfast.

[David Woods ran a hardware and toy warehouse at 2, Skipper's Lane (now Street), Belfast. In 1808 the concern was in the hands of one Mary Woods.]

WOODS
[No longer extant. James Wood of Smithfield bought this plot in August 1829.] Family burying place of the late James Woods.

WOODS
[Polished black granite.] In loving remembrance, James Woods who died 15th October 1856. His sons: James who died 12th May 1867, Robert who died 10th March 1890. His wife Margaret who died 21st March 1899. His son-in-law Thomas CRAIG, who died 27th December 1914. His daughter Margaret, wife of above Thomas Craig died 4th March 1921 aged 79 years. "Until the day break and the shadows flee away".

[Administration of the estate of Margaret Woods of 166 Albertbridge Road, Belfast, widow, who died 21 March 1899, was granted at Belfast 9 June 1899 to Margaret Craig, same address, married woman, the daughter. Effects £53 16s.5d.

James Woods, senior, who died in 1856 at the age of 55, was a copper- and tinsmith living at 13, Ormeau Street, off Ormeau Road, Belfast. His son Robert was a 40 year old clerk whose address is given in the burial register as the Union Workhouse. Thomas Craig, a school-teacher living on the Albertbridge Road, died in 1914 aged 62.]

WOOLSEY
See MATHERS

WORKMAN
[Twin tablets in pedimented entablature topped by three urns, secured to south wall in a high-railed enclosure. First part of inscription is on pediment.] Erected by Robert and John Workman, jr. in memory of John Workman their father who departed this life 3rd April 1846 aged 70 years, and Helen Workman their mother who died 27th October 1859 aged 79 years.

Also in memory of Maria, third daughter of John Workman (jnr), who departed this life 22d Nov. 1845 aged (3) years. Edward Kelswell his eldest son who died 26th August 1860 aged 20 years. Alfred John his youngest son who died 11th September 186(0) aged 14 years. Louisa Elizabeth his second daughter who died at Bournemouth, 20th Dec. 1866 aged 29 years. Also in memory of John Workman their father who died at Bournemouth, 16th Jan. 1867 aged 59 years. And also his wife Maria Workman who died 19th February 1871 aged 63 years. And Ellen her eldest daughter, wife of A.D. LEMON, who died 9th September 1914 aged 79 years.

Also in memory of William, second son of John Workman who died [blank]th Oct 1848 aged (4) years. And also Eliza his third daughter who died 18th May 1853 aged 12 years.

[Letters of administration of the personal estate of Louisa Elizabeth Workman of Edgcumbe, Sydenham, county Down, spinster, who died 20 December 1866 at Bournemouth, Hampshire, England, were granted at Belfast 23 March 1867 to Archibald Dunlap Lemon of Holywood, county Down, esquire, the administrator of John Workman deceased, the father and sole next of kin of said deceased. Effects in G.B. and Ireland under £2,000.

Letters of administration of the personal estate of John Workman of Edgcumbe, Sydenham, Strandtown, county Down esquire, who died 16 January 1867 at Bournemouth, Hampshire, England, were granted at Belfast 16 February 1867 to Archibald Dunlap Lemon of Holywood, county Down, esquire, the nominee of Maria Workman (the widow) and Ellen Lemon (the daughter), the sole next of kin. Effects in G.B. and Ireland under £80,000

The will of Maria Workman of Edgecumbe, Strandtown, county Down, who died 19 February 1871, was proved at Belfast 10 March 1871 by the oaths of Archibald Dunlap Lemon of Edgecumbe, Strandtown, esquire, and Thomas Workman and John Workman, both of Belfast, esquires, the executors. Effects in U.K. under £20,000.

John Workman, senior, was born in 1775/6, son of Robert Workman of Saltcoats, Ayrshire, and Elizabeth Boyd. He married Helen Millar of Saltcoats and came to Belfast in 1800 with £20,000 from his father to set up in business. In Belfast he lived at 9 Donegall Square East, a terrace which he built. His younger brother Robert (1790-1860) joined him in 1807 and they set up as muslin manufacturers with a warehouse in Upper Arthur Street. This Robert was father of the Rev. Robert Workman of Knockbreda who was buried there.

John Workman had 2 sons:

1. Robert Workman (1804-1870) married in 1833 Jane Service (1815-1895) and lived at 81 King Street and later at Ceara, Windsor Avenue. He and his brother continued the textile business and built the warehouse at 9-15 Bedford Street. He had 15 children, most of whom survived and married.

2. John Workman (1807-1867) married Maria Watts (1807-1871) and lived at Edgecomb, Strandtown, Belfast.

See Deane: *Belfast Natural History and Philosophical Society, Centenary*

Volume (1921); Garner: *Robert Workman of Newtownbreda* (1969); Clarke: *Gravestone Inscriptions, County Down*, Vol. 2, (2nd ed., 1988).

Eliza Workman, who died on 18th May 1853 aged 12, is described in the burial register as being the daughter of Robert Workman of Pakenham Place, Belfast.]

WORKMAN
See SMITH

WORTHINGTON
[Flaking.] Sacred to the memory of Ann Jane Worthington who departed this life the 23rd September 1853 aged 56 years.

[Anne Jane was the wife of John Worthington, an accountant living at 32, Gloucester Street, Belfast. Initially she was buried in the Strangers' Ground, and one year later her body was re-buried in this plot.]

WRIGHT
[Flaking.] Erected by Thomas Wright of Belfast, in memory of his daughter Mary Ellin Wright, who departed this life 4th Octr 1824 AE 2 years & 9 months. Also his daughter Jane who died in infancy. Mary Ellen his daughter who died 2nd August 1835 aged 9. His father James who died 12th January 1837 aged 68. His son Hugh who died 4th June 1846 aged 23. His wife Jane who died 13th February 1850 aged 45. Likewise Ellen KELLY, mother of Jane Wright, and grandmother of the above named children, who departed this life 18th May 1850 aged 73 years.

[Thomas Wright was a dealer in old furniture at 13, Smithfield in 1831. By the early 1840s the concern was being run by his wife Jane and their son Hugh, also of Smithfield, was a cabinet-maker. James Wright was a labourer living in Hudson's Entry, Belfast (nowadays Gresham Street).]

WRIGHT
[Twin tablets in marble Gothic entablature secured to south wall in enclosure formerly high-railed, now removed.] Sacred to the memory of Robert Wright, of Fortfield, who departed this life on the 23rd of May 1846 aged 64. "Blessed are the dead who die in the Lord, from henceforth: Yea, saith the Spirit, that they may rest from their labours and their works do follow them". Rev. XIV.13 Also to the memory of Margaret, wife to the above, who survived him 21 years. She entered into rest on the 29th of November 1867 aged 79. "So he giveth his beloved sleep". Psalm CXXVII. "Them also which sleep in Jesus will God bring with him" Thess. IV. 14. Also to the memory of their grandson John Henry Iever, son of the Rev. Adrian Henry and Charlotte Elizabeth LUTMAN. He died on the 23rd of June 1864 aged three years and eleven months. "Is it well with the child? It is well". 2nd Kings IV Ch., (26v.) Also Margaret, daughter of Robert and Margaret Wright, who died at the Bridge of Allan, 31st March 1870 aged (5)2. "I will give you rest". Matt.XI,28.

[The will of Margaret Wright of Donegall Square and late of No. 3 Queen's Elms, Belfast, widow, who died 29 November 1867 was proved at the Principal Registry 8 January 1868 by the oaths of John Hind of the Lodge, Belfast, linen merchant and Edward Wright of Flora Ville, Donnybrok, county Dublin LL.D. barrister-at-law, the executors. Effects under £7,000.

The will of Margaret Wright of Fortfield, county Antrim, spinster, who died 31 March 1870 at Bridge of Allan, Scotland, was proved at the Principal Registry 18 June 1870 by the oaths of John Hind of the Lodge, Belfast, county Antrim, esquire, and Edward Wright of the Boltons, Brompton, Middlesex, LL.D., the executors. Effects under £5,000.]

[Robert Wright was born in Newry, county Down in 1781/82 and was probably related to John Wright, proprietor of the *Newry Reporter*, one of several newspapers serving that town in the mid-nineteenth century. The parents of John Lutman lived at Dundonald, county Down.]

WRIGHT
See BROWN and HIND

WYLIE
See DICKEY

YEATES
[Flat stone on the ground.] The family burial place of William Yeates, Cornmarket. Samuel Henry Yeates died 14 July 1842 aged 6 months. Margaret Yeates died 1st August 1843 aged 13 years. Also the above named William Yeates died 26th August 1843 aged 43 years.

[William Yeates was a baker and flour merchant at 28, Cornmarket, Belfast. The burial register describes him as being 39 at the time of his death.]

YORK
[Very worn marble in headstone, surmounted by draped urn, now broken and lying face downwards.] (Sacred to the memory of) Alice York, (County Derry, obit September 15th 18(3)1. Most deeply lamented, having devoted her whole life in doing good. The stone is erected by Mrs. COCHRANE as a dear memorial of her love and gratitude. The remains of the above named Mrs. Alice Sophia Cochrane, obit September 6th 1879, are also interred here.

[Alice York's interment is not registered in the burial books. Mrs Alice Cochrane lived at 74 Carlisle Street and was 90 years old at the time of her death.]

YOUNG
[Marble tablet, formerly protected by a sheet of glass, in carved entablature, with rosettes and acanthus leaves at top, and secured to dividing wall, in high-railed enclosure. Arms: (now lost) Three rosettes and horizontal band in chief. Crest: Fist brandishing a spear?] Sacred to the memory of James Young, of Belfast, who departed this life on the 11th of April 1846 aged 73 years. Also his son William John who died 23rd September 1818 aged 7 years. His daughter Mary who died 5th March 1834 aged 17 years. His daughter Harriet who died 1st

March 1845 aged 17 years. His daughter Jane ANDERSON who died 16th June 1846 aged 26 years. Also Mary Young, the widow of James Young, who died 21st November 1872 aged 88 years.

[The will of Mary Young, formerly of Belfast, and late of Blantyre near Hamilton, Lanarkshire, widow, who died 21 November 1872 at Blantyre aforesaid, was proved at the Principal Registry 13 December 1872 by the oath of Robert Young at No. 2 Clarence Street, Belfast, architect, the son, the sole executor. Effects under £100.

James Young was born at Dundrod, County Antrim. In the 1800s he was operating a woollen and haberdashery concern at 37, Rosemary Lane, Belfast (now Street), moing to 84 High Street by 1819 and finally to 19, Donegall Street ten years later. His final residence was at Abbeyville, Whiteabbey. He was one of the Spring Water Commissioners appointed in 1837. He was the father of the Rt. Hon. Robert Young, P.C., J.P. (1822-1917), founder of Young & McKenzie, architects, and thus the grandfather of Robert M. Young, (1851-1925), antiquarian and architect. See Young: *Belfast and the Province of Ulster in the 20th Century* (1909).]

YOUNG

[Small marble tablet secured to north wall, in a low-railed enclosure. Young! moulders here, 1829.

[John Young was born at Rutherglen in 1781, eldest son of George Young. He entered Glasgow University in 1808, graduated M.A. in 1813 and LL.D. in 1821, and was appointed Professor of Moral Philosophy at the Belfast Academical Institution in 1815. A year before he died "the students of Dr Young presented their teacher with a silk gown, in token of their great esteem and in accepting the gift the learned Professor said amongst other things 'I have endeavoured to train you so that you may be imbued with an ardent and unalterable love of truth, and it is my dearest wish that this could be written, with justice, on my tomb'". He died on 9 March 1829 and his funeral was accompanied by his students in special mourning gowns and caps of their own devising. No one can explain why he has such a simple memorial or the reason for the exclamation mark after his name. See Addison: *The Matriculation Albums of the University of Glasgow* (1913); Fisher and Robb: *Royal Belfast Academical Institution, Centenary Volume* (1913); Hayward: *Belfast through the Ages* (1952).]

YOUNG

[Headstone broken and now lost. It has been supplemented from the Society's records.] Erected by Elizabeth Young to the memory of her husband John Young who departed this life June 29th 1836 aged 43 years. (Also her daughter Christian who departed this life July .. 1836 aged 10 years. Also the above named Elizabeth Young who departed this life 19th .... aged 54 years. Also their daughter Mary CLELAND) who departed this life 15th October 1851 aged 34 years. Robert Cleland who departed this life 24th September 1866 aged 70 years.

[John Young was an innkeeper and spirit grocer at 60, Grattan Street, Belfast. Robert Cleland was a publican at 5, Donegall Quay, Belfast.]

Memorial tablet to Professor John Young (1781-1829). The significance of the exclamation mark is unknown (photograph R.W.M. Strain).

YOUNG

[Small headstone.] Erected in memory of Dorothea Young, of Drum, County Monaghan, died at Belfast 30th May 1851 aged 88 years.

[Dorothea Young was the widow of William Young, of Rockcorry, county Monaghan. She spent her final years at 34, Gloucester Street, Belfast.]

YOUNG

[Face down, but recorded in Inscription book.] Erected by Margaret Mercer Young, in memory of her beloved husband John Young who died 2nd January 1857 aged 82 years. Also her son William who died 25th February 1853 aged 31 years. Also her son Robert who died 27th February 1857 aged 30 years. Also Clara, wife of James Young Soltr, 1st August 1845 aged 25 years. His infant son, March 1848. Also his daughter Margaret Wright Young, 3rd February 1853 aged two months. My beloved husband, the above-named James Young, solicitor, died 30th March 1865 aged 52 years. Also the above-named Margaret Mercer Young, died 16th May 1870 aged 80 years.

[The will of Margaret Mercer Young of Great Victoria Street, Belfast, county Antrim, widow, who died 15 May 1870 at Belfast aforesaid, was proved 1 June 1870 by the oaths of David Brown, merchant, and Anna

Mercer Brown his wife, both of Holywood, county Down, and Margaret Jane Orr, wife of Hugh Orr of Belfast aforesaid, gentleman, the executors. Effects under £700.

John Young was an iron merchant with premises at 15, Marlborough Street, Belfast; both he and his son Robert, a master mariner, lived at 9, Dock Street. His two other sons William and James were both solicitors, the latter practising at 3, Arthur Square with a branch office in Capel Street, Dublin. James lived at Fox Lodge, Ballymacarret.]

YOUNG
See DOE and LINDSAY

Looking west across the Cholera Ground, 1970s (Photograph R.W.M. Strain).